THE ILLUSTRATED
HISTORY OF
SCOTLAND

CHRIS TABRAHAM
with photographs by COLIN BAXTER

▲ *King Robert the Bruce (1306-29), one of the great figures in the history of
Scotland, looks out across his kingdom from the royal castle of Stirling.*

OYSTER PRESS
ANACORTES · WASHINGTON

▲ The mighty Stones of Stenness have dominated the gently rolling landscape of mainland Orkney
for 5000 years. But what use our remote ancestors put such 'monuments' to is a mystery, like so much of their story.
A great ceremonial meeting place for prehistoric Orcadians seems the most likely explanation.

CONTENTS

INTRODUCTION

'...the past is a foreign country: they do things differently there...'

(*From the prologue to* The Go-Between, *L P Hartley, 1953*)

If there is one thing we learn from history it is – we never learn from history, which is a great pity because history can tell us as much about ourselves as about those who have gone before.

History has taught me two things. First, nothing in this world is for ever, no matter how much we might wish it otherwise. 'Change', as Sandy Fenton puts it in his absorbing little book on island blackhouses, 'is an inevitable part of life, to be accepted not ignored'.

The second is – the more we change, the more we stay the same. We may have come a long way since our remote ancestors walked the earth – invented wheels and ways to kill people, learnt to communicate only for us then to go and sit in front of the 'telly' – but we are still basically the same under the skin, a complex mix of emotions: selfish, proud, loving, despairing.

At this basic level the history of Scotland would be the same as that of any nation in the world. It is the detail that sets us all apart, and the detail of Scotland's history is as complicated as any. Not quite as confusing, perhaps, as Sellar and Yeatman would have us believe in their masterful 'spoof' history of Britain, *1066 And All That*, but not far off it!

The Scots (originally Irish, but by now Scotch) were at this time inhabiting Ireland, having driven the Irish (Picts) out of Scotland; while the Picts (originally Scots) were now Irish (living in brackets) and vice versa. It is essential to keep these distinctions clearly in mind (and verce visa).

History isn't an exact science, and those who write it inevitably bring their own baggage. You'll find I'm no exception. I'll also come clean from the start: I'm English, from west Cumberland. So what, do I hear you ask, is an Englishman doing writing Scottish history? But then what is nationality but an accident of time and place? Saint Patrick, too, was a Cumbrian, and he became patron saint of Ireland. I'm no saint, but if I'd been born 800 years ago, I'd have been a Scot; 1300 years ago a Strathclyde Briton; before then who knows? To try to be as objective as possible, you'll see I quote extensively from those who were around at the time – not that they were necessarily objective, but at least they were there!

I've loved history since I could walk and talk, and I've thoroughly enjoyed researching and writing this book. It has taken me into pastures that I scarcely knew existed, and I am the richer for it. I hope when you've read it you will be too.

Slainte
Chris Tabraham

◀ *Kildrummy Castle, in deepest Strathdon, Aberdeenshire – 'the noblest of northern castles' – is a tangible link with Scotland's medieval past. In 1306 its formidable walls sheltered King Robert the Bruce's queen, Elizabeth, and their daughter, Marjorie, from the rampaging English army of Edward I, 'Hammer of the Scots'. Four hundred years later, in 1715, a Jacobite army marched out from those same walls in an attempt to return a Stewart to the throne of Great Britain.*

But when the King
  Edward heard say
How Neil Bruce held
  Kildrummy
Against his own son
  stalwartly;
He gatherit a great
  chivalry [knightly army],
And toward Scotland
  went in hy [haste].

(From John Barbour's epic poem The Bruce*)*

5

SCOTLAND

Orkney Islands
Knap of Howar
Noltland
Westray
Rousay
Sanday
Stronsay
Mid Howe Tomb & Broch
Gurness Broch
Skara Brae
Maes Howe
Ring of Brogar
Stones of Stenness
Kirkwall
St Magnus
Hoy
Scapa Flow Naval Base 1917, 1919 & 1939
Isbister Tomb
South Ronaldsay

Muckle Flugga Lighthouse 1858
Unst
Muness
Yell
Sullom Voe Oil Terminal 1978
Scalloway
Lerwick
Clickimin Broch
Shetland Islands
St Ninian's Isle
Mousa Broch
Jarlshof

Lewis Lighthouse
Dun Carloway Broch
Lewis
Stornoway
Lewis Chessmen
Calanais Stones
Uig
← Annexation of Rockall 1955
● Evacuation of St Kilda 1930
Harris
Rodel
North Uist
Lochmaddy
Dunvegan
Portree
Skye
Braes 1882
Kyle of Lochalsh
South Uist
Lochboisdale
Barra
Kisimul
Castlebay
Borreraig Clearance Village
Rum
Kinloch
Mallaig
Coll
Breachacha
Tiree
Tobermory
Mull
Staffa Fingal's Cave
Iona
Moy

Lochinver
Ardvreck
Lairg
Ullapool
Gairloch
Applecross
Eilean Donan
Glenshiel 1719
Glenelg Brochs
Caledonian Canal 1822
Fort Augustus
Kingussie
Glenfinnan Monument 1745
Tioram
Mingary
Ardtornish 1462
Stalker
Duart
Dunstaffnage
Oban
Bonawe 1753
Kilchurn

Dounreay 1955
Thurso
Castle of Mey
Strathnaver 1814
Wick
Sinclair and Girnigoe
Dunbeath
Dunrobin
Helmsdale
Strathoykel 1792
Spinningdale
Carbisdale 1650
Tain
St Duthac
Invergordon
Aluminium Smelter 1965
Moray Firth
Burghead Fort
Elgin
Spynie
Cathedral
Banff
Fraserburgh Lighthouse 1787
Inverallochy
Cairnbulg
Dingwall
Fort George
Nairn
Brodie
Alness
Leod
Cawdor
Auldearn 1645
Culloden 1746
Balvenie
Huntly
Fyvie
Cruden Bay
Inverness
Caledonian Canal 1822
University of the Highlands and Islands 2001
Haughs of Cromdale 1690
Ballindalloch
Picardie Stone
Mons Graupius 83
Harlaw 1411
Urquhart
Kildrummy
Alford 1645
Craigievar
Fraser
Loch an Eilein
Corgarff
Lumphanan 1057
Aberdeen
Aberdeen 1495
Robert Gordon's 1992
Ruthven Barracks
Drum
Crathes
Dalwhinnie
Braemar 1715
Balmoral
Dunnottar
Blair
Caterthuns Fort
Edzell
Kinneff
Corpach Paper Mill 1965
Inverlochy 1645
Fort William
Killiecrankie 1689
Meigle Pictish Stones
Aberlemno Stones
Nechtansmere 685
Montrose
Glencoe 1692
Dunsinnan 1054
Dunkeld Cathedral
Glamis
Arbroath Abbey
Menzies
Moot Hill Scone
Huntingtower
Dundee 1967
Broughty
Dundee
Tay Bridge 1879
Clach nam Breattann
Tippermuir 1644
Perth
Treaty of Perth 1266
St Andrews
Bell Rock 1811
Dupplin Moor 1332
St Andrews Cathedral
Aberfoyle
Sheriffmuir 1715
Falkland Palace
Loch Leven
Kirkcaldy
Stirling Castle
Bannockburn 1314
Dunfermline
Dirleton
Prestonpans 1745
Dunbar 1296 & 1650
Helensburgh
Antonine Wall
Edinburgh
Pinkie 1547
Greenock
Dumbarton Rock
Craigmillar
Largs 1263
Bothwell Bridge 1679
Berwick-upon-Tweed
Glasgow
R. Clyde
See opposite
Lanark
Peebles
R. Tweed
Kilmarnock
New Lanark 1788
Biggar
Melrose Abbey
Kelso Abbey
Flodden 1513
Ayr
Abington
Hawick
Cumnock
Wanlockhead
Culzean
Mull of Kintyre 1994
Otterburn 1388
Inveraray
Carnasserie
Dunadd Fort
Colonsay
Lochgilphead
Crinan Canal 1801
Dunoon
Jura
Keills Cross
Rothesay
Islay
Bowmore
Gigha
Skipness
Lochranza
Finlaggan
Kildalton Cross
Brodick
Arran
Machrie Moor Stone Circles
Campbeltown

← Annexation of Rockall 1955
→ Forties Oil Field 1967
→ Piper Alpha Oil Platform 1988

R. Nith
Glentrool 1307
Lockerbie 1988
Dryfe Sands 1593
Hermitage
Lochmaben
Solway Moss
Gretna Rail Crash 1915
Threave 1455
Dumfries
Caerlaverock
Sweetheart Abbey
Ruthwell Cross
Chapel Cross 1955
Stranraer
Glenluce
Ruthwell Cross
Carlisle
Dundrennan Abbey
Hadrian's Wall
St Ninian's Cave

NORTHERN IRELAND

0   10   20   30mls
0 10 20 30 40kms

ENGLAND

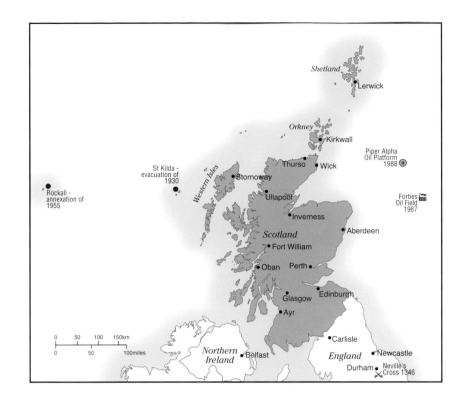

Key

Ancient monument	🏛
Castle	🏰
Scene of conflict	✕
Disaster	✺
Historic house	🏚
Industrial site	🏭
Lighthouse	🗼
New town	★
Religious site	✠
Treasure site	🗝
University	📖
Other	●

Inset map labels: Shetland, Lerwick, Orkney, Kirkwall, Thurso, Wick, Piper Alpha Oil Platform 1988, St Kilda - evacuation of 1930, Stornoway, Ullapool, Forties Oil Field 1967, Rockall - annexation of 1955, Western Isles, Inverness, Aberdeen, Scotland, Fort William, Oban, Perth, Glasgow, Edinburgh, Ayr, Carlisle, Northern Ireland, Belfast, England, Newcastle, Durham, Neville's Cross 1346

Scale: 0 50 100 150km / 0 50 100miles

CENTRAL SCOTLAND

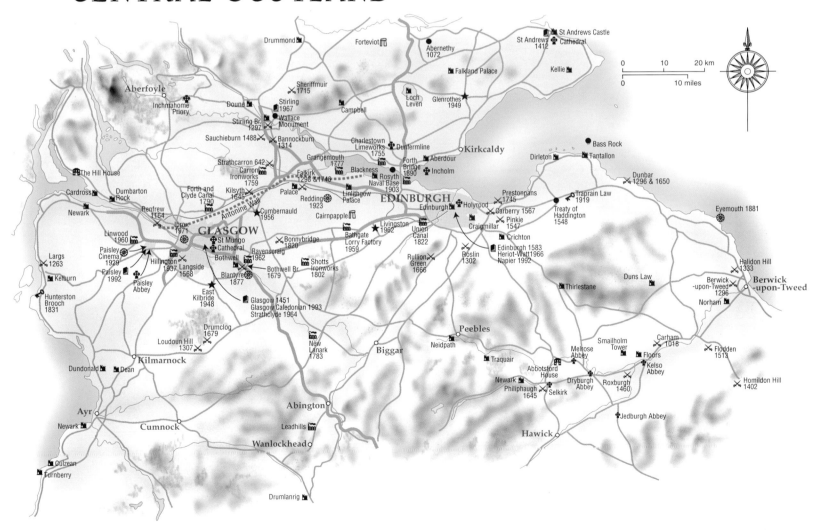

Drummond, Forteviot, Abernethy 1072, St Andrews, St Andrews Castle, Cathedral 1412, Kellie, Falkland Palace, Loch Leven, Glenrothes 1949, Aberfoyle, Sheriffmuir 1715, Inchmahome Priory, Doune, Stirling 1967, Campbell, Kirkcaldy, Bass Rock, Tantallon, Dirleton, Wallace Monument, Stirling Br. 1297, Sauchieburn 1488, Bannockburn 1314, Strathcarron 642, Charlestown Limeworks 1755, Dunfermline, Aberdour, Dunbar 1296 & 1650, The Hill House, Carron Ironworks 1759, Grangemouth 1777, Falkirk 1298 & 1746, Blackness, Forth Bridge 1890, Rosyth Naval Base 1903, Incholm, Cardross, Dumbarton Rock, Forth and Clyde Canal 1790, Kilsyth 1645, Palace, Redding 1923, Linlithgow Palace, EDINBURGH, Prestonpans 1745, Traprain Law 1919, Eyemouth 1881, Newark, Renfrew 1164, Cumbernauld 1956, Cairnpapple, Edinburgh, Holyrood, Carberry 1567, Pinkie 1547, Treaty of Haddington 1548, Linwood 1960, Ibrox 1971, Antonine Wall, GLASGOW, Bonnybridge 1820, Bathgate Lorry Factory 1959, Union Canal 1822, Craigmillar, Crichton, Largs 1263, Paisley Cinema 1929, Paisley 1992, St Mungo Cathedral, Hillington, Ravenscraig 1962, Langside 1568, Bothwell, Shotts Ironworks 1802, Rullion Green 1666, Edinburgh 1583 Heriot-Watt 1966 Napier 1992, Roslin 1302, Halidon Hill 1333, Kelburn, Hunterston Brooch 1831, Paisley Abbey, Blantyre 1877, Bothwell Br. 1679, East Kilbride 1948, Glasgow 1451 Glasgow Caledonian 1993 Strathclyde 1964, Duns Law, Thirlestane, Berwick-upon-Tweed 1296, Berwick-upon-Tweed, Norham, Drumclog 1679, Loudoun Hill 1307, New Lanark 1783, Biggar, Neidpath, Peebles, Smailholm Tower, Carham 1018, Flodden 1513, Dundonald, Dean, Kilmarnock, Traquair, Abbotsford House, Melrose Abbey, Floors, Kelso Abbey, Homildon Hill 1402, Ayr, Newark, Cumnock, Abington, Leadhills, Wanlockhead, Philiphaugh 1645, Newark, Selkirk, Dryburgh Abbey, Roxburgh 1460, Hawick, Jedburgh Abbey, Culzean, Turnberry, Drumlanrig

Scale: 0 10 20 km / 0 10 miles

ORIGINS

(2,800,000,000 BC - AD 79)

> '...the nation of the Scots is of ancient stock...'
> (Abbot Walter Bower, in his introduction to Scotichronicon, c. 1440)

For Scots to walk this earth, they need the ground beneath their feet. This chapter looks first at the creation of the land of Scotland, a fascinating drama that took 2,800,000,000 years to unfold, before exploring the history of our remote ancestors during the first 8000 years of human life.

CREATION

Imagine the history of the Earth compressed into one calendar year, with our planet being born just after midnight on New Year's Day. Dinosaurs would have made their appearance just in time to celebrate Christmas, and you and I arrived right on the stroke of midnight on 31 December. It is a humbling and sobering thought.

The creation of the landmass called Scotland is a fascinating story in which our country inched its way northward from Antarctica towards and across the Equator, propelled by great continents slowly moving about the globe, repeatedly colliding with each other, joining up and breaking away. It is a story in which the awesome forces of nature – earth, air, fire and water – were forever creating and destroying the surface of the Earth. At one stage, impossible as it might now seem, Scotland was separated from England by a great ocean wider than the Atlantic.

And we aren't finished yet. Scotland continues to creep ever closer to Europe at the rate of about the width of your wrist each year. And we, its inhabitants, are still in the grip of the Ice Age, with more glaciers due to carpet the Highlands in perhaps 50,000 years time – that's less than six minutes away!

> Continents, although permanent for whole geographical epochs, shift their positions entirely in the course of ages.
> (Sir Charles Lyell, native of Kinnordy, in Angus, writing in 1875.)

21 May (2800 million years ago)...

Scotland begins to take shape. The hard, unyielding rock known as Lewisian Gneiss that today forms swathes of the north-west Highlands and Islands

◀ *The Stone-Age village of Skara Brae, on Orkney, is a truly special place. The maze of snug stone houses and sheltered covered passageways was built over 5000 years ago, before even Stonehenge was begun, and abandoned a little over 600 years later, just as the great pyramid at Cheops was nearing completion. Skara Brae may not be quite the oldest settlement surviving from Scotland's remote past – the stone houses at Knap of Howar on the nearby island of Papa Westray are even older – but it constitutes by far the best-preserved Stone-Age village surviving in northern Europe.*

'Rock Legend'
~ JAMES HUTTON ~

'...no vestige of a beginning - no prospect of an end...'

(From John Playfair's biography of James Hutton)

There was a time, and not all that long ago, when people believed in the Biblical story of the Creation and blithely accepted that our Earth was just a few thousand years old. They believed that the rocks had been laid down during Noah's Flood, and that the fossils were the remains of those unfortunate creatures unable to get into his Ark. Mr and Mrs Hutton's wee boy, born in Edinburgh in 1726, changed all that, and by the time of his death 71 years later, the world had begun to appreciate that Planet Earth was infinitely older and far more complex than that.

Geology wasn't very fashionable in 1749 when the young James Hutton took on a small farm in Berwickshire. Soon the nearby rock formations at Siccar Point, south of Cove harbour, began to intrigue him, setting him on a path that took him across Wales and England as well as his native land in the quest for answers. A canny observer and a meticulous recorder, he eventually presented his theories on the creation of the Earth to an astonished public. Not surprisingly, given the Bible-based culture of the day, his theories aroused intense controversy.

Undaunted, in 1768 Hutton forsook the farming life for the intellectual stimulus that the 'enlightened' city of Edinburgh provided. There, appropriately, he took up residence in a house looking across to Arthur's Seat. He mixed with

▲ *This fine portrait of James Hutton (1726-97) was painted by the equally famous Scottish figure, Sir Henry Raeburn. The Edinburgh-born Raeburn (1756-1823) began his working life apprenticed to a jeweller but soon developed a penchant for portrait painting. This study of Hutton, painted when Reynolds was barely out of his 'teens, was an early manifestation of his prodigious talent. Raeburn, like Hutton, became one of the stars of the Scottish Enlightenment.*

some of the great names of the Scottish Enlightenment. He took one, his friend John Clerk, to see a drainage trench being dug in Frederick Street, and demonstrated to him how our rocks could be made in more ways than one, and did not necessarily have to involve the sea. Hutton took another, John Playfair, who became his biographer, to Siccar Point to see for himself those

rocks that had first aroused his curiosity. The visit clearly made its impact on the noted philosopher and mathematician, for he later wrote of his unforgettable experience:

The mind seemed to grow giddy by looking so far into the abyss of time; and while we listened...we became sensible how much further reason may sometimes go than imagination can venture to follow.

Hutton died in 1797, shortly after publishing his mould-breaking *Theory of the Earth*. By then his second theory – that the Earth had been created by a continuing cycle of erosion, deposition and vulcanism, and would indeed continue to be so shaped until the end of time – had begun to receive acceptance. Since his passing, geology has become a respectable and hugely important science, and great scholars have trodden in Hutton's footsteps.

Two fellow Scots stand out for special mention; Sir Charles Lyell (1797-1875), a native of Kinnordy near Kirriemuir, who advanced the theory of 'continental drift', and Hugh Miller (1802-1856), from Cromarty, who through his trade as a stonemason became a specialist in the study of fossils. But these and others would not have achieved what they did had it not been for James Hutton's pioneering efforts. Not for nothing is he known as 'the father of geology'.

seems perfectly at home where it is now, 60° north of the Equator and bearing the brunt of the harsh Atlantic storms. Incredibly, though, its birth took place far away to the south, not far from Antarctica. We have come a long way since then.

For the next six months (1800 million years), the rock lies deep within the bowels of the Earth. But around mid October (1000 million years ago) it breaks through the crust to form a bleak, desolate landscape, devoid of colour save for the muddy slime. Once exposed to the elements, the rock begins to erode. Vast amounts of pebbles, sand, silt and mud are deposited, slowly solidifying into the sandstone that now forms the impressive Torridon range of mountains with its stupefying array of mighty peaks. More debris is swept into the encircling oceans. And there it accumulates and settles over millions of years.

20 November (500 million years ago)...

Scotland begins to inch its way north. The submerged sediments, unable to resist this mighty force, buckle and fold over the land to create today's northern and central Highlands. Some of the deepest rocks are subjected to such fierce temperatures that they melt and thrust their way through to the surface where they cool into the huge masses of granite that characterise much of Aberdeenshire and form the jagged Black Cuillin peaks on Skye. Life now begins as myriads of tiny creatures appear in the seas around.

29 November (400 million years ago)...

As the rest of Britain and Europe hoves into sight, more ocean sediments are thrust up and over the desolate land; we call them the Southern Uplands. Meanwhile, further north, a four-footed amphibian, equipped with a tail for swimming and toes for crawling, takes its first faltering steps on land near Elgin – hence his (or her) name *Elginerpeton*.

Scotland continues its slow drift northward, and erosion continues to reprofile the surface of the

▲ *You can readily imagine the enormous power of the melting ice at the end of the last Ice Age, as it moved across the land gouging out the rock of the Cairngorm Mountains to create the Lairig Ghru (meaning Pass of Drurie). Scotland, up until then, would have been under ice with the exception of north-west Lewis and some of the mountains in the western Highlands and Islands. Sheltered spots close to the sea in the west may have been missed, but eastwards there was no sea until the melt water created the North Sea, cutting Scotland off from Scandinavia.*

▲ The extraordinary columns of stone forming Fingal's Cave, on the island of Staffa, Argyllshire, were formed around 60 million years ago, during an epoch of violent vulcanism deep in the earth's core that resulted in the creation of the Atlantic Ocean. Felix Mendelssohn, who visited in 1829, was so moved by the awesome sight of the waters rising and falling at the entrance to the cave that he composed his Hebridean Overture as a result.

land. Mighty mountain peaks higher than the Himalayas are worn down and the resulting debris is spread over the lower ground, to harden and form the flagstones of Orkney and Caithness. Volcanoes too begin to contribute to the landscape – the most famous, Arthur's Seat in Edinburgh, born on 3 December (340 million years ago). By 6 December (300 million years ago) Scotland nears the equator.

Colonisation of the land by plants and animals gets underway in earnest. Rainforests sprout up, thriving on the heavy rains and steamy humidity. The stone stumps of trees discovered more than a century ago by quarrymen in what is now Glasgow's Victoria Park – 'Fossil Grove' they nicknamed it – once formed part of a tropical jungle stretching across Scotland's Central Belt. Around the trees crawl primitive creatures, drinking from shallow lagoons fed by hot springs bubbling up from the ground. Fossils found near Bathgate in 1984 included an ancestor of Mr Toad and 'Lizzie the Lizard', proclaimed the world's first reptile.

11 December (250 million years ago)...

As Scotland crosses the Tropic of Cancer, the searing heat takes its toll on our emerging land. Deserts form and blustering winds create great dunes of orangey-red sand that we now see in the buildings gracing Glasgow's streets. Gradually the torrid temperatures ease, and on land reptiles such as crocodiles crawl around. All except one that prefers to stalk about on its hind legs – the dinosaur, fossils of which have been found on Skye, Scotland's 'Jurassic Park'.

Scotland now enjoys a climate much like we experience on our Mediterranean holidays. In the waters large sea monsters resembling our whales and dolphins appear; their sheer size has earned them a fearsome reputation, yet their only crime was a passion for seafood. How these strange creatures evolved is not fully understood, but it seems probable that their ancestors were once 'landlubbers'. Up to this moment, the story of evolution has been one

'God's Treasure-House in Scotland'
~ LEADHILLS & WANLOCKHEAD ~

'In whase dark bowels...miners howk and sift'

(From Alexander Wilson's Epistle to William Mitchell, *written at Leadhills, 1790)*

High in the Lowther Hills, barely 40 miles (64 km) from the centre of Glasgow, are the two highest villages in Scotland – Wanlockhead (1500 ft / 450 m) and Leadhills (1300 ft / 400 m). But both have another claim to fame – the rich minerals that lie deep beneath them.

The Lowther Hills are part of the Southern Uplands, whose folded and faulted greywackes, mudstones, shales and cherts were laid down 450 million years ago. Later movements deep in the earth's crust caused fissures to open, and into these flowed the mineral ores that have since become world renowned. It was not so much the primary ores of lead, zinc, iron and copper that attracted the attention of mineralogists, although these were the most successful commercially; it was more the diverse range of secondary lead minerals, including Leadhillite and Lanarkite, they contained.

But it was gold that drew men to this remote spot time and again. We have no direct evidence for mining here in ancient times, but that must be a distinct possibility given the longevity and density of prehistoric settlement in Upper Clydesdale (the oldest mesolithic site in Scotland, 10,000 years old, was found recently near Biggar). The Romans, too, could well have exploited the minerals, given their presence in strength in the Nith and Clyde valleys to west and east.

Mining is first mentioned in the early thirteenth century when a perambulation of the Lindsay estate of Crawford refers to 'the mine' on Broad Law just to the north-east of Leadhills, probably the one

worked by those industrial entrepreneurs, the Cistercians of Newbattle Abbey, near Dalkeith. We hear little thereafter until the sixteenth century, when the search for gold reached its peak. The Crown of Scotland, on display in Edinburgh Castle, was fashioned from Leadhills gold; James V wore it for the first time at the coronation of his queen, Mary of Guise,

▲ *David Allan (1744-96), a lad of humble Alloa origins, earned his artistic reputation as 'the Scottish Hogarth' painting the commonplace rather than the special. They included a fascinating set of four paintings illustrating the process of lead manufacture at the Earl of Hopetoun's mine at Leadhills, commissioned in 1786. The one shown here is entitled* Inside the Smelter House.

in Holyrood Abbey in 1540.

The Leadhills 'Gold Rush' came later that century as adventurers from England and abroad joined the Scots themselves in a frantic search for the precious substance. Perhaps the most notable was an Englishman, Sir Bevis Bulmer, who according to his biographer, Stephen Atkinson, 'won much wealth and muckle honour on the five muirs'. It was Atkinson who bestowed the byname 'God's Treasure-House in Scotland'. Bulmer died in poverty; other seekers met

equally tragic ends. Spare a thought for poor George Bowes who in 1576 found 'a small vaine of gold.' Desperate to keep it a secret he sealed it. Alas, before he could return to make his fortune he died in a mining accident in his native Cumberland and his secret died with him.

It now seems doubtful there are veins of gold in 'them thar hills'. What gold exists is probably alluvial gold, found by panning. Colonel Borthwick, director of the Leadhills mines, wrote in 1684 of the gold being found 'by passing the earth through searches [riddles], and the same brought down with speats [spates] of raine. I have seen pieces of it as big as a cherry. It is exceeding fine gold'. The lead miners who laboured here until the early twentieth century took to searching for gold in their spare time to augment their wages, and in 1893 the Leadhills miners presented a gold ring to Princess Mary of Teck on the occasion of her marriage to the future George V. Today, the chill waters of the Lowther Hills play host each year to the Gold Panning Championships.

Here mountains raise their
   heath'ry banks,
Ranged huge aboon the lift,
In whase dark bowels, for lead tracts,
Swarm'd miners howk and sift.
A wimplan [wandering] burn
   atween the hills,
Thro' many a glen rins trottin';
Amang the stanes an' sunny rills
Aft bits of gowd [gold] are gotten;
(From Alexander Wilson's *Epistle to William Mitchell,* written at Leadhills 1790).

▲ The great Ring of Brogar, on Orkney, still contrives to impress and overawe the modern visitor, as it must have been intended to do when built almost 5000 years ago. It has been estimated that it took around 80,000 man hours just to dig out the surrounding ditch, let alone hew and erect the 60 tall stones that originally formed the 'ring'.

▶ When the last Ice Age melted away some 10,000 years ago, the exposed mountainous wastes of the Scottish Highlands were quickly cloaked in vegetation, particularly pine trees. Remnants of that ancient Caledonian pine forest can still be seen, as here in lonely Glen Affric, Inverness-shire. Into those woods came wild animals, and following hard on their heels our oldest ancestors, in search of food.

of progression from sea to land. Now nature decides the sea isn't that bad after all.

26 December (65 million years ago)...

Catastrophe! A mighty explosion rocks Scotland and the rest of the planet throughout Boxing Day morning. The dinosaur and a host of other creatures become extinct. What caused it? The massive meteorite, perhaps, that is thought to have smashed into the Earth at this time? Or maybe volcanoes such as those thundering off the west coast of Scotland from Ailsa Craig to St Kilda, spewing their dust and gases high into the atmosphere and blocking out the sun's rays? The extraordinary columns of cooled lava at Fingal's Cave, Staffa, are the most spectacular results of this vulcanism, part of a much larger shifting of the Earth's plates that results in the formation of the North Atlantic. Whatever the cause, Scotland finally bids farewell to North America.

8 p.m., 31 December (2 million years ago)...

The New Year revelries begin to get into full swing just as Scotland suffers its first 'deep freeze'. Great ice sheets envelop the land. At its most merciless, the ice reaches over 3280 ft (1000 metres) high, 16 times higher than the Scott Monument in

Edinburgh. The enormous mass of ice weighs down heavily upon the land, depressing it by several fathoms.

In between each freeze comes a period of global warming. As the ice sheets melt, they move across the land, scratching and tearing at its surface. The softer rocks succumb to the enormous pressure and are gouged out, creating the straths and glens we admire today.

11 p.m., 31 December (11,000 years ago)...

More global warming brings the last Ice Age to an end, and in so doing creates one of Scotland's great natural beauties – Loch Lomond. As the last ice-cube melts away, the land, relieved of its burden, breathes a sigh of relief and rises up, to create what will become in time the world's best links golf courses. But the melting ice also causes the seas to rise up and envelop the lowest land. Until this time Scotland has been physically joined to the rest of Europe, and separated from Scandinavia only by a narrow inlet off the Arctic Ocean. Now that dry tundra slowly sinks beneath the waves to form what is now the North Sea. The 29,730 square mile (77,000 square km) of landmass we now call Scotland is finally born, after a pregnancy lasting 3000 million years.

REMOTE ANCESTORS

Humans first set foot in Scotland after the ending of the last Ice Age some 11,000 years ago (9000 BC). What name they gave to the bleak landscape they encountered, where reindeer grazed and polecat prowled, is a mystery, like so much of their story. They were a restless folk, roving about the land, never far from water, in the relentless search for food, remaining in one place only long enough to leave behind the odd campfire and the remains of their last meal.

Amid the gloom there are faint traces to be had

▲ *Quite why our Stone-Age ancestors chose to build this great stone circle at Calanais on the Isle of Lewis almost 5000 years ago is a mystery, but it may have served as some kind of astronomical observatory.*

'The most attractive explanation . . . is that, every 18.6 years, the moon skims especially low over the hills to the south. It seems to dance along them, like a great god visiting the earth. Knowledge and prediction of this heavenly event gave earthly authority to those who watched the skies.'

(Patrick Ashmore, in his insightful guidebook Calanais: The Standing Stones, *2002)*

of the wild natives of the district, of fierce warriors from other lands; but complete pictures of the doings of those old times can be found only in the galleries of the imagination. (John H Dixon, in *Gairloch*, 1886).

When our ancestors first arrived, they encountered a landscape slowly recovering from the ravages of the melted ice. As the temperature rose – by 6500 BC it had reached on average 2°C higher than today – thin soils began to carpet the rocky ground. Grasses, shrubs and bushes took root and thrived, followed by forests of hazel, elm and oak spreading out from the Lowlands to the north-east, leaving the sturdier pines and birches to wrestle with the more mountainous Highland wastes. With the forests came animals large and small, from ferocious bears to the harmless vole. And following the animals came humans, in search of food.

Our ancient forebears were 'hunter-gatherers'. They not only hunted the wild animals but also gathered plants, berries, fruits and nuts, and made full use of the abundant life teeming in the inland lochs and rivers as well as in the encircling seas. They made primitive tools from stone, wood and animal bone, and lived in tent-like structures.

There is no doubting life was tough. But we have to blot out all those fanciful nineteenth-century images of 'noble savages' – stereotypes saying more about our Victorian predecessors than about our oldest ancestors. New evidence is emerging to suggest that they were more in control of their natural environment than we assume. They might have led a nomadic life, but rather than simply roam around in an endless quest for food, they appear to have begun taming their environment, so beginning the process of land-management that has resulted in the modern landscape.

On Colonsay a large pit packed with hundreds of thousands of hazel shells was recently

'The Lost Village in the Sand'

~ SKARA BRAE ~

'Northern Europe's best preserved stone-age village'

It was a particularly harsh winter in Orkney in 1850. The rollers crashed against the shore of the Bay of Skaill more fiercely than usual and the storms ripped savagely at the sand dunes. The laird of Skaill, braving the elements, saw something odd emerging from the shifting dunes. His curiosity aroused, he started exploring. Very soon he had exposed an immense midden, and within that midden the ruins of ancient dwellings. The laird had stumbled across the lost Stone-Age village of Skara Brae, built in 3100 BC, before Troy was founded, and abandoned 600 years later, just as the great pyramid of Cheops was nearing completion.

Had Orkney been blessed with trees, then Skara Brae would surely have been built of wood and not survived. That it has done is down to the plentiful Orkney flagstone. The stone buildings still stand to eaves height, and, even more amazingly, most of the furniture, fixtures and fittings inside the houses have survived as well. Visiting Skara Brae is a magical experience. As you stand and peer down into the houses beneath you, you can scarcely credit that you are staring at something over 5000 years old, older even than Stonehenge. There in the centre of the main room is the hearth with a little seat beside it; cosy box beds lie to either side; and at the far end facing the entrance doorway is a tiered dresser or cupboard looking for all the world like the wooden one

your granny had. All that is missing from the scene is the Sunday roast, the sheepskin blankets and the prized possessions on display in the dresser – and the residents as well, of course.

▲ *Skara Brae from the air. When the village was lived in around 5000 years ago, it was not beside the sea, for nature had yet to crash through the cliffs to create the Bay of Skaill. When the villagers were in residence, the settlement was located beside a more sheltered freshwater loch.*

The houses might look small and cosy from above, but in fact each had a floor area measuring about 48 sq yd (40 sq. m), some two-thirds the size of a modern semi-detached, two-bedroom bungalow. It is impossible for us to say

how many of a family each house was expected to accommodate because we don't know enough about the way they led their lives – whether they were polygamous, for example. Given that most Stone-Age people did not live beyond the age of 30, it may be that each house was home to an extended rather than a nuclear family.

Archaeological excavations down the years have cast a bright shaft of light on the inhabitants' way of life. They farmed the surrounding land, growing barley and a little wheat, and rearing cattle, sheep, goats and a few pigs. They fished the shallow coastal waters for a rich seafood harvest of cod, lobster and mussels. They hunted deer and caught seabirds for their flesh and eggs. They made clay pots and tools of stone and bone; they decorated themselves with bone jewellery and possibly also coloured themselves with a mixture of red ochre and fat. They seem even to have practised primitive medicine, for puffballs were found whose inner tissue might have been used as a blood-clotting agent.

Equally there is much that we do not know about them. Where did they come from? What contact did they have with other communities? Why did they abandon their village? But these enigmas cannot detract from the fact that this little cluster of buildings nestling in the sand-dunes beside the Bay of Skaill still remains the best-preserved Stone-Age village in northern Europe.

For 4000 years the hunter-gatherers roamed the land. The wild landscape gradually became home to them, as they returned year upon year to old and familiar haunts. Their primitive stone tools, at first useful only for catching fish and game, developed into implements capable of felling trees and tilling the soil. By 4000 BC, our remote ancestors had begun to put down tentative roots, literally, by growing cereals. We don't know why, or how, they turned their hand to farming, but the move proved irreversible.

Farming represented an entirely different approach to food production. Wild animals continued to be hunted, but certain breeds – cattle, sheep, goats and pigs – were now tamed and domesticated to ensure a more sustainable supply of food, drink and other products. While natural plants were still harvested, certain crops, like wheat, barley and flax, were more carefully nurtured to achieve the same end – a kind of prehistoric genetic engineering. Both activities required a more settled way of living.

These first farmers have left behind much more than their hunter-gatherer predecessors; not just the refuse from nature's larder but more permanent structures like houses and fields, ceremonial temples and burial tombs. As a consequence we know a good deal more about them.

For one thing, they were certainly not primitive. Could 'noble savages' have built the monumental Maes Howe in Orkney, or lived in those wonderful houses at nearby Skara Brae, all too eerily like our own, with their beds, dressing tables, even flushing toilets? All these in an age before Stonehenge and the great pyramids of Egypt were built? Most certainly not. Such ruins silently tell of a cultured, inventive and resourceful people.

But a circle has no beginning or end.
The symbol holds. People in AD 2000 are essentially the same as the stone-breakers and horizon-breakers of 3000 BC.

▲ *The monumental tomb of Maes Howe, in Orkney, dispels any lingering doubts we might harbour that our remote ancestors were 'noble savages'. So sophisticated is the tomb's construction, with its gigantic interlocking stones, that had the best architect of our present generation designed it they would be truly proud of their achievement.*

▶ *The stone circles on Machrie Moor, Arran, are lonely reminders of a hidden ancient world. For beneath the peat lie burial cairns and cists, hut circles and settlements, field walls and plough marks, all testifying to the intensive use to which our early farmers put this fertile land, until the decline in the climate and the formation of the peat forced them to move elsewhere.*

discovered, its entire contents apparently dumped in the same season. The harvest points to the gatherers not just collecting the nuts, but actively managing the island's hazel trees to increase the annual return. Such scraps of evidence may give us only a few, tantalising facts, but they do hint at additional possibilities. The Colonsay find implies a substantial communal effort, perhaps with different groups coming together for a while. We have no direct evidence for our remote ancestors wearing clothes, but the tools of bone, antler and stone found suggest they had clothes, bedcovers, tents and boats made from hide.

The study of modern hunter-gathering societies, like those in southern Africa, can help to 'flesh out' the picture. They suggest that our forebears had a lot of spare time in which they did very little but rest, that they stayed in quite small groups, meeting very few other people during the course of their lives, that theirs was an egalitarian society and they had little thought for personal possessions. We have come a long way since then!

Of course, there is so much that we don't know about them, nor will ever know. What language did they speak? Did they marry? What were the respective roles of men and women? Well, it might all have been an awfully long time ago, but it is fascinating nevertheless to think that, although these first 'Scots' have been joined by many incomers since, there remains something of them in all of us.

(George Mackay Brown in his introduction to *Brodgar Poems*, 1992.)

Another thing is clear: they didn't live in splendid isolation. Take their polished stone axes, traded over enormous distances. One axe made at Creag na Caillach, in Perthshire, Scotland's only known axe factory, has turned up in leafy Buckinghamshire! And another from Cairnpapple, the ceremonial site high in the Bathgate Hills of West Lothian, had been imported from as far afield as North Wales.

Much mystery shrouds our earliest farmers. Fortunately, because many of their burial tombs have yielded up skeletal remains, we can at least picture for the first time what our remote ancestors looked like, and learn something about the life they led. The chambered tomb at Isbister, in Orkney, nicknamed 'the tomb of the eagles' because of the large amount of bones and talons from sea eagles discovered there, has produced the best-studied stone-age community to date in Scotland – 342 individuals from across the age range; only the very young were absent. From the contents of this grisly sepulchre we discover that they were slightly smaller than us, and that their life expectancy was a good deal less. Most died soon after reaching the age of 25, and only a handful, mostly men, reached the ripe-old age of 50. The rigours of childbirth would certainly have contributed to the earlier demise of the womenfolk, but deformities found on their skulls showed also that a number of women carried loads by means of a 'brow-band'.

The Isbister tomb offers us a snapshot of what we may regard as a typical stone-age community. It was mostly a young (by our standards), hardworking population, in which almost everyone, including the children, would have played their part – working in the fields, tending the animals, hunting, gathering and fishing. Reaching the grand old age of 50 may well have bestowed a special respect and status on those so blessed.

MAKING METALS

After 4000 BC, there came changes and innovations, indicating a dynamic, developing society. But one change stands out above all others: the discovery, around 2000 BC, of metals. The introduction of gold, copper, tin and bronze into the everyday lives of our remote ancestors must have been as revolutionary as the introduction of plastic in the modern era; life would never be the same again.

The appearance of metals coincided with another significant change – the replacement of communal burial tombs by ones containing just one individual, probably a 'chief'. The two were probably linked. The transition suggests that the egalitarian life of the hunter-gatherers had given way to a hierarchical system, in which a select few exercised power over the many. Maybe these same leaders also controlled the production and distribution of the new metals. Such power would have been hugely important given that the metals were comparatively rare and required to be traded over considerable distances. Apart from the gold-bearing rivers of Sutherland and Lanarkshire, there were no gold deposits then known in Scotland, and the most likely source would have been Ireland; tin, which when mixed

▲ So much of the story of our remote ancestors is a mystery, no 'evidence' more enigmatic than those cup-and-ring-marked rocks they left behind, such as this example at Cairnbaan, Argyllshire.

◄ The chambered tomb on the Orkney island of Rousay served as the cemetery for a small community of Stone-Age farming families. When excavated, nine corpses were found lying in the stalls, crouched on their sides and facing into the central space. Three more skulls had been placed upright on a bench, and the remains of at least 15 other people were scattered about the chamber, suggesting that the tomb was no sealed sepulchre but one whose grisly contents were continually being visited, and added to, by their descendants.

▶ *Mousa Broch, in Shetland, is the best-preserved of a type of building that is unique to Scotland. Reaching to a height of 43 ft (13 m), the double-skinned walls, featureless save for a single low entrance, are a powerful reminder of the troubled times in Scotland that confronted our Iron-Age ancestors as the climate worsened, peat formed and cultivatable land became increasingly scarce.*

▼ *The rickle of stones called Dun Ringill hugging a cliff-edge overlooking Loch Slapin, on Skye, is all that remains of an Iron-Age defensive structure, or dun, occupied by a local warlord around 2000 years ago. It was still being lived in 1000 years later, probably by the chiefs of Clan MacKinnon before they relocated to Caisteal Maol beside Kyleakin.*

with copper produces bronze, could only have been mined in Cornwall. Possession of these precious metals must have bestowed a very special status on those controlling the means of production.

The appearance of bronze was once taken as evidence of an 'invasion' by other peoples. Few hold to that view now. It seems more plausible that the metals, like the stone axes that preceded

them, were traded, and that their appearance simply had an effect, albeit profound, on the nature and structure of the existing communities. Certainly farming remained the dominant activity for the majority of the population, which continued to grow and expand into hitherto uncultivated upland pastures. An ox-yoke from Argyllshire is the oldest evidence for traction animals in Britain, and the oldest cartwheel, dated to about 1100 BC, was found at Blairdrummond Moss, in the Forth valley, in the nineteenth century.

As 1000 BC approached, Scotland's climate began to deteriorate horribly. Quite why is unclear, though there is evidence for intense volcanic activity around this time, which unquestionably contributed by throwing great clouds of sulphurous dust high into the atmosphere and blocking out the sun's rays; the eruption of Hekla, in Iceland, in 1159 BC had such a devastating effect on Ireland's climate that the oak forests there took 18 years to recover. Just think – 18 years without a harvest, in an age without 'fridges'! The colder, wetter weather encouraged peat to form, making crop-growing increasingly difficult and harvests more

~ WHO WERE THE CELTS? ~

'there's not a team like the Glasgow Celtic'

(Parkhead football chant)

The popular notion persists that at some date around 700 BC, Scotland was conquered by the Celts. These woad-painted, sword-wielding warriors from central Europe had already overrun most of the Continent; now they arrived at these shores, subdued the natives and made this land their own. By such means did Scotland become part of a European-wide Celtic society stretching from Ireland to eastern Europe, a culture that would in time defiantly resist the armed might of Imperial Rome. The truth is very probably something quite different.

The idea that our history evolved only through a cycle of invasions, colonisations and displacements is relatively recent. It originated in the nineteenth century through archaeologists attempting to explain how certain material objects or physical structures sharing close characteristics came to be found dispersed over huge distances. Hence the invention of the 'Beaker folk', who at the start of the 'Bronze Age' created a form of pottery that is found widely across Europe. The creation of the 'Celts' as an all-conquering race followed the same logic. It was based largely on the discovery of decorative metalwork from a lake near La Tène in Switzerland, of a type also to be found across great swathes of Europe. Archaeologists put 2 + 2 together – and came up with 5. They presumed that language and material culture (art, architecture and so forth) could be spread only through conquest.

That there was a tribe called the Celts is undeniable. The Greeks referred to the 'Keltoi' in the sixth century BC, and subsequent Roman authors wrote of the 'Celtae'. By Julius Caesar's time in the first century BC, these Celts were clearly inhabiting southern and central France. Nowhere is there any hard evidence that these same Celts had invaded and conquered Scotland several centuries earlier.

What there is evidence for, though, is of several closely related languages linking the peoples of a substantial part of northern and western Europe – and these tongues, which included Scots Gaelic, Pictish, Cumbric and Brittonic, have been

▲ *The hallmark of Celtic art is its fundamentally flowing abstract character overlain with subtle symbolism. A perfect example is this marvellous bronze cap designed to be worn by a pony, found at Torrs, in Kirkcudbrightshire, and dating from a century or so before the time of Christ.*

labelled 'Celtic'. The error archaeologists made in the nineteenth century was to equate this linguistic spread with the material evidence. So how could language spread if not through conquest?

The answer is that it could just as easily have been spread through the processes of exchange and trade. As far back as Stone Age times, highly prized commodities like stone axes were traded over immense distances. During the Bronze Age the rare metals of gold and tin were similarly 'exported'. In order for goods to be traded, merchants would have needed to converse. Even if their respective languages were quite different and mutually unintelligible, some form of common language would have been required. This was after all how Swahili developed in more recent times, a fundamentally Bantu tongue modified by Arabic through the extensive East African trade and now spoken by 30 million people world wide.

That said, there might conceivably have been some small-scale conquests, or movements of tribes, from the Continent of Europe into Scotland during the pre-Roman era. Caesar himself wrote of the Belgae, whose southern boundary marched with that of the Celtae, having crossed to southern England some time before 100 BC, and it may be that similar encroachments were made along Scotland's eastern coast. It is also conceivable that the arrival of the Belgae put pressure on the indigenous population and forced them north in search of pastures new. Famine and disease may also have prompted such wholesale movements of people.

Notwithstanding the passage of time, there is still a unique bond uniting the 'Celtic' peoples, chiefly those of Scotland, Man, Ireland, Wales, Cornwall and Brittany. There is no doubting the common culture, of language and music, that identifies us, that marks us out as being from a common root. But it is most unlikely that our Scottish link with the Celtic tradition all came about with a single conquest, as attractive and as fascinating as that idea sounds.

▲ *Lonely broch towers tend to reinforce the standard image of them as defensive 'bolt-holes'. Recent excavations, however, show that they were quite elaborate farmhouses – defensive yes, but capable of housing an extended family in some style. The broch at Midhowe (pictured above), on the Orcadian island of Rousay, had a 'fully furnished' interior including a water cistern, fireplace and partitioned rooms.*

▶ *Excavation at the imposing Iron-Age broch tower of Dun Charlabhaigh, on Lewis, reveals that people had been living inside it, on and off, throughout most of the first millennium AD, the age of the 'invaders'.*

uncertain. Up till then the trend had been towards expansion of farmland; now the whole process went into reverse. The result was a growing competition for usable land, an economic pressure that resulted in an increasingly hostile social environment.

Then, around 700 BC, another technological advance was made – the ability to forge iron, a harder, more durable metal than bronze. It can only have made it easier for man to wage war. But iron's arrival had another significance. Whereas copper and tin ores were rare, iron ore was far more widely available. At a stroke, the power of those aristocratic élites controlling bronze production was rendered worthless. From now on, control of the land and of those dwelling on it would reside in the hands of a much larger number of locally based warrior chiefs.

One of the tangible legacies of this 'Bronze-Age crash' was a prolific boom in the building of fortifications. These came in all shapes and sizes –

great hill-forts girdled about with banks and ditches, modest palisaded homesteads, and artificial islands called crannogs. Scotland's Iron-Age inhabitants even produced their own unique fortification – awesome broch towers, none more striking than Mousa, in Shetland, still standing over 42 ft (13 m) high.

At first glance, such strongholds present a bleak picture of society in a constant state of warmongering, of a breakdown in law and order, of families and whole communities perpetually sheltering behind their rude defences in fear and trepidation. But that need not have been the case. If we see the advent of iron as breaking the power-base of the 'bronze masters' and transferring that power down from the few to the many, then we might just as easily see these fortifications as expressions by the new petty chiefs of their new-found wealth and status, just as the barons in medieval times perceived their mighty castles.

INVADERS

(AD 79 - 850)

> 'From the fury of the Northmen, O Lord, deliver us'
> *(A prayer offered up by the beleaguered monks of Iona around AD 800)*

Throughout the first millennium AD wave upon wave of invaders washed up onto Scotland's shores – Romans, Scots, Angles and Vikings. This chapter explores the profound impact each had upon the indigenous peoples – the Britons and those elusive Picts.

ROMANS

In the spring of AD 79 the armed might of Imperial Rome marched northward over the Cheviot Hills and entered Scotland in strength. At their head was Gnaeus Julius Agricola, governor of Britain; his objective – to fight 'battle after battle till we have reached the end of Britain'. By the end of that summer, the seasoned commander had advanced his battle-hardened legionaries as far as the River Tay.

Ptolemy, a second-century geographer from Egypt, helpfully named the Celtic tribes then inhabiting the northern part of the British Isles. South of the Forth and Clyde were four tribes: the Votadini in eastern Scotland, the Selgovae in the centre, the Novantae in the south-west and the Damnonii across the Clyde and Kelvin valleys. To the north were a further twelve tribes, from the Venicones in Fife to the Cornavii in Caithness. Beyond were the Orcades (Orkney), not named by Ptolemy but whose king had submitted to the Emperor Claudius in AD 43 during the initial conquest of Britain. Agricola's son-in-law and biographer, Tacitus, brackets these northern states together under one name, the Caledones, or Caledonians; the name Dunkeld means 'fortress of the Caledones' and the peak Schiehallion, 'fairy hill of the Caledones'. It was the Caledonians who most defiantly resisted the Roman menace.

There was clearly very little the native tribes inhabiting southern Scotland could do in the face of Agricola's 25,000 battle-hardened troops. They seem to have accepted their lot, adjusted to the new political order and become part of the Roman Empire. But as Agricola looked north beyond the Tay at the end of that first campaigning season he would have known that the tribes confronting him would not so easily be subdued. There in what the Romans called the Caledonian Forest lurked, so they thought, an enemy of 'half-naked savages with reddish hair and large limbs'. The Caledonians saw things differently, of course; they were 'the last people on earth, the last of the free'.

◀ *The Picts defeat an invading Anglian army – a scene from the beguiling carved stone in the churchyard at Aberlemno, in Angus. Aberlemno lies just 6 miles (10 km) north of the battle site of Nechtansmere (Dunnichen), where in 685 King Bridei's Picts routed King Ecgfrith of Northumbria's Angles. Does this stone depict that momentous event perhaps?*

'Scotland's First Battle'

~ MONS GRAUPIUS ~

'to fight battle after battle till we have reached the end of Britain'

(From Tacitus's Life of Agricola)

▲ *The dark and brooding peak of Bennachie, in the Garioch of Aberdeenshire. Could this be the 'Mons Graupius' Romans wrote about as providing the backdrop for their great victory over the Caledonian tribes in AD 83?*

The battle of Mons Graupius, AD 83, is the first recorded battle in Scotland's history. The Caledonian tribes had until then resisted Rome's invitation to a pitched battle, adopting the more tried and tested tactics of 'hit and run'. Only the previous year an audacious night attack had almost won them the scalp of the mighty *Legio IX Hispana* – the Ninth Legion. But the time had come for those whom Tacitus called 'the last people on earth' to stand and fight.

Precisely where the battle was fought is not known; maybe it never will be. Inspired guesses cover a swathe of north-east Scotland from Dunning in Perthshire to the vicinity of Culloden near Inverness. Perhaps the prominent hill of Bennachie in Aberdeenshire, 1732 ft (528 m) high and overlooking the great Roman camp at Logie Durno, fits best with Tacitus's 'Graupian Mountain'.

(A medieval clerical error resulted in 'Mons Grampius', and the error stuck; hence the Grampian Mountains.)

Prior to the battle, the Caledonians made detailed preparations, sending their women and children to places of safety and electing as their leader Calgacus, 'a man of outstanding valour and nobility'. Calgacus – his name means 'swordsman' – has the distinction of being Scotland's first named inhabitant.

Calgacus drew his troops up across the hillside, the front line with the chariots on the level ground below the mountain and the remainder rising up the gentle slopes behind – in total some 30,000 men. In the valley before them stood the might of Imperial Rome, 8000 auxiliaries, 5000 cavalry and an unspecified number of legionaries; over 20,000 all told.

Before battle commenced, the two opposing generals made speeches to galvanise their men. Agricola's, predictably enough, alluded to the bravery of the Roman army and the cowardice of the enemy, stressing that victory that day would complete the conquest of the island of Britain. Obviously that ascribed to Calgacus is pure invention, a conceit by Tacitus to moralise on the theme of 'the innocent savage uncontaminated by decadent Roman ways'. It is nevertheless stirring stuff, as patriotic in its language as the Declaration of Arbroath, and as bellicose in its tones as Winston Churchill at his best:

We are the last people on earth, and the last of the free. Our very remoteness in a land known only by rumour has protected us up to this day. But now there is no people beyond us, nothing but tides and rocks and, more deadly than these, the Romans. It is no use trying to escape their arrogance by submission or good behaviour. They have pillaged the world; when the land has nothing left for men who ravage everything, they scour the sea. If an enemy is rich, they are greedy; if he is poor, they crave glory. Neither East nor West can sate their appetite. They are the only people on earth to covet wealth and poverty with equal craving. To robbery, butchery and

▲ *This bronze visor mask, found at the Roman fort of Trimontium (Newstead), near Melrose, could have been worn by a member of any one of the well-paid cavalry units stationed there during the Roman occupation of Scotland.*

rapine they give the lying name of 'government' They make a desert and call it peace.

With these words supposedly ringing in his men's ears, Calgacus made the first move, deploying his charioteers. The Romans had long since abandoned the chariot as an instrument of battle, and the Caledonian charioteers were soon routed. An exchange of missiles followed, and then a Roman infantry advance. In the close fighting the shorter stabbing swords of the Romans proved more than a match for the longer slashing swords of Calgacus's troops. The greater mass of Caledonians waiting in reserve could hold off no longer, seized their moment and bore down on the enemy, in the fashion of the classic Highland Charge of later centuries, threatening to turn their foe. Agricola responded by deploying his reserve cavalry. The Caledonian advance was halted, then turned and pressed back into the woods where they momentarily rallied before the combined Roman infantry and cavalry finally broke their resistance. They fled deeper into the forest 'deliberately keeping apart from each other; they penetrated far into trackless wilds', the victorious Romans in hot pursuit. By nightfall the death-count was: Caledonians 10,000, Romans 360. Brave Calgacus must have made his escape, since had he been either captured or killed Tacitus would surely have trumpeted the fact.

Agricola's victory proved short-lived, his objective of 'reaching the end of Britain' thwarted by the Scottish climate and Roman politics. Mons Graupius may have been Scotland's first recorded battle, but it certainly wasn't the last.

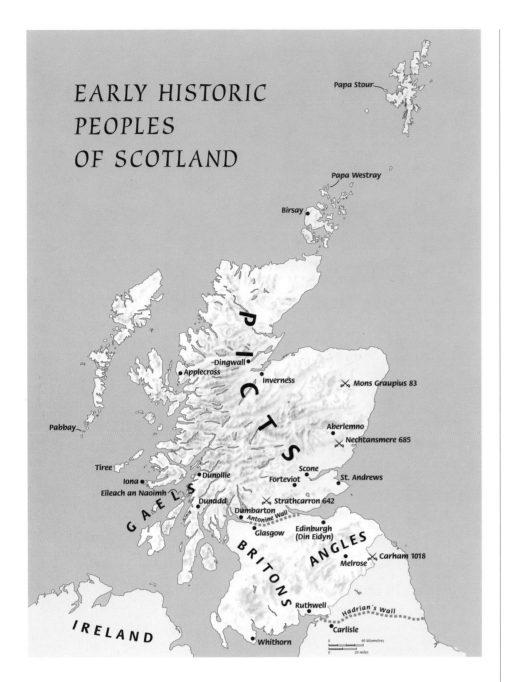

EARLY HISTORIC
PEOPLES
OF SCOTLAND

Papa Stour

Papa Westray

Birsay

P
I
C
T
S

Dingwall
Applecross
Inverness
✕ *Mons Graupius 83*

Pabbay

Aberlemno
✕ *Nechtansmere 685*

Tiree
Scone
Iona
Dunollie
Forteviot
St. Andrews
Eileach an Naoimh
Dunadd
✕ *Strathcarron 642*

G
A
E
L
S

Dumbarton
Antonine Wall
Glasgow
Edinburgh (Din Eidyn)

B
R
I
T
O
N
S

A
N
G
L
E
S

Melrose ✕ *Carham 1018*

Ruthwell

Hadrian's Wall

Carlisle

IRELAND

Whithorn

40 kilometres

20 miles

▲ *This map shows
how the four 'peoples'
occupying Scotland in the
aftermath of the Roman
withdrawal around 400 –
the native Picts and
Britons, and the invading
Gaels and Angles – were
disposed. The arrival
of the marauding Vikings
after 800 rearranged
this political map
considerably.*

Agricola's advance into Caledonia was put on hold for a time. Emperor Vespasian had died in 79 and Titus (79-81) was not inclined to move. Not even the appearance of a Caledonian bear at the opening ceremony of the Coliseum in Rome in 80 could persuade him to change his mind. But Domitian (81-96) gave Agricola the 'green light' to push north. The unleashed general spent the following two summers (82 and 83) campaigning in the Caledonian Forest. He narrowly avoided disaster in the first, when the Caledonians almost succeeded in wiping out his Ninth Legion, but he achieved a great victory as the second drew to a close, at the battle of Mons Graupius, fought somewhere in north-east Scotland. Mons Graupius is the first recorded battle fought on Scottish soil.

But Agricola was denied the ultimate prize, conquest of all Britain. On the orders of the emperor, he returned his troops to their winter quarters in the south of Scotland while he himself headed for Rome and retirement. He would have had mixed feelings at leaving; on the one hand regret at not completing his mission, on the other relief at escaping the Scottish climate: 'wretched', Tacitus described it, 'with its frequent rains and mists'.

But the Romans returned. Around 140 the legionaries were back in Scotland busily constructing a new frontier to replace Emperor Hadrian's stone wall built barely 20 years earlier. The Antonine Wall, named after Emperor Antoninus Pius, was built only of turf, but even today impressive stretches of it can still be seen snaking and twisting for almost 40 miles (65 km) along the crags of Scotland's Central Belt between Old Kilpatrick on the Clyde and Bo'ness on the Forth. The Antonine Wall became Imperial Rome's most northerly frontier.

But no sooner had it been built than it too was abandoned. By 163 the legionaries were back once more behind Hadrian's Wall, leaving only isolated garrisons out-posted across southern Scotland. Then in 208 came Rome's last attempt at conquest, this one commanded by Emperor Septimius Severus in person; he even brought with him from Rome his prestigious praetorian guard. The historian, Cassius Dio, leaves us in no doubt as to Severus's intentions: 'They [the Romans] should let nobody escape, not even the children hidden in their mothers' womb'.

Twice the massed ranks of legionaries with their auxiliaries entered Caledonia – and twice they withdrew. Severus, undaunted, prepared for a third time, but his health failed him and he died unexpectedly at York. Just like another great would-be conqueror of Scotland one thousand years later – Edward I of England in 1307 – Severus was denied his ultimate prize, ground down by the very effort of it all. With Severus's passing, there was only one direction now for Rome – retreat southward and away from Scotland.

But what of the native tribes, particularly those within the Roman pale, during all this time of Roman marching and counter-marching? Alas, as far as written sources go we have only Rome's side of the story. Tacitus wrote of them 'now guarded and watched over on all sides, with such judicious care, that they became part of Britannia'. What the 'guarded and watched over' made of the situation can only be guessed at. There does seem to have been an accord between the southern Scottish tribes and their Roman 'guardians'. If we harbour visions of our forebears attempting to fight off the mighty Romans from behind the banks and ditches of those formidable Iron-Age hill-forts that abound throughout Scotland, like that on Eildon Hill North overlooking the legionary fortress of Trimontium, 'the three mountains', then we would do better to forget them. Recent archaeological investigations have shown that these strongholds had been abandoned as defensive strengths long before the Roman Eagle appeared in the skies. There is also a suspicion that some natives, probably local warlords, were doing rather well under the Roman occupation. The few Lowland brochs that were built, like those at Buchlyvie and Leckie, west of Stirling, have produced such rich assemblages of Roman goods that they hint at their owners having both the wealth and the freedom to build and live in the grand style.

What we don't know first-hand we can guess at from comparable situations elsewhere in Rome's sprawling Empire. The Romans would have imposed taxation on the cowed and defeated population; in fact they were the first to introduce coinage to Scotland, although the majority of people would have paid their taxes in kind, not cash. Other impositions would have included forced labour to build and repair the lengthy road network, and conscription into the Roman army for those of fighting age.

Hostility to the Romans never dimmed in all the time the Romans were here. Both Hadrian's and Antonine's walls were responses to continuing unrest. Whether that unrest was solely down to 'our friends in the North', the Caledonians, is unclear. What is clear is that by the reign of Emperor Commodus (180-92), 'the tribes in the island crossed the wall which

separated them from the Roman legions, did a great deal of damage, and cut down a general and his troops'. By the time Septimius Severus had taken the imperial purple in 197, there was clearly collusion between tribes for 'the Caledonians instead of honouring their promises had prepared to defend the Maeatae'. This is the first mention of the Maeatae, who inhabited the land lying to the north of the Antonine Wall; their name lives on in places such as Dumyat, 'fort of the Maeatae', north of Stirling. The governor of Britain, Lupus, 'had no choice but to buy peace from the Maeatae for a considerable sum of money'. Here is our first evidence for peace treaties between Rome and the northern states, and of the uneasy truces between them.

Severus's campaigns, whatever their primary objective, do seem to have checked the incursions on Rome's most northerly frontier, because for the rest of that century nothing further is heard of the Caledonians or the Maeatae. But when they next appear, it is with a new name. In 297, Eumenius wrote of *Picti*, 'painted people', raiding down Scotland's eastern coast and across Hadrian's Wall. The northern tribes seem finally to have

◀ *Scotland has the distinction of possessing the most northerly frontier the mighty Roman Empire ever built – the Antonine Wall. Stretching across the Central Belt from Clyde to Forth, it was constructed in the 140s, not of stone like Hadrian's Wall, but of turf. A particularly good stretch of the Wall can be seen at Bar Hill, in Dunbartonshire. This view of Croy Hill, near Cumbernauld looks along the line of the ditch towards the western end of the Wall, at Old Kilpatrick.*

'Scotland's Lost Nation'

~ THE PICTS ~

'the last people on earth, and the last of the free'

(From Tacitus's Life of Agricola)

The Picts come charging onto the pages of history in AD 297, when the Roman panegyrist Emmenius tells of them raiding his beloved Roman Empire. They tiptoe quietly out during the course of the ninth century, absorbed into either the new Scottish kingdom or the Viking earldom of Orkney. They have left behind no written accounts of themselves, just some useful lists of kings and a few mainly indecipherable oghams scratched onto stone. What we know of them we know only through the writings of others, of Romans like Emmenius, of Anglo-Saxons like the Venerable Bede, and of the Scots, their neighbours to the west. They are our oldest ancestors, descended from the ancient tribes of northern Britain, and yet we know scarcely anything about them.

So ignorant were we until recently that a legion of myths had sprouted up about them down the centuries. The Romans had them 'living in tents, unclothed and unshod, sharing their women and bringing up all their children together'. Bede wrote of them coming from a faraway country and without women so that they had to beg for wives; hence the supposed Pictish tradition of succession through the female line. And an anonymous twelfth-century Norwegian described them as being: 'little more than pygmies in stature, working marvels in the morning and evening but who at midday entirely lost their strength and lurked through fear in little underground homes.' It wasn't all that long ago that the Iron-Age underground storehouses, known as souterrains, in eastern Scotland were called 'Picts' houses'. The reality was, of course, very different.

Picti was the name given them by the Romans. It simply meant 'the painted people', a reference perhaps to their custom of decorating or tattooing their bodies. What they called themselves we do not know. They inhabited much of Scotland from the Forth and Clyde to Shetland. Their roots lay in the many tribes that occupied that same territory throughout prehistory. They gradually confederated, doubtless in response to the Roman menace, and by 600 they had merged to become one nation, ruled over by one paramount chief, or over-king. Real power, though, was held by under-kings, or warlords, operating at a more regional level. In this the Picts were no different from other Celtic societies. Tradition has it that there were seven such under-kings, all descended from Cruithne, the eponymous father of the Pictish nation. Each ruled a province named after one of his sons – Cait (Caithness), Fidach (Ross and Moray), Ce (Mar and Buchan), Fotla (Gowrie and Atholl), Circinn (Angus and the Mearns), Fortriu (Strathearn and Menteith) and Fib (Fife).

We know most about the Picts through their fighting and warring. When we first encounter them they are resisting the Roman menace. No sooner had the shadow of Rome faded from the land than other threats emerge, most threateningly from their erstwhile allies in the 'Barbarian Conspiracy', the *Scotti*, or 'pirates', who encroach from the west. Next come the Angles, Germanic incomers from the Continent, and later the Viking hordes descending from the north. Their carved symbol stones bear silent witness to this warrior society, who are depicted armed to the teeth with sword, spear, shield and horse. The gruesome account of the ritual drowning of an under-king, Talorgen, by his overlord, the mighty Oengus I, in 739, is testimony to the fundamentally Celtic nature of Pictish society.

But the Picts were men and women also, who farmed the land, fished the rivers, lochs and seas, played games, cracked jokes, made love, died and were buried. This peaceful side to their nature is evident in place-names (such as those beginning with *pit*, meaning 'part' or 'share', eg. Pitlochry, 'stony share'), and becoming increasingly more apparent through archaeological excavation as the vestigial remains of their homes and cemeteries are discovered. But it is also there for all to see in those wonderful symbol stones. These unique creations, dotted about Pictland from Fife to Shetland, and festooned with beasts, birds and fishes, mirrors, combs and crescents, display a remarkably cohesive cultural unity for such a far-flung nation. Even more remarkably, through their decorative devices and Christian symbolism, they declare themselves to be truly international in outlook.

Pictland ceased to exist in the ninth century, absorbed into the expanding kingdom of the Scots. Tradition holds that it was Kenneth mac Alpin who was the first of the Scots to rule over the Picts also around the year 843; in reality it wasn't that straightforward. Previous Scottish kings had lorded it over Pictland, whilst Pictish rulers had likewise held sway over the Scots. But Kenneth's reign marked the watershed, and from his time on it was the Scots who imposed themselves on 'the fierce men of the east'. By 900 the customs, institutions and language of the Gaels held sway; the Picts were history.

collaborated to form a 'united states' that would more effectively deal with the Roman threat. As the next century dawned so their raids increased in intensity and frequency. Rome responded as best it could, but to little avail. Peace treaties were made, then just as easily broken. Emperors came, like Constantine the Great in 312, and just as quickly went away again. By 367, the Romans were bemoaning the 'barbarian conspiracy' of Picts and others 'visiting a never-ending series of disasters' on Rome. By then, any lingering ambitions the Romans had of conquering Scotland were well and truly buried.

What then of Rome's legacy for Scotland? Very little in all truth. Not one inch of it was ever fully within the Roman Empire. There was no civilian rule, no towns, no country villas as there were on the other side of Hadrian's Wall, just military rule, here and there, and on and off. Not even Rome's great road network has survived to guide today's road planners; just as the modern A68 reaches Scotland it parts company with ancient Rome's Dere Street.

GAELS

When the Picts raided the Roman frontier in 367, they were not alone; among their fellow 'conspirators' were a people the Romans called *Scotti*. The name may simply mean 'pirates'. They certainly came from across the sea, for their homeland was Ireland. They clearly liked what they saw, for by the time the Roman menace had gone, they had begun to colonise the western seaboard of Scotland. Unlike the Romans, they were here to stay.

Tradition holds that the Scots, under their legendary leader Fergus Mór, crossed the narrow but treacherous North Channel from the Glens of Antrim to the rocky coast of Argyll around AD 500. In reality, they had infiltrated well before then. The vacuum created by Rome's retreat may well have been the cause.

The Romans may have called them Scotti; they called themselves Gaels ('Goidil' in Old Irish). Like the Picts and Britons they were a Celtic people, but their Gaelic tongue was quite different from that

spoken by the tribes of northern Britain. The very name 'Argyll' comes from the Gaelic *Earra Ghaidheal*, 'coastland of the Gael'.

The Gaels were organised into kindreds, or extended families, called *cenéla*. Their Argyll lands came to be divided between four *cenéla*, Loairn, nGabhráin, nOengus, and Comgaill, each named after its founder. We even know the territories of each: Cenél Loairn in northern Argyll, in what is now Lorn, Cenél nGabhráin in Knapdale and Kintyre, Cenél nOengus, in Islay and Cenél Comgaill in Cowal. Their kings ruled from imposing fortresses such as Dunollie, beside Oban, and Dunadd, in Kilmartin Glen.

▲ *What are we to make of the 200 or so mysterious Pictish symbol stones that abound in Scotland from the Firth of Forth to the Northern and Western Isles, such as that pictured here, the Picardy Stone, near Insch in Aberdeenshire, with its incised double disc and Z-rod, serpent and Z-rod, and mirror? All we can say with confidence is that they are unique to the Picts, for no other European society has left such an absorbing but thoroughly enigmatic legacy.*

▲ This depiction of a West Highland galley, or birlinn, now in Iona Abbey Museum, may have been carved on Iona or Mull around 1500, but it serves to illustrate that the sea was in the blood of every Gael, from the time of their arrival on Scotland's shores over a thousand years earlier.

We know all this because a remarkable document survives from those far-off days, the *Senchus Fer nAlban* ('The History of the Men of Scotland'). This is Britain's earliest census, 400 years older than William the Conqueror's *Domesday Book*. Drawn up in the seventh century, it records the composition of each *cenél* in extraordinary detail – the townships within each kindred, the number of households within each township, the names of householders and so forth: '...Eógan Garb has 30 houses, his wife is Crodu, daughter of Dallan, son of Eógan, son of Niall...'

Its purpose was to provide the king with an assessment of the number of fighting men at his command, and for every 20 houses he could count on 28 men. But these were sailors, not soldiers, for this was a maritime nation and the navy was all-important. By the reckoning of the *Senchus*, the king could count on a fighting force of nearly 2000 men in 140 seven-benched ships, 14 men per ship. Hardly surprising then that it is the Gaels who

provide us with the first recorded naval battle in Britain's history, fought between Cenél nGabhráin and Cenél Loairn in 917.

When the Gaels first crossed to Argyll they were pagan, just like their Pictish neighbours. But by the end of the fifth century they had become Christian, thanks in the main to the missionary work of St Patrick, the son of a Roman official who, when just a young lad, was snatched from his home somewhere in Cumbria by a band of raiders and taken across the Irish Sea as a slave. It is possible that St Columba's parents, Fedelmid and Eithne, were converted as a result of Patrick's later missionary work.

Columba wasn't the first Irish saint to cross to Scotland; nor was he the last. The trail had been blazed by St Brendan of Clonfert, who crossed to Scotland and established holy places on Tiree, and, most evocative of all, his isolated retreat of Eileach an Naoimh, 'island of the saints', in the Firth of Lorn. But Brendan was a restless soul, never content to remain in one place for long, and Scotland was but a stopping-place along intrepid journeys that took him north through the Outer Hebrides and the Northern Isles on to the Faroes and Iceland – and, who knows, maybe to North America also. Not for nothing is he known as St Brendan 'the Navigator'.

Brendan, Columba and other Gaelic holy men were the people who, through their constant journeyings, spread the Christian word, not only among their own people but to nations far beyond: to the Picts of eastern and northern Scotland and the Angles of Northumbria.

Wondrous the warriors who abode on I[ona],
Thrice fifty in monastic rule,
With their hearts on the main sea
Three score men a-rowing.
(From the *Old Irish Life of Columba*.)

It almost defies belief that such journeys were possible given their flimsy skin-covered curraghs and the lack of navigational aids save the very stars themselves. But the proof that they did so is there for all to see today, in the plethora of place-names incorporating *papa*, the old Irish word for 'father', found sprinkled about in the most remote of locations – for example the two Pabbays in the Western Isles, Papa Westray in the Orkney Islands and Papa Stour in the Shetland Islands. That these same *papar* ventured even further into the unknown is proved by the existence of Papey, a little island off Iceland's east coast. It was a perilous business, and not all these saintly men survived the perils of the deep. Abbot Failbe mac Guaire of Applecross was 'drowned in the deep with his sailors, twenty-two in number' in 737. Doubtless there were many others who died for their faith in similar circumstances.

During Columba's time, the kings of Argyll held sway not only over their own Scottish colony but over their traditional Ulster homelands also. The situation was not to last; a severing of the umbilical cord was inevitable. The end came in 637 when King Domnall Brecc was beaten in battle at Mag Rath, in County Down. The defeat cost him his Ulster lands.

Meanwhile, Gaelic relations with their neighbours to the east, the Picts, Britons and Angles, fared little better. Early expansionist hopes initially met with success but then suffered a severe setback in 603 with King Áedán's defeat at the hands of the Northumbrians at Degsastan, a battle site that has so far proved elusive but may be Addinston (Áedán's Stone), near Lauder. Domnall Brecc, Áedán's successor, lost twice to the Picts before finally coming to grief in 642 at Strathcarron, in Stirlingshire, fighting King Owen's Strathclyde Britons.

The subsequent history of the Scottish Gaels is of internal strife between the various kindreds, interspersed with warring against external foes, particularly the Picts. In time, however, relations between the two became tempered by more peaceful contacts, including intermarriage between the ruling dynasties. The missionary work of their holy men, which resulted in the Picts converting to Christianity, helped to oil the diplomatic wheels. Óengus I mac Fergusa (729-61), the great Pictish king who, having overcome all his rivals for the Pictish throne in 729, then went on to defeat the Gaels also, had a Gaelic name, as did his father, strongly hinting that Scots blood coursed through his veins. By the close of that century we even find kings ruling over the two nations simultaneously; a formal union between the two nations was clearly in the offing.

ANGLES

The Picts and Scots weren't the only 'barbarian conspirators' raiding beyond Hadrian's Wall in 367. Saxons, too, had sailed across the North Sea to plunder the rich farmlands of eastern England. These Germanic invaders were followed by others, including people from the region of Angulus, modern-day Schleswig-Holstein in northern Germany. The Angles put the 'Eng' in England. By the sixth century they had established colonies in eastern Yorkshire and along the coastal plain of Northumberland. The new Anglian kingdom of Northumbria (literally 'north of the Humber') soon emerged. It was the most powerful Anglo-Saxon kingdom until the rise of Mercia and Wessex in the eighth century.

The neighbouring British kingdoms soon sensed danger. The people of Rheged, the British kingdom

▲ The repeated pillaging of Iona by the Vikings around 800 forced the abbot and brethren to relocate to Kells in Ireland. It seems that among the possessions they took with them was the lavishly illustrated gospel book we know today as the Book of Kells.

The page shown here depicts the four gospel writers, Matthew, Mark, Luke and John. The design is remarkably similar to gospel books produced elsewhere and to artwork on Pictish symbol stones, confirming that the monks on Iona kept in close touch with their fellow brothers in Christ elsewhere.

'Sons of the Rock'

~ THE BRITONS OF STRATHCLYDE ~

'a strongly defended political centre of the Britons called Al Cluith (Clyde Rock)'

(From The Venerable Bede's A History of the English Church and People, *c. 735)*

On a lonely hillside in Glen Falloch, in the shadow of Ben Lomond, stands a boulder, Clach nam Breatann, 'the stone of the Britons'. It is said to mark the northernmost extent of the ancient British kingdom of Strathclyde. That territory once covered a huge swathe of western Scotland, and at its height in the tenth century extended from the Lennox, the area around Loch Lomond, south across the Solway Firth into Cumbria, where another lonely boundary marker, the Rere-Cross in the Stainmore Pass, east of Penrith, marks the southernmost limit of their lands.

The Britons, with the Picts, are Scotland's oldest inhabitants, the descendants of those tribes named by Ptolemy in the second century AD, which included the Votadini, the Selgovae, the Novantes and the Damnonii. Like the Picts, they emerged from the ashes of the Roman Empire relatively unscathed – the Votadini as the British kingdom of the Gododdin, the Selgovae and Novantes as the British kingdom of Rheged, and the Damnonii as the British kingdom of Strathclyde. But whereas the people of the Gododdin and Rheged were conquered by the Angles of Northumbria during the course of the seventh century AD, the Britons of Strathclyde, in their heartlands around the Clyde valley and the Firth of Clyde, survived the repeated incursions of Angles, Picts

and Gaels alike. And until their eventual incorporation into the kingdom of Scotland in the early eleventh century, they remained leading power brokers throughout the later Dark Ages in Scotland. *Dun Breatann*, 'fortress of the Britons' – now Dumbarton Rock – was the impregnable fastness from which their kings exercised that power.

Dumbarton Rock is everything you imagine the stronghold of a mighty Dark-Age warlord to be. The brute mass of hard, volcanic rock rises up almost sheer from the dark waters of the rivers Clyde and Leven that meet and swirl around its base. From its twin peaks one can see for miles around, westward to the mountains of Cowal, south across

the Clyde to the green Renfrewshire hills, eastward to Glasgow, and northward over the Vale of Leven to the snow-capped summit of Ben Lomond beyond. It was from Dumbarton Rock that the powerful kings of Strathclyde held sway – kings like Coroticus, to whom St Patrick wrote around 460, castigating him for raiding a fledgling Christian community in his adopted Ireland, and Donald, who ended his days in 975 a pilgrim in the Eternal City of Rome.

The Britons of Strathclyde have generally received a poor press down the centuries, perhaps because they have left little account of themselves. Yet they are the unsung heroes of the Dark Ages in Scotland. Although caught in a vicelike

▲ *The twin peaks of Dumbarton Rock served as the 'capital city' of Strathclyde for centuries. When Prince Duncan of Strathclyde became King Duncan I of Scotland in 1034, Strathclyde was formally integrated into the Scottish kingdom, and Dumbarton, 'Clyde Rock', was abandoned to the seabirds.*

▲ *The modern-day 'Sons of the Rock', aka Dumbarton Town F.C., seen pictured here in 1896. Like their ancestors, the Britons, they are 'great sturdy men'!*

And yet it wasn't the Vikings who benefited from their victory. The storming of Dumbarton Rock forced the beleaguered Britons to look to the Scots for aid. By now the Scots were in the ascendant following Kenneth mac Alpin's takeover of Pictland in the 840s, and it didn't take long for them to take control of Strathclyde also. They had its king, Artgal, assassinated, and the remnant of his once-mighty war-band expelled from their lands. The ousted warriors soon put their fighting skills to good use, helping the king of Gwynedd, north Wales, defend his realm from the incursions of the English.

Thereafter, Strathclyde became a client-kingdom of the Scots, and under the protection of their kings it flourished once more. With the Anglian kingdom of Northumbria no more, and the Viking menace marginalised, so the Strathclyde Britons moved south into the vacuum and reclaimed most of the lost Cumbrian lands. The kings of Strathclyde even called themselves the kings of Cumbria. Such now was the relationship between Strathclyde and Scotland that the rulers of Strathclyde were seen as heirs-apparent of the Scottish throne. That is why, in 1018, the last King of Strathclyde, Owen the Bald, fought alongside King Malcolm II of Scotland at the battle of Carham, and how, in 1034, on Malcolm II's death, his grandson, Prince Duncan of Strathclyde, ascended the Scottish throne as King Duncan I (Duncan is better known to history as the King murdered by Macbeth.) From 1034 Strathclyde as a political entity was no more, now fully integrated into the Kingdom of Scotland. But old habits die hard, which explains why, in 1113, Prince David (later King David I) was permitted to govern southern Scotland, including Strathclyde and Cumbria, while his elder brother, Alexander I, ruled as King of Scots.

grip between the Picts to their north, the Gaels to their west and the Angles to their east and south, these 'great sturdy men' valiantly resisted all attempts to subdue them. It was the Britons of Strathclyde, under King Owen, who checked the advance of Domnall Brecc's Gaels into central Scotland, at Strathcarron in 642, and who through Bridei, son of King Bili of Strathclyde, put the Anglian war-machine into reverse at Nechtansmere in 685. At first sight it might appear odd that the offspring of a king of Strathclyde could rise to become a king of the Picts, but marriage alliances between ruling dynasties were just as essential then as they are today.

The Strathclyde Britons, like their fellow Britons to the east and south, spoke an ancient form of Welsh. The very name 'Strathclyde' derives from *Ystrat Clud*, 'the valley of the Clyde', and many of their place-names survive today, including Lanark (*llanerch*, 'clearing'), Paisley (*basaleg*, 'basilica' or church), Bathgate (*baeddgoed*, 'boar wood') and, of course, Glasgow itself, *glasgau*, 'green hollow'. It was to this green hollow that Strathclyde's greatest son,

St Kentigern, came in the late sixth century to establish a church that would in time become the religious heart of a huge diocese reaching from the Clach nam Breatann to the Rere-Cross.

The kingdom of Strathclyde almost didn't make it through the Dark Ages. Having fended off the Picts, Gaels and Angles, by the middle of the ninth century they were facing a new threat – the Vikings. In the late spring of 870, Olaf of Dublin, overlord of the Scottish and Irish Vikings, met up with his compatriot Ivar Beinlaus, 'the crippled', fresh from his capture of York, and together they laid siege to Dumbarton Rock. Weeks turned into months, and still the 'sons of the Rock' held out, until finally they were 'wasted by hunger and thirst'. The victorious Vikings stormed the Rock 'and carried off all the riches that were within it and afterwards a great host of prisoners were brought into captivity.' Two hundred longships transported the booty and slaves back to Dublin. Strathclyde was all but destroyed, and Dumbarton Rock disappears from the annals of history until the thirteenth century.

▶ *The Ruthwell Cross, in Dumfriesshire, is one of the great legacies from the Anglian occupation of Scotland. Scenes from the life of Christ and depictions of the early church are framed by texts in Latin and Anglian (Old English) runes. Through word and picture, the priests would have used this eighth-century preaching cross as a teaching aid, helping them continue to bring the gospel message to the local people three centuries after St Ninian of Whithorn first introduced Christianity to their ancestors.*

The earliest Christian memorials surviving in Scotland today are to be found in the south-west of Scotland, at Whithorn and Kirkmadrine. Dating from around 450, they predate the coming of the Anglian invaders, and testify to a thriving Christian community in the area.

Christianity had actually been introduced under the auspices of the Romans; and St Patrick, Ireland's patron saint, was himself the son of Calpurnius, a Roman civil administrator and Christian deacon, and the grandson of Potitus, a priest.

that straddled the northern Pennines and took in Galloway also, were the first to suffer when their attempt to storm the Angles' fort at Lindisfarne around 590 failed and their king, Urien, was killed. Rheged was soon under the Anglian heel.

Shortly afterwards, the Gododdin, the descendants of the Votadini, under their king, Mynyddog Mwynfawr 'the magnificent', carried out a similar pre-emptive strike. Gathering around their king in the taper-lit hall atop the stronghold of Din Eidyn, in Lothian, his warlords, numbering some 300 strong, pledged themselves to fight, and if needs be to die, for him, before riding out from the rocky fastness on the long road south.

His drinking horn was handsome in the hall of Eidyn, His kingliness was spectacular, his mead was intoxicating.
(From Aneirin's poem Y Gododdin.)

It is estimated that some 24,000 men advanced on the Angles, finally doing battle with them at Catraeth, probably Catterick in Yorkshire. It proved as disastrous a gamble as Urien's assault on Lindisfarne. Scarcely any of the Gododdin survived the slaughter, among them Mynyddog's bard, Aneirin, who wrote a blow-by-blow account of the whole sorry episode. Lothian was soon overrun by the Angles, and by 638 even mighty Din Eidyn had fallen. From this time Scotland's capital city became known by its English name of Edinburgh.

The threat posed by the Angles was a major worry not just for those British kingdoms most directly concerned but also for those further removed from the theatre of war. When Urien of Rheged embarked on his fatal assault on Lindisfarne, he was joined by King Riderch and his Strathclyde Britons. Mynyddog's Gododdin were similarly supported by other Britons, including warbands from Strathclyde and Gwynedd in North Wales, as well as heathen Pictish warlords from beyond the Firth of Forth. The Gaels, too, joined the struggle, losing at Degsastan in 603. In the aftermath of that victory, the Anglo-Saxon chronicler boasted of his nation's achievement with the words: 'No king of Scots dared afterwards lead an army against this nation'. How wrong he was.

The conquering Angles did not stop at Edinburgh; emboldened by their success, they crossed the Forth and penetrated deep into Pictish

territory. They made similar gains in the west and by 684 were even attacking Ireland's east coast. But events began to conspire against them in the following year.

In 685, King Ecgfrith of Northumbria embarked on a major expedition against King Bridei's Picts. Bede records that he 'rashly led an army to ravage the province of the Picts. The enemy pretended to retreat, and lured the king into narrow mountain passes.'

The battle of Nechtansmere, fought near Dunnichen in Angus on 20 May, was a disaster for the Northumbrian king, who fell along with many of his troops. The victorious Bridei had a great stone carved with a pictorial story of the battle in honour of his triumph, and this still stands in the now tranquil surroundings of Aberlemno churchyard, a little to the north of the battlesite. In the bottom right-hand corner is a helmeted Anglian warrior lying dead while a raven picks at his skull – a depiction of the once-mighty Ecgfrith of Northumbria himself.

Nechtansmere put the Anglian advance into reverse, and they were eventually forced back south across the Forth. They continued though to make inroads into the territory of the Strathclyde Britons to the west, reaching their full extent around 750 with the conquest of Kyle (the northern part of Ayrshire). By now the Anglian kingdom of Northumbria was immense, reaching from the Firths of Forth and Clyde in the north to the Humber and the Mersey in the south. The peoples brought within its compass,

▲ *The lovingly restored medieval abbey on the island of Iona, Argyllshire, stands over the very site where St Columba set up his monastery around 563. The tiny gabled building to the left of the main abbey door is known as St Columba's Shrine, and tradition links that spot to the place where the holy man's body was first laid to rest.*

'Dove of the Church'
~ SAINT COLUMBA ~

'His relics and holy remains are on earth with honour and reverence...and his soul is in heaven'

(From Abbot Adomnán's Life of Columba, c. 690)

On Saturday 8 June 597, Columba, frail with age, journeyed with his servant, Diarmait, to a barn on his beloved Iona. It was what he had come to love doing most, pottering about his island community. As Columba paused to rest, a white horse trotted up – and wept into the old man's lap. The horse knew what the servant had just heard from his master's own lips, that this was to be Columba's last day on earth. Later, as the midnight bell tolled for the coming day, the elderly cleric breathed his last in the abbey church he himself had built over 30 years before. Columba, the simple monk who had shaped the destinies of great men and bequeathed to the world one of its greatest centres of intellectual and artistic activity, was dead.

We know little of Columba's early life. He had been born in 521 in the Derryveagh Mountains of Donegal. He was of the blood royal, a son of the house of Tír Conaill, who could count Niall of the Nine Hostages (who gave his name to the mighty Uí Néill warlords) among his illustrious forebears. Two of his cousins became high kings of the Uí Néill, and Columba might have become king himself had his parents

▲ *The St Columba window in the north transept of Iona Abbey, designed by William Wilson in 1965. No contemporary images survive of the holy man, just captivating word-pictures from his biographer and successor as Abbot of Iona, Adomnán.*

not sent him into the Church. They had originally called him Crimthann, 'the fox' but later he was given a new Christian name, Columba – in Gaelic, *Colum Cille*, 'dove of the Church'.

But in 563, at the age of 42, advanced years for those times, Columba left his native land, and set sail for Argyll with just 12 companions, including his devoted Diarmait, for company. But why? Adomnán, his biographer, despite his desire to depict Columba in a miraculous light, offers a clue by informing us that before Columba came to Scotland he had been excommunicated, and then reprieved, by a church synod meeting in County Meath. Adomnán, for obvious hagiographic reasons, does not state the nature of the 'crime', but it seems that it may have been linked to Columba's involvement in the bloody battle of Cúl Drebene fought in 561, in which the northern Uí Néill triumphed over their southern kinsmen. The *Annals of Ulster* record that the victory was brought about 'through the prayers of Columba', but Columba's part in the slaughter may not have been confined to prayer. Adomnán himself testifies to Columba's fiery temper, and describes 'a livid scar which remained on his side all the days of his life'. Had Columba actually fought at Cúl Drebene, and been injured in the process, it could well explain his excommunication, his subsequent reprieve and within two years his decision to leave behind the green land of his birth for the rocky shores of Argyll.

Columba arrived in Argyll not as a missionary, for the people there were his people, Gaelic-speaking and already Christian. Rather he came as their priest. Where he spent his first months we do not know, for the mysterious island of *Hinba* has never satisfactorily been located. By 573, however, he had settled on Iona, and it is that tiny speck of land on the western seaboard that has become inextricably linked with Scotland's most loved saint. It was from Iona that the holy man travelled among the Gaels of the Cénel Loairn, just like a priest visiting his parishioners. We read of him journeying through 'the rough and rocky district of Ardnamurchan', of him passing along the shores of the Firth of Lorn, of sailing across to Coll, Islay and the south of Skye, baptising, marrying, burying and admonishing his flock. No one is too mighty or too meek for Columba, friend of kings, farmers, even thieves.

Occasionally Columba leaves his adopted Argyll. Several tiring journeys are made across the 'spine of Britain', the Great Glen, into the kingdom of the northern Picts, to the court of King Bridei at Inverness. This certainly was missionary work, for the Picts at that date still worshiped their pagan gods. It is during one such visit that Columba encounters a 'water-beast' in the River Ness, the first recorded sighting of the monster we know as 'Nessie'!

When Columba reached the river

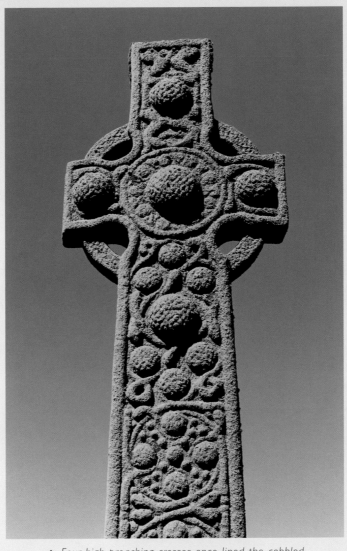

▲ *Four high preaching crosses once lined the cobbled Street of the Dead leading to St Columba's Shrine. They included St Martin's Cross (pictured here), sculpted from a single slab of stone around 775, and adorned on one side with rich carvings of bosses and serpents and on the other with Biblical scenes.*

bank, he saw a poor fellow being buried; and the buriers said that, while swimming, the man had been seized and most savagely bitten by a water beast. Notwithstanding, the holy man ordered Lugne, one of his companions, to swim across to the other side and bring back a boat. Lugne obeyed without delay, but the monster suddenly swam to the surface

and with gaping mouth and great roaring rushed towards the man in mid-stream.

While all there were struck down with extreme terror, the blessed man raised his holy hand and commanded the

savage beast:

'Do not touch the man; turn backward speedily.'

The beast, as if pulled back with ropes, fled terrified in swift retreat. (Abbot Adomnán, in his *Life of Columba*, c. 690.)

During his long life, Columba founded other monasteries. But it is with 'the island of Io' that the saint is most intimately linked. He was by no means the only holy man working amongst the Gaels and taking the word of God to the Picts and other pagans. St Moluag, for example, came across from Ireland in the same year as Columba. In fact, it is said that the two raced each other to take occupation of the more favoured island of Lismore, closer to the Scottish mainland; Moluag won. But it was Columba who became the spiritual father to so many people, great and small, near and far. And it was Iona that grew into a leading centre of spiritual, intellectual and artistic activity of its day, and whose impact was felt far beyond Argyll.

Shortly after returning to his monastery from blessing the barn on that June Saturday, 'Colum Cille' climbed the little hill, Cnoc nan Carnan, looked down upon his creation and uttered these words:

On this place, small and mean though it be, not only the kings of the Gaels with their people, but also the rulers of barbarous and foreign nations, with their subjects, will bestow great and especial honour.

Today, over 1500 years after his passing, that 'small and mean place' continues to offer comfort, solace and inspiration to people from all over the world who make the pilgrimage to its shores.

▲▶ *Shetlanders celebrate the Viking pagan festival of Up-Helly-Aa (or Uphalliday) in Lerwick on the last Tuesday of January each year. The climax is reached when a thousand and more guisers brandish their flaming torches through the darkened streets of Shetland's capital before setting fire to a replica Viking longship.*

whether Briton, Pict or Gael, were subjected to a new culture and a new language, English. Although the Angles of Northumbria have been gone from southern Scotland for more than a thousand years, the countryside is littered with the place-names they left behind, like Newbattle (-*botl*, 'dwelling'), Polwarth (-*worth*, 'enclosure') and most commonly of all names incorporating -*ham*, 'village or homestead' (eg, Tyninghame, 'Tyne-dwellers' village'). Most crucially, though, it is their language, albeit modified, that lives on today as our mother tongue – Scots.

VIKINGS

In 793 the tranquillity of the Anglian monastery on Lindisfarne, off the Northumbrian coast, was shattered when a host of men emerged from the sea 'like ravenous wolves' to slaughter the brethren and plunder their treasures. The following year they struck again, this time in the Northern Isles of Scotland. In 795 it was the turn of those poor souls living on Iona, Skye and along the coast of northern Ireland to feel their wrath. And so it went on, year after year...798 the Hebrides...802 Iona again...806 Iona yet again. The prayer went up: 'From the fury of the northmen, O Lord, deliver us'. The Vikings had stormed onto the pages of history. The invader had become the invaded.

 Forth the people quickly carried

 From the ships the shields of many;

 Then was heard the dismal howling

 Of the gray wolf o'er the corpses.

(From the *Orkneyinga Saga*, written down around 1230.)

Quite why the Vikings embarked upon their orgy of violence just as the eighth century was drawing to its close remains a mystery. Perhaps the need for more land was at the root of it all, for although Scandinavia was vast, most of it was composed of mountainous waste, impenetrable forest and intractable bog. Much of the population in the west clung to the rocky coastal margins formed by the deep fjords of Norway, like barnacles on the bottom of a boat. Perhaps the only means of expansion open to these inlet people (the word *vik* means 'inlet') was to take to the seas and search for new lands elsewhere. And the most logical place for these Vikings to look was 'west over sea' to northern Britain, to the land of the Picts, Britons, Gaels and Angles. Kirkwall was, after all, nearer to Bergen by sea than Stockholm.

Thoughts of colonising new lands, however, may have been the result, and not the cause, of the initial forays. Judging by the appalling catalogue of murder, rape and pillaging recorded by the chroniclers of the time, the prime motive seems simply to have been sheer piracy. Such hit-and-run raids were made possible thanks to the Viking longship, which could slice its way through the seas like the proverbial knife through butter. Certainly it

'The Quiet Life'

~ JARLSHOF, A VIKING FARM ~

'They shall beat their swords into ploughshares, and their spears into pruning-hooks'
(From Isaiah II.IV.)

Perched on a low cliff edge at the southern tip of Shetland stands a ruined shell of a building. Anciently called 'the Old House of Sumburgh' it is now better known by the name bestowed on it by Walter Scott in his novel *The Pirate:* Jarlshof.

Jarlshof, the building, isn't particularly old, but the site on which it stands is. At the end of the nineteenth century, violent storms ripped open the cliff to reveal a large and complex settlement reaching far back into prehistory.

But the chief fascination of Jarlshof is not its ancient remains but its Viking farm. Within a generation or so of the first recorded sighting of the Viking longships off the coast of Britain shortly before 800, a Viking family uprooted from their home in western Norway and made a new life for themselves here at Sumburgh. Over the ensuing centuries, succeeding generations lived and farmed

at Jarlshof, until well after Shetland had come under Scotland's control in 1469.

The archaeological excavations carried out in the early 1950s didn't just reveal the long-lost buildings of the Viking farm; they shed important new light on this period in Scotland's history. Up to that time, the image of the axe-wielding, horn-helmeted Viking storming ashore from his longship to murder and pillage held sway in the popular mind; to an extent it still does. And there is no gainsaying the terror these Northmen struck in the hearts of those unfortunate enough to be caught in their path.

But what the 'dig' revealed was 'the other side of the coin': Viking families going about their peaceful ways 'every year and all year round', generation upon generation. Farmhouses being built, extended, modified and demolished; so, too, outbuildings and field-dykes. Amid

the foundations a wonderful range of objects was discovered, painting a picture of a people working the land and fishing the seas, not forever waging war. There were fine articles of dress-wear beautifully crafted from animal bone, cooking utensils and other household items fashioned from the local steatite and clay, assorted farm implements, like iron sickles and stone hones, fishing-tackle such as line sinkers and fish hooks – even the games they played in the long winter evenings, scratched onto pieces of slate.

One piece of slate stands out in particular as portraying a peaceful people. On it is scratched a ship. But this was no longship built for war; it was a merchant vessel under sail. The Vikings were certainly a maritime people *par excellence*, but the sea-lanes were used as much by merchants and traders as by 'the warriors of the western sea'.

▲ *The foundations of the Viking longhouse at Jarlshof, built by incomers from western Norway some time during the ninth century, stand 'cheek by jowl' with the ruined houses of earlier inhabitants who once lived at this southern tip of Shetland.*

▲ These wonderful chess-pieces, made from walrus ivory by someone somewhere in the Viking world, possibly Trondheim, in Norway, around 1100, were discovered quite by chance in 1831 in sand dunes close to Uig, on the west side of Lewis.

The soldiers (we call them 'castles' or 'rooks') shown biting their shields were 'berserkers', harking back to 'the good old days' when Viking warriors worked themselves into a frenzy before battle. We get the phrase 'going berserk' from them.

▶ A Viking fleet sets sail on yet another blood-thirsty cruise, as wonderfully depicted by a twelfth-century artist. The descendants of those same Vikings would continue to be a thorn in the flesh of the Scottish 'kingdom' until the Treaty of Perth in 1266 formally brought their control of the western seaboard to a close.

is difficult to see a colonising motive behind the first decade or so of raids, which mostly had as their goal the isolated monasteries of the holy men, dripping with treasures of gold and silver. Only this bloodlust by a people who still worshipped their pagan gods, like Odin and Thor, can explain why, time and again, they targeted Iona. The raid of 806 alone saw 68 brethren cut down by the Vikings' axes, leaving Abbot Cellach with no option but to abandon temporarily Columba's monastery and build a new life back home in Ireland.

But the violent raiding soon gave way to colonising. The green and fertile low lands of the Orkneys and eastern Caithness would certainly have presented a most welcoming sight to these 'warriors of the western sea'. Even the rockier landscapes of Shetland and the Hebrides would have held out the promise of a reasonable life, as good as anything back home in Norway. And so they began to settle, at first possibly only in small groups, and perhaps only for the summer season, close to the shore and the seas which had carried them thither. From about the middle of the ninth century the process of colonisation was underway in earnest. Later sagas tell of the Orkneys, *Orkneyjar*, falling under the sway of Sigurd the Mighty, and of the Hebrides, *Sudreyjar* 'the southern isles' (the diocesan name 'Sodor' comes

from this), being conquered by a Viking chief rejoicing in the name of Ketil Flatnose. The threatened Gaels coined a new name for the Hebrides – *Innse Gall*, 'islands of the foreigners'.

The Vikings were set for a lengthy sojourn. To this day their presence lives on – in the Shetland dialect, in customs like Up-Helly-Aa, Lerwick's celebration of the pagan Viking festival of *Uphalliday*, and in those remarkable ruined Hebridean blackhouses that housed man and beast under one roof and belong in the Viking longhouse tradition. But the Viking legacy lives on most conspicuously in place-names. You can't travel anywhere in the former Viking dominions without encountering names containing *sund*, 'sound' (Baltasound), *nes*, 'headland' (Sandness), and *bolstadr*, 'farm' (Scrabster). Such names suggest a peaceful settlement of the land, rather than the rapine that marked the Vikings' arrival on the scene, for the Viking invaders, like the Gaels and Angles who preceded them, became farmers first and foremost, and warriors only when the need arose. They were also, perhaps surprisingly, a law-abiding and democratic-minded people, meeting together in 'things' to discuss matters of common concern. Dingwall, in Easter Ross, barely 11 miles (17 km) north-west of Inverness, shows just how far the Vikings penetrated the ancient homeland of the Picts.

The Vikings, of course, didn't stop at the British Isles. They went on, north-by-north-west, in the wake left by the curraghs of the holy fathers, to people the Faroes, Iceland and the coastal fringes of Greenland; they even 'discovered' America 500 years before Columbus set eyes on it. At its height, the Viking 'empire' extended from the chilly waters inside the Arctic Circle to the warmth of the Mediterranean, from the deserted wastes of Newfoundland to the wealth of Samarkand and the silk road to China. The Vikings had a profound influence world-wide. But most importantly for us, they had a fundamental effect on the political landscape of northern Britain. It was their arrival off the west coast around 800 that forced the Gaels to look increasingly eastward to Pictland. As events dramatically unfolded during the course of the ninth century, the Vikings proved to be the unwitting midwives at the birth of the new nation – Alba.

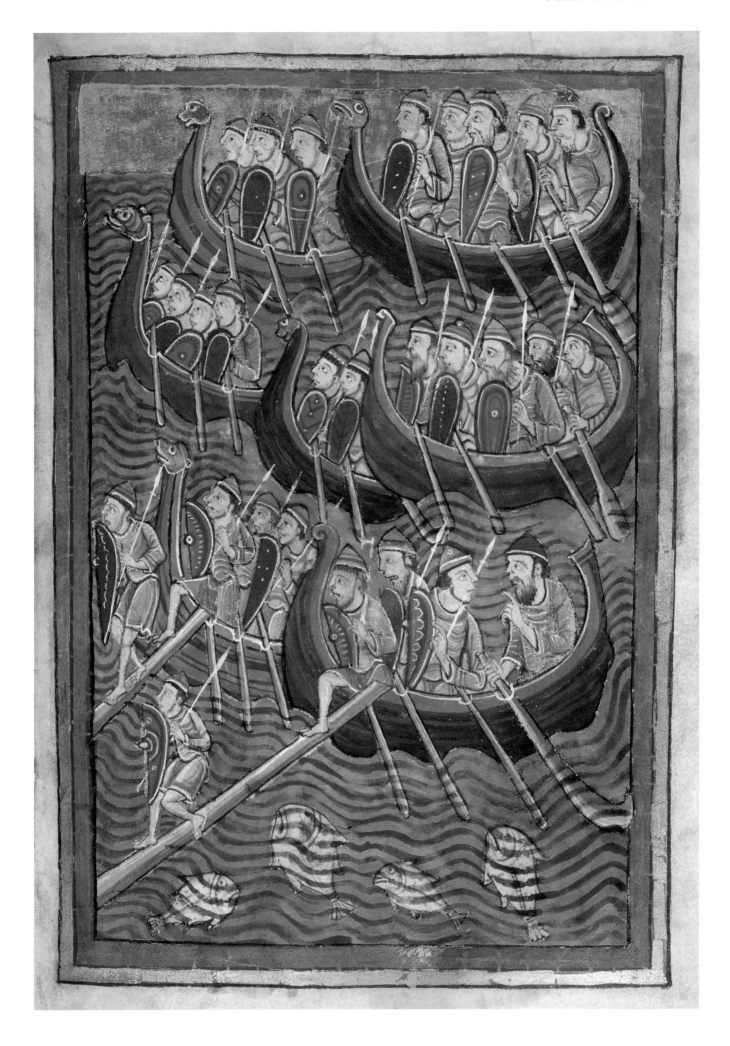

KINGDOM

(850 - 1286)

'God bless the Pepill and the King'

(An acclamation from the Scottish medieval enthronement ceremony)

AD 843 is enshrined in Scottish history as the year Kenneth mac Alpin united Scotland and Pictland. Life of course is never that simple, but certainly from that time the Picts begin to fade from the scene and the Scots take centre stage. This chapter explores the complex transition from tribal kingdoms to nation state; from Alba to Scotland.

ALBA

The Scots were still rooted to Argyll when the first Viking longships appeared on the horizon around 800. When a century later the Scots and the Picts did battle with the Vikings in Strathearn, they fought alongside each other not as allies but as one nation – Alba. The political landscape of Scotland had undergone momentous change in those 100 years.

The rich farmlands of Pictland were being eyed covetously by the Scots long before the Vikings appeared on the scene. But with the Vikings threatening from the west, the Scots now had every reason to move eastward. The figure traditionally held to have forged the union between Scots and Picts is Kenneth mac Alpin.

Kenneth 'son of Alpin' was born just as the Vikings began to strike terror in the hearts of his people. By 840 he was their king, and turning his gaze upon the throne of Pictland also, a nation lately thrown into turmoil following a crushing defeat at the hands of those same Vikings. The story goes that, around 843, Kenneth invited the feuding Pictish warlords to feast with him at Scone, in the heart of their own kingdom. There he treacherously slaughtered them. Kenneth now ruled over both peoples as one king, Kenneth I. This man of obscure origins, whom later genealogies claimed was descended from the legendary Fergus Mór, was destined to found a royal dynasty that continues to rule to this day.

Kenneth moved swiftly to secure his newly won prize. Scone, the Pictish king-making seat, became the administrative heart of the new united kingdom, while Dunkeld, an important Pictish

◀ *Dunkeld means 'fort of the Caledonians', and this beautiful place beside the River Tay was doubtless a settlement from ancient times. King Kenneth I (834-858) made Dunkeld his main ecclesiastical centre when he moved from Argyll after the union of Scotland and Pictland around 843. Shortly afterwards, the remaining relics of St Columba were brought from Viking-ravaged Iona and buried in these comparatively peaceful Perthshire surroundings. The later medieval cathedral church probably lies over the spot where they were laid to rest.*

▲ The rocky hillfort of Dunadd dominates Moine Mhor, 'the great moss', in Argyllshire's Kilmartin Glen. On its saddle-backed summit are two footprints and a basin hollowed out of the rock, most likely to have been put to use during the inauguration ceremony for a new king.

religious centre, became the home of the remaining precious relics of St Columba, brought from their hiding-place on Iona. Kenneth himself moved his court from the rocky fastness of Dunadd to the palace of Forteviot, in Earn's green valley. And there he died, in 858.

First to reign in Albany, tis said,

was Kenneth son of Alpin, warrior bold.

He expelled the Picts, reigned twice eight years

and in Forteviot met his death.

(A verse from Walter Bower's *Scotichronicon*.)

The creation of the new united kingdom was not achieved so easily, of course. The process had begun long before Kenneth came to power and ended only after he had long been laid to rest. Later chroniclers would bestow on him the honour of being 'the first to reign in Albany', but it was only as the tenth century dawned that the two peoples began confidently to think of themselves as a new nation. The Scots called it *Alba*, the Gaelic name they had until then given to the entire island of Britain. (The title 'Duke of Albany' has occasionally been used for royal princes since that time.)

Kenneth and his successors didn't have their troubles to seek. In 849, a huge Viking fleet threaded its way down past Argyll, spreading yet more panic and grabbing yet more land. The

Viking host also struck right at the heart of the new kingdom, not once but time and again. In 903 they invaded for the last time. For months they looted the countryside around Dunkeld until coming to grief in Strathearn. As the Scots charged into battle that day, they carried at their head the casket housing the relics of St Columba – the national treasure we know as the *Breacbannach* or Monymusk Reliquary. Four centuries later that same talisman would bring victory to their descendants on the field of Bannockburn.

By now the Vikings were coming under pressure not only from the Scots but from a resurgent Anglo-Saxon England also. Alfred 'the Great', King of Wessex, had won a remarkable victory over the Vikings, at Edington in Wiltshire in 878, and by his death in 899, could with justification claim to be the first King of England. It was the Vikings' destiny to be the unwitting midwives at the birth not only of Scotland but of England also.

By 927 the reconquest of the lost Anglian lands by the rampaging English army was all but complete. Now there were effectively just two great powers controlling the island of Britain – England and Alba. Athelstan of England was determined that there be just one, and in 934

'Throne of Scotland'

~ THE STONE OF DESTINY ~

'So the king sat down upon the royal throne – that is, the Stone'

(From John of Fordun's account in his Chronica Gentis Scotorum of the inauguration of King Alexander III, 1249)

In the Crown Room in Edinburgh Castle, on display beside those other ancient symbols of Scottish sovereignty, the Honours of Scotland, lies the Stone of Destiny, sometimes known as the Stone of Scone. It hasn't been there long, for it was returned to Scotland as recently as St Andrew's Day 1996 from Westminster Abbey, where it had lain for 700 years.

The precise age of the Stone is unknown. The sandstone from which it was hewn is millions of years old, but what is far from clear is at what date it was fashioned as a royal throne. A few cling to the belief that the Stone is the *Lia Fail*, the 'fatal chair', that legend holds served as Jacob's pillow that night he dreamed his dream at Bethel, and was subsequently brought from Egypt to Ireland and ultimately Scotland by the descendants of Scota, the daughter of Pharaoh. Some see the Stone as an ancient Pictish throne adopted by the Scots when Kenneth mac Alpin united the two kingdoms around 843 and took control of Scone, the Picts' king-making centre. Others would have the Stone as a forgery of 1296, the shrewd Abbot of Scone having taken the precaution of hiding the original prior to the arrival of Edward I of England at the monastery gates. And there are some who view the present Stone as a fabrication of more recent times.

So if ever ye come on a Stane wi' a ring,
Jist sit yersel' doon and proclaim
yersel King;
For there's nane wid be able tae
challenge yer claim
That ye'd crooned yersel' King on the
Destiny Stane.

▲ *The Moot Hill at Scone was the place where the Pictish kings of Fortriu were enthroned. From the time of King Kenneth I (834-858), Scone came to be described as the hill 'of melodious shields', a reference surely to the clashing of shields at the acclaiming of a new king. The later chapel now gracing the summit was used for the last coronation ceremony of a king of Scots – King Charles II in 1651.*

Wi' a tooreli-ooreli-ooreli-ay, etc
(From Johnny McEvoy's song *The Wee Magic Stane*.)

But it isn't what it <u>is</u> that's important; it is what it represents. The Stone of Destiny is a powerful icon of Scottish nationhood, a tangible symbol linking the present generation of Scots back through the centuries to their distant forebears. It may not be the only coronation stone existing to the present time – Emperor Charlemagne's throne in the cathedral at Aachen, Germany, is perhaps the best known – but it is certainly the most revered. Compare its veneration to that accorded the stone at Kingston, south London, on which the Anglo-Saxon kings from Edward 'the Elder' (900) to Edmund 'Ironside' (1016) were crowned; that stands out in the open encircled by traffic.

Had the Stone of Destiny not been stolen in 1296 and removed to London, then it is highly probable that the Scots might not have come to hold it in such high regard. The Stone, imprisoned in a foreign land and out of reach, became a talisman of Scottish independence. It was its very inaccessibility that raised it high in the national consciousness, and ultimately led four Scottish students to risk all on removing it from the Coronation Chair and smuggling it back across the Border over Christmas 1950. It was later found in Arbroath Abbey and returned to London.

Somehow, since its 'official' return on St Andrew's Day 1996, the Stone of Destiny has lost something of its magic, its potency. Perhaps when it is taken south to Westminster again, as it must be under the Constitution for future coronations of British monarchs, some of that magic will return.

Now, this stone is reverently kept in that same monastery for the consecration of the kings of Alba; and no king was ever wont to reign in Scotland, unless he had first, on receiving the name of king, sat upon this stone at Scone, which, by the kings of old, had been appointed the capital of Alba.

(From John of Fordun's account of the inauguration of King Alexander III in 1249.)

▶ The magnificent Keills Cross, beside Loch Sween in Argyllshire, was erected in the eighth century, probably by papar, or holy men, living on the nearby island monastery of Eilean Mor. These early parish priests would have rowed across to the mainland and used the high cross as a focus of Christian worship.

MILLENNIUM SCOTLAND - AD 1000

Scotland in AD 1000 was very different from the country we inhabit day. For one thing the population was a fraction of the present total of over 5 million, perhaps numbering only some 300,000 souls. For another it was nowhere near the same extent. Certainly substantial inroads had lately been made into Anglian-held Lothian and the British kingdom of Strathclyde, but nothing had yet been formally settled. The Vikings, too, continued to hold sway over much of northern and western Scotland. That stranglehold would be formally acknowledged when King Edgar (1097-1107) handed over the Western Isles, Skye and the Argyllshire islands to King Magnus of Norway.

The Scotland of a millennium ago had no cities, no towns, no money other than foreign currency, and no industry to speak of apart from that associated with farming – and waging war. Most of the population was scattered about the realm, not heavily concentrated in the Central Belt as it is today. A few lived in villages, but most dwelt on isolated crofts. There were no roads, just muddy tracks twisting their ways through a landscape dominated by marsh and bog that would remain until the eighteenth-century 'improvers' came along. Getting around would have been far easier by boat, particularly in the west with its deeply indented coastline and expanses of inland lochs.

The land dominated society in those far-off times, and working it preoccupied most people's everyday lives. What ground that could sustain crops was given over to the plough, but most was used to pasture cattle, sheep and goats. As winter approached stark decisions had to be made as to which animals to keep and which to slaughter and salt away. The feast of Martinmas (St Martin's Day, 11 November) became the time for doing this, whence the Scots word 'mart' for a fattened beast. Martinmas was one of four 'quarter days' that divided up the farming year; the others were: Candlemas (2 February), when the candles and tapers to be used in the local church in the coming year were carried in procession; Whitsun (15 May), a date traditionally associated with the hiring of servants; and Lammas (1 August), or 'loaf mass',

invaded Alba in strength. The grandson of Alfred 'the Great' now faced Constantin, grandson of Kenneth mac Alpin. The two weren't to know it, but the opening shot in that campaign was to herald a bitter struggle between the two countries that would last, on and off, for the best part of 700 years. Not for nothing are the English known by the Scots as 'the auld enemy'.

For the rest of that century, the two powers fought to gain mastery of the other. As their armies marched and counter-marched across what is now northern England and southern Scotland, the Britons of Strathclyde and the Angles of Lothian were caught in the cross-fire. Their days were numbered.

Around 954, King Indulf led his Scots south across 'the Scottish Sea', as the Firth of Forth was known, and captured Edinburgh. The fertile lands of Strathclyde and Lothian lay tantalisingly before them.

As the sun set on the first millennium AD, the victorious Scots had reached the salt-marshes of the Solway and the swift-running waters of the Tweed. By now the Gaelic name Alba too was fading from people's lips, to be replaced by its Latin equivalent – Scotia.

the equivalent of today's Harvest Thanksgiving.

Perhaps just as important as the land to the Scot of a thousand years ago was kin. Everybody, no matter what rank or station in life, belonged to a kindred or *clann*, and could thereby claim descent from a common ancestor. At their head was *ceann cineil*, the 'chief of kin'. Clan membership is still much enjoyed today by many people across the globe, but in those days it was a far more serious business. Being 'one of the clan' all too often meant having to leave the croft and loved ones to fight for the chief. It also served another important purpose. In those days of the blood-feud, justice was meted out according to your status in the clan. For example, if you were a thane, and therefore in the senior hierarchy, your 'blood money' rating was 100 cows. So, if you were killed, your clan would expect 100 cows from your murderer's clan as recompense.

Such was Scotland in the year 1000, a heady brew of Celt, Angle and Viking. They would have come in all shapes and sizes, just like us, but generally they were smaller, though only by the odd inch, and they didn't live as long. All, though, had one thing in common – they were Christian and intensely God-fearing. Even the Vikings had become imbued with the spirit of Columba. Quite how they all heralded the new millennium is not recorded. Perhaps it was with rejoicing: more likely it was with fear and trepidation that Judgement Day was at hand. In the event the year 1001 brought just more of the same – the daily grind, interspersed with much warring.

SCOTIA

On the south bank of the River Tweed, in Northumberland, is Carham, a peaceful spot, its little church surrounded now only by tree-studded green pastures. It was not always so.

The Battle of Carham in 1018 is one of the defining moments in Scotland's history. Malcolm II's rout of the English there effectively set the seal on Scotland's claim to Lothian, and firmly established her south-eastern Border on the Tweed. 'Carham 1018' has become almost as memorable to Scots as 'Bannockburn 1314'.

As the victorious Scots moved across the Forth

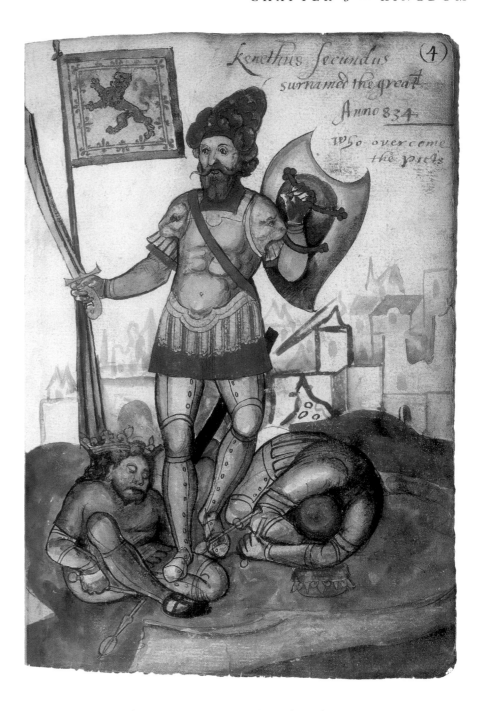

to avail themselves of their new prize, they brought with them their Gaelic language. It was the furthest south the tongue was to reach. The Gaelic legacy lives on in names such as Balerno (*baile airneach*, 'settlement of the sloe-tree') and Auchendinny (*achadh an-t Sionnaigh*, 'field of the fox').

Yet Scotland's history after 1018 might have been so very different. Malcolm's victory was only made possible because a Dane, Cnut (or Canute), had recently grasped the English throne. Before long, Cnut of England became King of Denmark and Norway also. And he might well have become King of Scotia too, had he not been beset by unrest in his native Scandinavia. In 1031 he even got as far as the Tay before having to withdraw to put

▲ *King Kenneth I (834-858), as portrayed in the sixteenth-century Seton Armorial. No contemporary likeness exists of the great king who united Scotland and Pictland around 843.*

'Hero or Villain?'

~ KING MACBETH ~

'All hail, Macbeth! Thou shalt be king hereafter!'

(from Shakespeare's Macbeth, *Act 1, Scene III)*

Ask anyone to name a Scottish king and they are almost sure to answer 'Macbeth'. Thanks to William Shakespeare and his 'Scottish Play', poor old Macbeth's name is synonymous across the globe with treachery, foul murder and base villainy. And yet nothing could be further from the truth.

We cannot really blame Shakespeare. He was after all a playwright writing fiction. Rather it is his sources we must criticise, chroniclers such as Ralph Holinshed, Shakespeare's immediate source, supposedly writing factual history. Walter Bower, the fifteenth-century Abbot of Inchcolm, wrote scathingly of Macbeth, likening his reign over the Scots to that of a rotten head above a healthy body: 'If the head aches, the rest of the body is sick'. Strong stuff. Yet from the few scraps of contemporary evidence available to us, the reality would appear to have been very different. Macbeth, the renowned warrior from Moray, reigned for 17 years, from 1040 to 1057, a rare feat in those days when kings were despatched so easily.

Macbeth, a grandson of either Kenneth II or III (his Gaelic name *MacBeathadh* means 'son of life'), was a battle-hardened leader as much through necessity as by choice. The province of Moray, of which he was mormaer or 'great steward', then lay at the northern limit of Scotia. Beyond stretched the ancient Pictish province of Cait (modern Caithness and Sutherland) but long overrun by the Vikings and now under the sway of Thorfinn 'the Mighty', Earl of Orkney. Thorfinn had another reason to hate Macbeth; as the grandson of Malcolm II he too had a claim to the Scottish throne. The two met in battle

several times, including a great sea-battle fought out in the treacherous waters of the Pentland Firth, between the Scottish mainland and Orkney. Victory went to Earl Thorfinn that day, and the saga-writer waxed lyrical:

Never was a battle shorter;
Soon with spears it was decided.
Though my lord had fewer numbers,
Yet he chased them all before him;
Hoarsely croaked the battle-gull, when
Thickly fell the wounded king's men;
South of Sandwick swords were
reddened.

(From the *Orkneyinga Saga*, c. 1220.)

But Macbeth lived to fight another day. The 'ruddy-faced, yellow-haired and tall' man whom the Vikings scathingly called Karl, Hunda's son, 'peasant son of a dog', contained the Viking menace. On becoming King in 1040, following his assassination of Duncan I, he contrived to snuff out the threats from within his realm also. By 1050 he was so confident of his hold on power that he departed on lengthy pilgrimage to Rome, the only king of Scots ever to visit 'the Eternal City'.

While there he was not just another 'face in the crowd', for it is reported that he 'scattered alms like seed corn'. Earl Thorfinn happened also to be in Rome around the same time, leading to speculation that the two mighty warriors had by now formed an alliance. We don't normally associate the words 'Viking' and 'Christian', but Earl Thorfinn was as devout in his faith as Macbeth. While King Macbeth and Queen Gruoch 'with the utmost veneration and devotion' were bestowing largesse on the monks of Lochleven, near Kinross, Earl Thorfinn

and his good lady, Ingibiorg, were building 'Christ's Kirk, a splendid church' beside their residence at Birgisherad (Birsay), in Orkney.

Macbeth was eventually overthrown not by Vikings descending from the north but by an alliance in the south between the late King Duncan's elder son, Malcolm, and Earl Siward of Northumbria. By now the English throne had returned to a descendant of the House of Wessex, Edward 'the Confessor', and it was with his blessing that Siward invaded Scotia in 1054. Macbeth was indeed defeated at Dunsinnan, north-east of Scone, as we all know from our Shakespeare, but he was not killed there. He withdrew north where he remained at large for the next three years. He was eventually caught and killed at Lumphanan, in deepest Aberdeenshire.

Scarcely had his body been laid to rest on Iona when his foes began to blacken his name. The heroic figures that were King Macbeth and his Queen Gruoch were fast on their way to becoming the treacherous villains portrayed by Shakespeare.

My thanes and kinsmen,
Henceforth be earls, the first that
 ever Scotland
In such an honour nam'd.
 What's more to do,
Which would be planted newly
 with the time,
As calling home our exil'd
 friends abroad,
That fled the snares of
 watchful tyranny;
Producing forth the cruel ministers
Of this dead butcher, and his
 fiend-like queen.'

(Malcolm III's closing speech in Shakespeare's *Macbeth*.)

down rebellion in another part of his sprawling North Sea 'empire'. A hoard of coins buried in haste at Lindores, in Fife, is testimony to the panic that swept through the realm as the Danes marched north. King Malcolm had escaped by the skin of his teeth.

Being king in those days was a risky business, and no sovereign from the time of Kenneth mac Alpin on was ever really free from either internal feuding or external warring. Most came to a sticky end; only three kings in 200 years – three out of 14 – died of natural causes!

King Grim reigned for the space of eight years
The son of Kenneth who was the son of Duf.
He was killed on the Plain of Bards
By Kenneth's son named Malcolm.
(A verse from Walter Bower's *Scotichronicon*.)

How someone became king in those days is still a puzzle. We are used today to the rule of primogeniture, whereby the eldest male heir succeeds to the throne. But that wasn't the case way back then. Not once between the reigns of Kenneth I and Malcolm II did son directly succeed father, and even the succession of a brother was exceptional. But all that was to change with the arrival on the throne of Scotland's most infamous king – Macbeth.

Macbeth (1040-57) reigned for 17 years, a remarkable achievement given the doubt surrounding his royal credentials and the relative remoteness of his power-base, the province of Moray in the north of the country. Later chroniclers blackened his name, among them Abbot Bower of Inchcolm who wrote of Macbeth's 'tyrannous regime' and of a 'loyal people refusing to submit any longer to their distressful subjection under a man of no higher rank than themselves'. Yet this was not how his own people necessarily saw him. To them he was 'the generous king', who brought prosperity to an impoverished country and who at his death was laid to rest on Iona alongside his valiant predecessors. How apt his

▲ *Macbeth, newly enthroned as King of Scots, plots the execution of Banquo and his son Fleance. George Cattermole (1800-1868) captures Macbeth on canvas just as we imagine him to have been thanks to Shakespeare and his 'Scottish play' – dark and devious. Macbeth was no murdering upstart but of the royal blood who reigned for 17 years – no mean achievement in those dark times.*

'...and with him,
To leave no rubs nor
*   botches in the work,*
Fleance his son, that
*   keeps him company,*
Whose absence is no
*   less material to me*
Than is his father's,
*   must embrace the fate*
Of that dark hour.'
(Macbeth, Act III, Scene I)

▲ The imposing abbey church of Dunfermline has a special place in the history of Scotland, and in the hearts
of its people. On this site, around the year 1070, the great warrior-king, Malcolm III, married his saintly queen, Margaret, a refugee
from an England lately thrown into turmoil by the Norman Conquest. The happy couple were subsequently laid to rest there, and the great
Benedictine abbey built over their tombs by their youngest son, King David I, replaced Iona as the royal mausoleum of Scotland.
David himself was also buried there, as was King Robert the Bruce, the victor of Bannockburn. Charles I was one of several
royal heirs born in the adjacent royal palace, in 1600, but his headless corpse lies buried in far-off Westminster Abbey.

name then – *MacBeathadh*, 'son of life'. This was no rebellious upstart but a sovereign confidently enthroned. That he was eventually undone at Dunsinnan cannot deny Macbeth his rightful place in Scottish history.

Macbeth was Scotland's last great Celtic king. His eventual successor, Malcolm III (1058-93), known as Malcolm Canmore (from the Gaelic *Ceann Mór*, 'great chief'), the victor at Dunsinnan, had spent most of his life in exile at the court of King Edmund 'the Confessor', where he became closely acquainted with Anglo-Saxon ways. And when many of those whom he had befriended there fled their homeland following the Norman Conquest in 1066, it was in Malcolm's Scotland that they sought shelter. Chief among them was Edgar 'the Aetheling', King Harold's heir, and his sister, Margaret.

It is said that Malcolm fell in love with Margaret in the instant they met. Margaret may have been an unwilling bride, but she bore Malcolm eight children, six sons and two daughters. Three sons reigned as kings of Scots, and a daughter as a queen of England. While Malcolm's shrewd diplomacy raised Scotland's profile abroad, and Margaret's piety undoubtedly took the rough edges off the Celtic character at home, it was their offspring who would prove their most enduring legacy. No more sharing the kingship around different segments of the royal house; the Canmore dynasty that henceforth ruled Scotland, and ultimately Great Britain up to the present time, would do so through the direct line of succession.

Malcolm III was implacably opposed to the Norman conquerors of England, and ended his days being killed by one at Alnwick, in Northumberland, in 1093. He had first experienced the might of the Normans in 1072 when William 'the Conqueror' invaded Scotland and got as far as Abernethy on the Tay. There William received the homage of King Malcolm before having to return south to quell lingering Saxon unrest. Little did the King of Scots realise, as he bent the knee before 'the Conqueror' that day, that therein would be sown the seed of English claims to Scottish sovereignty that would dominate British politics for the next five hundred years.

NORMANS

Norman knights had first appeared in Scotland in 1052 at Macbeth's invitation. Sadly, their renowned fighting qualities didn't stand them in much stead for they were all killed at Dunsinnan two years later. It wasn't until the reign of David I (1124-53), the youngest of Malcolm and Margaret's sons, that they began to arrive in large numbers. There wasn't a Norman 'conquest' of Scotland as such, like there had been of England, for they were invited to come and settle. And it wasn't just Normans who 'flooded' into Scotland, but Bretons and Flemings as well. David's grandsons who succeeded him, Malcolm IV (1153-65) and his

▲ *King Malcolm III (1058-93) and his second queen, Margaret, as portrayed in the sixteenth-century Seton Armorial. The inscription reads: 'K. Malcolme 3 surnamed Canmoir Began his rayne, 1057. He maried Margaret dochter to Edward 'ye outlaw' sone of Edward yronsyd [ironside] king of England and wer buryed at Dunfermlyne'. The artist got the date wrong; clearly Macbeth's nephew, King Lulach (1057-58) was of no interest to him!*

▲ *From the air the medieval burgh of Edinburgh takes on the classic shape – a straight main street (the High Street) leading to the royal castle. The view actually takes in two twelfth-century burghs, for Canongate ('the canons' way') beyond was established under the watchful eye of the Augustinian abbey of Holyrood.*

building mints for the striking of coin. He established towns across the land to help regulate trade and stimulate economic growth. He created a national justice system and a new local government structure administered by sheriffs. He reorganised the Church by reforming the overarching diocesan structure and introducing at a local level a new parish system. And to help him to put all this in place he transformed land-tenure by introducing the 'feudal' system whereby people held land (called a fee or feu) from their superior in return for military service. It is difficult to overstate the impact all this had on the Scots. Not a single soul was unaffected. And the reforms were set to last. Today we take coins for granted, and most of us live in cities and towns. The 'shires' and parishes still persist despite modern bureaucratic attempts to remove them. And there are those among us who recall paying 'feu duty', albeit to someone we had most likely never met and certainly not in return for armed protection!

It was not only the political, social, economic and religious landscape that changed beyond all recognition; the physical landscape too was fundamentally affected. The new towns might not have been large by today's standards, but they would have seemed huge in the eyes of twelfth-century Scots. The new cathedrals and monasteries might have taken years to construct, but they must have presented awe-inspiring sights in the landscape, unlike anything they had ever seen before. And all across the land formidable castles were rising up for the new lords and ladies to live in, and stone parish churches for all to pray in.

While David and his grandsons were the architects of change, it was the Normans, Bretons, Flemings and others who provided the tools and the building materials. A few were the king's personal friends, but many more were lords of lesser rank. All though were 'vassals' (from the Latin *vassallus*, 'servant'), bound by the oath of fealty or allegiance to serve their lord in exchange for the privilege of holding land. And land in those days meant power. Many of our Scottish surnames are derived from these incomers, including three of the most famous names in Scottish history – Bruce, Stewart and Wallace. It was the same with Christian names – Malcolm,

brother, William 'the Lion' (1165-1214), who earned his byname when he adopted the Lion Rampant as the royal arms, continued the process. By the time William (even his Christian name was a Norman one) passed peacefully away at Stirling Castle, the transformation from Celtic state to feudal kingdom was effectively complete. David and his heirs had brought about profound and irrevocable change to almost every conceivable aspect of national life.

What David put in train was little short of a revolution. He introduced money into the realm by

Duncan and Edith were becoming old-fashioned; the 'in' names at the baptismal font were now William, Robert and Isabel.

Mounted mail-clad knights and ladies sporting strange names weren't the only newcomers; monks too, attired in strange habits, flocked to Scotland in droves. The monastic life was nothing new of course, but the successors of the 'holy fathers' had long abandoned their high ideals for more worldly ways. Corruption was rife. The Culdees, or *Céli De*, 'the servants of God', who had by Malcolm Canmore's reign come to dominate the spiritual life of the nation, might have lived in community with each other, but many were married and holding important positions they regarded as hereditary. There was need for change.

Change had already swept through the cloisters of mainland Europe. It began with the founding of the Order of Cluny, in deepest Burgundy, in 909 and spread like 'wildfire'. Other orders followed Cluny's lead in the quest to return to St Benedict's 'first principles' of poverty, chastity and obedience. They included the Tironensians, established in 1109 at Tiron, near Chartres, who became the first

of the 'reformed' Benedictine orders to come to the British Isles when David invited them to settle at Selkirk in 1113 (they were relocated to Kelso 15 years later). Others followed, including the Augustinians, renowned for their learning, who became associated with royal centres like Scone and Holyrood.

But it was the Cistercians who had the greatest impact on Scotland. Established at Citeaux, near Dijon, in 1098, their uncompromising insistence on poverty and labour attracted many disenchanted with the secular world to join their ranks. They established their first Scottish house at Melrose, in Tweeddale, in 1136, and the austere life they pursued was perfectly summed up by Aelred, Abbot of Rievaulx, the man who had engineered their arrival in Scotland:

Our food is scanty, our garments rough; our drink is from the stream and our sleep is often upon our book. Under our tired limbs there is but a hard mat; when sleep is sweetest we must rise at bell's bidding. Self will has no place; there is no moment for idleness or dissipation; everywhere peace, everywhere

▲ *Gracing the banks of the Jed Water, in Roxburghshire, stands the impressive ruined abbey church of Jedburgh. Built by the black-robed Augustinians around the mid-twelfth century, it was founded on the orders of King David I himself, to demonstrate to Scots and English alike the simple fact that his writ extended to the very fringes of his kingdom. But it was equally a spiritual place, where the prayers perpetually offered up by the canons therein were deemed to offer the hope of eternal salvation to those suffering the evils of the earthly world in which they lived.*

▶ *The power of 'holy mother church'. This larger-than-life statue of a bishop, in the grounds of Elgin Cathedral, once stood high up on the central crossing tower for all to see. Elgin Cathedral, the chief church of the bishops of Moray from the thirteenth century through to the Reformation of 1560 (the* cathedra *was the bishop's special seat), was the ecclesiastical focus of a vast diocese reaching from the River Spey in the east all the way to the west coast.*

serenity and a marvellous freedom from the tumult of the World.

The Cistercians went out of their way, literally, to help them to focus on the *Opus Dei*, 'the work of God', for they sought out remote places 'far from the concourse of men'. One contemporary wrote: 'Give them a wilderness, and in a few years you will find a dignified abbey in the midst of smiling plenty'. Whether their hard physical labour earned them their reward in Heaven God alone knows. But they unquestionably reaped a rich harvest on this earth, for themselves and for Scotland. They were renowned sheep farmers; the monks of Melrose

alone had some 15,000 sheep chewing their way across the Southern Uplands from the Lammermuirs to Carrick.

The monks flourished because Scottish society was intensely God-fearing; the dread of purgatory and the hope of an eternal life thereafter were present in the minds of all. To become a monk was the closest one could come on God's Earth to leading a blameless life. But not everyone could join a monastery, so paying someone else to do your praying for you was considered the next best thing. Giving to the monks was like taking out a spiritual insurance policy, so Scots great and small, rich and poor, gave to the Church. Everyone was obliged to render a teind, or tenth, of their yearly income. Many gave more than that, but no one more than King David. It was later said of him that he was 'a sair (sore) saint for the Crown', and he clearly dug deep into the royal coffers to set up so many monasteries. Add to that all the other costs of his 'revolution' – the castle-building, the town planning, the fact that to entice so many feudal lords to his realm he had to 'farm out' so much of the Crown estate – and one can begin to see why he earned this accolade.

But David wasn't a poor king of a poor country. He was immensely wealthy, thanks to the fact he had at his disposal the silver-rich mineral deposits high up in the north Pennines. The area around Allanheads is now more famous for its later lead-mining heritage, but in the twelfth century it provided the mints of Europe with much of their silver. David had grasped the opportunity presented by the civil war that had broken out in England following the death of his brother-in-law, Henry I, by invading the northern counties of England and annexing them. When David himself died in 1153, it wasn't at Dunfermline or Edinburgh or at any of his other Scottish residences but at Carlisle. For David was king not only of Scotland but of northern England also.

David was king in Scotland for twenty-nine years, warily discerning what was provident;
After he fortified the kingdom with castles and arms, the king died an old man, at Carlisle.
(An entry in the *Melrose Chronicle* for the year 1153.)

'The Normans are Coming'

~ SCOTLAND'S SURNAMES ~

'What's in a name? That which we call a rose
By any other name would smell as sweet.'

(From Shakespeare's Romeo and Juliet *Act III, Scene II, 1595.)*

Scottish surnames like Bruce, Stewart and Wallace, feel as Scottish as tartan and tweed. But they owe their origin not to ancient Gaelic ancestors but to twelfth-century incomers from the other side of the English Channel.

Everybody has a surname nowadays, but in twelfth-century Scotland they weren't at all common. Most people would have been known by their Christian name and further identified by their father's name – as in Macbeth mac Findlaeth, Walter fitz Alan or Thorfinn Sigurd's son.

Another way of distinguishing between people of the same name was to bestow nicknames on individuals that seemed apt, such as 'the Conqueror' and 'the Lion', or if you weren't so lucky 'Flatnose' and 'Barelegs'. The practice of taking the surname from one's occupation – like baxter (baker), lorimer (harness-maker) and webster (weaver) – had yet to take on.

By the twelfth century it was becoming more common to link a person to the place they either lived in or hailed from. Whence the Balliols (after Bailleul-en-Vemeu in Picardy where they originated), the Douglases (from Douglas in Clydesdale, where William 'de Dowlas' settled after uprooting from Flanders) and the Murrays (named after the province of Moray where Freskin, another Fleming, settled about 1150).

Most Normans settling in Scotland came by way of England rather than directly from across the Channel. However, some brought their Norman 'place-names' with them. The Giffords hailed from Longueville-la-Gifart, near Dieppe, the Haigs from near Cap de La

Hague on the north-west tip of the Cotentin, the Rosses from Rots and the Sinclairs probably from St Clair-sur-Elle. The Somervilles (Graveron-Semerville) and the Turnbulls (La Tremblay-Omonville) had once been neighbours in the Seine valley north-west of Paris, while the Menzies were from even further afield, Rheims in Champagne. The Colvilles, Corbets, Frasers, Grahams, Mowbrays, Ramsays and the rest have yet to be 'run to earth'.

Undoubtedly the most famous Scottish surname betraying its Norman origins is Bruce. The family hailed originally from Brus, a village not far from Cherbourg; it is now spelled Brix. Sir Robert de Brus was highly connected at the court of Henry I, David I's brother-in-law, and was already lord of Cleveland, in north-east England, by the time he appeared in Scotland in 1124. He was clearly one of David's confidantes, for not only was he entrusted with the vast lordship of Annandale, hard by the English Border, but the charter sealing the deed was among the first, if not the first, to be granted by David as king. Eight generations on, another Robert de Bruce would become king himself.

Several surnames were picked up in England *en route* to Scotland. They include Barclay, derived from the manor of Berkley, in Somerset, from where Walter 'de Berkeley', Malcolm IV's chancellor, had come, and Mowat (derived from Mold, 'Le Mont Haut'), which clearly originated in the Welsh Marches.

But the most famous Welsh immigrant is Wallace. The name 'le

Waleys' literally means 'the Welshman', and the great Scottish patriot's ancestors would have come north with their lord, Walter, the High Steward, who had an estate in Shropshire. A William Wallace held Stenton, in East Lothian, but the surname is more commonly found linked to the Stewart patrimony in the west of Scotland. Richard Wallace gave his name to Riccarton (Riccardes-tun), near Kilmarnock, and he could well have been the forebear of Sir William Wallace of Ellerslie, victor of the Battle of Stirling Bridge.

Two surnames derive from the post their 'chiefs of kin' held at the Scottish royal court. The Durwards were hereditary 'doorwards', ushers who were responsible for checking the credentials of those wishing to enter the king's presence. The Stewarts were hereditary stewards, to whom fell the daily running of the king's household. The family were 'old hands' at stewarding, having previously served the Bishop of Dol in distant Brittany. One of them, Alan, crossed to England with Henry I and was in time rewarded with a portfolio of estates across ten English shires.

On his death, Walter, the third son, seeing little prospect of advancement in either country, decided to chance his luck in Scotland. By 1136 he was King David's high steward, with a major landholding centred on Renfrewshire and Ayrshire. Ultimately, Walter's move proved astute, for whereas his elder brother, William founded a great English baronial dynasty, the earls of Arundel, Walter himself became the progenitor of a royal dynasty that would one day rule Great Britain.

'Glory of a Golden Age'
~ GLASGOW CATHEDRAL ~

'a great fabrick, with a lofty steeple built by St Mungo'

(Reverend Thomas Morer, who visited in 1715)

The great cathedral of Glasgow is one of the outstanding architectural glories of Scotland's 'Golden Age' in the thirteenth century. The Reformation and the Industrial Revolution may have taken their toll of the 'great fabrick', yet it remains the only medieval cathedral on the Scottish mainland to survive virtually complete, its awesome scale and intricate ornament brilliant testimony both to the strength of belief, and the power and majesty of its Church, in that bygone age.

Reverend Morer wasn't alone in mistakenly believing that the mighty edifice was the work of St Kentigern, or St Mungo as he is more affectionately known. Most of what we know of this sixth-century holy man is the stuff of later legend, but that he became bishop of a sprawling diocese corresponding in size to the British kingdom of Strathclyde is beyond doubt. It is said that he built his church in *Glasgau*, 'the green hollow', and that when he died in 612 he was laid to rest on the site where the magnificent cathedral dedicated in his honour now stands. Bishop Jocelin (1174-99) did much to promote the cult of St Kentigern and shortly before his death embarked on an ambitious building project designed to enhance the experience of the countless pilgrims to his tomb. In July 1197, as part of the celebrations to mark the dedication of the new work, the prelate instigated a week-long fair to be enjoyed by the people of his cathedral city. Glaswegians enjoy the 'Glasgow Fair' holiday to this day.

Early in the thirteenth century the decision was taken to rebuild anew, for this was the great age of cathedral building throughout western Europe, and something of a 'golden age' for Scotland. The new seat of the bishops of Glasgow ('cathedra' meant 'the bishop's throne') took almost the entire century to build.

The intention of the Church authorities was threefold: to build an eye-catching structure that would dominate the landscape for miles around; to provide a

▲ *Throughout the Middle Ages, Glasgow Cathedral dominated its surroundings, demonstrating to all who gazed on it the power of 'Holy Mother Church'. By the time this fine view was painted by an unknown artist in the early nineteenth century, the Royal Infirmary on the right, designed by Robert Adam and built in the 1790s, had begun the process of rivalling its neighbour for mastery of the Glasgow skyline.*

stunningly beautiful interior space wherein the cathedral canons could maintain the daily round of services; and to create a fitting pilgrim route to the relics and tomb of one of the nation's leading saints. The names of those who created the wonder, the architects and masons, joiners, glaziers and labourers, remain unknown to us, but the fruits of their labours stand as silent witnesses to their belief, their skills and their art; the spacious elegance of the choir, the bewitching gloom of the crypt

beneath, and soaring over all the slender pinnacle of the spire.

Standing in the vast, echoing space of the nave, one can imagine the scene on perhaps the busiest day in the cathedral's calendar, 13 January, St Kentigern's festival day. Throngs of pilgrims crowding expectantly through the great west doors, jostling for a place in the queue that would lead them along the narrow aisle past the High Altar to the shrine containing the holy relics, where a sight, perhaps even a touch if one was lucky, might bring comfort, maybe even a cure for some affliction or another. Thence down the cold stone stair into the crypt beneath, towards the candle-flames flickering over the saint's tomb. And all the while the monotonous chanting of the canons, the murmuring of pilgrims praying, and from on high the great bells in the lofty spire ringing out across the city and the countryside beyond.

In its medieval prime, the great cathedral dominated the little town beside the Clyde that sprouted up in its shadow. But with the coming of the 'Tobacco Lords' and the Industrial Revolution in the eighteenth century, the rapidly expanding city shifted its centre of gravity westward to a new municipal and commercial heart around George Square. The cathedral's 'lofty steeple' was left to vie with chimneys and cranes, and latterly tower blocks, for the skyline it had once had to itself. But although the cathedral today may no longer be physically at the centre of the city, it remains a vital part of civic life, for without the cathedral there would be no city.

SCOTLAND

In Malcolm IV's reign (1153-65) the phrase 'the kingdom of Scotland' was used for the first time. The country over which the king of Scots now ruled had never extended so far. The Northern Isles and Hebrides still lay beyond the realm, but areas once under the sway of the Vikings, like Caithness, Argyll and Galloway, were now coming increasingly under the influence of the Scottish Crown.

The writ of the king of Scots now also extended into England, as far south as the River Ribble in Lancashire and the River Tees in Yorkshire. But the gains proved hard to hold on to, and for the next 50 years and more there was constant tension in the area, occasionally erupting into open conflict. Life must have been unbearable for the poor Border folk caught in the middle.

It was early morning and the dawn scarcely breaking when the proud company of [Scottish] knights arm themselves. First they attacked the town of Belford. They spread themselves out all over the countryside. You could have seen Flemings tying up peasants and leading them off roped together like heathens. Women flee to the church only to be snatched away naked, leaving behind their garments and their valuables.

(Eye-witness account by Jordan Fantôsme, a clerk at the court of Henry II of England, of King William's invasion of Northumberland in 1174.)

Fantôsme's mention of Flemings raises the intriguing issue of nationality – what did being 'Scottish' or 'English' mean in those days? The men who followed William's 'Lion Rampant' into Northumberland in 1174 were an assortment of nationalities – Scots, Gallovidians, Normans, Bretons, Flemings – and English as well of course, the descendants of those who had fled north after 1066. There must have been quite a number in the 'host' unsure as to where their loyalties lay. Some of the Normans must have found it particularly awkward having to go into battle against their kinsmen. Take John de Vaux, lord of Dirleton in East Lothian. His brother was not only lord of the Cumbrian manor of Gilsland but also keeper of Carlisle Castle when the Scots

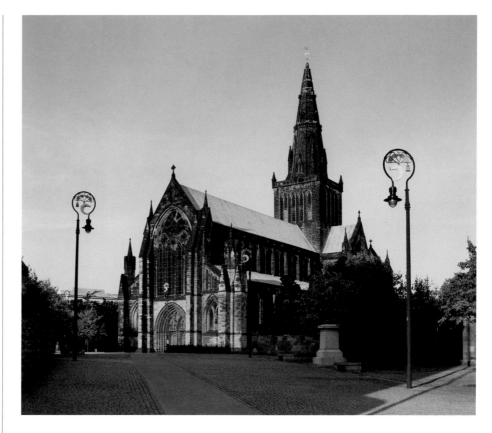

besieged it. Such divided loyalties would continue to vex people on both sides of the divide until the bitter Wars of Independence of the fourteenth century finally forced them to choose one or the other.

Communication must have presented a problem too. With the creation of Alba, Gaelic had become the 'mother tongue', and as the kingdom expanded so did Gaelic, finally forcing out the Welsh language spoken by the Strathclyde Britons and almost expunging the Old English of the Angles. But the immigration of so many Anglo-Norman landlords and monks progressively reversed that trend. While Latin continued as the 'official' language of church and charter, the language now spoken at the royal court, and in the knightly echelons of the 'host', was Norman French.

But that is not what many of those accompanying the new lords spoke. Being mostly of English origin, they spoke 'Inglis' – not quite the tongue of the seventh-century Angles but one that had become heavily laced with Scandinavian grammar, vocabulary and pronunciation following three centuries of Viking rule in England. This was the language that began to permeate Scotland.

By the fourteenth century 'Scots' had become

▲ *The awe-inspiring cathedral of Glasgow is a remarkable testament to the 'golden age' of the Alexanders in the thirteenth century. Next to St Andrews, in Fife, it was the most ambitiously planned cathedral in medieval Scotland. The arms of the city of Glasgow, depicted on the lampposts, were inspired by some of the miracles associated with Glasgow's patron saint, Kentigern.*

*This is the bird that
    never flew,
This is the tree that
    never grew,
This is the bell that
    never rang,
This is the fish that
    never swam.*

(Glasgow children's rhyme recalling the four images from St Mungo's life now incorporated in the city's coat of arms.)

the common tongue of all Lowland Scots from the Border north to Aberdeen, including those in the upper classes who had previously spoken French. Only those living in Galloway continued to speak Gaelic well into the seventeenth century.

The Earl of March, in a letter to Henry IV of England dated 1400, made no excuse for writing in Scots and not French because 'the tongue is maire cleare to myne understanding'. By now Scots was becoming the 'official' language of Parliament. It was even beginning to infiltrate 'Norn', the language of the Vikings spoken in the Northern Isles. As Gaelic retreated back to its ancient heartland in the west, the *Gaidhealtachd*, there were doubtless many instances such as that said to have beset the good folk of Inverness in the seventeenth century when 'one halfe of the people understand not the other'!

One English word calls out for special mention. During the course of the twelfth century, and the country's transition from Celtic twilight to European dawn, the names Alba and Scotia passed into history. From now on, the country would be known by its English name: Scotland

HOW THE WEST WAS WON

On 5 July 1217, Alexander II (1214-49) crossed into England at the head of another great Scottish army. The mission came to nothing and effectively ended any claim Scotland had to Northumberland. Eighty more years would pass before a hostile army crossed that frontier, with devastating results. Meanwhile, Alexander wisely elected to sue for peace with Henry III of England, and the years that followed were relatively calm on the southern border, leaving Alexander and his son, Alexander III (1249-86), free to press on with the task of reclaiming the lost lands in the west.

When Alexander II came to the throne, over 400 years had elapsed since the first Viking longships appeared off the west coast, and more than a century since his great-grand-uncle Edgar had formally ceded the Hebrides to Norway. In truth neither crown could claim it had ever exercised royal control over this vast and sprawling archipelago. Bergen was a long way from Barra, and the Scottish kings had long since lost interest in the land of their fathers. Into the vacuum had stepped powerful local warlords who ruled almost independently of whichever crown happened to claim sovereignty. They not only acted like kings, they called themselves 'kings'.

By the early twelfth century one warlord reigned supreme, Somerled, self-styled 'king' of Argyll, a vast power-base extending from Lorn to the distant Uists. Only the kings of Man, who controlled Lewis and Skye as well as Man, could compete with the man whose very name bears witness to his Viking roots – *sumarlidi*, 'summer-raider'. Such was his power, and such his ambition, that he even ventured to invade Scotland, sailing up the Clyde in 1164 at the head of a huge fleet of 160 ships. It proved his undoing; he was killed near Renfrew, and his head taken to Glasgow Cathedral as a trophy.

> The deadly leader, Somerled, died, in the first
>   great clash of arms.
> He fell wounded by a spear and cut down
>   by the sword;
> Their savage leader now laid low, the wicked
>   turned and ran,
> But many of them were butchered in the sea
>   as on dry land.
> They sought to clamber from the blood-red
>   waves into their ships,
> But were drowned, each and all, in the
>   surging tide.

(From a poem written by a canon of Glasgow Cathedral.)

Somerled's demise saw his vast 'empire' fragment as his sons divided up their inheritance. Dougal, the eldest, became 'King of Argyll' and it is from him that the MacDougall clan is descended. Ranald, the second son, assumed the title 'king of the isles', and although he himself didn't found a clan, his two sons, Ruari and Donald, did; the MacRuaries aren't that common today but you'll be hard pushed to find a telephone book anywhere in the world that doesn't have a MacDonald in it.

If Somerled's invasion set the antennae twitching at the Scottish court, then the Norman invasion of Ireland in 1171 had the alarm bells ringing. By 1181 they had taken control of eastern Ulster, and with Galloway and Kintyre within sight from the Antrim coast Scotland's western border was looking increasingly vulnerable. It was time to strike. Before 1200, Walter, the second High Stewart, moved across the Firth of Clyde and reclaimed Bute, the Cumbraes and Arran for Scotland. He built a mighty castle at Rothesay to secure his prize. More gains followed. One by one the descendants of Somerled were forced into swearing allegiance to the Scottish Crown.

King Haakon of Norway was compelled to respond. In 1263 he commanded the fleet in person, sailing from Bergen in a great oak ship specially built for the occasion, with a gilded dragon at its prow. But high summer was almost over by the time Haakon sailed through the strait between Skye and the mainland that now bears his name – Kyleakin, 'Haakon's Narrows' – and when at last the fleet rounded the Mull of Kintyre and anchored off Largs, September too had run its course.

The battle of Largs (1-2 October) was not so much a full-blown encounter, more a series of bloody skirmishes in which first one side and then the other seized the initiative. It may never have happened at all had a howling gale not sprung up from the west, causing Haakon's ships to drag their anchors and blowing them perilously close to the Ayrshire coast. Some crews were forced ashore,

▲ *The departure of the Vikings from the western seaboard of Scotland in 1266 after more than 400 years saw the emergence of new lords. They included the Macneils of Barra, who held sway locally on behalf of the Scottish kings from their island fastness of Kisimul Castle.*

▲ King Alexander III
(1249-86) being
inaugurated King of Scots
on the Moot Hill at
Scone in 1249; from the
fifteenth-century history
of Scotland,
Scotichronicon, by Abbot
Bower of Inchcolm.
On the left is the king's
Highland bard who
'suddenly fell on his knee
before the throne and,
bowing his head, hailed
the king in his mother
tongue [Gaelic] and
recited the pedigree
of the kings of Scots'.

▶ St Andrews Cathedral,
'headquarters' of the
Scottish Church from the
tenth century until the
Reformation in 1560.
In its prime the longest
church in the realm,
it was completed in
Alexander III's reign.

where they encountered stiff resistance. As dawn broke the following morning, Haakon too went ashore and battle was well and truly joined. Eventually, the superior numbers of the Scots, fighting on horseback as well as on foot, took their toll and Haakon's Norwegians had no option but to claw their way back to their ships as best they could. Many didn't make it, cut down or drowned in the chilly waters of the Clyde. As Haakon's fleet sailed away, the victorious Scots watched from the shore. It was the last the Scots would see of the Norwegians in the west.

King Haakon never made it back to Norway. Battling through fierce autumn storms took its toll of the ageing king, and he got no further than Kirkwall. His death snuffed out any lingering hope Norway harboured of continuing dominion over the Scottish Hebrides. One by one the 'sons' of Somerled transferred their allegiance; there was little point remaining true to the Norwegian flag if the Norwegian fleet could not command the sea-

lanes. When in 1266 Magnus of Norway and Alexander III of Scotland agreed to a formal hand-over and set their seals on the Treaty of Perth, the final curtain came down on over four centuries of Viking rule in the west.

Scotland was now becoming recognisable as the country it is today. Only Orkney and Shetland remained beyond the realm. For the rest of Alexander's long reign, Scots enjoyed a period of sustained peace and not a little prosperity – they even began to think of themselves as 'Scots', not Normans, Flemings or whatever. To their children and grandchildren, who had had to endure the horrific events of the Wars of Independence, Alexander's reign was seen as a 'golden age' – peace with England, the 'wild west' reconquered and a booming economy.

Then – disaster! It had all been gladness and joy when, on 14 October 1285, Alexander wed his second queen, Yolande, in the splendour of the abbey church at Jedburgh. He was 44, she young and beautiful. The heir to his throne was his three-year-old granddaughter, Margaret, daughter of the king of Norway; hence her soubriquet 'the Maid of Norway'. Now, as the abbey bells rang out and the wedding guests sat down to a feast the like of which had never been seen before in Scotland, there was every prospect of a male heir.

But within five months Alexander was dead. Anxious to return to the loving embrace of his French queen, then residing at Kinghorn on the Fife coast, he ignored the advice of his companions not to go beyond Inverkeithing, the night being dark and stormy, and pressed on by a precipitous clifftop path. His body was discovered the following morning. For the first time in almost 200 years, the dynastic succession was in crisis. Scotland's 'golden age' was at an end.

Alas for tomorrow, a day of calamity and
misery! Because before the stroke of twelve a
strong wind will be heard in Scotland the like of
which has not been known since times long
ago. Indeed, its blast will dumbfound the
nations and render senseless those who hear it;
it will humble what is lofty and raze what is
unbending to the ground.

(The prophecy of Thomas 'the Rhymer', foretelling
the demise of King Alexander III in 1286.)

WARS WITH ENGLAND

(1286 - 1371)

> 'Scots wha hae wi' Wallace bled, Scots, wham Bruce has aften led'
>
> (*The opening lines of* Scots Wha Hae, *by Robert Burns, 1793*)

The integrity of Scotland as a nation was never so threatened as during the time of Edward I of England, 'Hammer of the Scots'. This chapter explores the background to Edward's invasion of 1296 and charts the extraordinary events and acts of heroism over the ensuing 100 years that secured Scotland's independence.

INVASION

Scarcely had Alexander III been laid to rest than the wrangling began about his successor. The fact that Parliament had acknowledged the late king's grandchild, Margaret the Maid of Norway, 'our lady and rightful heir' didn't prevent certain magnates from voicing their concern that the heir was a female. She may have been the sole surviving descendant in the direct line, but up to that time no woman had ever reigned as queen anywhere in feudal Europe, let alone Scotland. Those with royal aspirations began to stake their claim, chief among them Robert Bruce, Lord of Annandale, and his neighbour, John Balliol, Lord of Galloway. The 'Guardians' appointed to steer the ship of state in the interim were in a quandary.

That they looked to Edward I of England for help may be considered an act of sheer folly to us who have the benefit of hindsight: a bit like inviting the 'big bad wolf' into the house! But the

Guardians would have deemed it the obvious, and most prudent, thing to do. After all, the two countries had been at peace, more or less, for decades, and their late sovereign and the King of England had been good friends, indeed brothers-in-law. Edward might have made noises about being 'lord superior' of the king of Scots, but hadn't Alexander put him firmly in his place with the riposte: 'No one has the right to homage for my kingdom for I hold it of God alone'? And when Edward offered his own son, Edward of Caernarfon, as Margaret's husband, they accepted with alacrity, subject to safeguards regarding the sovereignty of Scotland of course, for it seemed to offer a suitable way out of the mire. The relieved Guardians immediately invited Eric of Norway to send his daughter, now aged seven, to Scotland. The poor lass got no further than Orkney. She breathed her last soon after arriving in Kirkwall at the beginning of September, dying possibly in the same chamber where her great-grandfather,

◀ *The equestrian statue of King Robert the Bruce (1306-29) overlooks the battlefield of Bannockburn where, in 1314, the great king sent 'proud Edward's army home to think again'. The Scottish victory over the English at Bannockburn did not bring an end to the bloody Wars of Independence with England; far from it, for they continued on and off for a further 50 years before both nations tired of the effort. But what Bannockburn did achieve was the unqualified support by the Scots for The Bruce as their sovereign king, after years of bitter internecine rivalry with the Balliols. Charles Pilkington Jackson's fine statue at the National Trust for Scotland battlefield site was erected in 1963.*

▲ The town of Berwick-upon-Tweed is 'English' now, and has been officially since 1482. But prior to that it was effectively Scotland's capital city, the premier town and seaport of the realm. From the moment in 1296 when King Edward I of England, 'Hammer of the Scots', crossed the River Tweed and captured the town, the luckless inhabitants were always going to be vexed as to which nation they belonged to; the debate continues to this day, and is highlighted by the fact that Berwick Rangers play their football in the Scottish League.

Haakon, had passed away 27 years before. Fate had determined that the Maid of Norway would never set eyes on the land over which she had nominally reigned for four years.

Queen Margaret's untimely death plunged the country into crisis once more, but doubly so for now there was no recognised heir, male or female. Civil war threatened as Bruce and Balliol vied for pre-eminence. The Guardians in desperation turned again to Edward of England for help. The opportunity was too good for the wily monarch to pass up. Edward came north to the Tweed with a large army, having first ordered his clerks to scour the archives for any shred of evidence that might advance his claim to the overlordship of Scotland. When the Guardians politely rebuffed him, declaring that they had 'no power to reply to your statement, lacking a king to whom the demand ought to be addressed', Edward simply invited the rival claimants, or competitors (there were now twelve of them!), to acknowledge him as their lord superior. All readily did so, for that seemed the only way they could remain in the race. Edward Plantagenet, King of England, Wales and Ireland, was cunningly negotiating his way to the throne of Scotland also. Mastery of all Britain was now within his grasp.

All that remained for Edward to do now was

determine which of the competitors would be his 'puppet-king'. An elaborate court was convened in the great castle at Berwick-upon-Tweed, then Scotland's main town and trading port, to which all the claimants were invited. The 'Great Cause', as the decision became known, dragged on for over a year, and took many a twist and turn. There were deals struck between rival competitors, even talk of dividing up Scotland. Gradually the competitors were whittled down until only Bruce and Balliol remained. There was little to choose between them. Both were descended from David I through his grandson Earl David, William the Lion's younger brother. But whereas the ageing Bruce was a generation closer to the great sovereign, the younger Balliol was from the more senior line. At last, Edward proclaimed in favour of John Balliol, and on St Andrew's Day 1292 King John (1292-96) was duly enthroned at Scone.

Poor John was doomed from the outset. First he was made to do homage to Edward, then told he had to travel to England to explain every decision made at his court. Humiliation was heaped on humiliation. Edward wished it so, prepared to 'turn the screw' until something snapped. The final twist came in 1294 when he demanded that John help him wage war against France. It was too much for the Scots, who had no quarrel with the French. They relieved John of much of his power, though not his crown, and in 1295 negotiated a pact of mutual military assistance with the French – the famous 'auld alliance'. Edward responded in the only way he could – he invaded Scotland. That single act heralded 300 years of bitter conflict.

The date Friday 30 March 1296 will be forever etched on the memories of the people of Berwick. The townsfolk had just celebrated Easter. Suddenly a 30,000-strong English army, with Edward at its head, stormed the town walls and ran amok through the streets. By Low Sunday 7500 men, women and children – two-thirds of

'Scotland's Lost Capital

~ BERWICK-UPON-TWEED ~

'the English possess, beyond the Tweed in the kingdom of Scotland, the singular fortress of Berwick'

(From C A Sneyd's A relation of the Island of England, 1500)

The bustling town of Berwick-upon-Tweed has a strange feel about it. It is _in_ England, but somehow it is not _of_ England. The pretty stone-walled houses with their red pantiled roofs lining the steeply sloping streets stubbornly refuse to conform to the image of a typical English north country town. Instead, they seem still to proclaim the town's ancient Scottish roots.

Berwick hasn't been Scottish since 1482, when the last brave defenders duly 'partit thairfra with bagg and baggages'. Indeed, for the two centuries before that it could hardly be deemed to have been Scottish either, for during the prolonged Wars of Independence it passed back and forth between the two countries like a bone between two dogs. But prior to the murderous events of 1296, this neat town, perched where the River Tweed meets the North Sea, had the distinction of being Scotland's largest and wealthiest town – not strictly speaking a 'capital city', but if you had asked any foreigner to name one Scottish town they would probably have said 'Berwick'.

Towns, or burghs as they were formally called, first appeared in Scotland in the early twelfth century. Berwick may have been the first; it is certainly the first to appear in the records alongside Roxburgh. Burghs weren't necessarily distinguishable from villages by their size alone but by the fact that they were licensed by the Crown to control the buying and selling of local goods as well as the import-export business. Berwick's geographical position facing across to the European mainland made it eminently suited for that purpose. It rapidly grew into a thriving market town and sea port.

No one shall buy any merchandise brought for sale to the burgh upon the bridge of Tweed or in the Briggate or outwith the ports of the town before that merchandise has reached the burgh market. Anyone convicted of so doing shall forfeit the goods he has brought, give a tun of wine to the gild or leave the burgh for a year and a day.
(From Berwick's Gild Statutes, 1249)

Standing in Marygate when the street market is in town, one gets an inkling of how it must have been all those years ago; throngs of people from the villages and countryside around jostling with each other to haggle with the merchants and traders for the farm foods and finished goods on sale – grain from England, cloth from the Low Countries, wines from Bordeaux and spices from the Orient sitting alongside the local produce. And behind the market stalls and merchants' houses, men and women toiling away in the wynds and closes at their craft or trade: waulkers and weavers working wool; skinners and souters making leather goods; baxters and brewsters, smiths, wrights and the rest.

The people of Berwick were a cosmopolitan lot – native Scots, English incomers as well as a healthy smattering of other European nationalities. Flemish and German merchants were particularly prominent, and both had hostels in the Seagate. During the horrendous events of March 1296, almost the entire Flemish colony was burnt to death when the blazing roof of their Red Hall crashed down on top of them. Add to these the crews of the trading vessels and fishing smacks tying up at the quayside, many of whom would be foreign too, and one has the picture of a throbbing town alive with noises – and smells!

The focal point of the town was the mercat (market) cross, and close by it the 'tron', the all-important weighing machine. At each entrance into the town were 'ports', gates controlling access into and out of the burgh. Other prominent landmarks included the parish church of St Mary and five friary churches. And rivalling these public buildings and monuments in the affections of locals and visitors alike would have been the alehouses and brothels; it was aye thus.

All this activity was controlled by regulations called 'customs', administered by the king's representative with the help of the burgesses. In all other burghs in the realm, the chief official was called *prepositus*, from which our word 'provost' is derived. But Berwick was so important that it was headed by a mayor assisted by four *prepositi*. As the town flourished, the burgesses developed their own merchant and craft gilds, and even adopted that ultimate symbol of corporate identity – the 'logo'. Berwick upon Tweed was the first Scottish town to have a Burgh Seal, in 1212.

Burghs existed, though, only by royal consent, and looming above the town was the formidable royal castle. Alas, most of this great medieval stronghold was swept away with the coming of the railway in the 1840s. But while you're waiting on Platform 1 for the 10.42 to Edinburgh Waverley, pause to reflect on perhaps the most momentous event that occurred on that spot on 17 November 1292 when Edward of England, in the splendid surroundings of the castle's great hall, finally gave his judgement; that John Balliol would be King of Scots.

▲ King John Balliol pays homage at the feet of King Edward of England in 1292. Just four years later, John's troubled reign as King of Scots was brought to a premature close by that same King Edward during a humiliating ceremony at Montrose Castle. The chronicler, Andrew of Wyntoun, describes the scene for us:

This John of Balliol
   deprived he
Of all his robes of royalty.
The fur they took out of
   his tabard [coat],
'Toom Tabard' [Empty
   Coat] he was called
   afterwards;
And all other insignia
That fell to king in
   any way,
Both sceptre, sword,
   crown and ring,
From this John, that he
   made king,
Wholly from him he
   took there,
And made him of his
   kingdom bare.

the population – lay dead or dying. It was said Edward only ordered a halt to the butchery upon seeing a crying child clinging to the bloodied skirts of his dead mother.

For two days streams of blood flowed from the bodies of the slain so that mills could be turned round by the flow.

(From Walter Bower's *Scotichronicon*).

The Scots now found themselves up against one of the most efficient fighting machines in Europe. The English had after all been waging war for most of the preceding century – on Crusade, in France, against the Irish and the Welsh, even against each other in the civil war of the 1260s in which Edward himself had almost lost his life. The Scots, by contrast, had had little recent experience of warfare save for the desultory victory at Largs. The battle fought at Dunbar on 27 April was a foregone conclusion. Within days the great royal castles of Roxburgh, Edinburgh, Stirling and Dumbarton had fallen, and within weeks John, abandoned by most of his subjects, had surrendered at another, Kincardine. In a humiliating spectacle beside the mercat cross in Montrose, the King of Scots was forced to hand back his crown, sword, sceptre and ring (the royal

regalia) to the very man who had entrusted them to him four years before. The rich fur from his tabard, or surcoat, was also taken from him, whence Balliol's nickname 'Toom Tabard', or 'empty coat'. Soon Edward was heading south, with John as his prisoner and the Scottish regalia and Stone of Destiny as trophies of war, sure in the knowledge he had conquered Scotland. He couldn't have been more wrong.

But who would lead the resistance? Many Scottish noblemen, knights and esquires had been killed or captured at Berwick and Dunbar, while hundreds more had subsequently been made to swear allegiance to the all-conquering king. A few magnates who had been implacably opposed to Balliol had even sided with the English king from the outset, including most notably Robert Bruce the younger, whose father, 'the Competitor', had died in 1295. While the English were slaughtering the townsfolk of Berwick, Bruce was holding Carlisle Castle for Edward, and after Dunbar had the temerity to ask for the throne now that Balliol was a spent force. 'Have we nothing else to do but win kingdoms for you?' was Edward's curt reply.

FIGHT FOR INDEPENDENCE: *William Wallace*

One person who didn't bend the knee to Edward of England was William Wallace. Perhaps this younger son of a minor Ayrshire lord (he was probably born at Ellerslie, near Kilmarnock, and not Elderslie, in Renfrewshire) was not of sufficient standing in society; more likely it was because he had already decided on rebellion. We know remarkably little about the life of Scotland's greatest patriot – most of it is the stuff of later legend – but we do know that no sooner had Edward left Scotland than Wallace's name begins to appear in English military despatches – 'that bloody man', he is called in one, 'the chief of brigands'. Withdrawing into the great forest of Selkirk, Wallace raised a guerrilla army that ambushed without warning and just as quickly vanished. In May 1297 he turned up the heat, killing Sir William Heselrig, the English sheriff of

Lanark, and carrying out audacious 'hit-and-run' raids into northern England. His lead inspired others. Sir Andrew Moray, heir to his father's vast northern earldom, had been captured at Dunbar and incarcerated in Chester Castle. But during that winter he escaped, returned to his home in the Black Isle and raised a second army. The two resistance fighters finally joined forces on the Abbey Craig, overlooking a winding in the River Forth and the mighty castle of Stirling, then in English hands.

The Battle of Stirling Bridge on 11 September 1297 might never have been fought at all if the Earl of Surrey, the victor of Dunbar, had had his way. But he was overruled by Hugh de Cressingham, Edward's treasurer. Cressingham, his accountant's mind working overtime, was anxious to get the whole show over and done with. But Stirling Bridge itself was so narrow that it could take only two horsemen abreast, and Surrey did all in his power to avoid crossing it, even sending two friars over to parley with Wallace and Moray. They soon returned with Wallace's stinging response still ringing in their ears: 'Tell your commander that we are not here to make peace but to do battle to defend ourselves and liberate our kingdom. Let them come on, and we shall prove this in their very beards.'

The English did 'come on', to the surprise and delight of the Scots. Wallace and Moray held back until they figured sufficient had crossed, and then they struck, charging down the slope, the points of their spears glistening in the autumn sun. It was a massacre. Those who had crossed over were cut down, others threw themselves into the river and were drowned by the weight of their chain-mail. In all 100 mounted knights and 5000 infantry were slain. The wily old Earl of Surrey had chosen not to cross and made his escape. Poor Cressingham was not so lucky; struck down in the heat of battle, his body was mercilessly flayed and pieces of his skin passed around the victorious Scots as a memento of their great victory.

There is no doubting Stirling Bridge was a disaster for the English, undoing at a stroke all of Edward's gains of the previous year. Not since Carham in 1018 had the Scots defeated the English in pitched battle. The victory was made all the

sweeter because a hastily assembled peasant army of foot-soldiers had seen off one of Europe's finest fighting machines. It was undoubtedly Wallace's finest hour.

Wallace had won the battle, but he knew he had not won the war. Edward invaded again. Confronted with another formidable force, Wallace could have been forgiven for resorting to guerrilla tactics once again. Instead, he chose to stand and fight, drawing up his men on rising ground near Callendar Wood, east of Falkirk. The day-long encounter was hard-fought and bloody, but when the noise of battle finally faded, it was mostly Scots cries of agony that rose into the evening air and Scots blood that coloured the sluggish waters of the Westquarter Burn. Many a

▲ *The pivotal importance of Stirling Bridge is reinforced in this map of Britain, drawn in the thirteenth century; truly, Stirling was 'the brooch clasping Lowlands and Highlands together'. Travellers beware, however. The cartographer not only exaggerates Stirling Bridge out of all recognition, but he gives the impression that the Western Isles (top left) were separated from the mainland only by a narrow river rather than the perilous expanse of the Minch.*

▲ *The graceful stone bridge over the River Forth at Stirling was not there in 1297 when William Wallace won his great victory over the English. The 'bridge' of the Battle of Stirling Bridge was made of wood and lay a short way upstream of (that is, beyond) the present one.*

wife was widowed and many a child orphaned on that July day in 1298.

Wallace managed to escape the field, but his defeat rendered him a spent force militarily. Viewed with suspicion by the great magnates, this man of lowly aristocratic birth was only ever going to be as good as his last victory. He resigned as military commander, and instead put the tremendous reputation he had won at Stirling Bridge to good effect by crossing to Europe and gaining audiences with the 'great and grand', including the king of France and the pope. He may even have visited King John himself, now living in exile on his ancestral estate in Picardy. By 1303 he was back home in the thick of things once more, and was last seen fighting a skirmish near Perth in September of the following year. By then Edward of England's patience had run out: 'Know that it is not our will that any word of peace be held out to him unless he places himself utterly and absolutely in our will.'

Wallace was eventually captured near Glasgow (the traditional place is Robroyston) on 3 August 1305. He was taken straight to London. There he was led through the crowded, jeering streets of the English capital to his show-trial in Westminster Hall, where he was accused of many crimes. Wallace pleaded guilty to them all except the main

one, treason; how could he be guilty of this, he replied, when he had sworn his oath of allegiance to King John of Scotland and not to King Edward of England? It made not one jot or tittle of a difference. He was found guilty on all counts. Once more he was dragged through the city streets. At Smithfield he met his grisly end – firstly hanged, and then cut down while still breathing and disembowelled. But still Edward lusted for more vengeance. And so Wallace's entrails were burnt before the cheering throng, and his head parted from his body and put on public display above London Bridge. Finally what was left of his torso was cut into quarters and taken separately to Newcastle, Berwick, Perth and Stirling where they would serve as a warning to anyone contemplating following in Wallace's footsteps.

It was perhaps more the manner of his dying, rather than anything he might have achieved when alive, that earned Wallace enduring fame and his place in Scottish history. For on that August day at Smithfield, the mighty Edward of England, one of the greatest military commanders medieval Europe was ever to see, had been reduced to little more than a ruthless tyrant pursuing a cruel personal vendetta against a humble Scottish patriot. No sooner had the breath left Wallace's body than the legend began.

FIGHT FOR INDEPENDENCE: *Robert Bruce*

The man who followed in Wallace's footsteps happened also to be an Ayrshire man – Robert Bruce, Earl of Carrick. But there the similarity ended, for whereas Wallace had been the younger son of a minor lord, Bruce was heir to a vast estate of lands, in England as well as in Scotland, and was a leading magnate of the realm. Furthermore, thanks to the efforts of his grandfather, Robert Bruce 'the Competitor', he had a claim to the throne itself.

There was another significant difference between Wallace and Bruce – the matter of national identity. Wallace would have had absolutely no doubt about his; although of Welsh descent, he himself had been born a Scot, and everything he owned, and everyone in his social circle, was Scottish too. With Bruce things were nowhere near so cut-and-dried. Yes, he too was of foreign lineage, and he too had been born a Scot, first seeing the light of day at Turnberry Castle on 11 July 1274. But although the Bruces resided chiefly in Scotland, like most Scottish aristocratic families they had extensive landed interests in southern England also, including a residence in London.

Until the momentous events of 1296, the matter of national identity had not been an issue to Bruce and his peers; more important was the social milieu in which they moved. One contemporary actually described Robert Bruce as an English nobleman with estates in Scotland. Bruce probably saw himself more as a Scottish nobleman with lands in England, but the most significant word for Bruce would have been 'nobleman'. He would have had far more in common, and been much more comfortable, with his English peers than with Scots like Wallace. But as the wars with England rumbled on, so the matter of national identity came more sharply into

focus. Gradually even great Anglo-Scottish magnates like Bruce had to decide which side they were on, Scotland's or England's.

Right from the start Bruce played a cunning game, supporting first one side then the other. Uppermost in his mind was the prospect of his becoming king one day. Initially throwing in his lot with Edward, he managed to avoid the débâcle at Dunbar, and carefully distanced himself from Wallace's revolt, choosing not to fight at Stirling Bridge. But with Wallace's defeat at Falkirk, Bruce stepped from the shadows. By now the impetus had rather gone out of Edward's attempt at conquest. English garrisons held the great castles, but the land itself was not so easily subdued. To achieve that Edward needed money, lots of it, but even his own people baulked at his ruthless taxation of them. Bruce, sensing the weakness of Edward's position, thought his cause would be better served if he appeared to lead his people, king in all but name. It was not to last. The intervention of the French early in the new century brought about the daunting possibility that his grandfather's old adversary, King John, might yet return to his throne. It was too much for Bruce. He returned to Edward's camp once more, and even attended the English parliament. It was a shrewd move. In 1303, Edward again invaded

▲ *Given its situation close by the treacherous sands of the Solway Firth and the Border with England, mighty Caerlaverock Castle, seat of the powerful Maxwell clan, was always going to be a target for Edward I from the time he invaded Scotland in 1296. That day came in the summer of 1300, and although the siege was over in under two days the event has entered the annals of history thanks to a dramatic eye-witness account by a herald in the English King's entourage:*

'In shape it was like a shield, for it had but three sides round it, with a tower at each corner, but one of them was a double one, so high, so long and so wide, that the gate was underneath it, well made and strong, with a drawbridge and a sufficiency of other defences. And it had good ditches, filled right up to the brim with water.'

▲ *Thrusting up from the tree-clad Abbey Craig, near Stirling, where in 1297 William Wallace and Andrew Moray planned their victory over the English at the Battle of Stirling Bridge, is the National Wallace Monument. This tribute to Sir William Wallace was supported by money collected from Scots world-wide in the 1850s. The resulting Victorian tower was designed by John T Rochead and at 220 feet in height with 246 steps, it dominates the surrounding countryside. It took eight years to build; an inauguration ceremony was held on 11 September 1869, the 572nd anniversary of Wallace's famous victory.*

Scotland in strength, sweeping aside all who had the effrontery to stand in his way. Bruce assisted, and was handsomely rewarded for his efforts. By early 1304 the Scots had surrendered. With Edward back in control, Bruce must have felt his time had come.

So why did Bruce choose that moment to risk all by plotting behind Edward's back? Had he reluctantly concluded perhaps that Edward had no intention of replacing the doomed King John with anyone but himself? Whatever the reason, three factors must have contributed to his decision: firstly, the death of his own father in Essex in March, leaving Bruce as claimant to the throne in his own right; secondly, the inescapable conclusion that King John was now effectively a spent force; and lastly, the age of Edward himself, 65 and surely not long for this world.

In June 1304, Bruce was helping Edward besiege Stirling Castle, the last of the country's strongholds to hold out. Bruce had even contributed several siege engines, for which he was right royally thanked. But even as the siege continued, Bruce was concluding a secret pact with one of Scotland's most fervent patriots, Bishop Lamberton of St Andrews. Bruce knew he needed the services of men such as this if his plan was to succeed.

It was probably just such a mission that

brought Bruce and John Comyn, Lord of Badenoch, together in the church of the Greyfriars in Dumfries on the 10 February 1306. The Comyns, leading allies of the Balliols, were the sworn enemies of the Bruces, but these were dark days for Scotland and long-harboured grudges needed to be buried, for the moment at least. But the two men were not to be reconciled. Tempers were raised, harsh words said, and soon the 'Red' Comyn was bleeding profusely from a stab-wound. Whether the deed was premeditated is doubtful, but Bruce now had no choice but to act, and act fast; there was no going back. Within hours he had captured Dumfries Castle, within days he had been absolved of his sins by Bishop Wishart of Glasgow, and within weeks he was enthroned as Robert I (1306-29) on the Moot Hill at Scone. The date was 25 March, almost ten years to the day since Edward of England had first invaded.

And then in haste to Scone rode he,
And there was crowned without delay
All in the manner of that day,
And on the royal throne was set.

(The inauguration of Robert I in 1306, from John Barbour's *The Bruce*.)

Gaining the crown was one thing, winning the country was another matter entirely, as Bruce soon found to his cost. Tempted into attacking the English garrison at Perth, he was caught off-guard at Methven and his force routed. The outraged Edward exacted terrible revenge on those who now fell into his grasp. Heads were despatched from bodies the length and breadth of the land. Even the ladies of the royal court were despicably treated. Countess Isabella of Buchan, who had had the temerity to place the circlet of gold on Bruce's head at his enthronement, was locked 'in a cage made in the likeness of a crown and suspended in the open air' from the battlements of Berwick Castle so that passers-by might stare at her. And there she remained for the next four years. How she survived her ordeal is a miracle.

Bruce meanwhile fled into the mountains with a handful of loyal followers. He was last seen leaving Kintyre in September, bound for his legendary encounter with the spider in a cave we know not where. When he re-emerged in 1307 in his native Carrick, it was with renewed vigour for the cause – an independent Scotland led by a sovereign answerable to no one but the pope. He had clearly learnt from his brief encounter at Methven. From now on there would be no pitched battle with England's mightiest; Bruce would achieve his goal through guerrilla warfare. Only when he felt the time was right would he confront the enemy head-on. It had been nine years since Falkirk; it would be another seven until Bannockburn.

Bruce's luck was in almost immediately. On 6 July 1307 mighty King Edward I of England finally breathed his last. He was 66 and wracked by ill-health, but there he was, preparing to invade yet again. He got as far as Burgh-by-Sands, west of Carlisle, with the object of his obsession in view across the shimmering sands of the Solway. Even in the hour of his dying Edward had not given up hope that he would conquer one day, instructing that his body be boiled and his bones carried into battle against the Scots! Robert Bruce, when later on he had experienced the sheer ineptitude of Edward I's son and successor, Edward II, concluded with relief: 'I am more afraid of the bones of the father dead, than of the living son. By all the saints, it was more difficult to get a half a foot of the land from the old king than a whole kingdom from his son!'

So died one of the greatest military commanders of the Middle Ages, and the greatest threat to Scotland's independence. During his life he was known affectionately by his subjects as Edward 'Longshanks', because of his commanding height. But in the sixteenth century someone scratched the words 'Hammer of the Scots' on his simple tomb in Westminster Abbey, and that

▲ *Mighty Stirling Castle sits atop its rocky perch, commanding the countryside for many miles around. So pivotal was the royal fortress's physical position in the realm that it brought the English here, time and again, during the bloody Wars of Independence. It was King Robert the Bruce's threat to the English, that if they hadn't relieved their beleaguered garrison holed up therein by Midsummer's Day 1314 he would take it by storm, that brought Edward II in person to Scotland – and to defeat at Bannockburn.*

'The Fight for Freedom'

~ BANNOCKBURN, 1314 ~

'Scots wha hae wi' Wallace bled,
Scots, wham Bruce has aften led,
Welcome to your gory bed, or to victorie''
(From Robert Burns's Scots Wha Hae, *1793)*

Over two days in June, 1314, on boggy carseland to the south of mighty Stirling Castle, the greatest battle in Scottish history was fought. Precisely where the encounter between Robert the Bruce and Edward II of England took place is still a matter of debate, like many great battles of history. But the sequence of events, and of course the outcome, are not.

The 'battle of Bannok' was a veritable 'David and Goliath' affair, an estimated 8000 Scots up against 17,000 English. The English supply-train stretched back down the road almost as far as Edinburgh 40 miles away. As if that wasn't enough, a large armada of ships sailed up the Firth of Forth from ports all along England's east coast. But the cracks in English discipline and morale were already beginning to show as they approached the Bannock Burn on the morning of Sunday the 23rd. Edward II was profoundly disliked by his subjects, and the long, tiring march north, made in haste so as to meet Bruce's deadline of the 24th, Midsummer's Day, for them to relieve their beleaguered garrison holed up in Stirling Castle, had only served to exacerbate the situation.

By then, Bruce and his four brigades, under the command of himself, his brother Edward, the Earl of Moray and 'the Good Sir James' of Douglas, were drawn up in the royal hunting forest south of the castle through which the king's highway from Edinburgh threaded. If the English were to take Stirling, they would have to come by there. The location, with higher ground behind, boggy ground below and good tree cover, allowed Bruce to keep his options open – he could engage or withdraw.

The English vanguard appeared on the afternoon of the 23rd. They had little knowledge of the strength or disposition of their enemy; nor did they much care, such was their supreme confidence. And when they saw a few Scots dotted about among the trees on the rising ground beyond the Bannock Burn, they charged forward. Battle was about to be joined.

But before they could engage, a remarkable episode unfolded that would have a profound effect on the whole course of events. Sir Henry de Bohun, a young English knight, spied a Scottish knight mounted on a small 'grey' a little apart from the rest. The gold circlet above his helmet told him that here was none other than the King of Scots himself. The opportunity for fame and fortune was there for the taking, and so, pricking his spurs deep into his horse's side, de Bohun galloped towards him. Bruce, armed only with an axe, dodged de Bohun's levelled lance at the very last moment and, as the two drew level, swung round and brought his axe crashing down on the Englishman's helm, splitting it and the young knight's head in two.

Bruce's lieutenants would advise him later, with some justification, that his recklessness could have seriously jeopardised the whole campaign, but the effect that their sovereign's single combat had on morale was immediate and crucial. Bruce's schiltrom, a thickly packed square of spear-wielding foot-soldiers bound together with rope for greater stability and looking for all the world like an enormous hedgehog, surged forward and met the English cavalry head on. The 'flower' of English chivalry found itself fleeing before the Scottish spears. Scarcely a Scot was scratched.

If Bruce still harboured any thoughts of withdrawing, they were dispelled as the armies bivouacked for the night, for into the Scots' camp crept Sir Alexander Seton, an East Lothian knight who until then had been on England's side. He told of the enemy's low morale and profound unease. Bruce listened attentively and decided he would stand and fight. The die was cast.

Just before daybreak on the following morning, Bruce heard mass and then went forth from his tent to rouse his men for the coming fight:

My lords, my people, those barons you can see before you, clad in mail, are bent on destroying me and obliterating my kingdom, nay our whole nation. They do not believe that we can survive. They glory in their war-horses and equipment. For us, the name of the Lord must be our hope of victory in battle. This day is a day for rejoicing: the birthday of John the Baptist. With Our Lord Jesus Christ as commander, Saint Andrew and the martyr Saint Thomas shall fight today with the saints of Scotland for the honour of their country and their nation.

With these words ringing in their ears, the Scots prepared for the coming fight. The battle itself was fought on slightly different ground. By the time the English cavalry had returned to the main force the previous evening their horses

▲ *The Battle of Bannockburn, Monday 24 June 1314: Jim Proudfoot's captivating depiction of The Bruce's great victory over the 'auld enemy', painted in 1977.*

were so exhausted that they were compelled to move down onto the marshy ground to water them. The added fear that the Scots might attack during the night meant that they could not relax their guard for one moment. By daybreak the English were ineptly positioned and weary from the vigil.

Then out of the gloom emerged the Scottish host, Edward Bruce leading, Moray and Douglas on either flank. The king held his brigade of Highlanders in reserve and out of sight. No sooner had the Scots come into full view than each man knelt down and prayed. 'What!' exclaimed the excitable English king, 'Those men kneel to ask for mercy.'

'You are right', ventured one of his lieutenants, adding: 'they ask for mercy, but not from you. They ask it from God.'

The Scots, rising as one from their orisons, advanced down the hill. The Earl of Gloucester led a headlong cavalry charge into Edward Bruce's schiltrom. Within moments he was unhorsed and crushed beneath the advancing spearmen, one of many casualties proud Edward's

army would suffer that day. Moray and Douglas joined the fray. For some reason, the English infantry were held back beyond the Bannock Burn. Even more inexplicably the main force of English archers was also too far to the rear, and by the time they were deployed it was too late for the knights at the front line. As the English arrows rained down from the skies, as many shot into the backs of their own men as into the enemy.

It was now that Bruce showed his general's worth. He ordered his small cavalry force to run down the archers and scatter them to the four winds. They did their job perfectly. Bruce scented victory. Seizing the moment, he slipped the leash off his own brigade. Their screaming rampage down the slope presaged the famous Highland Charge that would one day be feared throughout the world. They crashed into the mêlée, pushing the English ever nearer to the boggy ground beyond. In their excitement, even the peasants guarding the Scottish supplies joined in, armed with anything that came to hand.

Thinking them to be yet more reinforcements, the English finally turned tail and fled, as best they could, across the intractable ground between the Bannock Burn and the Forth. Many were drowned, others were cut down either by their pursuers or by their own comrades desperate to get away. So full of dead and dying bodies was the Bannock Burn that it was said a man could cross without getting his feet wet. By the end of the day, one earl, 70 knights and thousands more unnamed Englishmen lay dead on the battlefield.

For Bruce, Bannockburn was the defining moment in his reign. It may not have seen off the English aggressor for good, but the victory secured for Bruce the loyalty of a grateful people and ensured his unshakeable grasp on the throne of Scotland.

Lay the proud usurpers low!
Tyrants fall in every foe!
Liberty's in every blow!
Let us do or die!
(The last verse of *Scots Wha Hae*, by Robert Burns, 1793.)

▲ *The powerful Comyn family, who as earls of Buchan, Badenoch and Lochaber held sway over much of northern Scotland in the later thirteenth century, had many great strongholds. They included Balvenie Castle (pictured here), in Glen Fiddich, Banffshire, chief seat of the 'Black' (as distinct from the 'Red') Comyn earls of Buchan. Arch-rivals of the Bruces, they were finally overthrown in 1308 at the Battle of Inverurie. Robert the Bruce's great 'herschip', or harrying, of Buchan that followed lived long in the memory of north-east folk.*

somehow seems the more appropriate epithet. But hammer as hard as he might, the man who captured Nazareth for the Crusaders, and conquered Wales, could not crack the Scots. On the contrary, King Edward's hammering, far from forcing a foreign people to submit to his will, succeeded only in forging them into a proud and truly independent nation.

> He invaded the Scots, broke up the realm by
> fraud, laid waste our churches, shut up our
> prelates in prison; He slew Christ's folk and
> seized the gold of the tithe. His sins are well
> known in all the world. England will weep
> when at last it lies in ruin. Scotland, clap your
> hands at the death of a greedy king. Give thanks
> to God now Robert has been crowned and
> guided in virtue's strength by the staff of
> salvation.

(From a poem written shortly after Edward I of England's death.)

Bruce took full advantage of his luck. Starting in the north of the country, he began evicting the English garrisons and neutralising their Scottish supporters. He was relentless and unforgiving, particularly with his old adversaries, the Comyns. At Inverurie he defeated and killed John Comyn,

Earl of Buchan, whose wife Isabella, was still dangling in her cage from the walls of Berwick Castle. Bruce followed it with a murderous rampage through the Earl's former lands. Men, women and children were killed, homes burned and crops destroyed. The 'herschip', or harrying, of Buchan would live long in the memory of north-east folk.

Meanwhile Bruce's bandwagon rolled on. In March 1309 he was able to hold his first parliament, at St Andrews. By 1312 he was taking the fight to the enemy, striking terror into the hearts of the people of northern England. So frightened were the citizens of Hartlepool at one point that they took to their boats in search of safety. An old Northumbrian rhyme sums up the feelings of the beleaguered population perfectly:

> From Goswick we've geese,
> from Cheswick we've cheese,
> From Buckton we've venison in store;
> From Swinhoe we've bacon,
> but the Scots have it taken,
> And the Prior is longing for more.

The looted plunder helped replenish Bruce's depleted war-chest. English garrisons continued to surrender until by the summer of 1313 only Lothian remained outwith Bruce's control. The latest news from France that John Balliol, 'King Nobody', had passed away only added to Bruce's feeling that the tide had turned in his favour.

On a dark and murky night in February 1314, the English garrison at Roxburgh capitulated to Bruce's great friend, 'the Good Sir James', Lord of Douglas. Mighty Edinburgh fell a month later to the Earl of Moray. As each fortress fell, Bruce ordered that it be 'razed to the ground' to prevent it from being of any further use to the enemy. Now the castles remaining in English hands could be counted on the fingers of one hand. They included Stirling. But the garrison there, cut off from their fellow countrymen, was gradually falling to hunger and disease. Bruce issued a defiant deadline to the English king – relieve the garrison by Midsummer's Day – or else. The gauntlet had been thrown down; it only remained to see if Edward II would pick it up.

He did. Precisely a week before the deadline Edward left Berwick at the head of yet another huge invasion force, estimated at over 2000 mounted knights and 15,000 foot-soldiers. Crossing the Lammermuirs by way of Soutra they reached Falkirk by the 22nd. A few veterans doubtless cherished memories of their great victory over Wallace there back in '98, mingled perhaps with dark thoughts about the débâcle at Stirling Bridge, now just 15 miles away. The following morning they set out to avenge that defeat.

Meanwhile Bruce had summoned 'the host' to muster in Torwood forest north of Falkirk. We can only guess at the numbers that had arrived from all the airts by the 22nd – perhaps some 7000 infantry, supported by just 500 cavalry. On the following morning, he pulled them back to a defensive position in the New Park, the royal hunting reserve south of Stirling Castle, overlooking the sluggish Bannock Burn.

And there he waited, for Midsummer's Day and the English to come. Two days later, on the field of Bannockburn, Bruce pulled off one of the greatest military victories in history.

Bannockburn did not finally win the war, but it succeeded in making Bruce's position as king well-

nigh unassailable. Yes, he still had enemies, within and beyond his kingdom, but who now could impugn the right of the victor of Bannockburn to be lord of his people?

But Bannockburn did not achieve for Bruce the prize he desired most – England's acknowledgement of Scotland as a fully independent nation. Despite his crushing defeat, Edward of England stubbornly refused to negotiate, and even contrived to thwart the Scots' overtures to the pope. Even after the Scots invaded Ireland in 1315 and had Bruce's brother, Edward, crowned king – even after the humiliating loss of Berwick in 1318 and the devastating raids into Yorkshire that followed – the English king still maintained his liege rights to 'my lands of Scotland'.

In desperation, 'the community of the realm of Scotland' despatched a letter in April 1320 to the holy father, Pope John XXII, setting out the case for the Scottish people. The famous Declaration of Arbroath, drafted very probably by Abbot Bernard of Arbroath, Chancellor of Scotland, and affixed

▲ *'For so long as there shall but one hundred of us remain alive, we will never consent to subject ourselves to the dominion of the English. For it is not glory, it is not riches, neither is it honour, but it is liberty alone that we fight and contend for, which no honest man will lose but with his life.'*

The closing words from the Declaration of Arbroath, 'addressed to the lord supreme pontiff by the community of Scotland' in 1320. It is likely that the 45 magnates representing the people of Scotland, who agreed to its drafting, met at Newbattle Abbey in Midlothian. Their seals were sent to the chancery of Abbot Bernard of Arbroath, Chancellor of Scotland and responsible for the letter. The seal impressions are seen here affixed to the actual parchment.

'Deadly Scourge or Divine Retribution'

~ THE BLACK DEATH ~

'From winter, plague and pestilence, good Lord, deliver us!'

(From Thomas Nashe's Summer's last Will and Testament, *1600)*

In 1296, on the outbreak of the Wars of Independence with England, the population of Scotland stood at around a million souls. A century later, that total had been reduced to 700,000, possibly less. But although many a Scot had been killed in battle, or died later from his wounds, the dramatic fall was mostly brought about by the 'Black Death'.

The 'pestilence', as it was known in medieval time (the name 'Black Death' became common only from the eighteenth century), first visited its deadly scourge on Scotland in 1349. The 'second pestilence' occurred in 1361, the third in 1379 and so on – 1392, 1401-3 and 1417. After that they gave up counting.

The way in which this painful death happened by the divine will was strange and unusual; once the swollen inflammation of the flesh had taken hold, life in this world lasted for a further two days. Everyone trembled at it with such fearful dread that children would not dare to visit their parents suffering in the last extremity; instead they fearfully shunned the contagion as they would flee from before a serpent' (From Walter Bower's *Scotichronicon*.)

The 'Black Death' swept through England before Scotland. Such was the state of war between the two nations that the Scots blamed the pestilence on the enemy, calling it 'the foul death of the English'. In truth, the 'Black Death' had broken out first in the much warmer climes of Asia in the 1330s, reaching Western Europe in 1347 and England the following year. As devastating as the 'Black Death' was in Scotland, the epidemic never reached the scale of tragedy seen elsewhere. For once, Scotland's cold weather came to its aid.

▲ *Victims of the 'Black Death' are consumed by Hell's gaping jaws; from a fourteenth-century manuscript. One of our nursery rhymes chillingly recalls the horrors of that truly awful plague: 'Ring a ring o' roses, A pocket full o' posies; Atishoo, atishoo, We all fall down.'*

The plague was spread by fleas on rats, and these vermin were everywhere, in the densely populated towns, on board merchant ships, thriving on the filthy living conditions that were the hallmark of the Middle Ages. Bubonic plague (from the Latin *bubo*, 'groin') made the glands in the armpit and groin swell up alarmingly. It was a long, debilitating illness, often resulting in death. But when that same bubonic plague struck those with damaged lungs (Greek *pneuma*, 'breath'), death was inevitable and swift.

It was the pneumonic form that visited its curse on Scotland. But although it struck with immediate, devastating effect it didn't linger as the bubonic plague was wont to do in warmer climes; consequently it didn't sweep like 'wildfire' through the land. The Highlands, with far fewer rat-infested towns and cooler temperatures, seems to have escaped its worst excesses, so much so that during the second outbreak in 1361, David II and his court travelled to Aberdeenshire to avoid becoming infected, as well as to escape the agonising cries and sights that prevailed in Edinburgh. This may explain why Scottish chroniclers rarely mention the plague; they devote more space to an outbreak of fowl pest!

There is no doubting the dreadful suffering of Scots during these pestilences. But if there was a silver lining to the cloud it was this. There are indications that by the fourteenth century the land was becoming overpopulated, thanks to the healthy economy bequeathed by the Alexanders' 'golden age'. Famine had already begun to affect the lower orders in society by the time the 'Black Death' arrived. As the fourteenth century drew to its close, the plague had contrived to make land more available, and food more plentiful for those fortunate enough to have survived the greatest demographic disaster ever to befall Europe.

To us the cause of the 'Black Death' is clear and incontrovertible – rats. But to the medieval world it was not vermin, but the wickedness of mankind at the root of it all. It was God's punishment for the sins of the world, and he visited his wrath on all, saints and sinners alike. Some today believe that Aids is likewise divine retribution. Will we ever learn from history?

with the seals of some 40 nobles, barons and freemen, remains one of the most inspirational missives ever written. It articulated the ancient right of the Scots to self-determination – a ringing endorsement of their fight for freedom and right to independence:

For as long as a hundred of us remain alive, we will never on any conditions be subjected to the lordship of the English. For we fight not for glory, nor riches, nor honours, but for freedom alone which no good man gives up except with his life.

But for all its passionate rhetoric, the Declaration brought forth no immediate positive response from the pope, just some weasel words informing them that he had written to Edward urging him to make an enduring peace with 'the aforesaid Robert, who says that he is King of Scotland'.

But Edward of England's star was declining fast, and he who had never shown anything approaching his father's mettle was deposed as king in 1327. Bruce seized the moment. On the very day (1 February) Edward III was crowned King of England in Westminster Abbey, the Scots crossed the Tweed and stormed Norham Castle. By the summer they had penetrated deep into northern England. It was too much for the English people, who had paid dearly, both in death and taxes. Negotiations began, and on 17 March 1328 Robert I set his seal on the Treaty of Edinburgh at Holyrood Abbey; the English parliament ratified it at Northampton on 4 May. Bruce had finally secured his prize. How he must have savoured that moment above all others in his momentous life, and how he must have read, and re-read, those words in the treaty concerning his beloved land of Scotland:

Separate in all things from the kingdom of England, assured forever of its territorial integrity, to remain forever free and quit of any subjection, servitude, claim or demand.

Robert the Bruce did not live long thereafter. He was already in his sickbed when he sealed the treaty, ravaged by leprosy it would seem. Knowing his end was near, Bruce betook himself west to that part of his kingdom most dear to him. He passed peacefully away on 7 June 1329, not in some mighty castle but at his manor of Cardross, close to where the Leven meets the Clyde. He was 55, a remarkable age given all that he had endured.

BRUCE VERSUS BALLIOL

Bruce's death and the accession of his five-year-old son David II (1329-71) prompted the English to interfere in Scotland's affairs yet again. Edward III was nothing like his father and everything like his grandfather. His achievements in battle – Crécy (1346), Poitiers (1356) – are the stuff of legend, and a king such as he was not going to allow the humiliation heaped on his father by the Scots to go unpunished.

The problem for David was the 'disinherited', those magnates who had been stripped of their lands and titles by his father and who were bent on recovering them. To bolster their claim they even persuaded Edward Balliol, the son of King John, to leave Picardy and join them; after all,

▲ King Robert the Bruce, just before he died in 1329, wrote to his successors urging them to make payments to the Cistercian monks at Melrose Abbey, in Roxburghshire (pictured here) 'to which through special devotion we have granted our heart for burial'; his heartless body was to be buried before the high altar at another monastery, Dunfermline, in Fife. And so it came to pass, but only after the embalmed heart had been taken on a most remarkable crusading journey by Bruce's close friend, 'the Good Sir James' of Douglas. Alas, the Black Douglas was killed at Teba in southern Spain fighting the Moors, and Bruce's heart was brought home and laid to rest in Melrose.

With gret worschyp
  he [the Earl of Moray]
  has gert bery
The kingis hart at
  the abbey
Off Melros . . .
(From John Barbour's epic poem, The Bruce.)

▶ The spectacular castle of Urquhart, beside Loch Ness, in Inverness-shire, first felt the wrath of the English in 1296, right at the very onset of the Wars of Independence. Sir Andrew Moray, who with William Wallace defeated the English at the Battle of Stirling Bridge a year later, had earlier attacked the English garrison but succeeded only in killing the English constable's son. But the ending of the prolonged English wars in the middle of the fourteenth century brought little peace to the beleaguered inhabitants of Glen Urquhart. During the long Stewart 'dynasty', the castle remained a continuing focus of attention as the royal Stewarts fought out their deadly duel with their arch-rivals, the MacDonald Lords of the Isles.

wasn't Edward the rightful King of Scots, not the upstart David Bruce? They sailed from the Humber in July 1332, a motley force numbering no more than 2000 men, and landed at Kinghorn, on the Fife coast, a week later.

'Oh how small a number of warriors was this to invade a kingdom then all too confident of its strength!', ran an entry in the *Lanercost Chronicle*.

The Scots were too confident for their own good. The battle of Dupplin Moor, south of Perth, on 11 August was a farce, the Scots, ill-led and confused, stumbling into each other rather than engaging with the enemy. The English archers got plenty of target-practice that day. With his path cleared, Edward Balliol made for Scone and was crowned Edward I of Scotland on 24 September. The late-lamented King Robert would surely have turned in his grave.

But Balliol hadn't sufficient forces to make any real gains and by Christmas he was back in England pleading with Edward III to aid him in his struggle. He very nearly didn't make it, for he was almost caught with his pants down, literally, while he lay abed in Annan; the scantily clad Balliol was lucky to reach Carlisle. Edward agreed to help, and soon the whole of Scotland was back under the English yoke. By the end of 1333, only five castles were holding out. They included Dumbarton, where the young David II and his English queen had taken shelter. It was now that the 'Auld Alliance' came to their aid. In May 1334 the couple arrived at mighty Chateau-Gaillard, overlooking the Seine north-west of Paris, as guests of Philip VI. And there they remained for the next seven years.

Edward III soon discovered that trying to conquer Scotland was as difficult and as costly as his father and grandfather had found. It was a bit like squeezing the air out of a 'lilo' – just when you had flattened one part, another part rose up. There were as many heroic deeds in this second War of Independence as in the first, not least 'Black' Agnes's robust defence of her imprisoned husband's castle at Dunbar in early 1338. The formidable wife of the Earl of March stoutly stood on the battlements withstanding all that the English could throw at her, hurling back abuse and taunting them. It was said that after each

incoming missile smashed against the castle walls, she would 'arrange for a very pretty girl to be sent, adorned like a bride for her husband, who with a white handkerchief held in her hand would gently rub the place of impact.'

By the time proud Edward withdrew to save himself further embarrassment, he had decided there was no glory to be had in Scotland. From now on he would focus his energies on becoming king of France. Balliol was a spent force, and by 1341 King David was back in his native land.

But it wasn't long before Philip of France was calling in the debt as the spirit of the 'auld alliance' allowed: 'The league between us (is) written not in parchment of sheepskin, but rather in the flesh and skin of men, traced not in ink but in blood shed in many places.'

In August 1346 the French were crushed at Crécy, and the Scots invaded northern England to create a diversionary tactic. It was rumoured that David was set on reaching London – and he did, but not in the way he would have liked. On 17 October, at Neville's Cross near Durham, his army was routed and he himself captured. He arrived in the Tower of London a prisoner, and there he languished for the next eleven years.

On 19 September 1356 Edward of England defeated the French at Poitiers, and the unfortunate French king soon joined the king of Scots in captivity. Edward had the prize he most desired at his mercy; Scotland was of little interest to him now except as a bargaining counter in the ensuing peace negotiations. Eventually David was ransomed and returned. He would never leave Scotland again. During the remaining years of his reign he displayed much of his father's mettle, putting down petty factions among his quarrelsome magnates, doing much to restore the machinery of government – and, despite the colossal ransom demanded by the English, putting the country's finances back onto some kind of stable footing. He died in Edinburgh Castle on 22 February 1371. He was just 47, but despite his two marriages and several mistresses he left no male heir. Within 14 years of the demise of the Balliol dynasty, the Bruce dynasty too was no more. It was the end of one of the most turbulent chapters in Scotland's history.

IACOBVS I D·GRATIA
REX·SCOTORVM

DYNASTY

(1371 - 1548)

'It cam wi' a lass, it'll gang wi' a lass'

In 1371, Robert the Stewart succeeded to the throne. So began the 300-year long dynasty of the Royal House of Stewart. This chapter charts the reigns of the first seven Stewart sovereigns, culminating in the arrival on the throne of Mary, Queen of Scots.

THE COMING OF THE STEWARTS

Shortly before he died at Falkland Palace, a broken reed of a man, on 14 December 1542, James V, seventh in the line of Stewart kings, was brought the news of the birth of his daughter, Princess Mary. He turned his face to the wall, muttered the immortal words, 'It cam wi' a lass, it will gang wi' a lass', then breathed his last. The king's prophecy would prove only partly true. The Stewart dynasty would certainly end 'wi' a lass', but the lass in question would not be his daughter, Mary, Queen of Scots, but his great-great-great granddaughter, Queen Anne.

The Stewart dynasty was the longest to reign over Scotland, for 343 years. The dynastic name was taken from the first of the line, Robert II (1371-90), who before his accession had been Robert the Stewart, the seventh to hold the prestigious office of steward in the royal household. But who was the mysterious 'lass' who brought the dynasty to power?

Robert the Bruce married twice. His first wife, Isabella, bore him just one child, a daughter Marjory. Marjory was barely in her 'teens' when she was captured by Edward I and imprisoned in a Yorkshire nunnery. But following her father's great victory at Bannockburn, she returned home and wed Walter the Stewart. Their child, Robert, succeeded to the thone 55 years later.

It must be questioned whether it was worth the wait. Robert II was undoubtedly a good man, 'humble and gentle, friendly in appearance, a cheerful man, an honourable king, witty in his responses, admirable in the way he carried himself, surpassing others in stature and the height of his body.' And yet, despite his commanding presence, he proved no leader of men, never happier unless he was back home at Dundonald Castle in his native Ayrshire, where he died in 1390. By then he was a spent force, his sons quarrelling among themselves and his kingdom wracked by unrest.

It should all have been so different. Robert's accession had coincided with an upturn in the

◀ King James I (1406-37) was the third monarch of the Stewart dynasty. Born in Dunfermline Palace, Fife, in 1394, he heard the news that he had succeeded his feeble father, King Robert III, in 1406 only after having been captured by English pirates off the Firth of Forth.

Eighteen years in captivity clearly concentrated his mind and put steel in his body, for he returned home in 1424, with a new queen, Joan Beaufort, daughter of the Earl of Somerset, and a new determination to reassert the authority of the Royal Stewarts. This portrait, by an unknown artist, depicts King James as a sovereign confident and assured.

▲ *On 17 June 1390,*
Alexander Stewart, the
third son of King Robert II,
but better known to
history as the 'Wolf of
Badenoch', emerged from
his mountain fastness in
the Cairngorms with his
band of 'wyld wykkyd
Helandmen', descended
on the town of Elgin and
burned down its cathedral.
The loss of this
architectural treasure,
'the lantern of the North',
moved Bishop Alexander
Bur to complain to the
Wolf's elder brother,
King Robert III:

'My church was the
ornament of the realm,
the glory of the kingdom,
the delight of foreigners
and stranger guests:
an object of praise
in foreign lands.'

economy, due ironically to the 'Black Death' The reduction of the population by over a third had greatly eased the pressure on land so that food was now reasonably plentiful, rents lower than they had been for a long while, and labour much in demand. The wool trade, Scotland's chief foreign currency earner, had never been in better shape, over 9000 sacks going for export in 1372 alone.

But it didn't take long for 'boom' to turn to 'bust' under the stewardship of the Stewarts. With 21 children, most of them illegitimate, 'King Bob' was reduced to buying them off with lands, titles and other assorted privileges. The three sons from his first 'marriage', to Elizabeth Mure of Rowallan – John, Earl of Carrick (the future Robert III – the name 'John' had become 'non PC', thanks to King John Balliol), Robert, Earl of Fife and Menteith (the future Duke of Albany), and Alexander, Earl of Buchan (the notorious 'Wolf of Badenoch') – in effect ran their father's realm. Soon these 'arrogant

and ill-disposed' offspring were at daggers drawn, Carrick frustrated by his father's stubborn refusal to die, Fife recognising his elder brother's ineptness, while 'the Wolf' (his heraldic crest was a wolf) became a law unto himself in his power-base in the north.

Things began to go awry in 1384 when King Robert slipped into semi-retirement and Carrick took the helm. Up to then, an uneasy truce had existed with England. But whereas Robert II preferred to keep the peace, Carrick was all for taking the fight to the 'auld enemy', egged on by his close allies, the Douglases. When Archibald 'the Grim', third Earl of Douglas, threw the English garrison out of Lochmaben Castle in February of that year, it was like waving a red rag at a bull. Back into Scotland stormed the English, no incursion more savage or brutal than that in 1385, led by Richard II in person. They burned and pillaged their way through the eastern Border country as far as Edinburgh. And so it went on, 'tit-for-tat': 1388 – Otterburn (Scottish victory), 1402 – Homildon Hill (English victory). But if 'normal service' had been resumed on the English Border, profound change was taking place in the Highlands.

A NATION DIVIDED

On 17 June 1390 'The Wolf of Badenoch' descended on Elgin with a band of 'wyld wykkyd Helandmen' and burned down its cathedral. Poor Bishop Bur was left to bemoan the destruction visited by this scion of the royal house of Stewart and his war-band on his beloved church: 'the ornament of the realm, the glory of the kingdom, the delight of foreigners and stranger guests, an object of praise in foreign lands.'

If that raid had taken place a century earlier, it seems most unlikely that the bishop of Moray would have written of 'wyld wykkyd Helandmen' for there was then no such distinction between 'Highlands' and 'Lowlands' as we understand it today. If there was any demarcation at all in 1300, it was between those who lived north and south of the Firth of Forth, the 'Scottish Sea', and not west or east of the Great Glen. And the distinction was solely linguistic; if you lived south of the Forth you spoke Scots, if north then Gaelic. By the 1350s that had all changed. The Scots tongue had now spread north across the fertile eastern Lowlands to Buchan in the north-east; Gaelic retreated to its ancient heartlands in the west.

Then the 'Black Death' struck, and as the population rapidly declined so did the pressure on land. The people in the Lowlands lucky enough to survive the deadly plague now had little reason to look elsewhere. And so by the time Robert Stewart came to the throne, Scotland had begun to take on a very different look, a kingdom divided into two not just by language but by geography also. It wasn't long before the Scots-speaking Lowlanders began to see in the Gaelic-speaking Highlanders a third distinction, a different way of life:

The manners and customs of the Scots vary with the diversity of their speech. For two languages are spoken amongst them, the

◀ *The right of burial on the holy island of Iona had been the preserve of the kings of Scots until the formal transfer to Norway in 1098 caused them to move the royal mausoleum to Dunfermline Abbey. By the thirteenth century, clan chiefs were emulating their royal ancestors by likewise being buried on Iona.*

Gilbride MacKinnon, whose fine monument is pictured here, was chief of his clan around 1275, and his lair in St Oran's Chapel was subsequently used by no fewer than five succeeding generations of MacKinnon chiefs.

The MacKinnons claimed ancestry back to Fingon mac Alpin, brother of Kenneth I, and held sway over their kin and tenants from Caisteal Maol, on Skye. They were firmly allied to the MacDonalds, Lords of the Isles, against the house of Stewart.

Gilbride's shield is carved with the ever-present Highland galley and, beneath it, an otter pursuing a fish, a sight one can still enjoy in the clear blue waters around Caisteal Maol.

'Seats of Learning'

~ SCOTLAND'S UNIVERSITIES ~

'Alma Mater'

(Latin for 'benign mother' and applied by students and former students to their university)

Shortly after Whitsuntide in the year 1410, Master Laurence of Lindores, theologian, gave a talk in St Andrews on the *Sentences* of Peter Lombard. But this was no ordinary talk; it was the first lecture to students of the new university of St Andrews, Scotland's first. When, four years later, Henry Ogilvie arrived in the cathedral city bearing Pope Benedict XIII's bull giving his consent to the undertaking, church bells rang, services were held, prayers and praises of thanksgiving were offered up, and everyone in the city was caught up in the revelry:

> They spent the rest of this day in boundless merry-making and kept large bonfires burning in the streets and open spaces of the city while drinking wine in celebration.

(From Walter Bower's *Scotichronicon*, 1440)

Up to that time, Scots wishing to go to university had had to head south into England, to either Oxford (Balliol College was founded by King John's father in 1266) or Cambridge, or abroad to places such as Paris, Orleans and Bologna. The latter became more popular once the outbreak of the Wars of Independence in 1296 made it harder for Scots to study at 'Oxbridge'.

Universities were at the top of the educational ladder. Below them were 'grammar schools' and 'song schools', in descending order, and these Scotland did have prior to 1410, and in abundance. All were run by, and largely for, the Church. Grammar schools (the equivalent of our secondary schools) were located in the cathedral precincts and in the towns (even Tranent had one) and catered for students wishing to develop their skills in Latin (hence the term 'grammar' – they even shouted at each other on the football field in Latin!), which was the official language of Church and State. Song schools (the equivalent of our primary schools) were more widespread, and instilled in their pupils the rudiments of reading and singing in Latin. Almost all were exclusively boys' schools, but there were a few girls' schools, including one at Aberdour, in Fife.

The creation of St Andrews University allowed young Scots (men only, of course) to extend their education without having to go abroad. They would 'go up' about the age of 15 and enter one of the faculties – theology, canon (that is, Church) law, civil law, medicine and the liberal arts, which ranged across a broad spectrum from philosophy, rhetoric and logic to music, arithmetic, geometry and astronomy. Within 18 months, if they were lucky, they would gain their bachelor's degree; two further years of study would get them their master's licence. The numbers graduating were nowhere near as large as today; about 10 a year in the first half of the fifteenth century, rising to 30 by 1500. Most then went into the Church, where they put their skills to good use both spiritually and temporally, serving as secretaries in the households of the nobility.

But in addition to all the worthy reasons for establishing his university, Bishop Henry Wardlaw of St Andrews, its first chancellor, had another – the need to stamp out heresy in the Church. By 1410 western Christendom had endured years of schism, with two rival popes holding court in different places. Heresy was rife and it was reaching Scotland. A university based in Scotland could only assist the country's leading cleric in his drive to stamp it out before it spread like wildfire throughout the realm. When the Great Schism finally ended in 1417, and Scotland recognised Martin V as the one true pope (the last nation to do so) it had been the arts faculty in St Andrews University that was instrumental in persuading Governor Albany to do so.

Bishop Wardlaw's creation blazed a trail. In 1451, Bishop Turnbull of Glasgow did likewise in his cathedral city. Glasgow was intended to complement rather than duplicate St Andrews by specialising in legal studies. And when Bishop Elphinstone of Aberdeen created King's College in February 1495, two more landmarks were reached. Firstly, laymen as well as clerics were admitted as students. Secondly, Scotland now had one more university than England.

Since then, a further eleven universities have joined the ranks – Edinburgh (1583), Strathclyde (1964) Heriot-Watt (1966), Stirling (1967), Dundee (1967), Paisley (1992), Napier (1992), Robert Gordon's, Aberdeen (1992), Glasgow Caledonian (1993) as well as the Open University (1969) and the innovative University of the Highlands and Islands linking on-line colleges as far apart as Stornoway, Lerwick and Perth. These institutions of advanced learning have changed out of all recognition since those heady early days – they even started letting women in after the passing of the Universities (Scotland) Act in 1889! But all owe a debt to the vision of Bishop Wardlaw and the oratorical skills of those inaugural lecturers who addressed Scotland's first students six centuries ago.

Scottish [*Gaelic*] and the Teutonic [*Scots*]; the latter of which is the language of those who occupy the seaboard and plains, while the race of Scottish speech inhabits the highlands and outlying islands. The people of the coast are of domestic and civilised habits, trusty, patient and urbane, decent in their attire, affable and peaceful, devout in Divine worship, yet always ready to resist a wrong at the hands of their enemies. The highlanders and people of the islands, on the other hand, are a savage and untamed nation, rude and independent, given to rapine, easy-living, clever and quick to learn, comely in person, but unsightly in dress, hostile to the English people and language, and, owing to diversity of speech, even to their own nation, and exceedingly cruel. They are, however, faithful and obedient to their king and country, and easily made to submit to law, if properly governed.

And this was written in about 1380 by an Aberdonian!

There was a kernel of truth in what John of Fordun wrote. Despite the introduction and spread of feudalism, with all its bureaucratic rules and regulations, the Highlanders had managed to retain their kin-based system based on deeds not words. 'The broadsword's charter is the birthright of that bold people; often without seal's impression do they impose tax or tribute', waxed one Highlander. Whereas Lowlanders hid behind the skirts of the law to appropriate new land, Highlanders took good old-fashioned direct action, leading war-bands, or caterans (from the Gaelic *ceatharn*, 'lightly armed warrior'), on raids into neighbouring territories and forcing the inhabitants to part with their wealth – in effect, 'protection rackets'.

That was how 'the Wolf of Badenoch' did his business, driving fear and trepidation deep into the hearts of the locals and forcing them to 'pay up'. And when the bishop of Moray refused to continue paying his instalments, 'the Wolf' and his caterans rode down from the mountains to the fertile plains of the Laich o' Moray and made him and his tenants pay dearly.

'The Wolf' was able to run amok in Moray largely because of the lack of effective local

magnates who might have contained his worst excesses. The north and north-east had formerly been the power-base of the Comyns, but they had been wiped out by Bruce and the noble families brought in to replace them had either run out of male heirs (like the Randolphs) or were more preoccupied with their estates in the south (the Douglases). But 'the Wolf' had been unable to extend his reign of terror into the western Highlands because two aristocratic houses had stepped into the power vacuum left behind by the demise of Balliol – the Campbells and the MacDonalds.

The origin of the Campbells (from the Gaelic

▲ *The buildings might be Victorian but the origins of the University of Glasgow reach back to the fifteenth century. On 7 January 1451 Bishop Turnbull of Glasgow gained approval to establish a new university, Glasgow's first and Scotland's second, probably in celebration of Glasgow's elevation to a burgh of regality the previous year. Today Glasgow has three universities.*

Na Caimbeulach, 'men of the twisted mouths') is obscure, but they had links with the Britons of Strathclyde, and even claimed they could trace their roots back to the legendary King Arthur. When Robert Bruce became king in 1306, Sir Colin Campbell had a modest landholding beside Loch Awe; by the time of Bruce's death in 1329 the family, rewarded for their loyal support, had acquired much of Lorn, Benderloch and Kintyre, most of it from the disgraced MacDougalls. They became sheriffs of Argyll, then in 1382 its royal lieutenants. The earldom of Argyll followed in 1457, the marquisate in 1641, and the dukedom in 1701. During most of that time they were fierce rivals of the MacDonalds, a bitter hatred that lives on in the national memory through the bloody Massacre of Glencoe.

The MacDonalds of Islay, unlike the Campbells, were Argyllshire born and bred, their eponymous founder the grandson of Somerled, Lord of the Isles. Not every MacDonald threw in his lot with Bruce, but Angus Og MacDonald did, fighting valiantly alongside his sovereign at Bannockburn.

One effort more, and Scotland's free!
Lord of the Isles, my trust in thee

Is firm as Ailsa's Rock;
Rush on with Highland sword and targe,
I, with my Carrick spearmen charge;
Now forward to the shock.

(The words of Robert Bruce, from Sir Walter Scott's epic poem *The Lord of the Isles*, 1814.)

Angus and his son John duly received their reward – the Lordship of Islay and extensive lands stretching from Kintyre to Lochaber. And when in 1346 John took as his first wife Amy MacRuarie, the sister and sole heir of Ranald, the last clan chief, and with her all the remaining Hebridean islands save Skye, it was as if Somerled's former dominion had been resurrected. John's second marriage, to Margaret Stewart, Robert II's sister, in 1350 simply underpinned MacDonald influence in the west. John MacDonald now styled himself *Dominus Insularum*, 'Lord of the Isles'. If he had been alive today he would surely have been known as 'Big Mac'!

But the mighty MacDonalds weren't content to stop there. By around 1400 they had opened a branch of MacDonalds in the Glens of Antrim, where they had strong historic links. John's son, Donald, also began to cast his covetous eyes over the fertile lands around the Beauly and Cromarty Firths to the east also. He was confident he could do it; who wouldn't be, with a 10,000-strong army at their command. In 1411 Donald MacDonald and his caterans struck, seizing Inverness before sweeping east across the Spey. As they advanced on Aberdeen, the only obstacle in their path was a rapidly formed force raised by Alexander Stewart, Earl of Mar and Donald's own cousin. The two came crunching together on 24 July, at Harlaw near Inverurie. Both sides claimed victory, although a later cynic would tell of each side thinking it had been beaten by the other. But indecisive as it was, the Battle of Harlaw was a landmark in Scottish history; it was the first fought between Highlander and Lowlander. The last would take place over three centuries later, at Culloden.

> Oh, came ye frae the Hielans, man?
> And came ye a' the wye?
> Saw ye MacDonal and his men
> Come marching frae the Skye?

(From a ballad popular in Aberdeenshire.)

MONARCHY RESTORED

By the time of Harlaw, the first two Stewart kings had come and gone. They were not much missed. Robert II had been likeable but lacking in leadership. His son, Robert III (1390-1406), was without any redeeming qualities whatsoever. The chronicler, Abbot Bower, who conceivably met him, was withering in his criticism. He records an imaginary conversation between Robert and his queen, 'the noble Annabel', in which she asks him what arrangements he was making for a monument to himself and what words he would have written thereon. He replies:

> I should prefer to be buried at the bottom of a midden. And write for my epitaph: 'Here lies the worst of kings and the most wretched of men in the whole kingdom.'

Poor Robert, nothing went right for him. In 1388, barely four years after becoming Regent to his inept father he was kicked by a horse and

permanently crippled. Thereafter his efforts to regain a grip on power were thwarted not just by his own inadequacies but by the rapidly worsening economic situation. Recent substantial devaluations in the weight of Scotland's silver coinage led to the English breaking the centuries-old parity in the exchange rate. In 1390 the rate stood at 1:2, and the phrase 'usual money of Scotland' replaced 'sterling'. The result was inflation. So much for it being the curse of the modern world!

The last straw in King Robert's sad reign came shortly before his death; in fact it may have hastened it. By now the king and his younger brother, the Duke of Albany, deeply mistrusted each other. Robert, for all his inadequacies, could see that Albany had designs on his throne, despite the existence of an heir-apparent, the 12-year-old Prince James. He therefore arranged for his son to be smuggled to France. Even that plan went horribly wrong. In February the young prince was rowed out from North Berwick to the Bass Rock to await ship. After a month enduring the company of the thousands of gannets nesting there, James was finally taken aboard a merchantman bound from Leith for the Continent. Almost immediately it was boarded by English privateers, James captured and taken to the Tower of London. On hearing the news, his father took to his bed in Rothesay Castle and breathed his last.

There was a suspicion that Albany had been

The MacDonalds, Lords of the Isles, ruled over their extensive lordship from a number of impressive castles, most notably Mingary and Ardtornish, on the Argyllshire mainland. But perhaps the most evocative of all their strongholds, Finlaggan, on the island of Islay, is not really a stronghold at all, more a work of nature – two islands, one large, Eilean Mor ('the big isle'), the other, Eilean na Comhairle ('Council Isle'), small. The two islands lay at the heart of the MacDonald hegemony until their forfeiture as the fifteenth century drew to its close.

'Into this Ile of Finlagan the Lords of the Iles, quhen thai callit thame selfis Kingis of the Iles, had wont to remain oft in this Ile forsaid to thair counsell: for thai had the Ile well biggit in palace-wark according to thair auld fassoun [fashion], quhairin thai had ane fair chapell.'

(From a document written 50 years after the downfall of the mighty MacDonalds.)

▲ *The gaunt, forbidding tower on the island of Threave, in Galloway, perfectly reflects the personality who built it in the mid fourteenth century, for Archibald 'the Grim', third Earl of Douglas, earned his nickname 'becaus of his terrible countenance in weirfair [warfare]', mostly spent dislodging the English from their 'bolt-holes' in the south of the country. But Threave was also the stage where the final overthrow of the once-mighty Black Douglases was played out, in the summer of 1455 in the presence of King James II himself.*

behind his nephew's capture. Whatever the truth of the matter, Albany certainly made the most of his good fortune. He was declared Governor of Scotland, the first there had been, and until his death in 1420, at the ripe old age of over 80, he brought strong governance back to the top, something sadly lacking under the two Roberts.

By most accounts he was a compassionate man, particularly in his dealings with the 'common folk'. He introduced no new taxes, and went out of his way to be seen by 'his people'; when for example the Sandgate in Ayr was narrowed to prevent the sand encroaching further, Albany attended in person and drove home the first stake.

But Albany also had a reputation for lining his own pockets. Abbot Bower described him as 'a man of great expenses and munificent to strangers'. He certainly lavished a small fortune on his magnificent residence of Doune Castle; it was a home fit for a king. Albany clearly had designs on the throne itself.

A clause inserted into a bond agreed with the Earl of Douglas made that abundantly clear, for it stipulated that the agreement would be null and void 'gif it happynis the Duc Albany grow in tyme to cum to the estate of king'. He didn't quite realise his ambition, hence his soubriquet, Scotland's 'uncrowned king'.

Four years after Albany's death in 1420, James I (1406-37) was back in his kingdom, determined to

make up for lost time. His first act was to dispose of Albany's heirs. Within the year he had the son, Duke Murdoch, and others in his family and retinue arrested and brought to Stirling. Most, including Murdoch, were beheaded. Among the released was Murdoch's gentleman servant, Sir Robert Graham of Kincardine; had the king known what lay in store for him at this man's hand, he would surely have despatched him also.

James next moved against the MacDonalds. After a cat-and-mouse action, he finally caught up with Alexander MacDonald in 1429 beside 'a bog in Lochaber'. James had him locked away in the rocky fastness of Tantallon, on the East Lothian coast and as far removed from the MacDonalds' family seat of Ardtornish, beside the Sound of Mull, as one could possibly get.

Such ruthlessness in a king had not been witnessed since David II's time. It won James sneaking admiration from most of his subjects, intense loathing from those few adversely affected. But James was treading a fine line. Strong rule might be welcome after years of royal ineptitude, but add in the ingredients of heavy taxation, petty restrictions on playing 'at the fut ball' and drinking in taverns after nine o' clock of an evening – all this while the king himself was lavishing money on magnificent palaces like Linlithgow and newfangled gunpowdered artillery – and there would inevitably be growing resentment.

The touch-paper of civil war was lit in 1436 as the king's gunners primed their weapons during the great siege of Roxburgh Castle, still in English hands.

There were in number more than two hundred thousand men-at-arms. But they waited there a fortnight doing nothing worth recording because of a detestable split and most unworthy difference arising from jealousy; so, after losing all their fine large guns, both cannon and mortars, and gunpowder and carriages and wagons and many other things utterly indispensable for a siege, they returned home most ingloriously without effecting their object.

(A somewhat exaggerated account from the near-contemporary *Book of Pluscarden*).

The episode was extremely expensive and deeply embarrassing for the Scots, and the knives, literally, were soon out for James. The end came on the evening of 21 February 1437. The king and queen were lodging in the Dominican friary at Perth when conspirators entered the grounds, among them Sir Robert Graham of Kincardine, the man set free by King James in 1425. James wrenched a plank from the floor and hid in the sewer below. All was in vain. The intruders burst in, and finding the room empty would have left had not one of their number suddenly remembered the sewer. The defenceless king put up a valiant struggle before sinking beneath the assassins' blows.

James II (1437-60) was just six years old when his father died, and didn't take the personal reins of government until he was 18. But from then until his untimely demise 11 years later at yet another siege of Roxburgh – the last in fact – he did more than show his mettle; he bared it for all to see.

The second James proved to be one of the most warlike monarchs Scotland ever had; his reign coinciding with the advent of gunpowdered artillery as a force to be reckoned with helped. He entered the arms race with gusto; he could afford to. The huge guns, called 'bombards', might be inordinately expensive, both to buy and to maintain and use, but he was married to Mary of Gueldres, niece of the Duke of Burgundy, arguably the richest man in western Europe. His uncle even presented him with two mighty siege guns in 1457, including Mons Meg herself, still on proud display in Edinburgh Castle. Alas, three years later James lay dying in a field near English-held Roxburgh Castle, felled by one of his own cherished bombards (not Mons Meg). He wasn't even 30. His grieving widow, fired up by her husband's untimely death, urged the besiegers to greater efforts and within days Roxburgh Castle fell to the Scots. Now Berwick alone remained in English hands.

SCOTLAND REDEFINED

It seemed to be the fate of the Stewarts that they would come to the throne barely out of their cots; James III (1460-88) was no exception. He was just eight when he received the crown in Kelso Abbey within a week of his father's demise. His 28-year reign achieved much that was long-lasting, but the king himself came to a sticky end, falling prey to the character-weakness that would ultimately prove the downfall of the Stewart dynasty – an unshakeable belief that they had a divine right to rule.

The personal turmoils of James III's reign (he was abducted at 14, imprisoned at 30, and murdered by his nobles at 36) should not detract from the real gains (and losses) made. One lasting legacy was the effective establishment of Edinburgh as the nation's capital. Hitherto the 'chief burgh of the kingdom' had been wherever the sovereign and his court happened to be, and where Parliament met; one month it might be Inverness, the next Ayr or wherever. But James III eschewed the peripatetic life and scarcely left Edinburgh during his reign, with the result that in all that time only one Parliament ever met beyond it. By now Edinburgh was the wealthiest of all the burghs, and by a good margin. More than half of the 'great customs' paid

▲ West Mainland, Shetland, looking towards Papa Stour. When Shetlanders and Orcadians awoke on the morning of 10 July 1469, they would have considered themselves Scandinavian; when they went to bed that night they were effectively Scottish, for on that day King James III of Scotland had married Queen Margaret, daughter of the King of Denmark, Norway and Sweden. This change did not impact at once, of course. The Northern Isles were only handed temporarily to the Scots as a pledge for the 60,000 florins King Christian I had agreed to pay as his daughter's dowry. But when the money never materialised, James III decided to keep the islands. Thus Scotland became the shape it is now, with the small exception of Berwick-upon-Tweed, lost to England in 1482, and the even smaller exception of Rockall, far out in the Atlantic, annexed to Scotland as recently as 1972!

But it was at the farthest reaches of James's realm, not in the 'heart of Midlothian', that the greatest changes would be made to the physical appearance of Scotland. The most significant change came in 1469 when James took as his queen Margaret, daughter of Christian I of Denmark, Norway and Sweden.

Up to that time the Scandinavian kings, the descendants of those Vikings who had once held sway over much of northern and western Scotland, still ruled in the Northern Isles, nominally at any rate. Since 1236 the earldom of Orkney had been held by a Scot and by 1450 the combined power of the earl and the Scottish Church had imbued the islanders with a growing sense of 'Scottishness', particularly in Orkney, less so in Shetland. The marriage treaty paved the way for the inevitable, the transfer of the Northern Isles fully into the hands of the Scottish Crown. It didn't happen overnight. The 'kingslands', or royal estates, in the Isles were handed over initially as a pledge for Queen Margaret's dowry. But King Christian never paid up, and James III took effective control a year later. And although Denmark was still raising the possibility of the Northern Isles reverting to them as late as 1749, in effect from 1469 Orkney and Shetland became part of Scotland.

But just as Scotland was expanding northward, it shrank in the south; not by very much but it was a sad loss for all that. Berwick-upon-Tweed had once been the wealthiest of Scotland's burghs. But the years since 1296 had been far from kind and its position right on the frontier, at the centre of a war-zone, had seen the inhabitants pass back and forth between the two competing countries so often they must have begun to wonder what nationality they were. More worryingly, they must have pondered whether their beloved town would survive at all. They only needed to look up-river to the smoking rubble that had once been the town of Roxburgh, second only in importance to Berwick in the 'good old days' of the twelfth century, to imagine where it might all end.

▲ *The Crown of Scotland was first worn by King James V on 22 February 1540 at the coronation of Queen Mary of Guise. Unlike the other 'Honours' – the Sword of State and the Sceptre – which are principally of Italian manufacture, the Crown is substantially Scottish, crafted by John Mosman, of the Edinburgh Incorporation of Goldsmiths, and created from Scottish gold mined at Leadhills.*

'Nothing earthly can be more...happy to Us...than... to see Our most dear son,.... Prince of this Our Realm placed in the Kingdom thereof, and the Crown Royal set upon his head.'

(From Mary Queen of Scots' Letters of Abdication signed at Lochleven Castle, in May 1568.)

to the Crown in 1479 came from the burgesses of 'Auld Reekie', thanks in no small measure to the stranglehold they had over the busy port of Leith; Aberdeen was next (at one-sixth), then Dundee, Berwick, Haddington, Perth and so on.

Edinburgh positively basked in the limelight. In and around the town there was feverish building activity, particularly churches; Trinity College (demolished in 1848 to make way for Waverley Station), St Mary's in Leith (now South Leith Parish Church) and a most unusual chapel dedicated to St Triduana in Restalrig. (Legend holds that Triduana responded to the unwelcome advances of a certain Pictish warlord by gouging out her eyes and sending them to him on thorns, and by this means became associated with the healing of eye complaints; perhaps James himself suffered 'with his eyes'.) Most importantly, the pre-eminence of the burgh kirk of St Giles in Edinburgh's High Street was formally recognised when it was raised to collegiate status in 1467.

'The Honours of Scotland'
~ SCOTLAND'S CROWN JEWELS ~
'The Croune, Sceptre and Sword of State'

On 4 February 1818, a distinguished group of men gathered on the stairs outside the Crown Room in Edinburgh Castle. Among them was Walter Scott, whose urgent pleas to the Prince Regent (the future King George IV) had resulted in the Royal Warrant granting the noted author and antiquary permission to search for the long-lost Crown, Sceptre and Sword of State – the ancient Honours of Scotland.

The group watched in silence as the king's blacksmith removed the masonry blocking the doorway. In the darkness beyond they spied a great iron-bound chest, which they approached with apprehension, for there was a suspicion that the chest was empty. The Honours had been ceremoniously locked away in 1707 following the Treaty of Union with England, but many believed that that ceremony had been a hoax. Let Walter Scott himself describe what happened next:

> The chest seemed to return a hollow and empty sound to the strokes of the hammer. The joy was therefore extreme when, the ponderous lid of the chest being forced open, the Regalia were discovered lying at the bottom covered with linen cloths, exactly as they had been left in 1707. The discovery was instantly communicated to the public by the display of the Royal Standard, and was greeted by shouts of the soldiers in the garrison, and a vast multitude gathered on the Castle Hill; indeed the rejoicing was so general and sincere as plainly to show that, however altered in other respects, the people of Scotland had lost nothing of that national enthusiasm which formerly had displayed itself in grief for the loss of these emblematic

Honours, and now was expressed in joy for their recovery.

The Honours of Scotland are the oldest royal regalia in the United Kingdom and among the oldest surviving in Christendom. They were shaped in Italy and Scotland during the reigns of James IV and James V and were first used together as coronation regalia at the enthronement of the infant Mary Queen of Scots in Stirling Castle on 9 September 1543. They had a relatively uneventful history, until they were taken from Edinburgh Castle in 1650 to be used at the crowning of King Charles II at Scone on New Year's Day 1651, in what proved to be the last Scottish coronation. By then Oliver Cromwell and his 'New Model Army' were already in the country, unexpectedly defeating the 'host' at Dunbar and capturing Edinburgh. Cromwell was determined to lay his hands on the Scottish Crown Jewels, to do what he had earlier done with the English ones – destroy them.

The Honours, unable to be returned to Edinburgh Castle following the coronation, were entrusted into the safekeeping of the Earl Marischal who was instructed to: 'cause transport the saidis Honouris to the hous of Dunnottar the Earl Marischal's well-nigh impregnable castle perched on an isolated headland in Kincardineshire thair to be keepit by him till farther ordouris.' By the end of September Cromwell's men were at Dunnottar in strength. Inside were just 40 men, two sergeants and their commanding officer, George Ogilvie of Barras, a local laird. They had the proud, if unenviable, distinction of being the only garrison now holding out against the English, for all Scotland's other castles had fallen.

The story of how the defenders of Dunnottar withstood the might of Cromwell's army for eight bitter winter months; of how the Honours were smuggled out from the castle under the very noses of the English and hidden beneath the floor of nearby Kinneff Kirk; and of how they lay buried there for eight long years until King Charles returned to his throne, is one of the most well-kent stories of Scottish history. The more entertaining, but highly implausible tale has Christian Granger, wife of the minister of Kinneff, and her serving-woman as the heroines of the piece. Having obtained permission to visit Lady Ogilvie in the castle, they smuggled the Honours out, the Crown concealed under Mrs Granger's skirts and the Sceptre and Sword in bundles of flax carried by her servant. Legend has it that the breaks visible in the sword blade and scabbard resulted from attempting to make the concealment of these lengthy items more effective. They could as easily have been snapped in two by the woman who is said to have been at the bottom of the cliff with her creel when the Honours were lowered by rope from the castle in the dead of night – the more prosaic but infinitely more believable story. The garrison surrendered shortly afterwards.

Poor Lady Ogilvie suffered with her life as a result of her role in protecting the Honours – she died while in prison. George Ogilvie somehow survived and returned to his castle of Barras. Unbeknown to anyone he kept a memento of his adventure, the elaborate Sword Belt. In 1790 it was accidentally discovered built into a garden wall at his residence, and was eventually returned to its rightful place in the Crown Room in Edinburgh Castle in 1892.

▲ *Powerful clan chiefs resided in powerfully impressive castles, and no castle comes more powerfully and impressively situated than Kilchurn, at the head of Loch Awe, in Argyllshire, seat of the Campbell Lords of Glenorchy. The Campbells had acquired so much territory by the fifteenth century that, in order for them to maintain control, the family had to split into various branches, known as sliochdan, each under its own chief but ultimately answerable to the clan chief. Kilchurn was built by Sir Colin Campbell around 1450, on his being entrusted with the Lordship of Glenorchy by his nephew, the first Earl of Argyll. Not everyone dwelling on Lord Glenorchy's estate would have been a Campbell through genuine kinship, but all owed their allegiance to the Campbell clan.*

After the fall of Roxburgh Castle to the Scots in 1460, things had begun to look more promising for the people of Berwick than for some considerable time. Over the Border, England was in turmoil as the Wars of the Roses waged between the rival houses of Lancaster and York. The civil wars came to the first of several climaxes in 1459-61 and resulted in the Scots not only seizing Roxburgh but also recovering Berwick in 1461, handed over by the beleaguered Lancastrians in return for sanctuary and the promise of military support. The usual repairs to the town's battered defences were put in hand by the rejoicing Scots, and then just as quickly abandoned on grounds of cost. James III himself spoke of 'the grete charge and coist that his majestes has now taking apone him to hald and ly on heis aune expense the garaysoun of 500 men of war in the said toune for the keping of the defens thereof to the grete honour and profit of the Realme.'

But the balance-sheet no longer made sense. The 'grete charge and coist' of holding Berwick far exceeded the paltry sum now rendered up in customs by the beleaguered burgesses. With the resolve to hold Berwick at any price gone, the town

became little more than a pawn in a chess-game, to be sacrificed for the greater good, whatever that might be. The crunch came during the political crisis of the summer of 1482, which came about because of the nobles' resentment of the autocracy of the king and the growing influence of a few 'lowborn' familiars promoted to important posts, people such as Archbishop Scheves of St Andrews, who had begun life at the royal court sewing his majesty's shirts! It resulted in the king's capture at Lauder in July. By now, the Wars of the Roses in England were temporarily on the 'back-burner' and Edward IV comfortably enough in control of his realm to meddle once more in Scotland's affairs. The citizens of Berwick saw the writing on the wall and packed their 'bagg and baggages'. On 24 August, while James still languished in his Edinburgh prison, his royal burgh of Berwick was formally handed over to the English; it has never changed hands since. And so it came about that in 1482, with the acquisition of the Northern Isles and the loss of Berwick upon Tweed, Scotland became the shape it is today – almost, that is – for Rockall, the tiny granite rock lying far out into the Atlantic, 200 miles west of St Kilda, was 'added' to the UK only in 1972.

THE THISTLE AND THE ROSE

On 8 August 1503, James IV (1488-1513) wed Margaret Tudor, daughter of Henry VII of England, in Holyrood Abbey, a union celebrated as 'the marriage of the thistle and the rose'. The English red and white rose was itself the symbol of a peaceful union after years of strife, adopted by Henry, of the House of Lancaster, on his own marriage to Elizabeth of York in 1486 at the close of the Wars of the Roses. Quite how the thistle came to be adopted by the Stewarts, though, is a mystery. James III was the first to use it, on his 1470 coinage, along with a new motto: *Nemo me impune lacessit*, meaning 'No one provokes me with impunity'; or, put more bluntly, 'Waur daur meddle wi' me'! Such motifs were the equivalent of today's 'logos', conscious attempts at rebranding by the powerful dynasties of western Europe. But unlike so many of our 'here today, gone tomorrow' logos, these Renaissance emblems have stood the test of time. At every bruising Calcutta Cup rugby match, the Scottish thistle intertwines with the English rose in a way unimagined by their creators all those centuries ago.

'Renaissance' means 'rebirth', and James IV's reign witnessed momentous change in many aspects of human life. The Spanish ambassador, Don Pedro de Ayala, wrote: 'There is as great a difference between the Scotland of old time and the Scotland of today as there is between good and bad.'

Whether many of the changes immediately and directly impacted on the common people must be doubted. Few of them would have been privileged to stand in the cathedralesque grandeur of the great hall' in Stirling Castle, or have heard the wonderful polyphonic strains of Robert Carver's music, or have gazed on the graceful beauty of the artistic works imported from the Continent, such as tapestries and altarpieces. Even fewer would have been able to afford the new books coming off

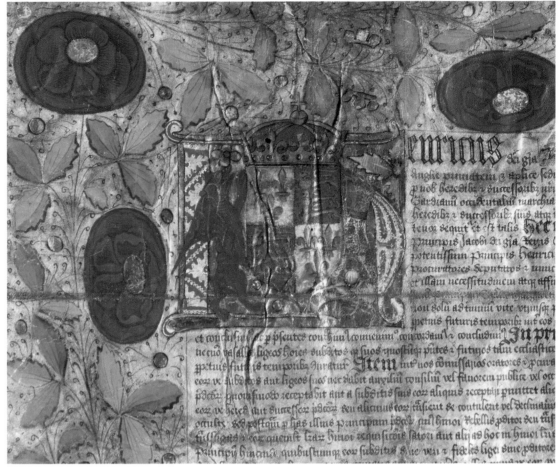

Scotland's first printing press, set up by Walter Chapman and Andrew Millar in 1508 in Edinburgh's Cowgate. More of James's subjects would have seen Mons Meg and the royal guns being trundled out from the new armaments factory in Edinburgh Castle, and stood in awe as his flagship, the *Great Michael*, was launched at nearby Newhaven in 1511; Louis XII of France declared it 'the greatest in Christendom' and eventually bought it.

Ayala painted a fascinating word-picture of the Scots at this pivotal time in Scotland's history. On the men, for example, he says: '[they] are not industrious, and the people are poor. They spend all their time in wars, and when there is no war they fight with one another.' Not so the women, apparently: '[they] are courteous in the extreme...really honest, though very bold. They are absolute mistresses of their houses, and even of their husbands, in all things concerning the administration of the property, income as well as expenditure. They are very graceful and handsome. They dress much better than here [i.e., in England].' And on the Scots generally: '[they] are

▲ Negotiations for a marriage between King James IV of Scotland and Margaret Tudor, elder daughter of King Henry VII of England, began in Melrose Abbey in the autumn of 1498. The happy couple were finally wed in Holyrood Abbey on 6 August 1503 – the groom was aged 30, his bride just a tender 13. They called it the marriage of 'The Thristill (thistle) and the Rose', after the respective coats-of-arms of the royal dynasties. The marriage treaty was joined by another pact between the two countries – the 'Treaty of Perpetual Peace' (pictured here). But perpetual peace was impossible between the 'auld enemies', and within ten years of the marriage King James lay dead on the battlefield of Flodden, in Northumberland.

'The Flower of Scotland'
~ FLODDEN, 1513 ~
'The flowers of the forest are a' wede awae'

On 17 March 1513, King James IV celebrated his fortieth birthday. Barely six months later he lay dead on the battlefield of Flodden, his throat cut half asunder and his body scarred by arrows and spears. Around him lay 5000 fellow countrymen, the 'Flower of Scotland'. Flodden 1513 was one of the worst defeats inflicted on Scotland by England.

The expedition into Northumberland had started out so confidently. On 22 August more than 20,000 men forded the Tweed near Ladykirk and with the aid of the 17 heavy guns hauled from Edinburgh Castle had soon brought the English Border castles of Norham, Etal and Ford into submission. By the evening of 8 September, they had advanced south along the west bank of the River Till and taken up a strong position on Flodden Edge, overlooking the village of Milfield. Such was the chivalric convention of the time that James had already negotiated with the Earl of Surrey, the English general, to do battle at noon on the following day.

It was a miserable morning the two armies awoke to, an infuriating mix of driving rain interspersed with spells of autumnal sun. The English, despite numbering about as many as the Scots, were at a distinct disadvantage, what with the Scots on the higher ground and the flat ground beneath their own feet spongy and soon churned to mud from all the rain. The noon deadline came and went, and still stalemate. Who would make the first move?

The Scots did. Their guns opened up first, in the mid afternoon. They made a frightful noise but most of the huge gun stones sailed harmlessly over the heads of the enemy. The lighter, more manoeuvrable English pieces, on the other hand, sliced paths through the Scottish ranks, massed into five battalions. It was more than the Earl of Huntly and Lord Home, spearheading the left flank, could bear and they rushed headlong down the hill, apparently without orders to do so. They soon had the English right flank in disarray. King James, leading the Scottish centre with the Earls of Crawford, Errol and Montrose, seized the moment and began advancing likewise. But then, suddenly, with the tide going Scotland's way, Huntly and Home withdrew and played no further part in the action; just why has never satisfactorily been explained. It proved the defining moment in the battle. James, his left flank now woefully exposed and his right flank of Highlanders led by Argyll and Lennox soon scattered by a strong English counterattack, found himself inextricably engaged with the armed might of the English centre.

It was a long, bruising encounter, going on well into the evening. No quarter was shown by either side, the Scots with their long pikes against the English with their shorter bills, a kind of spear-and-axe combined. Slowly but surely the bills won the day, slicing the heads off the enemy pikes and forcing the Scots to resort to their swords. Gradually the Scots withdrew from the field, until only the cries of the wounded and dying and the sound of the English looting their victims rose into the night sky.

Over 5000 Scots lost their lives on that fateful day in Northumberland against 1500 English dead. Hardly a single family in the land was left unaffected by the slaughter, from the highborn to the common foot-soldier. They were called the 'Flower of Scotland', and the biggest flower of them all was King James himself. He got within a spear's length of his opponent, the Earl of Surrey, that day before finally succumbing to the hail of blows on his person; such was the fine line between ignominious defeat and glorious victory.

I've heard them lilting,
at the ewe-milking,
Lasses a' lilting, before dawn of day;
But now they are moaning
on ilka green loaning;
The flowers of the forest
are a' wede awae.

(From Sir Walter Scott's *The Flowers of the Forest: A Lament for Flodden*.)

But what happened to the body? King James's bloodied corpse was discovered by an Englishman, Lord Dacre, the morning after the battle, lying at the bottom of the hill down which he had so courageously led his men. Dacre had it disembowelled, embalmed and taken to Berwick; from there it made the long journey south to the monastery of Sheen in Surrey. But then came the Dissolution of the English monasteries, and with it the dismemberment of King James's body. 'But since the dissolution of the house, I have been shewed the same body so lapped in lead, thrown into an old waste room, amongst old timber, stones, lead, and other rubbish. Since the which time, workmen have for their foolish pleasure hewed off the head.' (From the *Annals of John Stow*, 1598.)

The head alone, still with its shock of red hair and red beard and giving off 'a sweet savour', was taken to a house in London, where it became something of a 'conversation piece' at dinner parties! But once that had tired, the head was buried in nearby St Michael's Church.

Today the monastery at Sheen is under a golf course, and St Michael's under an office block. It seems unlikely that the remains of one of Scotland's greatest kings will ever be returned to the land he once ruled.

handsome. They like foreigners so much that they dispute with one another as to who shall have and treat a foreigner in his house. They are vain and ostentatious by nature. They spend all they have to keep up appearances. They are courageous, strong, quick and agile.'

But while it was a case of 'in with the new', it wasn't necessarily 'out with the old'. Some things in life never change, and that included the ancient rivalry between Scotland and England. As the future Pope Pius II ruefully observed on a visit to Scotland in 1435: 'nothing pleases the Scots more than abuse of the English'. The marriage of 'the thistle and the rose' might have been intended to secure a lasting end to hostilities, but it proved in the event to have no effect whatsoever; after just eleven years of 'perpetual peace', the two nations were at each other's collective throats once more.

Henry VIII's invasion of France in the summer of 1513 was the catalyst, giving James little option but to abandon the idea of perpetual peace with England and instead support France in her hour of need. The Battle of Flodden was one of the heaviest defeats inflicted on Scotland; 5000 Scots – among them the king himself, two bishops, two abbots, nine earls and 14 lords – made the ultimate sacrifice on that dreich autumn day.

The disaster put the nation on 'bikini alert'. Town defences were hastily repaired and new ones built, like the Flodden Wall around Edinburgh.

> For as meikle as thair is ane greit rumour now laitlie risen within the toun, touching our Soverane Lord and his army...we chairge straitlie and commandis...within this burgh, that all maneir of persounis, nybouris within the samyn, haif readie thair fensabill geir and wapponis for weir, and compeir thairwith...at jowing [ringing] of the comoun bell, for the keiping and defens of the toun against thaim that wald invaid the samyn.

(Proclamation by Edinburgh Town Council on the morning after Flodden.)

But the invasion never came. Henry was too preoccupied with strutting about on an altogether bigger stage, France, to be bothered with pressing home his advantage. Gradually things returned to normal on the Border, an uneasy truce broken only by the sounds of cattle being rustled back and forth across the frontier by the notorious 'steel bonnets', the Border reivers.

But normal service wasn't resumed entirely. Cracks were now appearing in the 'auld alliance', led in Scotland principally by the anglophile Earl of Angus, whom Queen Margaret Tudor had married after barely a year playing the grieving widow. But it wasn't so much Angus's machinations that would prove the alliance's undoing, but more the tendency of the French king, François I, to stall when asked to send aid to the Scots. The flamboyant meeting between François and Henry at the Field of the Cloth of Gold, near Calais, in 1520, in which the two attempted to broker an end to the lasting enmity between the two nations while their knights jousted in 'the lists', can hardly have inspired much confidence in the 'auld alliance' among the Scots. Yet still they persevered with it – and paid the price.

A new factor was also emerging that would prove the ultimate undoing of the 'auld alliance'.

▲ Stirling Castle was the stage on which strutted the sovereigns of the royal house of Stewart. And there is no more perfect a backdrop against which to pose than the sumptuously ornate royal palace, built around 1540 by King James V as a residence befitting his new Queen, Mary of Guise. Alas, the King never lived long enough to enjoy his 'dream home', for he died in 1542, just as the French and Scottish stonemasons and joiners, plumbers, smiths and glaziers were packing up their tools.

▶ *Mary of Guise (1515-60), daughter of the Duke of Guise-Lorraine, wed King James V in St Andrews Cathedral on 12 June 1538; for both it was their second marriage.*

When James unexpectedly died at nearby Falkland Palace four years later, the determined dowager-queen, a devout Catholic, took it upon herself to confront the emerging Protestant threat. She would have taken great comfort from hearing the news of John Knox's capture at St Andrews Castle in 1548, and rejoiced that he was now a galley-slave aboard one of her country's ships. Little did she know that she would encounter the fiery Protestant preacher again, shortly before her death in Edinburgh Castle in June 1560. Her body lay under a mortcloth for three months before the Protestant lords allowed it to be taken to France for burial.

The mother of Mary Queen of Scots lies at rest in Rheims Cathedral, not far from her birthplace, Bar-le-Duc.

In 1517, Martin Luther railed against the unregulated practice by the Church of selling indulgences, remittances of penances to a sinner. His protest fanned the flames of a movement that became known as Protestantism and quickly spread through northern Europe. Scotland was soon engulfed in its fire.

Scotland had seen heresies before, but the 'heresy' of the new Protesters was more easily spread thanks to the Renaissance, chiefly for the humanism it espoused, away from the mysterious and divine view of the world to a more practical and human one, leading people increasingly to question the infallibility of the pope and the all-pervading power of his church.

Parliament tried to stem the Protestant tide, first by passing an act against bringing Lutheran books into the country, and then in 1528 burning Patrick Hamilton, a Lutheran preacher, at the stake. To no avail. The dissenting voices grew in numbers and noise-levels, particularly in the towns. The sixteenth century saw a prodigious growth in the population, up by half as much again, the first real increase since the devastation wrought by the Black Death in the fourteenth century. And although only one Scot in ten lived in a town, the impact of the population explosion was felt far more acutely in the cramped wynds and closes than in the wide-open countryside. Towns became overcrowded, and the poor and discontent within them more conspicuous. The conditions for revolution were almost in place.

Shortly after James V's death in 1542, following another inglorious foray by the Scots into northern England, negotiations opened with the 'auld enemy' to try to secure a marriage between his heir, the babe Mary Queen of Scots (1542-67), and Prince Edward of England, then aged five. By now Henry VIII had formally broken with Rome, annexed the monasteries and declared himself head of the Church of England. In Scotland there were many who sympathised with this action, not just in the towns but also among the lairds and nobles. To them a dynastic union with Protestant England was more attractive than one with Catholic France. But before the seals could be affixed to the parchment, the Earl of Arran, the regent, with the advice of Cardinal Beaton of St Andrews, called the deal off. Henry, furious he had been denied the opportunity to get control of Scotland through the back door, decided to crash in through the front. In May 1544 he dispatched the Earl of Hertford north with a huge army to 'turne upset downe the cardinalles town of St Andrews sparing no creature alyve within the same.'

In the event Hertford didn't make it to the cathedral city, but he did besiege Edinburgh and run amok through the Borders. Back came the English the next year, not once but twice, the second time just as the crops were ripening under the late summer sun. There would be no harvest to speak of that year. Henry's aggression, known as the 'rough wooing', proved no more effective than his politicking. On the contrary, it only succeeded in persuading some anglophiles to become anglophobes instead. Such was the ferocity on the Border that pacts were made between families who had been at 'daggers drawn' for years; they included the Kerrs and the Scotts. Only in the west did there remain a strong pro-English faction, spearheaded by the Earl of Lennox and supported by clans like the MacLeods and MacLeans who had their own axes to grind.

But all this 'rough wooing' didn't stop the Scots from clamouring increasingly for reform of the Catholic Church. In 1546, the year Henry called a

temporary halt to his far-from-amorous advances, the Protestants took the law into their own hands. Incited by the appalling sight of one of their own, George Wishart the preacher, being burned at the stake in front of St Andrews Castle, they turned on the instigator of the crime, Cardinal Beaton himself. They stormed his residence, murdered him and hung his naked body from the castle walls. It was the opening scene in the drama that was the Scottish Reformation.

But the final act was still some way off. In the autumn of 1547, Hertford, now Duke of Somerset, was back in Scotland with his English 'wooers'. On 10 September, at Pinkie, on the outskirts of Musselburgh, he crushed the Scots. So great was the slaughter – 10,000 Scots – that the discarded pikes of the vanquished were said to resemble 'rushes strewn about a chamber'. As he staggered from the battlefield, the Earl of Huntly was heard to mutter 'I like not this wooing'. This time Somerset was not for going

home. He set up garrisons encircling Edinburgh, from Eyemouth to Broughty Ferry, and took over Haddington for his HQ, heavily fortifying it. And there for the next 18 months he remained, biding his time.

But in 1547 two of the leading players departed the stage – Henry VIII and François I. While Somerset, now Lord Protector of England, continued his late sovereign's warlike policy towards Scotland, François's successor, Henri II, prepared to step up the action against England. He laid siege to English-held Boulogne, and dispatched more troops to help besiege Haddington. The grateful Scots showed their appreciation by agreeing to let their Mary marry the Dauphin, François. By August 1548, the young queen was safely in France. Queen Mary left behind in her wake a kingdom beleaguered by a foreign invader, riven by internal factionalism – and still avowedly Catholic. When she returned twelve years later she found a very different country.

▲ *What pitiful sights the townspeople of St Andrews must have witnessed at their local castle in the two years 1546 and 1547. Firstly, in March 1546 poor George Wishart, the Protestant preacher, being burned at the stake; then, less than two months later, the naked corpse of his murderer, Cardinal David Beaton, being dangled from the castle battlements wrapped only in a pair of sheets; and finally, in April 1547, the bedraggled Protestants as they filed out through the castle gates to a new life as galley-slaves of the French following the ending of a six-month-long siege.*

THE ROAD TO UNION

(1548 - 1707)

'Rex Britanniae Magnae et Franciae et Hiberniae'

The Reformation of 1560 transformed not just the religious life of the nation but other vital aspects such as education and social welfare. It also heralded closer ties with Protestant England. This chapter explores the stirring times that led ultimately to the creation of the United Kingdom of Great Britain and Ireland.

REFORMATION

In July 1548, a French fleet anchored off Dumbarton Rock. Shortly afterwards a small boat put out from the castle pier and headed towards the oared vessels. Sheltering in the stern was little Mary Queen of Scots. With its precious cargo safely aboard, the fleet threaded its way out of the Firth of Clyde for France. Little did the young Queen know that in one of the escorting men o' war toiled a galley-slave whom she would much later call 'the most dangerous man in all the realm'. For pulling at an oar of the *Notre Dame* was John Knox, father of the Scottish Reformation.

John Knox was born in Haddington soon after Flodden. His life had been unexceptional until he met George Wishart, the Protestant preacher, in 1543. Suddenly his whole world was transformed. Captivated by the charismatic Angus man, Knox abandoned his law practice and joined him. He took to walking in front of his master brandishing a two-handed broadsword to protect him from his

many enemies. It was not enough to prevent Wishart from being arrested by Cardinal Beaton in 1546 and burned at the stake in front of his captor's episcopal residence in St Andrews. But when a group of Protestant lairds captured the castle shortly afterwards, Knox soon joined them, and he was still there when the garrison surrendered in July 1547. John Knox's 'career' as a galley-slave was about to start.

On his release, Knox crossed to England rather than return to his native land. By now the 'auld enemy' had become Protestant, thanks to Henry VIII rejecting the authority of the pope (next to God, Henry knew best!) and sacking the country's rich monastic houses. Knox had known for some time that if Scotland was ever to become Protestant it would have to turn its back on the 'auld alliance' with Catholic France and join with its southern neighbour to create a Protestant Britain. The first step to Union with England had been taken.

Knox might never have returned to Scotland at all had Queen Elizabeth of England not taken great

◀ St Giles' Kirk, in Edinburgh's High Street, played a major role in the turbulent years that led down 'the road to union'. The Mass was sung there for the last time in March 1560; shortly thereafter a different sound was heard – the Revd John Knox, its first Protestant minister, haranguing the congregation on the evils of 'popery'. In March 1603, shortly before he left for London, King James VI bade his Scottish subjects 'farewell' therein, promising he would return often; he came back just once. And the elevation of the burgh kirk to the status of cathedral, albeit briefly, by King Charles I in 1633 led directly to the National Covenant, and ultimately to the downfall of the Stewart dynasty.

'Scotland's Tragic Queen'

~ MARY QUEEN OF SCOTS ~

'grief and pain shall be my due'

(From a sonnet by Mary to her cousin, Elizabeth of England, in 1568, after fleeing Scotland)

She lived just 44 years. Thirteen were spent in hiding in France, and 19 as a prisoner in England. Only 12 were spent in the land of her birth, and one of those was as a prisoner too. She was queen in two countries, and would have been queen in a third also. She was three times married, and three times widowed. She never saw her father, miscarried of twins, and almost died in a fire in her Stirling residence. What a life! Truly, Mary was Scotland's tragic queen.

The tragedy began on 14 December 1542. While she lay sleeping in her cradle in Linlithgow Palace, her father, James V, died at another, Falkland, 30 miles away. The little babe found herself Queen of Scots; she was just six days old.

The tiny queen soon became a fragile pawn in a very bitter chess game played out between the kings of Protestant England and Catholic France. For this was the time of the Reformation and northern Europe was aflame. Henry VIII of England saw Mary's marriage to his son, Edward, as a way of securing a union between Scotland and England, with himself as supreme leader, naturally; Henri II of France was determined to thwart his scheming namesake. Such was the ferocity of Henry of England's marriage overtures (he kept despatching large armies over the Border) that they became known as 'the rough wooing'. His stratagem back-fired. In 1548 Mary was secretly smuggled to France. And there, 10 years later, she married her childhood sweetheart, François, Henri's son. Within a year, Mary found herself

▲ *Mary Queen of Scots, by an unknown artist.*

Queen of France as well as Scotland. She was just 'sweet 16'.

Yet more tragedy struck. In 1560, Mary lost first her mother, Mary of Guise (they had seen each other just once in all the time Mary had been in France), then her husband, François II. Mary was devastated.

Have the harsh fates ere now
Let such a grief be felt;
Has a more cruel blow
Been by Dame Fortune dealt
Than, O my heart and eyes!
I see where his bier lies?

(From an ode penned by Mary on the death of her first husband, François II.)

After mourning her dear departed, Mary had to return to the real world, and that meant returning to Scotland, for there was no future for the dowager-queen in her adopted France. There was, though, every prospect of Mary securing her third crown, that of England, should her cousin, Queen Elizabeth, 10 years her senior, die childless. But even here Mary's luck was out, for although the 'Virgin Queen' didn't disappoint in that regard, Mary didn't live long enough to benefit.

It was a much changed queen who returned to Scotland in 1561 to begin her personal reign. Initially all went well. Despite her attachment to Catholicism, her undoubted beauty and charm enabled her to win over her Protestant subjects – all, that is, except the fiery preacher, John Knox, who would have no truck with Catholics of any shape and size, least of all female ones! Would that the same had been true of her personal relationships with other men; but here she was weak and vulnerable, and herein was her downfall.

With Darnley it was love at first sight, sheer unadulterated lust. As soon as she set eyes on him early in 1565 she declared him to be 'the lustiest and best proportionit lang man' she had ever seen. A brief and passionate courtship soon led to marriage, Mary's second, Darnley's first. She was 22, he 18. So besotted was she with his manly charms that she singularly failed to see the debauched womaniser that lurked within. The couple were soon estranged. The petulant Darnley now attracted around him, like fleas about a rotting carcass, those bearing grudges against the Catholic queen. It culminated in the brutal murder of David Rizzio, Mary's Italian secretary, during a supper-party in her apartment in Holyroodhouse on the evening of 9 March 1566. The Italian clung to his queen's skirts as the knife blows rained down on him. Darnley's own dagger was later found near the bloody scene.

It is a wonder Mary didn't miscarry as a result of this appalling episode. She had conceived Darnley's child in the heady weeks following their wedding and was six months' pregnant at the time. Now, for her better protection, Mary moved to the secure surroundings of Edinburgh Castle, and there, on the morning of Wednesday 19 June, she gave birth to her only child, a boy, Charles James, the future James VI of Scotland and I of England; the name Charles was later quietly dropped because of its Catholic redolence.

Mary had by now fallen uncontrollably in love with another – James Hepburn, Earl of Bothwell. But whilst Mary's attraction to the youthful Darnley was understandable, what did Mary see in the dastardly Bothwell to make her act as rashly as she did? Bothwell was 10 years her senior, a known ruffian, and already married. Yet she was besotted by him, even after he had taken her off to his castle at Dunbar in April 1567 and raped her. It was truly a fatal attraction.

For him I've spurned my honour, and disdained
The only way true happiness is gained.
For him, I've gambled conscience, rank and right.
For him, all friends and family I've fled,
And all respectability I've shed:
In short, with you alone will I unite.
(From a sonnet written by Mary to her beloved Bothwell.)

Mary's reign hurtled towards its seemingly inevitable end. On 15 May the couple were married at Holyrood, only to be parted a month later on the field at Carberry, near Musselburgh. The lovers never saw each other again. Bothwell fled north, ultimately to die languishing in a Danish prison. Mary too was imprisoned, on the island of Lochleven. And there on 24 July she was

▲ Mary first visited Lochleven Castle near Kinross (pictured here) in 1561 as guest of its lord, William Douglas; in 1567 she returned as his prisoner! It was here, on an upper floor in the tower house, that she was forced to abdicate in favour of her infant son, James. But Mary contrived to escape her watery prison, helped by another Willie Douglas who looked after the boats. It was to no avail, and she was soon a prisoner of her cousin, Queen Elizabeth of England.

forced to abdicate in favour of her son, who had been taken from her shortly after his birth and whom she had not seen since.

Mary Queen of Scots would not so easily be unthroned. On 25 March 1568, with the help of her jailers, she escaped her island prison, rallied an army about her and at the battle of Langside, near Glasgow, on 13 May attempted to regain

her crown. But like the rest of Mary's hopes, this too was doomed to fail. Mary fled south to England and the safety, so she thought, of her cousin Elizabeth. It proved her last, and fatal, decision.

There in England Mary remained, a prisoner both of her cousin and her emotions. Grief and pain had dogged her life; now they remained her constant companions for the rest of her days. Her end was neither swift nor sweet, for she was beheaded at Fotheringay Castle on the morning of Wednesday 8 February 1587. It took the executioner two blows to sever her head from her body. She was just 44.

Mary Queen of Scots has subsequently become the most written about, the most talked about, of all Scotland's sovereigns. So how significant was her reign? 'Not very' has to be the honest answer. The most important event of her reign was the Reformation, and that took place before she returned from France to rule in person. In truth, Mary's reign was a diverting episode in the long history of Scotland. But what a diversion! Mary was undoubtedly one of Scotland's most colourful, most appealing sovereigns. Perhaps this was inevitable – Mary was after all the first female to ascend the Scottish throne, if we discount the equally tragic 'Maid of Norway', who never saw her kingdom and never was crowned queen.

Mary adopted as her motto *En ma fin est mon commencement* – 'In my end is my beginning'. Why she chose it remains a mystery, like so much of her short, tragic life, but it has proved the perfect epithet. Her significance may not have been so profound when she was alive, but since her demise she has become one of the towering figures of Scottish history. In the hour of her departing began the legend that has become 'Mary Queen of Scots'.

▲ *John Knox, minister of St Giles', Edinburgh, preaching to the Protestant Lords of the Congregation; an evocative painting by Sir David Wilkie (1785-1841), the most celebrated Scottish artist of his day.*

exception to his anti-feminist *First blast of the trumpet against the monstrous regiment of women*, a diatribe fulminating against the evil regimes of two Catholic queens, Elizabeth's elder sister, 'Bloody Mary', and Mary of Guise, mother of Mary Queen of Scots and Queen-Regent of Scotland. When he arrived back in Scotland on 2 May 1559, the Reformation process was already well under way; on New Year's Day that year the 'Beggars' Summons', advising all friars to abandon their premises in favour of the poor and infirm by 'flitting Friday' (12 May), had been nailed to each friary door. Knox returned just in time to use that date to maximum effect. On the Thursday before (the 11th), he preached his first sermon back on Scottish soil in the burgh kirk of St John's at Perth. His tirade against Catholicism and idolatry soon had the congregation in a fury. They tore down the church's elaborate furnishings, and when that was done they moved on to the monastic houses

elsewhere in the town. Knox had ignited the first powder keg of the Reformation. Soon explosions were being heard all over the land; within the fortnight, for example, Ayr Town Council had ordered a stop to the celebration of the mass. On 7 July Knox was installed as the first Protestant minister of St Giles', in Scotland's capital city.

The transition was not without its difficulties. Mary of Guise sought renewed French assistance, and the port of Leith was taken over by them and heavily fortified. They even secured parts of Fife, a hot-bed of the Reformation. Mary of Guise couldn't resist the temptation to sneer at Knox: 'Where is now John Knox's God? My God is stronger than his, yea, even in Fife.'

The Reformers responded by appealing to Queen Elizabeth, and English troops were soon training their guns on Leith. An uneasy stand-off ensued, broken only when Mary of Guise died in Edinburgh Castle on 11 June 1560. Within a month all three countries had signed the Treaty of Edinburgh, and the foreign troops were soon on their way home. Parliament moved swiftly to secure the Reformation. In August it approved a Protestant Confession of Faith. The country now stood shoulder to shoulder with half of Europe in renouncing papal authority and the celebration of the mass. This was revolution and these were stirring times.

The Reformers' vision of a neighbourly society, godly, educated and humane, took an age to implement, but the foundations were put in place with the adoption of Knox's *Book of Discipline* late in 1560. The primary aim was to return the Christian faith to the Word of God as contained in the Bible. But there were other aspirations which ultimately changed the whole structure of society – discipline, education and social welfare. The 'top down' approach to religion practised by the Catholic Church was abandoned in favour of a more democratic process in which the parish – its minister, elders, or presbyters (from the Greek *presbytos,* 'old man') and congregation – was central. Each parish was expected to provide a school 'for the virtuous education and godly upbringing of the youth of this Realm', as well as make proper provision for the poor, not 'stubborn and idle beggars' but 'the widow and fatherless, the aged, impotent or lamed, your poor brethren, the labourers and manurers of the ground, that they may feel some benefit of Christ Jesus now preached to them.'

The *Book of Discipline* provided the building blocks for a new kind of society, but implementing it would not be easy. Unlike the other Protestant countries of Europe, Scotland did not have a Protestant ruler at its head. The demise of Mary of Guise in June had been followed in December by the death of her daughter Mary's first husband, François II. Arrangements were put in hand for the 18-year-old Dowager-Queen of France to return to Scotland to begin her personal reign as Queen of Scots. Mary Stewart (it was she who introduced the French form 'Stuarte' or Stuart) arrived at Leith on 19 August 1561. On the following Sunday, she celebrated mass in her chapel at Holyrood. When calls were made for 'the idolater priest' who had officiated to be done to death, Knox replied in exasperation: 'Who can stop her?' Ruler and ruled were on a collision course.

MOTHER AND SON

Queen Mary's personal reign was short and far from sweet. Throughout she was beset by troubles, both of her own making and foist upon her. But whether it was her unshaking devotion to Catholicism, her political judgement, or her complex love-life that proved her undoing we will never know. Perhaps it was a combination of all three, and more.

Mary had her first meeting with Knox within days of her return – although 'encounter' might be a more appropriate word, for Knox, who remained implacably opposed to Mary's rule to his dying day (24 November 1572), is said to have harangued the young queen and upheld the right of her subjects to resist she who was 'indurate against God and His truth'. But although Mary remained faithful to her Catholicism in her personal life, she displayed a willingness to accept 'the state of religion her majesty found universally standing at her arrival in this her realm'. All in all Queen Mary may be deemed to have played a very thorny religious card astutely. Would that the same had been true of her personal life.

Perhaps it was inevitable that Mary's reign would be wracked by scandal. She was young, tall, athletic, and very attractive. Above all, as a young widow she was the most eligible woman in the realm, if not Europe. Little wonder that she

▲ *The subjects of this double portrait, Queen Mary and her son, James VI, could never have 'sat' for the unknown artist responsible. The painting was executed in 1583, when she was 41 and he 17; yet mother and son had not seen each other since shortly after the Prince's birth in Edinburgh Castle in 1566.*

▲ In common with all monarchs, Mary was expected to make regular 'royal progresses' around her realm, to 'show herself' to her people. That is what brought her to Jedburgh, close by the English Border, in October 1566. There she heard the news that her lover, James Hepburn, Earl of Bothwell, had been wounded in a skirmish by 'Little' John Elliot of the Park, a reiver of note, and was lying gravely ill at his castle at Hermitage (pictured here), in Liddesdale. Mary rode in haste across the bleak moors to be at his side; the tryst lasted two hours. On her return, Mary's horse stumbled into a bog, and the Queen of Scots almost lost her life as a result.

brutal murder of the queen's secretary, David Rizzio, at Holyrood in March 1566.

Mary was six-months pregnant at the time, and on 19 June gave birth to her only child, a son James, within the confines of Edinburgh Castle. It was the one brief ray of sunshine in an otherwise storm-laden sky. By now Mary was amorously involved with another, James Hepburn, Earl of Bothwell. It was Bothwell, not Darnley, who organised Prince James's baptism in Stirling Castle on 17 December; Darnley wasn't even invited.

But was it Bothwell who also arranged for Darnley's murder shortly after? Mystery still surrounds the incident that took place on the night of 10 February 1567 when an explosion rocked the house in Edinburgh where Darnley was staying. The king's body was found in the garden; he had been strangled. Did Mary have prior warning? Who were the perpetrators? It seems we will never know the answer, although that doesn't stop the speculation even today.

did not have suitors to seek. The Earl of Arran was so obsessed by her that he was driven insane. Foreign suitors queued at her door, among them kings (France, Sweden and Denmark), sons of kings (Don Carlos of Spain), sons of the Emperor Charles V (the Archdukes Charles and Ferdinand), and dukes themselves (Nemours and Ferrara). In the event Mary took as her second husband one who was her equal in age, looks and athleticism. He was also her cousin. His name – Henry Stewart, Lord Darnley, grandson of Margaret Tudor by her second marriage. Mary took an instant shine to him.

Mary may also have been attracted by the fact that Darnley also had a good claim to the English throne. It was no secret that Mary coveted Elizabeth's crown. Marriage to the dashing Darnley, with every prospect of heirs, could only improve the likelihood of her succeeding the 'Virgin Queen'. And so they were wed. The union proved a disaster.

Mary very soon discovered that Darnley was an all-round thug. She began to distance herself from him. The frustrated Darnley, who was so much a Protestant that he hadn't even bothered to attend his own nuptial mass, became the focus for those who felt their queen was leaning too far towards the Catholic camp. The rot set in with the

Mary married Bothwell on 15 May. It was the final scandal in a reign that had seen too many already. For her long-suffering lords the union was the final straw, and now that they had Prince James in whom they could place their trust, they sought to remove Mary from the stage. A month after the wedding they confronted their queen and Bothwell at Carberry, on the outskirts of Edinburgh. Bothwell scuttled away before he could be caught, leaving his bride to face the music alone. Mary was taken to Lochleven Castle, and there in her island prison on 24 July she was compelled to abdicate in favour of her son. King James VI (1567-1625) was crowned at Stirling within the week. Mother Mary, still just 24 years old, was condemned to be a prisoner for the rest of her days.

O my Lord and my God, I have trusted in Thee.

Oh my dear Jesus, now liberate me.

In shackle and chain, in torture and pain,

I long for thee.

In weakness and sighing,

in kneeling and crying,

I adore and implore Thee to liberate me.

(Poem said to have been composed by Queen Mary herself on the morning of her execution at Fotheringay Castle, Wednesday 8 February 1587.)

Not that her son's early reign was any freer of political intrigue and potential disaster. There were occasions when he too was in mortal danger – bizarre episodes like the 'Ruthven Raid' in 1582, when he was seized by disenchanted Protestant magnates and held against his will in Ruthven Castle (now Huntingtower), near Perth, and of course the notorious Gunpowder Plot of 1605, a botched attempt by English Catholics to blow up the Houses of Parliament and with them James.

But these isolated incidents cannot detract from the real progress achieved in James's long reign. In the closing decades of the sixteenth century, Scotland began to cast off its medieval armour, stained by centuries of bloodfeuds and the sweat of vassal and serf, and clothe itself with a new mantle, one in which a stronger central government formed a new relationship with those ruling at the local level. While traditional local authorities – the sheriffs, major landlords and the Church – continued to wield power, they were increasingly marginalised by the growing authority of central bodies such as Parliament, the Privy Council and the Law Courts. Add to these the introduction of a regular system of taxation from the 1580s, and the adoption in 1600 of 1 January as the date when the calendar year should start (prior to this time it had begun on 25 March; it would be another century and a half before England followed suit!), and we have Scotland on the cusp of a new dawn.

James was motivated by the need to impose his authority on a kingdom recently ravaged by internal strife. He fervently believed in the 'divine

▲ *The imposing palace of the Stewarts at Linlithgow, which King James I began to build in the 1420s. The first open-air performance of Sir David Lindsay's play Ane Satyr of the Thrie Estaitis took place here; and two royal births, James V in 1512 and Mary in 1542. The room where both were probably born was in the 'north quarter' and in 1583 King James VI's 'maister o wark' reported that that entire side of the palace was in danger of collapse. His warning went unheeded, and in 1607 it came crashing to the ground.*

'Family Feuds'

~ BORDER REIVERS AND HIGHLAND CLANS ~

'Rest not untill ye roote out these barborous feudes'

(King James VI's advice to his son, Prince Henry, in his Basilicon Doron, *1598)*

It was bitterly cold that November day in 1571 when a band of men, led by 'Edom o' Gordon', descended into Strathdon, Aberdeenshire, and surrounded the lonely tower of the Forbeses at Corgarff. The laird himself was away, but trapped inside were his wife, their family and servants. Margaret Forbes stubbornly refused the Gordons, their sworn enemies, entry. And so the Gordons decided to smoke them out. They set a fire that soon engulfed the tower. Margaret and those under her protection, 24 souls in all, were burned to death.

Then oot it spak her eldest son,
On the castle head stood he:
'Gie ower your house, mother,' he said,
'Or the fire will gar us dee.
(From the ballad, *Edom o' Gordon*.)

Family feuds bedevilled life in late medieval Scotland. But it was on the fringes of the realm that the feuding was at its most intense and brutal. There, far removed from the tentacles of central government, waging war was a way of life, the participants well practised in the black art of inflicting the most unimaginable hurt on their enemies.

Take for instance the assassination at Waternish around 1580 of all the sons of Iain MacGhille Challum McLeod, laird of Raasay, by his cousin Ruaridh MacAllan McLeod of Gairloch, nicknamed *Nimhneach*, 'venomous', for no good reason other than that Iain had married a Mackenzie; having accepted their uncle's kind invitation to dine with him, one by one the sons were murdered as they entered his house. Or the callous murder in 1596 of Nicholas Bolton of Mindrum 'an honest Border yeoman' by

Sir John Kerr of Spielaw; the latter, having enquired of his wife where her husband was, went over to him as he worked his fields and, as the unfortunate Bolton doffed his cap to his superior, Kerr 'drew owt his sword and cutt him three blowes upon the head, and left the rest of his companie to cutt him all in peces'.

Such feuds, if kept within the warring families, could be overlooked by the authorities. But when they spiralled out of control, as they often did, blind eyes could not be turned. The 'battle' of Dryfe Sands, near Lockerbie, in December 1593 resulted in the death of 700 Maxwells, including Lord Maxwell himself, Warden of the Scottish West March. And yet this 'stramash' between the Maxwells and the Crichtons, described as 'one of the bloodiest family fights on British soil', had began 18 months earlier with the simple theft of a horse by one Border reiver from another. Such lawlessness would not be tolerated by James VI, who was determined to eradicate this cancer from his realm.

King James saw the Borders very differently from the Highlands. Up till now feuding on the Border had been viewed as no bad thing, a constant thorn in the side of the English. But with the prospect of him becoming king of England, there was no place for robbery, blackmail, arson, kidnapping and murder in the new political landscape of which he dreamed. The incident that brought matters to a head followed an untroubled (for once) day of truce held near Kershopefoot in the spring of 1596.

William Armstrong of Kinmont,

'Kinmont Willie', a notorious reiver, had attended that day. As he returned homeward along the Liddel Water, he was waylaid by Englishmen and bundled off to Carlisle Castle. There was no good reason for the kidnapping, and according to Scott of Buccleuch, the Keeper of Liddesdale, it was in clear breach of the truce. A diplomatic wrangle began, with letters passing back and forth between the Scottish and English authorities, to no avail. The high-spirited Buccleuch decided there was nothing for it but direct action. And so, on the night of Sunday 13 April ('Black Sunday' the English later called it) a band of reivers, among them Armstrongs and Elliots, broke into the mighty fortress and freed Kinmont Willie.

Wi' coulters and wi' forehammers,
We garr'd [made] the bars bang merrilie,
Until we came to the inner prison,
Where Willie o' Kinmont he did lie.
(From the *Ballad of Kinmont Willie*, in Sir Walter Scott's *Minstrelsy of the Scottish Border*.)

The English called it an outrage, and the repercussions embroiled both sovereigns. The affair led to the setting up of a joint Border Commission and the wholesale rooting out of the worst offenders. Hundreds of reivers were rounded up and hanged, others were simply removed from the scene, including one particularly problem clan, the Grahams, who were transported lock, stock and barrel to Ireland in 1606, ironically to help their king pacify another problem area. By 1609, after witnessing a mass hanging of reivers in Dumfries, the Earl of Dunfermline wrote with smug satisfaction to his majesty: 'The Earl of Dunbar has purgit the

Borders of all the chiefest malefactors, robbers and brigands as Hercules purged Augeus the king of Elides his escuries. The Middle Shires are now as quiet as any part in any civil kingdom in Christeanity.'

His proud boast proved well founded. By the time James VI and I passed peacefully away in London in 1625, his once wild and lawless Borders were no more ungovernable than almost any other part of his three kingdoms.

Almost...but not quite! If there was a rival to the Borders it was the Highlands. The only factor in the area's favour, from James's point of view, was that it was further removed from the heart of his kingdom. Whereas Border feuds often erupted onto the streets of Edinburgh, the endemic lawlessness in the Highlands generally went unnoticed, and unpunished, by the central authorities – even horrendous deeds like the burning to death of an entire congregation of Mackenzies whilst at prayer by their most hated foes, the MacDonalds, in 1603.

James could so easily have ignored the Highlands, for by now the descendants of Fergus Mór had long turned their backs on their ancient Gaelic homeland. James, born and brought up a Lowlander, was clearly not overly impressed with the Highlands, or its warring clansmen: 'As for the Hie-lands,' he wrote, [there are] two sorts of people: the one, that dwelleth in our maine land, that ar barborous for the most parte yet mixed with some shewe of civilitie; the other dwelleth in the Iles...are alluterlie barbares.'

But James didn't ignore them. After all, didn't he have a divine right to be treated with the respect God's representative deserved, even by

Highlanders? And so he set about sorting them out. If anything, the clans were more ruthlessly treated than their southern counterparts. James might have had a divine right to rule, but he had a most ungodly way of showing it. Executions and transportations were the order of the day.

The 'rooting out of the barborous and stubborne' clans effectively began in 1597 when all Highland landlords,

▲ *Corgarff Castle, in Upper Strathdon, Aberdeenshire, was the setting for an horrific tragedy in November 1571, the result of a bitter feud between two local clans, the Forbeses and the Gordons.*

great and small, were compelled to produce valid titles to their land. If they failed they were expelled, simple as that. The lands forfeited were then entrusted to 'civilised' people, Lowlanders by and large, like the 'Gentlemen Adventurers' of Fife who got the MacLeod lands in Lewis. 'New Towns' were to be established at Campbeltown (originally Lochhead), Inverlochy (now Fort William) and Stornoway, likewise populated by Lowlanders, or at least those from trustworthy clans – the Gordons, the Mackenzies, and of course the Campbells.

James was not to know that it would be the Campbells who would soon play a leading role in the downfall of his blessed Stewart dynasty. Perhaps if he

had listened to what his own Bishop of the Isles wrote, things might have turned out differently: 'Neither can I think it either good or profitable to his majesty or this country to make that name [ie Campbell] greater in the Isles than they are already or get to root out one pestiferous clan and plant in one little better.'

But the mastery of the clans would not stop there. James also tried his hand at forcing the Highlanders to stop speaking Gaelic. The *Statutes of Iona*, agreed with the heads of clans in 1609, included a clause requiring that the sons of men of substance be sent to the Lowlands for their education. It was a simple next step to making it illegal for anyone to hold property unless they could read, write and speak English, which James did in 1616. The first book printed in Gaelic (*Foirm ne n-Urrnuidheadh*, Knox's Book of Common Order) had been published as recently as 1567. Now barely a half century later the Gaelic tongue, once the language of the majority of Scots, was in danger of being forced out of existence.

As things transpired, James's attempts to stamp out the 'barborous feudes' in the Highlands proved nowhere near as successful as his pogrom against the Border surnames. Today as we drive over the rolling moorland of Liddesdale, 'the bloodiest valley in Britain', it is hard to envisage that this was once a region of endemic lawlessness, where surname was set against surname and national identity often relegated to second-place. Not so the mountainous, rugged Highland wastes, where the old medieval rivalries were still being played out at Culloden more than a century after Jamie Saxt had been laid to rest in far-off Westminster Abbey.

▶ *John Speed's wonderful map shows how the kingdom of Scotland looked around the time of the Union of the Crowns in 1603. Of particular interest are the marginal illustrations portraying 'Scotch' and 'Highland' men and women. It is as if they were from different countries. King James himself obviously felt they were, and showed his contempt when he wrote of his Highland and Island subjects in 1599: 'The people that dwelleth there [the Highlands] are barbarous for the most parte and yet mixed with some shewe of civilitie. The other that dwelleth in the Iles are alluterlie barbares, without any sorte or showe of civilitie.' So much for the concept of James's 'United Kingdom'. And therein were sown the seeds of the mistrust that would one day be harvested on the bloody battlefield of Culloden.*

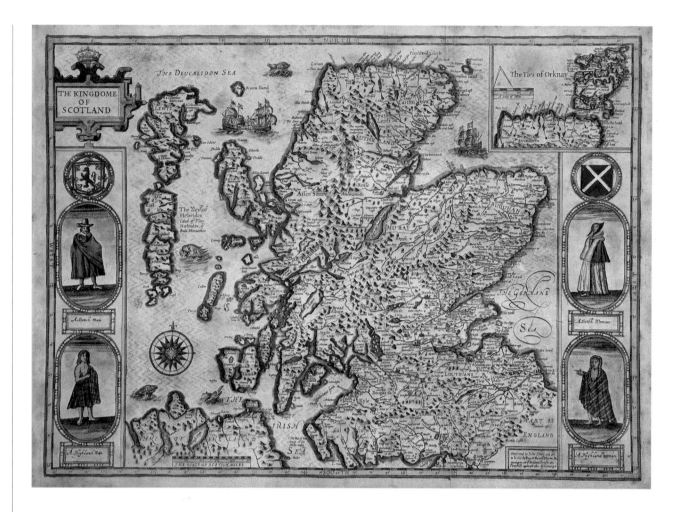

right of kings'. Kings were answerable only to God, and if there was a bond between king and courtier it was like that between father and child. Many of his subjects felt differently, their thoughts articulated to the King himself by Andrew Melville, the theologian, in a bad-tempered encounter at Falkland Palace in 1596: 'Thair is twa Kings and twa Kingdomes in Scotland. Thair is Christ Jesus the King, and His Kingdom, the Kirk, whase subject King James the Saxt is, and of whase kingdome nocht a king, nor a lord, nor a heid, but a member!'

James's stance, for it to command respect, demanded tact and diplomacy. And therein lay the seeds of dynastic ruin. James, for all his faults, possessed such qualities; his son, Charles I, singularly lacked them. The writing was on the wall for the Stewarts.

There was another concern, though, that exercised James's mind even more – the possibility that he might become king of England one day. Almost from the time he could talk, James had the vision of becoming king in both countries, what he called the 'perfect union' – Great Britain. As the

years passed and Queen Elizabeth remained unmarried and childless, so James became increasingly focused on achieving this goal. He did his utmost to keep on the right side of his aunt, negotiating a treaty with England in 1586, forsaking his own mother in her dying hours in 1587, and aiding the English in their hour of need in 1588 when the Spanish Armada threatened.

James's long end-game succeeded. On 26 March 1603, he was aroused from his slumbers in Holyroodhouse by an agitated messenger newly arrived hot-foot from London. Queen Elizabeth had passed away and would James VI of Scotland care to accept the invitation to become James I of England also? It was a rhetorical question. One of the greatest ironies in British history was about to unfold: after centuries of English monarchs attempting to wrest the throne of Scotland, it was a Scot who would seat himself on the throne of England. Had one stood in the ghostly stillness of Westminster Abbey after the coronation ceremony on 25 July, one might just have heard the body of Edward I, 'Hammer of the Scots', ever so slowly rotating in its grave!

TRIPLE CROWNS

James VI of Scotland's coronation as James I of England was the fulfilment of a dream. Another step had been taken along the road to Union with England. James preferred to be called *Rex Britanniae Magnae et Franciae et Hiberniae*, 'King of Great Britain and France and Ireland'. 'Great Britain' was his own invention, part of his grand plan for the union of the two kingdoms of Scotland and England. The reference to France was pure nostalgia, nothing more, for the English Crown had long surrendered all claim to that land. Ireland, invaded by England in the 1160s, retained a measure of independence but continued to present major problems for the English government. Poor Wales didn't even merit a mention, for 'the land of the dragon' had effectively lost its fight for independence with the death of Owain Glyn Dwr in 1416.

The moment James crossed into England, Scotland's destiny was irrevocably altered. There were indeed great benefits to be had by the move, not least for those living in the Border lands. As James journeyed south, he saw the ancient Border, over which much blood had been spilled, disappearing before his eyes: 'Where I thought to have employed you with some armour, I employ only your hearts, to the good prospering of me in my success and journey.'

Certainly Scotland and England were set to bury their differences, or at least fight them out without resorting to the battlefield – mostly. But there was a 'down side' for the Scots. Although James had promised to return to his northern kingdom regularly, in the event he made it back just once, in 1617. The attractions of London were evidently too much for a monarch who, despite his strict Calvinistic upbringing, was known for his hard drinking. Effectively from 1603 Scotland had an absentee monarch, and almost inevitably in view of their respective sizes Scotland would be the poor relation.

The effects of the new constitutional relationship were felt immediately. Where the sovereign was, there would be his fawning courtiers, drawn to the royal presence like moths to a candle flame. Down the road to London went the cream of Scottish society, following, and wallowing, in the king's wake. Even those who held Scottish positions of State preferred to reside in London and travel north only when necessary. And with the nobility went their extensive households; the population drift to the south-east of England had begun.

Not everyone looked to England for advancement after 1603. A good number crossed to Ulster to help James attempt to destroy the Gaelic culture there. From 1606 on, whole districts were 'cleared' of the native Catholic inhabitants and 'planted' with Scottish Protestants. Well-nigh 50,000 Scots had settled in Ulster by 1650. Surnames hitherto confined to the Scottish Lowlands, such as Hamilton and Turnbull, now became commonplace in Northern Ireland. James's Ulster 'plantation' was state terrorism on the grand scale, of which even Stalin would have been proud! But, as King James's *Authorised Version of the Bible*, *Deuteronomy* V, 9, published in 1611, says: 'for I the Lord thy God am a jealous God, visiting the iniquity of the fathers upon the children unto the third and fourth generation...'. So profound was the impact of James's policy of ethnic cleansing on Ulster that the

▲ *By the time of King James VI's departure for London and the English throne in 1603, Edinburgh was firmly established as Scotland's capital city, and its castle as 'the first and principal strength of the realme . . . where His Majesty's jewels, moveables, munitionis and registaris are kepit'. Among the King's jewels were the ancient Honours of Scotland, locked away in a strongroom in the royal palace. Before each sitting of the Parliament in the High Street, the Crown, Sword and Sceptre were carried in a solemn procession to Parliament Hall, where they lay, centre stage throughout the proceedings, signifying the presence of the absent sovereign.*

shock waves are still being felt to this day.

Emigration wasn't just confined to England and Ireland. Countless more were drawn to Europe where they took full advantage of the boom in international commerce resulting from the new peace. Many became respectable merchants and traders, but many more were humble pedlars roaming the countryside. These 'drifters' darkened the reputation of the Scots abroad. One Member of the English Parliament, in a debate about possible Union with Scotland, had the effrontery to warn his fellow MPs about the likely impact of the Scots on his nation with these damning words: 'We shall be over-run by them, as cattle pent up by a slight hedge will over it into a better soyle. Witness the multiplicities of the Scots in Polonia.'

As in Ulster, Scottish surnames embedded themselves in the local culture as the incomers married local lasses, and names such as Ramzy (Ramsay), Czochranek (Cochrane) and Makalienski (Maclean) still survive. One of the best-known descendants of a Scottish emigrant is the Norwegian composer, Edvard Grieg, whose forebears were Greigs from Aberdeenshire.

The damaging reputation was offset by the high standing of the Scottish soldier abroad, finding a new arena for his fighting skills now that Scotland and England were largely at peace. Many became mercenaries, enlisting in the armies of Sweden and Russia. The outbreak of the Thirty Years' War in 1618 put the Scottish soldier in demand as never before.

The period after 1603 also marked the beginning of Great Britain's colonial days. It fell to James to embark on the quest for empire in earnest when he oversaw the successful establishment of Britain's first colony in America, Virginia, named in honour of Elizabeth, the 'Virgin Queen'. The foundations of the British Empire were laid as those English settlers cut the sods to build their new homes.

The Scots too sought for a slice of the action, and were granted it in 1621 when Lord Stirling received title to Nova Scotia. Stirling had devoted his life to dreaming up money-making schemes; now he embarked on his greatest ploy, the colonisation of 'New Scotland'. Parcels of land were sold to those willing to part with the necessary cash. The additional lure of a baronetcy was dangled in front

of the noses of Scotland's wealthy. They didn't even have to leave Scotland to become barons of Nova Scotia; a short trip to the Castle Hill in Edinburgh, where they received a token handful of good old Scottish soil, would suffice. Thus the myth was born that the Castle Esplanade belongs to the Province of Nova Scotia! The 'project' soon foundered.

James maintained in his old age that he was able to 'sit and govern [Scotland] with my pen: I write and it is done'. But he couldn't do that without an effective postal service, so he ordered one to be set up between Edinburgh and Berwick, to link up with the existing service from Berwick south; to make matters easier for the 'postie', he had a bridge built across the Tweed – it is there yet. His long reign is distinguished by other notable achievements, among them the establishment of the first registers of births, marriages and deaths. It is doubtful if any of those deaths was caused by the new fashion for smoking tobacco, but James was certainly the first to speak out against the 'weade'. In his *A counterblast to tobacco* he flagged up the stupidity of those who indulged, causing 'the filthy smoke and stink thereof to exhale athort the dishes and infect the air'. If only his subjects had listened to him.

James died peacefully in his bed in Hertfordshire on 27 March 1625. He was 58 years old. For 57 of those he had reigned unhindered. Given the dark circumstances surrounding his birth this was a most remarkable achievement; no king of Scots had ever reigned so long.

KILLING TIMES

On hearing the sad news of the King's demise, the Scots poet William Drummond of Hawthornden bemoaned: 'The world which late was golden by thy breath is iron turned, and horrid, by thy death.' They proved prophetic words.

Things might have turned out differently had Charles I (1625-49) not chosen to return to the land of his birth for his Scottish coronation in 1633. All he succeeded in doing, by his arrogance and insensitivity, was exacerbate a delicate situation created by an absentee sovereign who had already done his level best to alienate them. The Scots had already paid more into Crown coffers in

'Consorting with the Devil'

~ SCOTLAND'S WITCHES ~

'When shall we three meet again – in thunder, lightning or in rain?'

(Shakespeare's Macbeth, *Act I, Scene 1)*

Spare a thought for Isobel Gowdie from Nairn. What unspeakable torture must she have endured to make her confess to such a catalogue of bizarre crimes, from sticking pins in a wax image of the laird's child and killing it; through making the local minister ill by swinging a bag with boiled toads and nail clippings over his bed; to killing a ploughman with little elf-arrows provided by 'Auld Nick' himself? For poor Isobel was accused of witchcraft by the 'godly folk' of Nairn in 1662 and found guilty. She was tied to a stake, strangled, then covered in pitch and burned to death.

Isobel Gowdie was far from alone. Between 1560 and 1700 almost 2000 Scots, most of them women, were executed for witchcraft.

Why witchery became such a feature of late medieval society remains a mystery. Two things are sure though – it was by no means confined to Scotland, and it affected Catholics and Protestants alike. Witches and warlocks were nothing new of course. The notion of 'the devil' as the embodiment of evil was integral to Christianity, and those who consorted with the devil were part and parcel of medieval spiritual life, just as real as the saints. But it is no coincidence that the rise in witch-hunting occurred in an age of momentous religious upheaval with its intense intellectual questioning of the old order. That Reformation Scotland should have joined in with such fervour is no surprise.

Once Parliament passed the 'Sorsarie Act' in 1563, making witchcraft punishable by death, there was hardly a corner of the realm that wasn't affected by witch-hunts at one time or another for the next 150 years. Only in the far

north-west and the Western Isles was it exceptional, coincidentally those areas least touched by the tentacles of the Reformation. And although it wasn't unknown for members of the nobility to be accused of witchcraft – the night Sir Robert Gordon of Gordonstoun died the devil's carriage was heard trundling up the driveway to his mansion – most 'witches' were from the lower orders. One can easily visualise the congregation in a kirk being whipped into a frenzy by the vitriolic words of some zealous Calvinist minister and then turning on one of their number generally perceived to be 'a bit odd'. 'Confessions' were extorted using instruments of torture like thumbscrews, or more commonly sleep-deprivation. Less conventional was the employment of a 'witch-pricker', a man who by the simple deployment of a sharp point over the body of the accused was capable of finding their 'witch-mark'.

It wasn't one long, sustained witch-hunt. Dumfriesshire, for example, didn't really 'get the bug' until after 1625, by which date Aberdonians had all but given up the chase. But the majority of victims suffered during certain 'epidemics' that swept through the nation – in 1590-7, 1628-30, 1649-50 and 1661-3.

The first epidemic was bizarrely related to James VI's return to Scotland following his wedding to Anna of Denmark in 1589. A coven of witches led by Euphemie McCalzean was found to have met with the devil at midnight in a North Berwick church and attempted to wreck the honeymoon couple's ship as it neared Leith. Apparently the devil saw in the King of Scots the 'greatest enemie hee hath in the world'. All 13 witches, needless to say, were found guilty and

burned on the Castle Hill in Edinburgh.

The final epidemic, following Charles II's return to his throne in 1660, was really an attempt to make up for lost time, because Cromwell had done his best to prohibit witch-trials from taking place. But the resumption of witch-hunting coincided with a growing revulsion at the whole sordid business, coupled with a questioning of the validity of confessions. Leading the attack on the witch-hunters was Sir George Mackenzie, the Lord Advocate, who paradoxically became better known as 'Bluidy Mackenzie' for his persecution of Covenanters.

The ruthless pursuit of witches didn't stop overnight. Hunts continued spasmodically thereafter, but by the time the most notorious witch-trial in history took place, that of the 'Salem witches' in Massachusetts, USA, in 1692, the practice was all but dead in Scotland. The last witch burned, an old woman accused of turning her daughter into a pony, died at Dornoch in 1722, but it got the sheriff-depute who presided over the proceedings into hot water as a result. When in 1736 the fledgling United Kingdom Parliament repealed the 1563 'Sorsarie Act', one of the most appalling and tragic episodes in Scotland's history was mercifully brought to an end.

And how Tam stood, like ane bewitch'd,
And thought his very een enriched;
Even Satan glowr'd, and fidg'd fu' fain,
And hotch'd and blew wi' might
 and main:
Till first ae caper, syne anither,
Tam tint his reason a' thegither,
And roars out 'Weel done, Cutty-sark!'
And in an instant all was dark!
(Tam's famous encounter in Alloway Kirk, from Robert Burns's *Tam O' Shanter*.)

the first two years of Charles's reign than they had in all the previous 25. Equally galling was their sovereign's religious stance, and when he was crowned according to the Anglican rite in St Giles, and further ordained that Knox's former kirk should become a cathedral, the Scots knew they had a fight on their hands.

Whether Jenny Geddes ever did throw her stool in St Giles that July day in 1637, during the first service held according to the *Book of Common Prayer*, and whether she shouted out: 'You daurna say Mass at my lug!' ('Don't you dare say Mass in my ear!'), seems doubtful. What is certain is that the introduction of 'that Booke' provoked a riot in Edinburgh, the effect of which quickly reached most corners of the land. Worse still for the ill-starred Charles, the tremors were felt in his other kingdoms also. Within a short while revolution had engulfed the entire British Isles. Everyone has heard of the English Civil War, with its Cavaliers

and Roundheads, but few realise that it all started in Scotland.

Whilst the initial reaction of the Scots to Charles's diktats was anger, the official response was pragmatic and measured. The 'thrie estaitis', profoundly disillusioned that their sovereign had chosen to ignore them, agreed to restate their right to defend their religion against popery's 'manyfolde ordoures' and 'wicked hierarchy'. They drew up a petition called the National Covenant, recalling God's covenant with the Israelites in *Exodus* VI:4, and urged all Scots to sign. On 28 February 1638, in Greyfriars Kirk, Edinburgh, the first signatures were collected from the nobility. Scots from all the airts followed; only in the north-east was there resistance of a sort.

Charles failed to take the hint. Despite the moderate tones of the National Covenant – it excluded any mention of abolishing bishops, and pledged the signatories to defend 'the King's

▲ *Thousands of gannets inhabit the Bass Rock, off North Berwick, today, but over 300 years ago the residents were state prisoners, mostly religious dissidents, or Covenanters. Among them was Revd Peden, minister of New Luce in Wigtownshire; he was arrested conducting a conventicle, or open-air worship, in Ayrshire, in 1673, and spent the next five years on the rock. A fellow inmate was a Dumfriesshire minister, John Blackadder, who would have no truck with Charles II's desire to foist bishops on his flock; he died in his rocky prison in 1686. The Bass Rock was Scotland's Alcatraz and Robben Island.*

▲ *Covenanters arrested during the Pentland Rising of 1666, and subsequently condemned to death, are marched down the West Bow, Edinburgh, on their way to their place of execution. Twenty-one were hanged, and many more were transported to a penal colony in the West Indies. As with so many of the victims, the artist of this painting is unknown to us.*

hope Charles harboured that his Scottish subjects would come to his aid were soon dashed when the two Parliaments signed the Solemn League and Covenant in 1643. The English Parliamentarian victory at Marston Moor, near York, on 2 July 1644, was achieved largely with the help of Scottish Covenanters. It spelt the beginning of the end for the monarch with the divine right to rule.

By now, though, cracks were appearing in the Covenanting ranks. Not all were convinced that they were right to resist the royal command; nor were they persuaded that a pact with Puritan England was necessarily in Presbyterian Scotland's best interest. Among them was the Marquis of Montrose, a leading signatory to the 1638 National Covenant. While the Royalists were being routed at Marston Moor, Montrose was embarking on a remarkable Royalist fight-back in Scotland. With just 5000 troops, mostly Highlanders and Irish Catholics, he won victory after resounding victory – Tippermuir, Aberdeen, Inverlochy, Auldearn, Alford, Kilsyth – until finally coming to grief at Philiphaugh, near Selkirk, on 13 September 1645. In that campaign alone, 6000 Covenanters lost their lives.

Even had Montrose won Philiphaugh, it is doubtful if it would have made any difference to Charles's cause. In May 1646 the King walked into the Covenanters' camp at Newark-on-Trent, in deepest Nottinghamshire, and surrendered. Nine months later the Scots handed their sovereign over to the mercy of Cromwell and headed for home. Two years later the English beheaded their – and Scotland's – king. The Stewart dynasty was temporarily eclipsed. England was now declared a republic.

How would the Scots react? Much as they resented their king, they were aghast at the news of his execution. With scarcely a thought, they snubbed Cromwell's offer to join them in union and proclaimed his son, Charles II (1649-85), king instead. Cromwell invaded in June 1650, and for the first time in almost a century an English army was once more on Scottish soil. The armies met at Dunbar that September, and two great generals who had fought shoulder to shoulder at Marston Moor, David Leslie (no relation of Alexander) and Oliver Cromwell, now opposed each other across the windswept northern slope of Doon Hill. But whereas

Majesty, His Person and Estate' – his majesty smelled revolution in the air: 'So long as this Covenant is in force, I have no more power in Scotland than as the Doge of Venice.'

Little did Charles realise what forces he was unleashing as he marched north with a large army. The Army of the Covenant, under the inspirational leadership of Alexander Leslie, who had earned his spurs in the Thirty Years War and risen to the rank of field-marshal in the Swedish army, advanced to Duns Law in June 1639 to resist the Royalist force. In 1640 they crossed into England and took Newcastle. In 1641 Ulster erupted when the Catholic population rose up and massacred the Protestant Scots recently foisted upon them. By 1642 England too was plunged into civil war. Any

Cromwell was free to command his smaller force, poor Leslie had bickering presbyterian ministers carping in his lug. The result was yet another 4000 Scots dead and another humiliating defeat. Those same ministers would soon regret their meddling; for the next 10 years Scotland was forced to endure Cromwell's 'United Commonwealth'.

No sooner had Charles returned to his throne in 1660 than he was exacting revenge. Examples were made of leading Covenanters like Archibald Campbell, Marquis of Argyll, who had placed the Crown of Scotland on his head that Ne'er Day at Scone in 1651 but who had had the temerity to defy Montrose – he was executed in 1661. The head of Johnston of Warriston, who had helped draft the National Covenant, followed soon after. The king even ordered that Montrose's skull be taken down from its spike above Edinburgh's Tolbooth, where it had been displayed since 1650, and given a state funeral! Such actions were bound to provoke – and they did. Some 300 ministers, almost a third of the total, left their churches and resorted to gathering with their parishioners in private houses. And when

the numbers attending their services grew, they took to meeting in fields, in what were known as 'conventicles'. The 'killing time' was about to begin.

In 1666 Government troops were carrying out their orders suppressing conventicles in the south-west, a hotbed of Covenantism. But they went far beyond their instructions, looting and raping their way through the douce countryside. It was more than the Covenanters could bear and in their frustration they marched on Edinburgh, over 1000 of them, to air their grievances. They got as far as the outskirts of the capital before being forced back into the Pentland Hills, hence the curious name the 'Pentland Rising'. And there on a cold November morning, at Rullion Green, they were caught by 'General Tam of the Binns' and his dragoons. Fifty were killed where they stood, another 21 were taken to the mercat cross in Edinburgh and hanged, yet more were bundled off to a penal colony in the West Indies. That, the authorities hoped, would teach them a lesson.

It didn't. The conventiclers stubbornly continued to gather in their fields, and the military

▲ James Graham, Marquis of Montrose, goes to the scaffold in Edinburgh on 21 May 1650, defiant to the last; a painting by the Victorian artist and Director of the National Gallery of Scotland, James Drummond. Even though he had helped draft the National Covenant in 1638, and had fought against Charles I in the early years of the civil wars, Montrose baulked at the extremism of Presbyterianism and threw in his lot with his sovereign. His brilliant generalship won him many successes in Scotland in 1644-5, but defeat at Selkirk forced him into exile. Returning in 1650, he lost his last battle at Carbisdale in Sutherland. His reputation, though, as: 'Scotland's glory, Britain's pride, As brave a subject as ere for monarch dy'd', was already secured.

▲ Glencoe, in Argyllshire, 'the narrow glen', became the 'Glen of Weeping' following the appalling massacre that took place there in the early hours of 13 February 1692. Thirty-eight men, women and children of Clan MacDonald were killed, some slaughtered in their beds by redcoats garrisoned at nearby Fort William, others frozen to death in the bitter winter snow as they tried to escape.

still did their best to stop them. And that was what John Graham of Claverhouse's men were up to on 1 June 1679 when they encountered a conventicle being held on an exposed Ayrshire muir. It should have been a formality, 'Bluidy Clavers' and his dragoons were more than a match for the Covenanters' pitchforks:

But up and spak cruel Clavers then,
Wi' hastie wit and wicked skill;
'Gae fire upon yon Westland men,
I think it is my sov'reign's will'.

But as soon as one of those pitchforks unhorsed Claverhouse, the result was never in doubt. The victorious Covenanters cheered as Claverhouse's troops fled the battlefield of Drumclog. Emboldened, they marched on Glasgow. By the time they reached Bothwell Bridge, north of Hamilton, they were 4000 strong and confident that the days of the 'tyrant and usurper Charles Stuart' were numbered. But blocking their path were

10,000 troops – and 'Bluidy Clavers' again. This time he got his revenge. Death, imprisonment and transportation were meted out in equal measure.

But still they resisted, their conviction made the stronger when the Duke of Albany, the future James VII of Scotland and II of England (1685-89), arrived in Scotland later that year to govern on behalf of his elder brother. James was even more determined to root out this Presbyterian heresy. He unleashed a reign of terror on the Covenanters so appalling that one minister, Robert Wodrow of Eastwood in Renfrewshire, called it 'the killing time'.

Although the numbers dying for their faith have become exaggerated over the intervening years – and far more would have died from famine and disease in the same period – there is no doubting the sheer brutality meted out in that dreadful decade. Thousands were killed in battle or murdered at prayer or in their homes, 362 executed, and many more incarcerated in grim holes like the Bass Rock, Scotland's Alcatraz. When Archibald Campbell's attempted rising in the West Highlands was snuffed out, the king ordered that: 'All men who joyned are to be killed or disabled ever from fighting again; And burn all houses except honest men's. Let the women and children be transported to remote Isles.'

The barbarity was taken to its most absurd limit in the following year when the body of the Revd Peden, one of the Covenanters' most fiery preachers, was exhumed from its burial-place in Auchinleck and taken to Cumnock for hanging!

Confrontation between king and country could not last. Matters came to a head in December 1688 when rioters broke into Holyrood Abbey and desecrated the burial vault of the Stewart dynasty that lay therein. Little did they know, as they vented their collective spleens, that their Stewart sovereign was already packing his bags for France.

But it was the English once more who dictated events in all three kingdoms. Already by the time of the Holyrood riot, the Protestant Prince William of Orange, Charles I's grandson, was in England with his wife Mary, James VII's daughter by his first marriage. By Christmas Day they had been proclaimed joint sovereigns of England. What would the Scots do? Would they maintain their allegiance to the rightful king, or would they throw in their lot with the new order? Was James VI's dream of a 'perfect union' with England to die or be continued? One thing was for sure – the notorious 'killing time' might be over but the 'grim reaper' was still honing his scythe in preparation for more.

UNION

When Parliament met in March 1689 to debate the royal succession, the house was equally divided between Jacobites (from the Latin *Jacobus*, 'James') and Williamites. When it decided a month later to offer the throne of Scotland jointly to William II (1689-1702) and Mary II (1689-94) the road to union was open again. But the Jacobites would not so easily submit. They might have lost the 'war of words', but they might still win the war itself. They did after all have the country's top military commander on their side; 'Bluidy Clavers',

scourge of the Covenanters, was about to become 'Bonnie Dundee', darling of the Jacobites.

Claverhouse headed for the Highlands where he knew he could recruit troops from the largely Catholic and Episcopalian clans. On 27 July he fought his first – and as fate would have it his last – encounter with Government forces. On the heather-clad slopes of Killiecrankie, he engineered a brilliant victory that was soon the stuff of legend.

 I fought at land, I fought at sea,

 At hame I fought my auntie-o;

 But I met the Devil and Dundee

 On the braes o' Killiecrankie-o.

(A verse from the ballad *The Braes o' Killiecrankie*.)

▲ *The Battle of the Pass of Killiecrankie, fought beside the River Garry in Perthshire on 27 July 1689, could so easily have resulted in an early return to the British throne of King James VII and II. Instead, the death of Viscount Dundee, the Jacobite general, in the very hour of his victory – he was mortally wounded by a stray bullet – soured the victory and the Jacobites, bereft of his leadership, failed to drive home their advantage.*

'Bonny Fighters'
~ SCOTLAND'S FIRST REGIMENTS ~

'Cuidich 'n Righ' - 'Help the King'

(The regimental motto of the Seaforth Highlanders, and now of the Highlanders)

It was no contest that day in 1666 on the windswept Pentland Hills outside Edinburgh; 1000 country folk armed with little more than pitchforks against soldiers neatly turned out in their bright scarlet coats and wielding bayoneted muskets. Rullion Green, fought between the Covenanters and the Scots Guards, was the first battle in Britain to involve a Scottish regiment. The concept of a regular standing army had been Oliver Cromwell's. His 'new model army' proved such a success that its continuation held its attractions for Charles II. Yet the cost was deemed too great by the parliaments of both countries and Charles was allowed only to retain a small permanent force for his personal protection, known as his Life Guard. And that is how the Scots Guards, Scotland's first official regiment, came into being in 1661.

> thair is none in airmes in all Scotland, aither native or stranger, except the leiff gaird for his Majesteis use and weill of his subjects.

(John Nicoll, in his *Diary of Public Transactions*, 1662.)

From this cautious start, the attraction of a standing army began to take hold, and before the seventeenth century had run its course another five regiments had been added to the strength.

The commander at Rullion Green, Lieutenant-General Tam Dalyell of the Binns, himself raised an independent cavalry force in 1678, which distinguished itself at Bothwell Bridge in 1679 and was formally incorporated into the standing army as the Royal Regiment of Scots Dragoons in 1681. Now called the Royal Scots Dragoon Guards, they were more popularly known as 'the Scots Greys' from the colour of their horses.

The Royal Scots had been raised in 1633 as Hepburn's Regiment of Foot, but they fought for the King of France not Great Britain! In 1661 they were added to the establishment but were not brought home until 1678 to help fight the Covenanters. The regiment became known as the Royal Scots in 1812, but are more popularly known as 'Pontius Pilate's Bodyguard' from their position as senior Regiment of the Line.

The Royal Scots Fusiliers, raised in 1678 as the Earl of Mar's Regiment but known as the Royal Highland Fusiliers since their amalgamation with the Highland Light Infantry in 1959, took their name from the weapon they carried, the fusil, a light flintlock musket less deadly than the matchlock version but much safer when used near gunpowder barrels; their prime job was guarding the artillery train. Ironically, the Fusiliers, formed to fight the Covenanters, became a popular regiment with the descendants of those same Covenanters, thanks to its recruiting base in Ayr, in the heart of Covenanting country.

The King's Own Scottish Borderers (the KOSBs) began as the Earl of Leven's Regiment, raised for the defence of Edinburgh in the heady days of March 1689 as Parliament debated who should be sovereign. The KOSBs soon tasted defeat, at Killiecrankie that same year.

The Cameronians (Scottish Rifles) were absent from Killiecrankie but soon earned their reputation as doughty fighters when they stopped the Jacobites dead in their tracks at Dunkeld shortly afterwards. The Cameronians actually began as a Covenanting force, 'the Mountain Men', who under their leader Richard Cameron fought valiantly at Bothwell Bridge against those same regiments they served alongside.

All these regiments had one thing in common – they were Lowland. In the Highlands, things were somewhat different. King Charles had authorised landlords sympathetic to his cause to raise independent companies of clansmen 'to keep watch upon the braes', and by 1700 'the Watch' comprised six companies; Campbell, Fraser, Grant, Menzies, Munro and Murray. General Wade's insistence that 'the plaid of each be as near as they can of the same Sort and Colour' saw the companies adopt the dark green and blue that is the hallmark of the famous Black Watch, *Am Freiceadan Dubh*, the first Highland Regiment incorporated into the British Army.

That was in the uncertain days before Culloden. Since then the Black Watch has been joined by other Highland regiments, including some of the most resonant names in British military history – the Seaforths (formed as the 78th Foot in 1778), the Gordons (the old 92nd established in 1794) and the Camerons (created by Cameron of Erracht in 1798). The outstanding bravery shown down the years by the descendants of those clansmen who were once held in such contempt by their fellow Scots from the Lowlands has rightly earned them the respect of their contemporaries and the reputation they hold to this day. Sir David Stewart of Garth, one of Wellington's generals, spoke of the Highland soldier 'considering courage as the most honourable virtue, cowardice the most disgraceful failing.' Adolf Hitler would put it more bluntly: 'Ladies from Hell!' he called the dreaded kilted Highlanders.

Had Claverhouse not been struck down by a stray bullet in the moment of his victory, the whole course of British history might have been different. But he was, and without him the Jacobite cause was doomed. The clansmen returned to their Highland homes, but their intervention on behalf of the exiled James would not be forgotten by the Government. More crucially, it reopened the mutual distrust that had long existed between Highlander and Lowlander. That loathing plumbed new depths amid the snows of Glencoe in the early hours of 13 February 1692.

The Massacre of Glencoe has entered the legend as yet another outpouring of hatred in the bitter feud between Campbell and MacDonald. But while it is true that soldiers from Argyll's regiment did the horrid deed, most weren't Campbells at all and the decision to exterminate the MacIans of Glencoe, a sept of MacDonald Clanranald, was taken at the highest level in Government. The reason for the blood-letting – excuse might be a more appropriate word – was that the ageing clan chief, Alasdair MacIan, had failed to swear his oath of allegiance to William and Mary by the 1 January deadline. The fact that he had managed to do so, despite the determined efforts of the authorities to

forestall him, was of no consequence. Someone had to serve as an example to the rest of the rebellious clans.

And so it was that troops from the newly built Fort William arrived in the glen. They availed themselves of the clan's hospitality for 12 days until, at the signal and in the dead of night, they rose from their beds and slaughtered all whom they found. Poor Alasdair MacIan was the first to be despatched, gunned down while still in his nightshirt. His good lady, falling on his prone corpse, was stripped bare, dragged outside and left to die in the freezing snow. By dawn, 36 men, women and children lay dead, either butchered by the redcoats or frozen to death. Glencoe, the 'narrow glen', had become at one fell swoop

the Glen of Weeping...melancholy, brooding,
the very valley of the Shadow of Death.
(From Thomas Macaulay's epic *History of England*.)

As appalling as Glencoe undoubtedly was, it was but a side-show compared to events happening elsewhere. William and Mary's arrival on the thrones of Scotland and England (though neither monarch visited their northern kingdom) had brought fresh impetus to the cause of unionism. But religion was no longer the driving force; economics were.

▲ *The Scots Greys, raised in 1678 to help King Charles II defeat the Scottish Covenanters, charge into the fray at Waterloo, 1815, to enable King George III to defeat the French. Lady Elizabeth Butler's famous oil painting, 'Scotland Forever', although painted many years after the momentous charge that began the battle, admirably conveys the fighting spirit of the Scottish soldier.*

▲ The rolling landscape of the Borders, seen here from above St. Mary's Loch, in Selkirkshire, was stained with human blood from centuries of bitter conflict between Scotland and England. In 1707 the two warring nations were politically joined, and although they have squabbled with each other intermittently ever since, they have managed to do so without recourse to the battlefield!

▶ Before 1707, the Palace of Holyroodhouse was central to the workings of the Scottish state. The Privy Council met in the Council Chamber, whilst the Commissioner to the Parliament, representing the absent sovereign, had his official residence in the north-west tower and over the main entrance. But all that changed after the Act of Union; the Scottish Privy Council and Scottish Parliament were no more.

Scotland had experienced something of a 'boom' during the seventeenth century. Edinburgh now rivalled Bristol as Britain's second city, and over 200 smaller burghs of barony had sprouted up since the Reformation, many of them along the east coast. And Glasgow finally emerged from Rutherglen's shadow, thanks to the growing trade with England's American colonies. Hitherto, the royal burgh of Rutherglen had been the main political and commercial focus on the Clyde – it was officially 'swallowed up' by Glasgow only in 1975. But from 1680 the country ran into stormy financial waters. A run of bad harvests was made worse by England declaring war on France. Former trading partners stopped trading with Scotland, forcing the Scots to rely increasingly on her southern neighbour. England exploited the new situation to the full. New solutions were needed.

It was William Paterson who dreamed up the idea of establishing a Scottish colony at Darien, on the narrow Panama isthmus in Central America. The Dumfries-born financier, founder of the Bank of England in 1694, saw the venture as 'the key of the universe', unlocking the door between the Atlantic and Pacific Oceans. It was an inspired idea, or so fellow Scots thought at the time, and in 1695 the 'Company of Scotland

trading to Africa and the Indies' was launched. Obvious difficulties, like the fact that Darien was an infested swamp, were brushed aside. Darien was the answer to Scotland's ills. The English thought differently, and with a little help from the appalling climate and the Spanish, Darien, renamed New Caledonia, proved a disaster, from the day the expedition set sail from the mother country in July 1698 to the humiliating moment two years later when the colony was abandoned; as fate would have it, it was April Fool's Day.

The Darien fiasco was an unmitigated, and expensive, embarrassment for Scotland as a nation. It was also a huge financial disaster for individual Scots who had invested vast sums in the venture. While ordinary Scots fulminated against the dastardly English and the underhandedness of their sovereign, the bankrupt investors thought only of how they might recover their losses. The only way they could see out of the mess was to achieve parity with England, and if that meant union then so be it.

And so the political debate hotted up, in both kingdoms. England would accept nothing short of out-and-out political union – a United Kingdom of Great Britain and Ireland under a secure Protestant succession and with a single Parliament, meeting of course at Westminster. The Scots preferred a federal solution. The English view prevailed. The debate over the proposed Treaty of Union dragged on through the winter of 1706. Perhaps if the people of Scotland had been given the chance to vote in a referendum, the answer to Queen Anne (1702-14) might have been a resounding 'no'. But this was Scotland 1707, not Scotland 1997, and political power was concentrated in only a few privileged hands. And when those select 147 hands went up on 16 January 1707, the majority voted for Union. Scotland was no more. As Chancellor Seafield brought the proceedings to a close, he sighed and muttered: 'Now there's an end o' an auld sang.'

UNITED KINGDOM

(1707 - 1815)

> 'The two kingdoms of Scotland and England shall be united into One'
>
> (*Article 1 of the Treaty of Union, 1707*)

This chapter tells the events of a momentous century that witnessed the creation of the United Kingdom and the demise of the ancient House of Stewart. It also experienced the 'Age of Enlightenment', innovation at home, in farming and industry, and the impact of revolutions abroad, in America and France.

STATE OF THE NATION

Scotland at the time of the Union in 1707 was a very different country from today. For one thing the population was far smaller – just over 1,000,000 souls, less than a fifth of the present total – and most of them lived in the Highlands and Islands, not squeezed into the Central Belt as the majority are now. Very few Scots were 'townies', probably one in 10, and of those, 30,000 resided in Edinburgh, maybe another 12,000 in Glasgow. The rest were dotted about the realm, from Lerwick to Stranraer, in towns numbering no more than 200 inhabitants.

Life for all but the privileged few was harsh, brutal, and often short. Life expectancy for those lucky enough to survive infancy was around 45 years of age. At the top of the social ladder were the aristocracy. Numbering no more than 100 noble families, they owned much of Scotland to a greater or lesser extent. Below them were the lairds, who

also owned land which they were allowed to pass on to their heirs. But whereas their predecessors had held land in return for military service, these latter-day esquires simply had to fork out the necessary cash. The old feudal order was almost gone. Only in the Highlands did it linger on until Culloden in 1746 put paid to the notion of kinship and military service for good.

For most Scots the prospect of owning the land they worked or the home they lived in was remote. Three out of four Scots were classed as peasants who rented their land, generally on short-term leases. A few were reasonably well-to-do tenants ('gudemen'), but most scratched a meagre living as sub-tenants – hinds (ploughmen), herds (tending the beasts), crofters and cottars. All, however, earned their living from working the land, growing and raising what they could for their own consumption, and selling what surplus there was, mainly to the towns. In those days, to earn

◄ *On 19 August 1745, Prince Charles Edward Stewart arrived at the head of Loch Shiel, in Inverness-shire. There, at Glenfinnan, he raised the standard of his father – called by his supporters King James VIII of Scotland and III of England, and by his detractors 'the Pretender'. Within the year, Charles's dream of restoring the Stewarts to their ancient throne lay trampled in the mud on Culloden Moor. The tower, built by Alexander Macdonald of Glenaladale, with its statue of the Prince, added later by Alexander's son Angus, remains an abiding monument to those first heady days of the last Jacobite Rising.*

▲ The countryside of Lowland Scotland looked very different in 1707 – no fields defined by neat hedgerows and stone dykes, just open land divided into broad strips, or rigs, each one allocated to the 'locals' roundabout. John Slezer captured that landscape in his 'prospect' of the old cathedral city of Dunblane, in Perthshire, published in his magisterial Theatrum Scotiae (1693). His wonderful engravings convey the physical essence of Scotland on the threshold of its political union with England. A hundred years later, that same landscape would look fundamentally different after the radical change brought about by the agricultural revolution.

a wage was a sign that you were way down the 'pecking order', a landless labourer perhaps, or a live-in domestic servant.

It wasn't just the make-up of the people that was different; so was the landscape. There were no neat fields spread across the countryside like a patchwork quilt, no trim hedgerows and drystone dykes. Villages were physically separated from the open muir around by just one boundary, the 'head dyke'. Within the dyke was the 'infield', or 'inbye', where the villagers grew their crops in narrow strips, called 'run-rig'. Oats and barley were the staple crops, oats for eating, and barley, the 'drink crop', to make beer and, increasingly, whisky. The beer, opined one observer, was 'strong enough to arm 'em against the coldness of the climate'. Vegetables such as pease, beans and kale, a kind of cabbage, added variety to the diet. But there were still no potatoes, which were only just beginning to appear on the dining tables of the aristocracy, and no turnips; the introduction of both during the eighteenth century would greatly change the lives of ordinary Scots.

Apart from the fertile south-east, much of the country was a pastoral and not an arable community, where the stock-in-trade, literally, were cattle, sheep and goats. It was normal for mothers and children to accompany the beasts to the summer grazings and remain with them there until the harvest, living in less substantial homes called 'shielings'; such a practice continued in the Western Isles until after the Second World War. The men meanwhile tended the crops, or went off to the fishing, leaving the grandparents to 'house-sit'. The more energetic children passed between the shieling and the croft with fresh milk for their grandparents.

B'e am dol chun ne h-airigh an t-am a b' fhearr sa bhliadhna air an tuath, am na leapa-fraoich fhallain agus na doigh-beatha fhallain, oiteag na mointich agus blaths na greine, an gruth agus uachdar a' bhainne... Chuala mi cailleachan is bodaich ag innse mu laithean is oidhcheannan sona na h-oige agus an uair sin a' caoidh s' ag ionndrainn nan amannan phriseil sin.

(Shieling time is the most delightful time of the rural year, the time of the healthy heather bed and the healthy outdoor life, of the moorland breeze and the warm sun, of the curds and the cream of the heather milk...I have heard old men and women waxing eloquent over these lightsome days and nights of their youth and again sobbing and sighing over awakened memories too tender for words.)

(From Alexander Carmichael's 'The Shieling' in *Carmina Gadelica, Ortha nan Gaidheal*, 1900.)

But what of the homes themselves? The landscape of Scotland is still liberally sprinkled with the remains of castles and tower-houses, the residences of the nobility and gentry. But of the homes of the peasants, who made up three-quarters of the population, there is now no trace above ground. We do, though, have first-hand accounts from early travel writers. All paint a word-picture of crude dwellings, cramped, damp and ill-lit:

The vulgar houses...are low and feeble. Their walls are made of a few stones jumbled together without mortar to cement 'em: on which they set up pieces of wood meeting at the top, ridge-fashion, but so order'd that there is neither sightliness nor strength; and it does not cost much more time to erect such a cottage than to pull it down. They cover these houses with turff of an inch thick, and in the shape of larger tiles, which they fasten with wooden pins, and renew as often as there is occasion; and that is very frequently done. 'Tis rare to find chimneys in these places, a small vent in the roof sufficing to

convey the smoak away. So that, considering the humility of these roofs, and the gross nature of the fuel, we may easily guess what a smother it makes, and what little comfort there is in sitting at one of their fires.

(From Revd Morer's *A Short Account of Scotland*, 1689.)

Across much of the country it was common in winter for the beasts to be housed under the same roof as their owners. One eighteenth-century woman recalled how she always knew it was time to put the porridge on when the family cow behind her urinated for the second time! Although this practice might appear primitive to us the presence of animals in the house was not without its advantages; not only did they provide a valuable source of heat, but the ammonia from their urine helped keep diseases like tuberculosis away.

But not all a peasant's beasts could be housed under his roof. With winter fodder at a premium, and with the turnip still to appear on the scene, hard choices had to be made after the harvest as to which animals to keep, which to drive to market and which to slaughter and salt away. The day in spring when the beasts were taken outside to the early grazings came to be known as 'lifting day', so malnourished were they they had literally to be lifted and carried outside.

In the absence of decent roads, the country folk had to transport their surplus produce to the towns along indifferent tracks threading over boggy muirs and down ill-drained glens. Markets and fairs were strictly controlled by the burghs, not surprisingly for therein lay much of their wealth. The burgesses, merchants and craftsmen who ran the towns made up only 5 per cent of the total population but they wielded immense power.

The towns presented a stark contrast to the clachans and touns of the countryside, none more so than the 'big four', Edinburgh, Glasgow,

▲ *Queen Anne (1702-14) receives a copy of the Treaty of Union from her Scottish Commissioners in 1707, painted by Sir Walter Monnington. The Act of Union, passed in the Scottish Parliament on 16 January and in the English Parliament on 19 March, effectively ended any prospect of a Catholic Stewart ever again ascending the throne of Great Britain. Its acceptance by Queen Anne was the catalyst for the second Jacobite Rising in 1708, and her death in 1714 led directly to the third in 1715.*

▲ *Eilean Donan*
(St Donan's Isle) has
a far from saintly past.
The ancient stronghold of
the MacKenzies of Kintail
beside Loch Duich in
Inverness-shire was
where, in 1331, the Earl
of Moray decorated the
castle walls with the
heads of 15 executed
men, and where in 1579
Donald Gorm MacDonald,
claimant to the Lordship
of the Isles, was killed by
an arrow during a siege.

At the start of the
1719 Rising, the castle
was garrisoned by
Jacobite troops, but they
weren't all Highland
clansmen for they
included 318 Spaniards.
All, though, went to their
defeat in the nearby Pass
of Glenshiel, shortly
before the castle was
blown to smithereens
by guns of the embryonic
Royal Navy.

Eilean Donan was
completely restored
in the early twentieth
century.

Aberdeen and Dundee. They might not have been very big – the whole of Glasgow in 1707 could have easily fitted into Kelvingrove Park – but they were densely packed and made up in height what they lacked in girth. In Edinburgh the tenements rose up so sheer from either side of the High Street that they blocked out the sun; one tenement, the 'great tenement', between Parliament Close and the Cowgate, soared to a height of fourteen storeys. Alongside the detached town houses of the nobility, in pride of place along the street frontages, were the premises of the burgesses, their trading premises at ground level and their comfortable residences overhead.

But above them again, on the upper floors and in the attics, and in the closes, or yards, behind the High Street, were the cramped rooms and dwellings of the 'unfree' of the burgh, ranging across the social spectrum from landladies to labourers. Such were the people who made up the bulk of the population, and yet just like the peasants in the countryside they had no rights or say in the running of their community. But whatever their station in life, all had to endure the 'downside' of town life, from chamber-pots being emptied on their heads from an upper floor (preceded or not by the cry of 'gardey-loo') to diseases like typhoid which thrived in the indifferent sanitation. St Andrews University even considered relocating to Perth in 1696 because 'the whole streets are filled with dunghill which are exceedingly noisome and ready to infect the air'. Plague was common, so too fire; the centre of

Edinburgh was devastated by such a conflagration just six years before the Union with England was trumpeted from its mercat cross.

Such then was the state of the nation at the Union. Some among the population saw the creation of the United Kingdom as the answer to the country's ills, others envisaged nothing but disaster. In truth, most of Queen Anne's Scottish subjects probably didn't much care one way or the other. As things turned out, Union brought neither benefit nor disaster in the short term; only after 1750 did Scotland begin to share in the economic miracle that came with Enlightenment and industry. By then Culloden had been fought and lost by the Stewarts.

JACOBITES AND HANOVERIANS

When the Jacobite army was finally routed on the Haughs of Cromdale, above Grantown-on-Spey, in 1690, William and Mary must have felt that their throne of Scotland was secure. When, shortly after, James VII and II was defeated at the Battle of the Boyne, in Ireland, and forced into exile once more, the joint sovereigns could be forgiven for thinking that their two other thrones, England and Ireland, were secure too and that the Stewart dynasty had been consigned to the dustbin of history. They couldn't have been more wrong.

In 1694 Mary passed away leaving William bereft – and childless. His chosen successor was his

wife's younger sister, Anne (1702-14). Unlike Mary, Anne had given birth to 17 children. Only one survived infancy and the hopes of an untroubled Protestant succession rested on the shoulders of the boy. But when he too died, in 1700, and with little prospect of Anne bearing more children, the succession was once more thrown into turmoil. Even before William fell from his horse and died in 1702, the English had made up their minds who would be next in line to the English throne after Anne; it would be Sophia, wife of the Elector of Hanover. Of all the possible candidates – and there was a ragbag of around 50 claimants scattered throughout the royal houses of Europe – Sophia alone could claim to be a Stewart (she was a granddaughter of James VI and I) *and* a Protestant.

As in 1689, Scotland was expected to fall into line. This time it wasn't minded to do so. The massacre of Glencoe and the Darien fiasco had cast such dark shadows over relations with England that Parliament was in no mood to cooperate. Their

response was the 1704 Act of Settlement, a classic piece of parliamentary obfuscation. Yes – the Scots would insist on their sovereign being descended from the House of Stewart, and yes – that person would also have to be a Protestant. But Parliament would be under no obligation to accept the person designated by the English, and their decision would be made only after the death of Queen Anne without issue. The move presented a major constitutional and political threat to England which had only recently embarked on a war with Catholic France and Spain. Just as in the days of the 'auld alliance', the threat of a Scottish army rallying to the aid of France and threatening England's northern frontier sent shock-waves through the English establishment.

And so the gloves came off. The English Parliament countered the Act of Settlement with their own Alien Act early in 1705, threatening the Scots that if they didn't accept the Hanoverian succession by Christmas Day that year they would

▲ *The Battle of Glenshiel, fought over the 9 and 10 June, 1719, brought an abrupt end to the fourth Jacobite Rising. Peter Tilleman's painting captures the action at the moment General Wightman's redcoats make their final assault on the Jacobite positions on the slopes of the Five Sisters of Kintail, by now largely abandoned by the clansmen and held only by the bemused Spaniards. The episode, though farcical, reinforced in the minds of the Hanoverian Government the need to keep a careful watch in the western Highlands, and led to the formation of the Black Watch Regiment in 1725.*

'Britain's Last Pitched Battle'
~ CULLODEN, 1746 ~

'There are reports of your having had another battle, but they only serve to increase my anxiety.'

(From a letter penned in Rome by James Frances Edward Stewart, the 'Pretender', to his son Carluccio, Prince Charles Edward Stewart, six weeks after Culloden. The letter is signed 'James R' - James Rex.)

On 16 April 1746, on a windswept muir a little to the east of Inverness, Prince Charles Edward Stuart's brave Jacobite soldiers were mercilessly cut down by the army of King George II. The Battle of Culloden proved the death-knell for the Jacobite cause. It also proved to be the last pitched battle fought on British soil.

There wouldn't have been a battle at all if Bonnie Prince Charlie had heeded the advice of his generals. Lord George Murray, his right-hand man, had urged withdrawal into the mountains from where they could carry out a guerrilla war, much as Bruce had done all those centuries before. The Jacobites were after all heavily outnumbered, barely 6000 men, exhausted and half-starved after their long march from Derby, up against 9000 crack Government troops, well fed and watered and ready for the fray. But Charles had stopped listening; ever since being overruled at Derby, he had retreated more and more into his shell, much preferring the company of his mistress, Clementina Walkinshaw, to that of his generals, and still stubbornly pinning his faith on the French riding to his rescue.

And there matters rested in the early morning of 16 April as the main Jacobite army bivouacked on the boggy ground of Culloden Muir. Barely had the men sunk into their rain-sodden sleep than news arrived of the enemy's approach. It was

decision time – fight or withdraw. Murray's protest that Culloden was 'not proper ground for Highlanders' (it was flat and not helpful to the main weapon in the Jacobite armoury, the Highland Charge) was brushed aside by Prince Charles: 'God damn it! Are my orders still disobeyed?'

▲ *The Jacobite flag flutters at the battlefield where over 1000 of Bonnie Prince Charlie's troops laid down their lives for the Stewart cause. A few days later, at Ruthven Barracks, near Kingussie, the ragged remnant of his men received a message from their erstwhile leader to look after their own safety 'in the best way they can'. Chevalier Johnstone expressed the emotions of all those present that day: 'This answer was as inconsiderate in Charles as it was heart-breaking to the brave men who had sacrificed themselves in his cause.' The dream had finally ended.*

They would stay and take on all that his cousin, William Augustus, Duke of Cumberland, could throw at them.

Precisely what Cumberland had at his disposal soon became clear enough. By mid morning 15 infantry regiments, 800 dragoons and a powerful artillery train had filed onto the field of battle 'like a deep sullen river'. They formed up on the north-eastern edge of the muir, their red coats and bayoneted muskets occasionally

glinting in the infrequent visits of the pale spring sunshine. Across the few hundred yards of blasted heath to the west were the Prince's men, including regiments from France and Ireland but mostly made up of Highland clansmen clad in tartan and wielding broadswords and targes – Camerons, Chisholms, Farquharsons, Frasers, Gordons, MacDonalds, MacIntoshes, MacLarens, MacLaughlans, MacLeans and Stewarts. As the betartaned Prince rode among them shouting words of encouragement, the heavens opened. It made a bad situation worse, for now the Highlanders would have to charge with the rain driving into their faces.

It was Cumberland who made the first move, shortly after luncheon; a portly young man, he wasn't going to be put off his food by a battle! A devastating opening salvo from his field-guns brought immediate death and destruction. When one young man standing close to the Prince was cut in two by a cannonball, Charles at once withdrew to the comparative safety of the rear. For fully 30 minutes Major Belford's guns poured their murderous contents into the Jacobite lines until Lord Murray, despairing of the Prince ever issuing the instruction to attack, himself gave the order.

Alas, by now carnage and confusion were running riot. Murray, leading the right flank, immediately found difficulty getting his message through to the rest of the front line; indeed, the MacDonalds out on the left may never have heard it. The great surge forward that was the celebrated Highland Charge quickly became a broken, ragged line, mercilessly exposed to the Hanoverians' muskets ranged before them. It was said that the men of Pulteney's Regiment 'hardly took their firelocks from their shoulders'. Many a man was cruelly cut down before he had had the chance to put his broadsword to its bloody work.

Then at last they engaged, the MacIntoshes crashing into the Hanoverian front line first, closely followed by Lord Murray's men. Barrel's Regiment buckled under the pressure, and 500 Jacobites stormed through 'in a cloud' to engage Sempill's Regiment in the second line. All was bedlam, shouts of anger and cries of despair ascending into the afternoon air in equal measure. One redcoat later described his experience:

It was dreadful to see the enemies' swords circling in the air. And to see the officers of the army, some cutting with their swords, others pushing with spontoons, the sergeants running their halberds into their opponents' throats, the men ramming their fixed bayonets up to the sockets.

As Lord Murray fought his way out of the fray to bring in the Jacobite second line, those still left standing from the first had not only to endure the swords, spontoons, halberds and bayonets confronting them but also the relentless hail of bullets pouring in from their exposed right flank, mostly from the muskets of Campbell's Regiment, the only Highland clan fighting on the Government side. Belford's guns too continued to wreak havoc, the grapeshot making 'open lanes through them, the men dropping down by wholesale'.

With the horror unfolding before their very eyes, the MacDonalds finally charged into the mêlée. But, cruelly exposed and short of muskets, they too dropped like flies before briefly coming to grips with St Clair's Regiment on the Hanoverian right. The cause by now though was clearly lost. With the humiliating spectacle of his faithful clansmen reduced to throwing stones at the Government troops in his eyes, Charles turned and left the field. The battle was over in under an hour.

That wasn't the end of the carnage though – far from it. As the remnants of Charles's army attempted to flee the field, Cumberland's redcoats advanced, stamping their way over the piles of Jacobite dead, 1000 in all. Unleashing his men on a savage bloody aftermath, Cumberland was later able to report back to his father, the king, that a further 1000 rebels had been slaughtered, as against just 50 redcoats. Belatedly he had celebrated his 25th birthday (15 April) in fine style. A relieved House of Hanover named the delightful flower Sweet William after him; his many detractors called him 'Stinkin' Billie' after a weed. The Highlanders knew him only as 'the Butcher'.

It was a ghastly sight to see some dead, some tumbling and wallowing in their blood, others not quite dead crying for mercy. We followed and slew them for three miles till the Dragoons were quite gutted with gore. (Private Will Aiken's account of the bloody aftermath of Culloden.)

▲ David Morier (1705-70) was the official war-artist for the Hanoverian King George II (1724-60), and this is his depiction of the bloody Battle of Culloden, which he entitled simply: 'An Incident in the Rebellion of 1745'. Some incident! Over a thousand dead on the battlefield, and, as it transpired, the end of the dream for the House of Stewart.

be treated as 'aliens', with all the dire economic consequences such ostracism would bring. The 10 dukes, 3 marquesses, 75 earls, 17 viscounts and 45 lords representing the people of Scotland shifted uncomfortably in their seats in Parliament House, in Edinburgh's Royal Mile. It was all very well standing up for the nation's rights and freedoms, but if one was reduced to penury as a result..? And so these largely unelected representatives grasped the olive-branch offered with the Alien Act – the promise of full constitutional and political union with England. Within two years Queen Anne was ruling over a United Kingdom and the House of Hanover was hovering in the wings waiting to enter the stage. One person was determined that day would never dawn.

The '08 Rising

James Francis Edward Stewart was just an infant when he was smuggled out of England by his father James VII and II in 1689. Now as the ink dried on the Treaty of Union, and with his father dead, he saw himself as the rightful king, James VIII of Scotland and III of England. Queen Anne mocked

her half-brother: 'he who pretends to my throne', she declared, hence James's other title 'the Pretender'. He wasn't long in launching his first bid for the throne.

At the outset of 1707 Louis XIV's France was in a bad way, having recently suffered another humiliating defeat at the hands of England. In the bloody aftermath of the Battle of Ramillies, Louis sought for help wherever it could be got, and his spies assured him that the glowing embers of Jacobitism, particularly in Scotland, provided one such source. And so it was that in March 1708 a French fleet bearing the Pretender and 5000 troops slipped through the 'British' Navy's blockade of Dunkirk and headed for Scotland. That was their sole success. Admiral Forbin, reluctant and despairing from the start, allowed only a handful of men to go ashore, at Pittenweem on the Fife coast, before beating a hasty retreat as soon as Admiral Bing's men o' war appeared on the horizon. James's pleas to be put ashore fell on deaf ears and by the end of the month he was back in his adopted land. An English prisoner who had witnessed his departure also observed his return:

We saw the person called the Pretender land, a tall, slight young man, pale smooth face, with a blue feather in his hat, and a star on his cloak; at his first going off they [the French] mightily huzzaed him with *Vive le Roi*, but were very mute at his coming back.

The '08 was over before it had started.

The '15

And there matters remained until the moment in August 1714 the people of the United Kingdom had been anticipating, or dreading: the death of Queen Anne and the accession of her distant cousin, George I (1714-27), the Elector of Hanover. Most poignantly for Scots, it heralded the end of the Stewart dynasty after three and a half centuries. As the new sovereign packed his bags for London, the Pretender made his second bid for the throne.

This time there was little hope of French assistance, for the ageing King Louis had recently negotiated a hard-won peace with the United Kingdom. This time James knew that support had to come primarily from within his kingdoms. He was in luck. Almost from the time King George set foot in England (he never bothered to visit Scotland) he succeeded in alienating key supporters in his government, among them the Earl of Mar. Mar, having accepted that his toadying to the new sovereign wasn't going to get him anywhere, headed back to his ancestral estate in Strathdon. And there at Braemar on 6 September 1715 he raised James's standard. He was confident of success, certainly in Scotland, and quite possibly in England and Wales too. The pockets of Roman Catholicism in the Highlands and Islands, the Borders and Dumfriesshire, were unashamedly Jacobite, and increasingly so were the Episcopalians, at their strongest in the north-east. Western clans like the MacDonalds could always be relied on to fight the Campbells, and as the Campbell chief, the Duke of Argyll, was also the commander of King George's army in Scotland, there was even more incentive for the MacDonalds to settle a few old scores. Only in Glasgow and the south-west, with its strong Covenanting roots and links with Protestant Ulster, was there scarcely any support for the Jacobite cause. The Edinburgh establishment would do what they were best at –

wait and see which way the wind was blowing.

It blew strongly for Mar in the early days of the Rising. Supporters flocked in droves to his standard. By the time he was approaching Stirling Castle, he had 8000 men, outnumbering Argyll by 4:1. It was the best chance the Stewarts had in the entire Jacobite-Hanoverian conflict to regain their throne, better even than Killiecrankie – and yet Mar blew it. More at home playing politics than soldiers, Mar hesitated at the vital moment. Rather than take Scotland while it lay at his mercy, he despatched part of his force into northern England to help the Jacobites there. By the time he had plucked up courage to tackle Argyll head on, the ratio was more like 2:1. Even then Mar should easily have taken the honours that cold November day at Sheriffmuir. He didn't. The two armies spent more time running away from each other than doing battle.

There's some say that we wan,
Some say that they wan,
Some say that none wan at a', man.
But one thing I'm sure,
That at Sheriffmuir
A battle there was which I saw, man.
And we ran and they ran,
 and they ran and we ran,
And we ran and they ran awa', man.
(From a contemporary ballad recording the Battle of Sheriffmuir, 1715.)

The whole desultory affair fizzled out into a draw, and when Mar at last departed the field he

▲ *There were roads of a sort in the Highlands before the eighteenth century, but it was the military situation during the Jacobite troubles that led to the road network we still largely rely on. General George Wade, the man responsible, secured from his Hanoverian paymasters the necessary funding to establish new routes – Fort William to Inverness, Dunkeld to Inverness, Crieff to Dalnacardoch and Dalwhinnie to Fort Augustus.*

Roads need bridges, and one of the finest is the Invercauld Bridge over the River Dee, near Braemar in Aberdeenshire. Built by Wade's successor as road builder, Major Caulfeild, in 1753, it is now by-passed, but the road of which it formed a part, built to facilitate troop movements between Blairgowrie and Fort George, east of Inverness, is still largely in use today as the A93 and A939.

'Had ye seen these roads afore they were made, You'd hold up your hands and bless General Wade.'

(Attributed to Major William Caulfeild, Wade's baggage master and inspector of roads.)

'A Symphony in Stone'

~ EDINBURGH'S NEW TOWN ~

'You Mr Somerville are a young man and may probably live to see all these fields covered with houses, forming a splendid and magnificent city.'

(Lord Provost Drummond, in conversation with the Revd Thomas Somerville, in 1725)

The plan was designed by a young, relatively unknown architect almost 250 years ago, an Edinburgh boy who would achieve very little else of moment in his sad life. But what a memorial to leave behind – Edinburgh New Town, perhaps the best example of classical town planning in the world.

The inspiration behind Edinburgh's New Town was George Drummond, the city's Lord Provost. In 1725, in his first heady days in office, he stared out across the Nor' Loch towards the low ridge called Barefoot's Parks, and envisioned the open fields spread out before him one day hosting a 'splendid and magnificent city', of broad level streets and handsome well-ordered houses. In the euphoria following the creation of the United Kingdom in 1707, Scotland's capital, so Drummond felt, deserved a centre reflecting its status as Great Britain's second city.

For there to be a 'new' town there must be an 'old' one. And there was – Provost Drummond's own place of work and residence, the higgledy-piggledy, steep, narrow, overcrowded and unbelievably dirty wynds and closes of the medieval burgh, where the high-born and the low-life rubbed shoulders, a city claustrophobically constrained within its tight defensive corset, the Flodden Wall, its inhabitants having nowhere to go but up, up into the sky, which they did to perfection. Robertson's Land, the 'great tenement' behind Parliament Hall, rose through fourteen storeys!

Provost Drummond had completed his fourth term in office by the time the proposals for a 'new town' were finally published in 1752; the wheels of local democracy turned just as slowly then, it would seem. And he had retired by the time a competition for final plans was announced in 1766. Indeed, he died that same year, before hearing who would realise his dream.

He would have been delighted with the panel's choice. Everything about James Craig's winning scheme proclaimed the vision of the new United Kingdom; the names of the streets and squares – Hanover (the dynasty that created the United Kingdom), George (its reigning sovereign), Queen (after his queen, Charlotte), Frederick and Princes (after three royal princes), Thistle and Rose (after the nations' emblems), St Andrew and St George (their respective patron saints; Charlotte later insisted that her name replace England's saint). Even the original plan (it was subsequently altered) submitted by the 22-year-old Craig resembled the Union Jack, one central square – George's Circus, what else – with the streets emanating from it!

The New Town wasn't intended for any old 'Tom, Dick or Harry'; it was to be a fashionable suburb, the preserve of 'people of fortune and a certain rank'. The necessary tradesmen, craftsmen and suppliers would be confined to the side streets, and the household servants and coachmen to the mewses in the narrow lanes behind. Architects of the calibre of Robert Adam, who contributed Register House, at the east end of Princes Street, and the north side of Charlotte Square, one of his truly great masterpieces, were invited by the aspiring owners to design houses that would grace this grand vision. It took a little time for the idea to take off – no-one likes to be first in 'the scheme' and surrounded by a builder's yard, do they? But gradually the 'magnificent city' rose up, and spread out north and west down to the Water of Leith and east towards Calton Hill. Adam, Playfair and the rest took Craig's basic melody and created 'a symphony in stone', despite the best efforts of the Edinburgh vandals!

In the night betwixt the 8th and 9th of July, some evil-disposed persons broke and destroyed several pieces of hewn work at the buildings carrying on at the west end of Princes Street, and likewise many work-tools. In order to lead to a discovery of the person guilty of said offences, the Lord Provost and Magistrates hereby offer a reward of TWENTY GUINEAS.

(A notice in the *Edinburgh Evening Courant*, Sat July 14, 1778.)

As the New Town filled, so the Old Town emptied. The separation was not without its pain. By 1823, Lord Cockburn was bemoaning the fact that the New Town had 'altered the style of living, obliterated local arrangements, and destroyed a thousand associations'. How often has that been said since, of communities that have been together for years, only to be broken up and dispersed, all in the name of progress?

Today, the 'Old' and the 'New' happily co-exist, and together form the busy heart of a great metropolitan city, each contributing its own unique blend of buildings and spaces. In 1999 Edinburgh Old and New Town became a World Heritage Site. How George Drummond would have loved that moment.

must have known he was sealing his sovereign's fate. The news from England that the English Jacobites had been routed at Preston simply served to ram home the point. The '15 was over, and with it the best chance the Stewarts had of reclaiming the throne.

The '19

Not that the Jacobite cause was lost for good. There were still those who would dearly have loved to see the Hanoverians sent packing. There were also countries other than France who saw in the Jacobites a potential source of irritation for the British Government. And that is how one of the most bizarre episodes in Scottish history, the '19, came about.

Poor Philip V of Spain found himself in deep trouble in 1718. A dramatic rearrangement of the deck chairs now saw Britain and France in an unholy alliance against him. A Jacobite diversion back in Britain would serve very nicely. The stratagem agreed with the Pretender was for a two-pronged landing in Britain, the main one in the far south-west of England and a diversionary one on Scotland's west coast. But as with the '08, a combination of weather, inept planning and half-heartedness combined to make the whole affair a farce. The main force never even got within sight of Cornwall, let alone landed on it. The diversionary force, however, did make it through the Atlantic storms – and that is how 400 bemused Spaniards found themselves half way up a mountain in Glenshiel on a warm sunny day in June 1719, staring at British redcoats freshly arrived from Inverness. By the end of the day, their Jacobite comrades had fled the battlefield, leaving them little choice but to surrender. By the time they were repatriated, Spain had patched up its quarrel with Britain and France – and nothing more was heard from the Jacobites for another 26 years.

The '45

On 23 July 1745 a small boat beached on the rain-sodden island of Eriskay in the Western Isles. First

ashore was a tall 25-year-old Italian gentleman rejoicing in the name of Charles Edward Louis John Casimir Silvester Xavier Maria Stewart. We know him better as 'Bonnie Prince Charlie'.

Almost from the time he could talk, Charles had one burning ambition in life – to reclaim the throne of Great Britain for his father, the Pretender. When the two parted tearfully in 1744, Charles promised his father: 'I go, Sire, in search of three crowns, which I doubt not to have the honour and happiness of laying at your Majesty's feet. If I fail, your next sight of me shall be in my coffin.'

Alas, the two were destined never to see each other again.

Charles must have thought that the fates were smiling kindly upon him as he left his father's court in Rome. The French, still smarting from defeat at Dettingen the previous year (the last battle, incidentally, to involve a British sovereign, George II (1727-60), in person), had resolved to invade Britain and install Charles as regent on behalf of his ageing father. But by the time he arrived at the Channel the fates had all but deserted him. The French invasion fleet assembled to carry him to his destiny had been scattered to the four winds in violent storms. Charles should have turned back there and then, but with characteristic stubbornness he soldiered on. Sailing secretly out

▲ Edinburgh New Town was begun over 200 years ago, took over 100 years in the building and extended over one square mile. The city's lord provost, George Drummond, the gentleman behind its creation, envisioned a 'splendid and magnificent city' reflecting the Scottish capital's status as the United Kingdom's 'second city'. He died before his dream could be realised, but those who visit the broad streets and graceful crescents today can enjoy what is perhaps the best example of classical town planning in Europe – truly a 'symphony in stone'.

of Nantes in early July of the following year, 1745, with just two small ships (one of which was soon wrecked), few arms and men – and crucially no French support – he landed on Eriskay to be urged by those greeting him to return home. He replied, 'I am come home'. By the time Prince Charles raised his father's standard at Glenfinnan, at the head of Loch Shiel, on 19 August, he had 1300 men.

Oh, what heady days they were and what excitement there must have been in the ranks as they threaded their way eastward through the mountains round past mighty Fort William and on towards Perth and the Lowlands, their progress made all the more easy thanks to General Wade's brand-new military roads! By mid September Prince Charles was holding court, and captivating the ladies with his charm, amid the grand surroundings of Holyroodhouse, ancient palace of the Stewarts. The sound of merriment therein was in stark contrast to the stony silence emanating from the Hanoverian garrison in the castle barely a mile away.

If only Charles had heeded the wise counsel of his lieutenants who urged him to consolidate his hold on Scotland before venturing south into England, then things might have turned out so differently. But he didn't. He was anxious to move on, and his daring victory over General 'Johnny' Cope's redcoats at Prestonpans in the early morning of 21 September, all over in the time it takes to boil three eggs, spurred him on even faster. 15 November, Carlisle; 30 November – Manchester; 4 December – Derby. And there beside the swirling River Trent he halted. The truth was slowly dawning on the would-be regent. There had been little outpouring of Jacobite sympathy on the long march south, little practical support. Even worse, there was no news that France had invaded England's south coast. With General Wade's brigade in their rear and the Duke of Cumberland's seasoned troops newly returned from the Continent, the Jacobite leaders, most of them from the Scottish Highlands, felt uncomfortably vulnerable. Carry on to London – death or glory – or beat a tactical withdrawal whilst there was still time. For once, Charles's stubbornness failed to win the day. They headed for home.

And there at Culloden, east of Inverness, on

16 April 1746 the remnants of Bonnie Prince Charlie's Jacobite army fell before the bayoneted muskets of George II's redcoats. Two thousand men, who had worn the blue bonnet and white cockade with pride, lay dead or dying on the windswept moor. And trampled into the boggy ground that awful April day, alongside the discarded broadswords and targes of the clansmen, was the last, lingering hope that Scotland might remain sovereign and free. The last pitched battle fought on British soil was over.

NORTH BRITAIN

Culloden is seen by many today as yet another war between Scotland and England, often mentioned in the same breath as Bannockburn (1314). It was emphatically not. Culloden was the culmination of a bloody civil war, the first to be fought in the new United Kingdom of Great Britain and Ireland, in which nationality played only a minor part. Jacobitism was a confusing flag of convenience for people with differing agendas – for those who simply wished to see the return of the ancient House of Stewart, for those who sought to overthrow Presbyterianism, and for those who despised the Union for whatever reason. Highlander was set against Lowlander, Scot against Scot. There were even members from the same

Fort George, beside the Moray Firth, lies a few miles east of Inverness and even fewer miles from the battlefield of Culloden. The Hanoverian garrison fortress was built in the bloody aftermath of that dreadful encounter as part of the military measures designed to prevent such a Rising happening again.

The fort took over 20 years to build and cost over £200,000, the equivalent of well in excess of £1 billion at today's prices. It was the single biggest construction project the Highlands had ever seen, overtaken only by Telford's Caledonian Canal early in the following century. And like Telford's canal, Major-general Skinner's Fort George still functions as originally intended.

Prince Charles Edward Stewart, painted by David Antonio. 'Bonnie Prince Charlie' was a youthful 25 years old when he first set foot on Scottish soil on 23 July 1745. He left it barely a year later, never to return. The 'bonnie prince' grew into a bitter ingrate and ended his days in 1788 an alcoholic on the streets of Rome, a century almost to the day that his grandfather, King James VII and II, had fled his British throne.

'Scotland's National Bard'
~ ROBERT BURNS ~

'I never had the least thought of turning Poet till I once got heartily in love, and then rhyme and song were, in a manner, the spontaneous language of my heart'.

(Robert Burns introducing his first poem, O! once I lov'd a bonnie lass, *1773)*

▲ *Robert Burns, portrayed posthumously by his good friend and fellow-traveller, politically and emotionally, Alexander Nasmyth (1758-1840). The love of nature and landscape that both friends shared is wonderfully expressed in Nasmyth's masterpiece.*

not just his contemporaries, and not just Scots, but people yesterday and today, and the world over.

Robert Burns's poems run the full gamut of human emotion. They reach into the heart and soul of each one of us. They show a humour, a warmth, a tenderness:

Wee, sleekit, cow'rin, tim'rous beastie,
O what a panic's in thy breastie!
Thou need na start awa sae hasty,
Wi' bickering brattle!
I wad be laith to rin an' chase thee
Wi' murd'ring pattle!

(*To a Mouse, on turning her up in her nest with the plough, November 1785.*)

They reveal an inner rage, a contempt for those in authority, for the pompous, hypocritical, sanctimonious bigot:

O ye wha are sae guid yoursel,
Sae pious and sae holy,
Ye've nought to do but mark and tell
Your neibour's fauts and folly!
Whase life is like a weel-gaun mill,
Supplied wi' store o' water:
The heaped happer's ebbing still,
An' still the clap plays clatter:

(*Address to the unco guid, or the rigidly righteous,* 1786.)

They rail against injustice, and speak up for the defenceless individual:

Then let us pray that come it may,
As come it will for a' that;
That sense and worth, o'er a' the earth,
May bear the gree [prize], and a' that.
For a' that and a' that,
It's comin yet, for a' that,
That man to man, the warld o'er
Shall brothers be for a' that.

(*For a' that and a' that,* 1794.)

And they weave words into wonderful tales that hold the child in us

He came into the world 'in a blast of Januar wind' on 25 January 1759, and left it on a warm summer's day 37 years later. The child born into poverty in the 'auld clay biggin' in Alloway village, near Ayr, laboured as ploughboy, flax-

dresser, farmer and exciseman, and died still a pauper in a meagre rented room in the town of Dumfries on 21 July 1796. His was a short, sad life, and yet this poor ploughboy contrived through his poetry to enrich the lives of so many,

▲ *Cutty Sark, from* Tam o' Shanter, *engraved by John Faed.*

Burns is to Scotland – her greatest poet. And yet this simple Ayrshire 'lad o' pairts' is greater even than that, for he has come to be revered across the continents, not just in English-speaking countries but in so many others as well; no country other than his own holds him in as great affection as Russia. What Englishman today can tell you off the tip of their tongue on what day William Shakespeare was born, or what German Bach or Beethoven? Yet as every 25 January arrives, all over the world men and women 'pipe in' the haggis and raise their glass of whisky to his 'immortal memory'. He wrote in his native Scots, but his words were universal.

> Should auld acquaintance be forgot.
> And never brought to min'?
> Should auld acquaintance be forgot,
> And auld lang syne?
> For auld lang syne, my dear.
> For auld lang syne,
> We'll tak a cup o' kindness yet,
> For auld lang syne.

(*Auld Lang Syne*, 1788.)

in thrall to this day, none more so than the bewitching *Tam o' Shanter*, written by the dying Burns in a single day:

> Tam tint his reason a' thegither,
> And roars out, 'Weel done, Cutty-sark!'
> And in an instant all was dark:
> And scarcely had he Maggie rallied,
> When out the hellish legion sallied.

(*Tam o' Shanter*, 1790.)

But above all they speak of love, of sheer, unadulterated passion of a young man for a pretty maid. It was love that first brought 'the heaven-taught ploughman' into poetry, and love that sustained him throughout his brief life.

> O, once I lov'd a bonnie lass,
> Aye, and I love her still;
> And whilst that virtue warms my breast
> I love my handsome Nell.

Burns was just 14 when he penned those words, perhaps his first fumbling foray into poetry; 23 years on, and with the breath fast departing his fevered body, he wrote his last verse with that same loving passion in his heart:

> Then come, thou fairest of the fair,
> Those wonted smiles, O let me share;
> And by thy beauteous self I swear,

> No love but thine my heart shall know.

(*Fairest maid on Devon banks*, 1796.)

Betweenwhiles Burns brought forth from his tortured heart some of the finest poems and ballads of love ever written in the English language, among them *Ae Fond Kiss*, and perhaps his best known, *Ye Banks and Braes* (1791):

> Ye banks and braes o'
>   Bonnie Doon,
> How can ye bloom sae
>   fresh and fair?
> How can ye chant, ye
>   little birds,
> And I sae weary fu' o'
>   care?
> Thoul't break my heart,
>   thou warbling bird,
> That wantons thro' the
>   flowering thorn:
> Thou minds me o'
>   departed joys,
> Departed never to return.

As Dante is to Italy, and Yeats is to Ireland, so Robert

▲ *Robert Burns 'in his own write' – the poet's original manuscript of* The Poet's Welcome to his Love-Begotten Daughter *(or* Welcome to his 'dear-bocht Bess), *composed in 1784 when he was 25.*

▶ 'Princes Street with the
Commencement of the
Building of the Royal
Institution', painted by
Alexander Nasmyth in
1825. Nasmyth was not
only a brilliant painter
of nature (see his portrait
of Burns on page 140),
he was also an architect
in his own right, as this
fascinating study of
Edinburgh's rising New
Town shows. Both he and
the architect of the Royal
Institution (now the Royal
Scottish Academy),
William Playfair (1790-
1857), were 'stars of the
Scottish Enlightenment'.

Whether Geordie Boyd
considered himself 'an
enlightened star' is
another matter, but it
is said that Edinburgh's
famous Mound, linking
the New Town with the
Old, began as a short-
cut in 1781, enabling
George Boyd's New Town
customers to continue
to patronise his tailoring
premises in the Old Town;
whence the Mound's
nickname – 'Geordie
Boyd's Brig'.

family who fought each other on that April day. If
anyone doubts this, read the sentiments by no less
a symbol of Scottish national identity than the
General Assembly of the Church of Scotland itself,
as expressed in a letter to the victor of Culloden
five weeks after the battle and at the very moment
the Duke of Cumberland was visiting untold
misery on the Highlands:

> The Church of Scotland are under peculiar
> obligations to offer their most thankful
> acknowledgements to Almighty God, who has
> raised you up to be the brave defender of your
> Royal Father's throne, the happy restorer of our
> peace, and at this time a guardian of all our
> secular and civil interests.

The faltering start to the Union had certainly
played into Jacobite hands. Economic benefits had
been few and far between, leading to frustration,
disillusionment – and eventually civil unrest. Two
notable urban riots had taken place between the '15
and the '45 – the Glasgow Malt Tax Riot of 1725, in
protest against the latest wheeze by Great Britain's
first Prime Minister, Robert Walpole, to squeeze yet
more blood out of the stone by extending the duty
to Scotland, and the peculiar Porteous Affair in
Edinburgh in 1736, sparked off when the blustering

captain of the city guard fired on a crowd gathered
for the execution of two popular smugglers, killing
four and injuring eleven others.

But by degrees the economic situation
improved. Economic indicators of this upturn
include the major rise in production of linen cloth,
'the staple and chief commodity of Scotland'
according to one contemporary – up threefold,
thanks to Government subsidies. This was the time
too when Glasgow began its prodigious growth
from small-time medieval burgh to wealthy
cosmopolitan city, thanks to its crafty exploitation
of the rapidly growing tobacco trade with England's
American colonies, an access officially denied it
prior to the Union. In the three decades from 1740,
the city fathers took Glasgow's stake in the British
tobacco trade from 10 per cent to a staggering 52
per cent. New banks joined the Bank of Scotland
(founded 1695) in assisting the wealth creators,
including the Royal Bank of Scotland in 1727 and
the British Linen Company in the very year
Culloden was fought. Within 20 years of Culloden,
the total assets of the Scottish banks had catapulted
from £600,000 to almost £4,000,000. Small
wonder, then, to discover that *Rule Britannia*, that
rousing celebration in song of the new Great

Britain, was composed by a Scot, James Thomson. Loss of national identity was but a small price to pay for increased prosperity.

The very name 'Scotland' was itself under threat after the Union. The London Government did its utmost to promote the concept of 'North Britain' in a vain attempt to rewrite history and devalue the contribution of the junior partner in the marriage. They never once thought to use the phrase 'South Britain' in place of England! Such arrogance merely served to heighten the Scots' determination to succeed in making 'a good fist' of things. The first issue of the *Scots Magazine,* published in January 1739, summed the situation up perfectly:

Though in many things calculated for the good of Great Britain, Scotland is little more than nominally considered, her distance from the seat of monarchy, instead of dispiriting, should prompt her sons to compensate for that misfortune by an extraordinary zeal in her service, to show themselves equal to the present disadvantage of their situation, and by an earnest exertion of their talents, revive that universal esteem which Scotland so justly acquired among her neighbours by the valour and learning of our ancestors.

They were prophetic words. Scotland was on the cusp of a truly astonishing new dawn, the 'Age of Enlightenment', a dazzling period of sustained intellectual thought and artistic creativity that almost set the heather alight and had the eyes of the world gazing in admiration on this once poor land on the edge of Europe. It had even the great Voltaire proclaiming: 'It is to Edinburgh that we must look for our intellectual tastes'.

The 'stars' of the Enlightenment were mostly university professors, ministers of the Kirk or lawyers – 'teachers, preachers, and pleaders'. Men of the calibre of David Hume, Scotland's greatest philosopher who put the 'light' into Enlightenment, Adam Smith, whose *Inquiry into the Nature and Causes of the Wealth of Nations,* published in 1776, established economics as a social science, James Hutton, the father of modern geology, the pioneering engineers James Watt and Thomas Telford, William Adam and his son Robert in the architectural sphere, the artists Henry Raeburn and Allan Ramsay, towering figures from

the world of literature like Robert Burns and Walter Scott – the list is almost endless.

But they didn't just materialise out of thin air. They were the natural products of an education system second-to-none in Europe, a system inspired by John Knox and his Reformers two centuries before and founded on the fundamental principle of universality, intellectual access for all – 'a grammar school in every parish, a high school in every town, a university in every city'. England in 1750 was still thirled to its two medieval universities, Oxford and Cambridge; tiny Scotland had five – St Andrews, Glasgow, Edinburgh and the two Aberdeen colleges. The Scots, it was claimed, were probably the best educated people in the world.

If a universal and respected education system provided the foundation for the Enlightenment, the circumstances in which Scots found themselves post-Union provided the spur. The Scots have a reputation for raising their game against the 'big guns', and in the eighteenth century they came no bigger than England. David Hume in 1757 posed the question: 'Is it not strange…we should really be the People most distinguished for Literature in Europe?', and then answered it with the observation: 'We have lost our Princes, our Parliaments, our independent Government, even the presence of our chief Nobility.

It was as if the departure of these stuffy bureaucracies, these overbearing individuals, had lifted a great burden from the shoulders of the

▲ *'Bird neuk' is an apt description of the rocky perch of Culzean (Gaelic cuil eun). And perched alongside the birds these past eight centuries has been a castle of the Kennedy clan. The present edifice, though, is not really a castle at all, but a handsome country seat built for the tenth Earl of Cassilis barely 200 years ago. Two of Scotland's great architects and artists, Robert Adam and Alexander Nasmyth, combined to create a house and landscape worthy of that remarkable age.*

'Giants in the Land'

~ THE STARS OF SCOTLAND'S ENLIGHTENMENT ~

'There is nothing which is not the subject of debate'

(David Hume in his Treatise upon Human Nature, *published in 1738)*

Sir Walter Scott called them 'giants in the land', the great men of the Scottish Enlightenment – philosophers and physicians, architects and engineers, each in their own way helping to take Scotland, and Europe, further away from the medieval world and forward into new pastures.

The 'giant' of them all, the man who put the 'light' into Enlightenment, was unquestionably David Hume. Born in Edinburgh in 1711, he abandoned his law studies and left home, lured to France by his love of history and philosophy. Three years of quiet contemplation resulted in his *Treatise upon Human Nature*, the first of his outstanding contributions to philosophical thought. It was initially received with disdain; Hume himself described it falling 'dead-born from the press', but it is often the case that change is the hardest thing to accept. And Hume's philosophical theories were certainly new – and provocative. A confirmed atheist in a profoundly religious age, when the Professor of Moral Philosophy at Edinburgh University was routinely expected to teach 'the Being and perfections of the one true God, the nature of the angels and of the soul of man', Hume took absolutely nothing for granted. He was an empiricist, who sought for truth only through proven fact. Little wonder, then, he was turned down twice for the Edinburgh chair!

Undaunted by the initial reception to his theories, Hume persevered, and in time his profound scepticism and questioning of orthodoxy shook his contemporaries and made them likewise question the fundamental concepts on which all knowledge and belief is founded. Although he was a friend of many 'enlightened' Scots, he was at the same time the figure who commanded their greatest respect. When he died in his native city in 1776, his reputation as the greatest philosopher Scotland had ever produced was firmly established. He remains so to this day.

...approaching as nearly to the idea of

a perfectly wise and virtuous man as perhaps the nature of human frailty will permit.

(Adam Smith, on hearing the news of the death of David Hume, in 1776).

The name of Adam Smith, a good friend of Hume, is perhaps the best known today. The son of a customs official in Kirkcaldy, Smith earned his reputation as the founder of modern economic science when his *Inquiry into the Nature and Causes of the Wealth of Nations* was published in 1776. Although in it he proposed that the invisible hand of market forces was a major factor in the development of trade – a view that prompted Karl Marx to label him a 'pioneer of capitalism' and one that has made him the unwitting champion of modern 'free-marketeers' – Smith was no advocate of unfettered 'laissez-faire' economics. On the contrary this 'giant' was by all accounts a man of benign disposition whose economic views were informed by the basic philosophy that 'sympathy is the foundation of all our moral sentiments'. In discussing the iniquitous practice of serfdom in the mining industry in his *Wealth of Nations*, Smith wrote: 'The work done by slaves, though it appears to cost only their maintenance is, in the end, the dearest of any.' No cold, calculating champion of the free market could have written that.

Both Hume and Smith, though,

would claim that the 'father' of the Scottish Enlightenment was a man most of us will have never heard of; Francis Hutcheson (1694-1746), son of a Presbyterian minister from Armagh. A predecessor of Adam Smith in the Chair of Moral Philosophy at Glasgow, Hutcheson's particular philosophy – that man has a distinct moral conscience – is said also to have influenced Thomas Jefferson when he drafted the Declaration of Independence. But it was not so much his writings that excited but his inspiration as a teacher. He was the first to break with tradition and lecture in English, not Latin, and Adam Smith was just one of many who benefitted from his erudition.

Enlightenment was to be found in fields other than philosophy. Everywhere, enquiring minds were questioning the old order and breaking new ground – literally, in the case of the agricultural improvers. In the field of medicine, the faculty at Edinburgh University, founded in 1726, soon became the leading medical school in the English-speaking world, thanks chiefly to four 'giant' Monros: John, who helped establish it, and his son, grandson and great-grandson, all called Alexander, who ran the school of anatomy much like a family business for well over 100 years. They were joined by other 'giants', among them the Lanark-born obstetrician, William Smellie, the gynaecologist William Hunter, and Andrew Duncan, who inspired the building of the Royal Asylum (now the Royal Edinburgh Hospital). Together they helped lay the foundations of modern medicinal practice.

Foundations of a different sort were laid by Scotland's architectural and engineering 'giants'. Robert Adam's confident grasp of classical architecture and ornament made the Kirkcaldy lad the most sought-after architect of his day, the designer of great country seats like Culzean, and city streets such as Charlotte Square, in Edinburgh's New Town. John Rennie, from East Lothian farming stock, became a great civil and mechanical engineer, building anything from corn mills to canals, dyeworks to docks. In his bridge-building he dispensed with the old-fashioned hump-backed variety and created level bridges so new that, at the official opening of his Musselburgh bridge in 1805, the 'Honest Toun's' provost declared: 'That's nae brig at a'. Ye dinnae ken when your on it or aff it!'

Rennie is buried in St Paul's Cathedral, London. His nearest rival, Thomas Telford, lies in nearby Westminster Abbey. He too designed bridges and roads, canals and harbours, and much more besides. And he became the first President of the Society of Civil Engineers; not bad for the son of an Eskdale shepherd who was educated in his local parish school. David Hume, who saw the role of family and education in one's formative years as being of vital importance to the moral life, would have been immensely proud of Telford's 'giant' achievement.

educated Scot. Freed from their stifling presence, Scots embarked on a rigorous and unfettered debate touching on all matters of the human condition – intellectual, moral and scientific. Scotland became one of the most 'clubbable' societies in Europe. All sorts of societies sprang up discussing an eclectic array of topics and issues, including the Aberdeen Philosophical Society, known as the 'Wise Club', and the even more pompous-sounding Select Society – of Edinburgh of course, where else? But as diverse as the interests of these many gatherings were, their participants were all of one mind on one particular issue – the role of women. Quite simply they weren't wanted. For all its 'enlightenment', Scotland was still 'a man's world'.

There was another section of society likewise excluded – Highlanders. The suspicion in which they were held by their Lowland compatriots was deep-rooted. Ever since the fourteenth century when the division first manifested itself, there was a contempt for, even a fear of, those living in the mountains and glens, with their alien speech, their strange customs and dress. Lowlanders even fell into the habit of disdainfully dismissing them as 'Irish', as if they didn't really belong in the same kingdom. Such mistrust was stirred into outright loathing during the Jacobite troubles, bringing home as it did to the predominantly Presbyterian Lowlanders the dreaded possibility of a return to 'popery' – and quite possibly absolute monarchy too.

Lowlanders were joined in their concerns by the Hanoverian Government. The longer Jacobite disaffection in the Highlands rumbled on, the more stringent and bloody were the measures they took to stamp it out. After the '15, estates were confiscated and the clansmen disarmed, but it didn't last. By 1717 all but the notorious Macgregors had been officially pardoned, and unofficially only those clans loyal to the Government had actually bothered to turn in their weapons!

But after the '45, the same mistakes would not be made a second time. Both in the field and at

◀ *David Hume, the philosopher and leading figure of Scotland's 'Age of Enlightenment', painted by his friend, Allan Ramsay (1713-84). Ramsay also co-founded with Hume the Select Society, Edinburgh's most prominent debating club, and earned a reputation not only as a portrait painter but also as a philosopher and essayist in his own right.*

'A Creative Lot'

~ SCOTTISH INVENTORS ~

'Scotland's sons compensate for their misfortune by an extraordinary zeal and an earnest exertion of their talents'

(From the leader article in the first issue of the Scots Magazine, *January 1739)*

I had gone to take a walk on a fine Sabbath afternoon. I was thinking upon the engine at the time, and had got as far as the herd's house [on Glasgow Green] when the idea came to my mind that as steam was an elastic body, it would rush into a vacuum, and if a communication were made between the cylinder and an exhausted vessel, it would rush into it, and it might there be condensed without cooling the cylinder. I then saw I must get rid of the condensed steam and injection water. Two ways of doing this occurred to me [and] I had not walked further than the Golf House when the whole thing was arranged in my mind.

James Watt's 'stroll in the park' that Sunday afternoon in 1764 changed the whole course of world history. He had started out wrestling with a problem in his head, and returned with a solution that would soon unleash the awesome forces that have become known as the Industrial Revolution – the steam engine.

The well-kent story of the young James alighting on his invention as he watched the kettle boil in his house in Greenock is the stuff of legend. He was certainly an inquisitive child, and as an 18-year-old had journeyed to London to try to make his mark. But ill-health soon forced him to return, and in 1757 he took up a post as a mathematical-instrument maker in Glasgow University. It was there that he perfected a machine that had been invented 1800 years earlier but which, despite the efforts of many great minds, was still hopelessly inefficient. James Watt's brainwave – the double-acting, self-regulating steam engine with its separate condenser – was

the key that unlocked the door of the Industrial Revolution.

But who unlocked the door to our modern scientific world? Who made radio, television, microwaves and thermal imaging possible? Step forward another James. But although we have all heard of James Watt, who among us can recall hearing the name of James Clerk Maxwell? And yet it is he who is justly acclaimed as the father of modern physics, 'the physicist's physicist'. Albert Einstein paid him the greatest credit when he declared: 'One scientific epoch ended and another began with James Clerk Maxwell.'

The Edinburgh-born, Galloway-bred lad first showed his prodigious talent at a remarkably early age; at 14 he had his first scientific paper (on how to draw the perfect ellipse) read to the august membership of the Royal Society in Edinburgh. By his 24th birthday he was Professor of Natural Philosophy at

Marischal College, Aberdeen, and by the time he was 30 he was holding a similar chair at King's College, London. The ultimate accolade from his peers came at the age of 40 when he was invited to become the first Professor of Experimental Physics at Cambridge and Director of the Cavendish Laboratory.

We have strong reason to conclude that light itself – including radiant heat and other radiation, if any – is an electro-magnetic disturbance in the form of waves propagated through the electro-magnetic field according to electro-magnetic laws.

Maxwell's own words, in a paper to the Royal Society in 1864, demonstrate his chief passion, and his principal contribution to humankind – the theory of electro-magnetism. So much of our technology owes its origins to Maxwell and his grasp of the basic principles of the universe. Einstein, who so freely

▲ *William Thomson, Lord Kelvin (1824-1907), the Belfast-born but Glasgow-bred scientist and inventor, gives his last lecture to his students at Glasgow University in 1899, aged 75. Lord Kelvin also gave us the first trans-Atlantic communication cable in 1866, and the Kelvin scale of temperature.*

▲ *James Watt (1736-1819),*
portayed here by John Partridge, unlocked
the door of the industrial revolution with
his perfection of the steam engine.

acknowledged his own debt to Maxwell, told of the 'profound change in the conception of reality' that Maxwell brought about, bringing to an end the epoch of Isaac Newton and heralding the modern scientific revolution.

But Maxwell didn't confine himself solely to the study of electro-magnetism. His penetrating intellect made fundamental contributions in other fields too: in thermo-dynamics (he founded the Kinetic theory of gases that led to the development of statistical physics), in mathematics (his particular gift was the ability to see phenomena in terms of relationships that could be defined by equations), in engineering (he defined most of the electrical units in use today), in nuclear energy (he provided Einstein with his key for unlocking the theory of relativity), and in space exploration (his brilliant theoretical study of Saturn's rings has recently been confirmed by a space probe). We even have him to thank for colour photography.

The baby born at no.14 India Street, Edinburgh, on 13 June, 1831, grew into a shy and unassuming man, by all accounts, and yet during his life he achieved 'greatness unequalled'. Today his birthplace serves as an international study centre of the James Clerk Maxwell Foundation, a fitting memorial to the man whose brain made 'one of the greatest leaps ever achieved in human thought.'

Alongside Watt and Clerk Maxwell stand many other Scots who have made their mark in the fields of engineering, physics and medicine. Many, Watt and Clerk Maxwell included, were from well-to-do families; others, such as Kirkpatrick Macmillan, the son of a country blacksmith, were just ordinary folk from ordinary families who had benefited from the best education system in Europe. Their names make for an impressive list for such a small country. The Scots truly were a creative lot. All, though, were Scots*men*, for Scotland was still very much a man's world.

Andrew Meikle (1719-1811), born East Lothian – threshing machine.

Joseph Black (1728-1799), born Bordeaux – discovery of carbon dioxide.

James Watt (1736-1819), born Greenock – steam pumping engine, etc.

Daniel Rutherford (1749-1819), born Edinburgh – discovery of nitrogen.

William Murdock (1754-1839), born Lugar, Ayrshire – gas lighting.

John Loudon McAdam (1756-1836), born Ayr – road metalling.

Charles Macintosh (1766-1843), born Glasgow – waterproofing.

David Brewster (1781-1868), born Jedburgh – kaleidoscope.

James Chalmers (1782-1853), born Arbroath – adhesive postage stamp.

James Beaumont Neilson (1792-1865), born Shettleston – hot-blast iron smelting.

James Bowman Lindsay (1799-1862), born Carmyllie, Angus – wireless telegraphy.

Patrick Bell (1799-1869), born Auchterhouse, Angus – mechanical reaper.

Robert Wilson (1803-1882), born Dunbar – ship propeller.

James Young Simpson (1811-1870), born Bathgate – chloroform.

James 'paraffin' Young (1811-1878), born Glasgow – paraffin oil.

Kirkpatrick Macmillan (1813-1878), born Keir Mill, Dumfriesshire – pedal bicycle.

Alexander Wood (1817-1884), born Cupar, Fife – pain-killing drug injection.

Lord Kelvin (1824-1907), born Belfast – electrical theory, first Atlantic cable, etc.

John Shanks (1825-1895), born Paisley – flushing toilet.

James Clerk Maxwell (1831-1879), born Edinburgh – electro-magnetism, etc.

John Boyd Dunlop (1840-1921), born Dreghorn, Ayrshire – pneumatic tyre.

James Dewar (1842-1923), born Kincardine-on-Forth – vacuum flask.

Henry Faulds (1843-1930), born Beith, Ayrshire – fingerprinting.

Alexander Graham Bell (1847-1922), born Edinburgh – telephone.

William Macewen (1848-1924), born Rothesay – development of antiseptic surgery.

William Ramsay (1852-1916), born Glasgow – discovery of 'noble gases' (helium etc)

Sir Alexander Fleming (1881-1955), born Darvel, Ayrshire – penicillin.

John Logie Baird (1888-1946), born Helensburgh, Dunbartonshire – television.

Robert Watson-Watt (1892-1973), born Brechin – radar.

▲ *James Clerk Maxwell (1831-79),*
is universally regarded as the father of
modern physics. Without him we
wouldn't have colour TV.

The Hanoverian Government's attitude to the Highlands, hot-bed of Jacobitism, in the aftermath of Culloden was double-edged. The 'stick' wielded by 'Butcher' Cumberland's redcoats was soon softened by the 'carrot' of economic regeneration. This included the building of a new town, Ullapool, beside Loch Broom, in Wester Ross, by the British Fisheries Society in the late 1780s. Further investment followed, particularly after the appointment by Parliament of Thomas Telford, the great Scots civil engineer, to spearhead a major initiative to improve road communication and harbour facilities. The Caledonian Canal, opened in 1822, is still in commercial use; so are substantial stretches of his 900 miles (1450 km) of 'parliamentary roads' and a good many of his 120 'parliamentary bridges', but, his 'parliamentary church' at Ullapool is now disused.

Westminster extreme measures were taken to repress what were seen as 'a barbarous people'. What Cumberland's redcoats perpetuated in the Highlands in the days and weeks after Culloden was little short of state-sponsored terrorism; and what Parliament decreed from the comfort of the Palace of Westminster was nothing short of a blatant denial of basic human rights to those who survived the horror. No opportunity was missed in the attempt to expunge all trace of Highland culture, including petty bans on the playing of the bagpipes and the wearing of the kilt.

From the 1st of August 1747 no man or boy shall on any pretence whatsoever wear or put on the clothes commonly called 'Highland clothes', that is to say the plaid, philibeg or little kilt. Every such person so offending being convicted shall suffer imprisonment without bail during six months and longer; and being convicted of a second offence shall be liable to be transported to any of His Majesty's plantations beyond the seas for seven years.

The Tigh-an-Truish Inn ('the house of the trousers'), beside the Clachan Bridge linking Seil Island to the Argyll mainland, is said to have been where returning Highlanders changed back into their kilts during this period of prohibition.

The measures, trivial or no, worked. Culloden and its aftermath put paid to the ancient clan system

and any lingering claim to authority and independence their chiefs might have clung to. Even as mighty Fort George, the Hanoverian army's garrison fortress within sight of Culloden, was being completed in 1769, the locals were calling it 'a white elephant'; and so it proved, for not a single shot was ever fired in anger from its awesome rampart. By the time Johnson and Boswell dined in the Governor's house there in the summer of 1773, the Highlands were largely peaceful and many a young Highland lad had passed through the fort's heavy gates to fight overseas. The white cockade of the Jacobite had been exchanged for the 'king's shilling'. With Britain once again at war with France, and with trouble looming in the American Colonies, the Government of George III (1760-1820) could use all the manpower it could lay its hands on, notwithstanding their supposed 'barbarity'. In 1766 Pitt 'the Elder' boasted to his king:

I sought for merit wherever it was to be found and found it in the mountains of the north. I called it forth, and drew into your service a hardy and intrepid race of men, who had gone nigh to overturn the State. These men were brought to combat on your side; they served with fidelity, as they fought with valour, and conquered for you in every part of the world.

So soon had the Jacobite cause become a thing of the past. The brutal reality of those 50 years of civil war became dimmed in the minds of most Scots, to be replaced by a dewy-eyed vision of a once-proud and independent race now peaceably incorporated into an increasingly prosperous United Kingdom. Such romanticism, ironically, was peddled in the main by Lowlanders such as Sir Walter Scott. Even Robert Burns got caught up in it. In his 'Bonnie Lass of Albany', written shortly after Bonnie Prince Charlie's death in 1788, Burns prepares to welcome the return to Scotland of Charles's loyal daughter, Charlotte:

We'll daily pray, we'll nightly pray,
On bended knees most fervently,
The time may come, with pipe an' drum,
We'll welcome hame fair Albany.

It was pure fantasy, and everyone knew it.

REVOLUTIONS

The Scot of 1800 would scarcely have recognised the Scotland of a century earlier, so dramatic had been the changes to the country in that time. Not only had the Union indelibly altered the political landscape; the physical landscape itself had also changed out of all recognition thanks to the agricultural 'improvers'. And hard on those heels had come technological innovation – the so-called 'industrial revolution'. The eighteenth century was the age when Scotland finally shook off its medieval shackles for good.

The transformation began in the countryside soon after the Union. John Cockburn of Ormiston was typical of the pioneering agricultural 'improvers'. A strong supporter of the Union and one of the new Scottish MPs sitting at Westminster, he set about improving his East Lothian estate. Influenced by what he had seen in England, and encouraged by his good friend, Charles 'Turnip' Townshend (so called because he had introduced the turnip into Britain, which did so much to revolutionise all-year-round stockholding almost overnight), Cockburn began to experiment with a new agricultural order. It was nothing short of a revolution, for it heralded the process whereby farming in Scotland moved from being a largely communal activity to one based on single farms. It wasn't just the landscape around Ormiston that was changing; it was the lives of its indwellers too.

▲ The familiar Lowland landscape of pocket-handkerchief-sized fields, typified here in the Forth valley, was created during the agricultural revolution of the eighteenth century which resulted in the radical 'enclosing' of the broad, open rigs that had existed for centuries.

Cockburn's tenants were encouraged to help bring in the new order. They were offered single-farm tenancies on generous, long-term leases, easily renewable so long as they 'took ownership' themselves and invested time and money in the transformation. Gradually the long, sweeping rigs that once sprawled about the farm-toun were replaced by neat, rectangular fields enclosed by hedgerows and dykes. The run-down cotts of the former joint-tenants were replaced by the detached farmhouses of the new farmers, whilst some of the displaced were rehoused in the new neat village of Ormiston, offering better homes and work premises, including a brewery and distillery, more suited to serving the new farms. Cockburn's experiment soon had his peers green with envy. Sir James Hall of Dunglass wrote gushingly:

His town is riseing exceedingly...blacksmiths,
shoemakers, candlemakers and baikers,
malsters, etc, make throng doeing.

The impetus spread furth of Lothian. The 'Age of Enlightenment' spurred on the process, agriculture taking its place alongside other emerging disciplines, such as geology and economics, as a suitable subject for enquiring minds. In 1723 the Honourable Society of Improvers in the Knowledge of Agriculture (the forerunner of the Highland and Agricultural Society whose annual 'Royal Highland Shows' at Ingliston continue to give pleasure to millions to this day) was founded in Edinburgh, and the cause

▲ *The industrial revolution that 'took off' towards the end of the eighteenth century transformed Scotland's urban landscape. Exploitation of the human as well as the natural resource by greedy employers was commonplace; an exception to the rule was New Lanark, the textile town set up below the dramatic Falls of Clyde by David Dale, himself a former textile worker. Thomas Garrett, a contemporary, extolled the virtues of Dale's industrial philanthropy: 'If I was tempted to envy any of my fellow-creatures it would be such men as . . . Mr Dale for the good they have done to mankind.'*

became a national one. But it was slow-going. Only by 1800 can the new agrarian economy be said to have made its impact on a greater part of the country from Portpatrick to Portmahomack. Even then great swathes of the Highlands and Islands remained largely unaffected.

The process was not without pain. The creation of single-farm tenancies made many a tenant landless. Forced evictions became commonplace, leading to untold misery for those directly afflicted. The first outward resistance came as early as 1724 with the Levellers' Revolt in Galloway, in protest at the creation of large 'black cattle' farms by the lairds at the expense of the 'little man'.

> The lords and lairds they drive us out from
> mailings where we dwell;
> The poor man cries, 'Where shall we go?'
> The rich says, 'Go to hell!'

(From the poem *The Levellers' Lines*, first published in 1841.)

At the other end of the country – Strathoykel, in Easter Ross – and at the opposite end of the century – 1792 – the locals too became greatly alarmed, this time at the proliferation of sheep farms. In that year they took matters into their own hands, rounding up all the woolly creatures they could lay their hands on – over 10,000 of them – and herding them south. They would have driven them out of the Highlands altogether had they not been intercepted at Dingwall by the Black Watch. Even though the great period of upheaval in the history of the Highlands, the infamous 'Clearances', was yet to come, the year 1792 lives on in Highland tradition as *Bliadhna Nan Caorach*, 'The Year of the Sheep'.

With agricultural improvement came technical innovation. The 'pocket-handkerchief' appearance of the Lowland landscape could not have been achieved with the old tools, the simple spade and the unwieldy plough pulled by 12 oxen. New implements were called for, and they came courtesy of 'enlightened' Scots: James Small, a Berwickshire farmer, who in 1763 designed a swing-plough capable of being drawn by just two horses, Andrew Meikle, mill engineer from East Linton, who in 1788 perfected the threshing machine, and Patrick Bell, from near Dundee, who in 1827 invented a reaping machine whose motion still beats in the heart of every modern combine-harvester. And alongside the new technology came new techniques – the widespread use of lime for improving soil fertility, and of course the introduction of the turnip and potato. By the end of the eighteenth century East Lothian, the cradle of the agricultural 'revolution' in Scotland, had been transformed from a county lagging behind the better farming areas of England to one in the lead, attracting international recognition.

Mr Rennie was acknowledged to be the most skillful and successful agriculturalist. Nor was the reputation he so justly merited confined to his native land. He corresponded with, and was visited not only by, the leading agriculturalists of England and Ireland, but many noblemen and gentlemen from France, Russia, Germany, Poland, Hungary and other European States seeking information to improve their domains. (From George Rennie of Phantassie's gravestone in Prestonkirk, East Lothian, 1828.)

So where did the unfortunate people displaced from the countryside go? A few took their chance and emigrated to the Colonies, others enlisted in His Britannic Majesty's fast-growing army and navy. Most, though, headed for the towns where they found a very different kind of work, in the factories that were rising up in the wake of the industrial 'revolution', and down the mines that fuelled their hungry boilers. In 1756, the fifth Earl of Elgin established the country's biggest lime works, on the north shore of the Forth, and, in its shadow, the village that bears his name, Charleston – Scotland's first planned industrial community. Three years later the mighty Carron Ironworks, on the opposite shore, was founded; by 1800 it had become the biggest ironworks in Europe, casting anything from gates to guns. It became a household name, thanks to the 'carronade', a deadly gun much admired by Lord Nelson and the Duke of Wellington.

But most of the dispossessed made for the huge cotton mills, for in the later eighteenth century cotton was 'king', not linen. The first cotton mills appeared in Penicuik and Rothesay in 1778, and by

1815 there were well-nigh 200 of them employing 100,000 people. A partner in the Rothesay venture, David Dale, himself a former weaver from Paisley, was also the prime mover behind the enormous mill-complex that harnessed the waters of the spectacular Falls of Clyde. New Lanark also employed over 2000 people, who came from all over the country; one street, Caithness Row, attests to its residents' roots. Today the village is better known for its association with Dale's son-in-law, Robert Owen, who succeeded to the business in 1799 and valiantly tried to carry through experiments in social engineering. His Co-operative Store strongly influenced the Co-operative Movement, and his wonderfully named Institution for the Formation of Character still dominates the centre of the World Heritage Site. Sadly, precious few other mill-owners, or any other industrialists for that matter, were as 'enlightened' as he.

None were less enlightened than the coal-owners and salt-manufacturers. Colliers and salters were the only people in eighteenth-century Scotland who were serfs – that is, they had no rights whatsoever. They toiled deep beneath the ground or sweated in the panhouses most of the hours God gave them, completely thirled to their masters, and unable even to move to another pit or pan. So too did their wives and children, all of whom laboured long and for little reward. One elderly East Lothian collier, speaking in 1842, recalled being:

first yoked to the coal work at Preston Grange

▲ Glasgow, for so long the poor relation of the royal burgh of Rutherglen, emerged from the shadows in the eighteenth century to become the leading town in the west. The growing trade with the American colonies, particularly in sugar and tobacco, was the catalyst. The first consignment of tobacco had been landed at the Broomielaw in 1674, when trade with England's colonies was still strictly illegal. But 1707 saw the barriers removed, and Glaswegian entrepreneurs maximised the opportunity presented. By the time John Knox painted this view of Trongate in 1826, the site of the former tron, or weighing machine, had been replaced by fine shops and coffee houses frequented by the city's 'tobacco lords'.

when I was nine years of age. We were then all slaves to the laird...if we did not do his bidding we were placed by the necks in iron collars called juggs and fastened to the wall, or 'made to go the rown'. The latter I recollect well, the men's hands were tied in face of the horse at the gin and made run backwards all day.

When this man was nine, the year was 1770 and Scotland supposedly an 'enlightened' land!

The migration of the landless from the countryside to the town, the servility of the collier and salter, and the increasing isolation felt by the business and professional classes from the centre of power, London, all created their own tensions in Scottish society. And as the British Empire expanded, so Scotland became open to new influences elsewhere across the globe. Revolutions furth of Scotland soon made their presence felt.

On 4 July 1776 the American Congress, despairing of ever getting more control over their own affairs from the British, signed the Declaration of Independence; the Revd John Witherspoon, born and bred in Gifford but by now Principal of Princeton Presbyterian College, New Jersey, helped draft the Declaration and was a signatory to it. The document was full of democratic sentiments such as 'accountability', 'freedom of speech' and 'no taxation without representation'. Such notions were soon crossing the Atlantic, courtesy of the tobacco trade, and being openly discussed in the coffee houses of Glasgow and Edinburgh. By the time America won its independence in 1783 the first 'congresses' had already appeared in Scotland, associations of tradesmen mainly, demanding electoral rights and a greater say in the running of their burghs. That they took their inspiration from what had happened in America was made evident in a letter to Witherspoon written in 1784 by another Scottish clergyman, the Revd Nisbet:

'People of fashion and such as would be thought courtiers still say that America might easily have been conquered, but the case is otherwise with the common people, who rejoice in that liberty which they are sensible they want, and which they hope to share.'

Five years on the word 'liberty' would be joined by two more, 'equality' and 'fraternity', to become the slogan of another revolution. The French Revolution was an upheaval as momentous as the War of American Independence, but because of its proximity to, and ancient ties with, Scotland, France presented a far greater threat to the stability of the country and the continuing prosperity of 'the Establishment' than the more distant colonies.

In the event the threat was more imagined than real. There was revolutionary fever in the air for a while. The year 1792 was particularly lively, with the creation of the Society of Friends of the People in Edinburgh, the 'official' vehicle for parliamentary reform. There was rioting too: 'wonderfully diffused through the manufacturing towns of this Country' according to the magistrates of Lanark, one of the worst affected areas. But many of the riots were not so much politically motivated as expressions of anger locally, against the growing numbers of sheep-farms in the Highlands and the enclosing of common land, the cause of the Lanark riot. And they certainly didn't represent a mass movement of the 'labouring classes' – far from it. One Government spy might have reported that 'the success of the French Democrats has had a most mischievous effect here. It has led them to think of founding societies into which the lower class of people are invited to enter.' But it soon became evident that the 'middle class' founders wished to have very little to do with the 'lower class of people' at all. The latter would have to wait another century, and take the lead themselves, before they got what was their rightful due in the industrial society they were labouring to create.

If one individual saved Great Britain from going down the road to revolution it was Napoleon Bonaparte. Somehow from the time 'the Little Emperor' emerged centre-stage in 1796 to take sole charge of French affairs, the shine went off democratic notions such as 'liberty, equality and fraternity'. Scotsmen joined with their brothers from the rest of the United Kingdom to enlist in the armed services in order to see off the menace. So great were the numbers that a huge, and it has to be said ugly, barracks was built in Edinburgh Castle to accommodate them. The New Barracks was begun in 1796, the year Napoleon wed his Josephine, and completed in 1799, the year Napoleon declared himself Emperor; 16 years later Napoleon met his Waterloo.

AN INDUSTRIAL SOCIETY

(1815 - 1914)

> 'When will the men cease to be worms for the proud to tread on?'
>
> *(From the diary of James Taylor, weaver from Fenwick, Ayrshire, 27 April 1847)*

The heroes of Waterloo returned to a country still dominated by working the land. The men who marched off to Flanders a century later left behind one of the most industrialised countries in the world. This chapter charts that dramatic transformation – the tensions in society wrought by post-war recession and famine, the phenomenal growth of heavy industry as the century wore on, and the increased clamour for political democracy, workers' rights and social justice that accompanied it.

HARD TIMES

On 18 June 1815, as the sun began to rise over the flat cornfields of Belgium, infantrymen from the 92nd Highlanders, 'the Gordons', surreptitiously clung to the stirrups of their comrades-in-arms, the Royal Scots Greys. Word had come that a large column of French infantry was fast approaching. Soon riders and pillion passengers were charging into the fray. The Battle of Waterloo, the set-piece that finally drew down the curtain on Napoleon's imperial dream, had begun.

Over 70,000 Scots fought in Wellington's armies. Now, with Napoleon vanquished, there was little need for 'cannon-fodder' and the demobilised heroes came back to pick up the threads of their peacetime lives once more. They

were in for a profound shock. No sooner had the cheers faded away than they discovered that their country was greatly changed from the one they had left a decade and more before. A bitter economic recession now gripped the land, brought on by the wartime disruption to the markets of Europe and America that even the demand for guns and warships had failed to counter. By 1815 supply had already outstripped demand, and the labour market was awash with the unemployed. The return of the 'demob-happy' Jocks merely made a bad situation worse.

The effects of recession were felt most in the towns of the Central Belt. These had grown phenomenally in the closing years of the eighteenth century as the Industrial Revolution took off; in just 50 years Dundee had more than doubled its

◀ *On 4 March 1890, the royal train carrying Edward Prince of Wales and his guests chugged across the Forth Railway Bridge to mark the official opening of John Fowler and Benjamin Baker's amazing cantilevered creation. All gathered that day, Gustave Eiffel included, declared it to be 'the eighth wonder of the world'. It was certainly a fitting culmination to a century that had seen Scotland transformed from a rural to an 'industrial society'.*

'Where Sheep May Safely Graze'
~ THE HIGHLAND CLEARANCES ~

'the misery of the congested, not of the dispossessed'
(Professor Smout in his A Century of the Scottish People, 1986)

One afternoon, as I was returning from my ramble, a strange wailing sound reached my ears at intervals on the breeze from the west. On gaining the top of one of the hills on the south side of the valley, I could see a long and motley procession winding along the road that led north. It halted at a point of the road, and there the lamentation became loud and long. There were old men and women, too feeble to walk, who were placed in carts; the younger members of the community on foot were carrying their bundles of clothes and household effects, while the children, with looks of alarm, walked alongside. Everyone was in tears. When they set forth once more, a cry of grief went up to heaven, the long plaintive wail was resumed, and after the last of the emigrants had disappeared behind the hill, the sound seemed to re-echo through the whole wide valley in one prolonged note of desolation.

Heart-rending words. They evoke sights such as we have seen all too frequently on our television screens of late, from war-torn Kosovo to the killing fields of Cambodia. But these words weren't penned by a recent war-correspondent; they were despatched from the Scottish Highlands in 1853.

The awful spectacle Sir Alexander Geikie witnessed that day on the winding road from Suisnish, on Skye, would have moved the coldest heart. Lord MacDonald was clearing the townships of Suisnish and Boreraig to make way for sheep. In truth there was

▲ *A ruined crofthouse at Boreraig, on Skye, once the home of an extended crofting family.*

little else his lordship could do. Since that day in 1846 when the deadly potato blight had struck, untold misery had inflicted itself on those living not just in Suisnish but throughout the Highlands and Islands. A huge relief effort had staved off the worst fears – starvation, disease and death – but it was no solution in the long term. The problem wasn't far to seek; there were simply far too many people for the hard, uncompromising land to sustain.

The infamous Clearances took place during the first half of the nineteenth century. But well before then, crofters had been leaving their homes in search of a better life. Some had trekked south to seek work on the rich farmlands of Lothian or in the new industries springing up across the Central Belt. One Skye crofter set out each spring from his home at Waternish to trudge all the way to a farm near Dunbar, then trudge all the way back again after the harvest, a round-trip of over 500 miles (800km); so desperate was he for work, and yet so reluctant was he to uproot from the land of his fathers. Others had opted for emigration, mostly to the wide-open spaces of Canada. But wherever they went, all shared one thing in common: they weren't pushed, they jumped of their own accord.

In those days it hadn't been in the landlords' interest to remove them. On the contrary, they needed as much cheap labour as they could lay their hands on to help them profit from the booming kelp industry. But even before the slump post-Waterloo, as cheap Spanish barilla flooded the home market, the first forced evictions were taking place, courtesy of the grand gentleman whose monumental statue stares down from the slopes of Ben Bhragaidh onto the good people of Golspie – George Granville, Marquis of Stafford, better known to Scots as the first Duke of Sutherland, and to one Scots-American as 'Evictor I'!

We and our fathers have been cruelly burnt like wasps out of Strathnaver, and forced down to the barren rocks of the seashore.
(Angus Mackay of Farr, in evidence to the Napier Commission on the Crofters and Cottars of Scotland, 1883-4.)

The notorious 'clearance' of thousands of families from Strathnaver between 1807 and 1821 is engrained in the national consciousness as the grossest act of inhumanity ever perpetrated by a Scottish landlord on his tenantry. Whole townships were uprooted from the land their ancestors had worked from time immemorial and transplanted to the rocky shores of the storm-lashed north coast. Those grim years are scarred with harrowing accounts of dreadful hurt inflicted on a cowed and terrified people. The heart-rending account of the burning to the ground of one house as the elderly grandparents cowered inside and the military looked on was no isolated incident.

But while it is right that we should never forget the horrific events that unravelled in Strathnaver in those years, it is also important that we put them in perspective. As Patrick Sellar, the Duke's factor, was wielding his stick of eviction, his employers were dangling the carrot of inducement in front of their tenantry's noses in an effort to persuade them out of the overcrowded glens. The planned village of Golspie was already rising from its foundations before 1807, soon to be followed by Brora New Town (1814) and Helmsdale (1818), where alone the Countess of Sutherland invested £14,000 in five years, on a fish-curing station, an inn, fine houses and a harbour designed by none other than John Rennie himself. Capital was put into other initiatives designed to give employment to the displaced crofters, including a coal-mine and a whisky distillery. Not all flourished, although Clynelish's fine single malt continues to give pleasure to many a discerning palate. The Countess seemed happy with what she saw from the windows of her fairy-tale castle at Dunrobin, if a little

caught up in the euphoria of it all; she described Helmsdale as looking 'more like a part of Liverpool than anything else, so handsome are the buildings and so great the bustle'.

The Countess was not alone. All across the Highlands, landlords were wrestling with the problem of overpopulation in similar ways, helped by Government grants and enterprises to

▲ A ruined crofthouse on Rousay, Orkney. In 1841 the population of Rousay was 976; by 1971 it was just 181, although there has been an increase since then.

improve the infrastructure. The great Scots civil engineer, Thomas Telford, was brought in to advise on the building of 'parliamentary' roads, bridges, harbours, even kirks and manses, and earned his nickname 'Colossus of Roads' as a result. People still avail themselves of his handiwork, most dramatically as they sail through the Great Glen on his Caledonian Canal, opened in 1822. The priority was to inveigle people out of the inland glens and onto the coast.

Houses were now placed separately on the new lots; and fevers and epidemics, which formerly had spread so fast, ceased to do so. Money was borrowed from government, and a great deal of draining and trenching was done. The surveying, measuring, planning and mapping near five

hundred crofters' lots was very expensive to the proprietor, Sir Kenneth Mackenzie.

This is a first-hand description of the creation of Gairloch, in Wester Ross, in 1845-46. The author takes pains to mention how terribly expensive it all was. What she fails to mention is the huge profit Sir Kenneth was by now making from the new sheep farms that had replaced the flattened communal townships that had once existed in the shadow of Ben Eighe and Slioch. The author was the Dowager Lady Mackenzie of Gairloch, Sir Kenneth's mother!

No sooner had Sir Kenneth seen his first tenants settle into their brand-new crofts when another disaster struck. But this one proved far worse than anything already inflicted on them by their landlords. Now nature intervened, blighting the potato crop on which the people had become so heavily dependent. It brought untold misery to the families toiling on their meagre parcels of land. Forced eviction, not just from the inland glens but from Scotland itself, was the only answer as far as the landlords could see. And so they went in their tens of thousands, from the islands of the Clyde to the northern tip of Shetland; to Canada, Australia and New Zealand. The ten miserable years following the outbreak of the potato famine in 1846-7 was the period of the real 'Highland Clearances'.

But the question remains – was there a more humane solution to the problem of overpopulation? What would have been the consequences had the people been left to go on trying to scratch a living from smaller and smaller plots of land? One thing is for sure – there remains no greater stain on the pages of Highland history than the infamous 'Highland Clearances'.

▲ The blackhouses at Centangaval, Barra, seem so much a part of the rocky landscape that you could believe they had been there for centuries. Yet crofting townships such as this, wonderfully captured on film by the pioneering photographer, George Washington Wilson (1823-93), himself from crofting stock in Banffshire, had barely been built when he 'snapped' it shortly before his death. The fishing boats crowding into Castlebay beyond suggest that the photograph was taken in the early summer when the herring shoals were passing north-eastward from the Atlantic to the feeding grounds around the Northern Isles. For much of the summer, the menfolk of Centangaval would have been away from home pursuing those 'silver darlings', leaving their wives and wains to tend the croft in their absence.

population to 26,000, and Greenock from just 3000 to a staggering 17,000. The industrial miracle had also seen Glasgow overtake Edinburgh as the largest city for the first time in the nation's history; by 1821 Scotland's industrial capital had 147,000 souls, a fivefold increase in just 60 years.

Such growth though was no longer a sign of expanding markets and increased production. It was brought about by the rising tide of immigrants displaced from the fast-changing countryside, Lowlands and Highlands, as well as from across the Irish Sea – all desperately seeking work. As unemployment spiralled upwards, so the misery and deprivation of the working class heightened. It affected not just the unemployed, reduced to near-starvation and begging on the streets, but also those still in work, who had to endure cuts in wages, and hikes in food prices, as well as worry about losing their jobs. In the cavernous cotton mills and the poky weavers' cottages, in the claustrophobic mines and the rat-infested back-streets, resentment grew apace. The ingredients for civil strife were ready and waiting to be cooked.

In a way it was unfinished business. The Napoleonic Wars had simply interrupted a growing clamour among the people at large for a greater say

in determining their affairs, spurred on by the revolutionary happenings in America and then France. If these peoples could gain their liberty and a greater democracy, then why not Scots? And so parliamentary reform and the extension of the right to vote (for men only, of course) became the cry of a wider section of the population. Now, with Napoleon defeated, they could cry again.

But this time it was different in one important respect. The rioting of the 1790s had largely been confined to more traditional centres like Lanark and Perth. After 1815 it was the seething mass of discontent in the new industrial heartland that took to the streets, in Greenock and Paisley, and most crucially Glasgow. The so-called 'Radical War' that sparked into life in 1816 and was so cruelly snuffed out by the authorities four years later was fought out mostly amid the growing squalor of the industrial west. The east of the country, even Edinburgh, was comparatively peaceful – 'quiet as the grave', so Lord Cockburn opined, 'or even as Peebles'!

Matters came to a head after placards appeared on the streets of Glasgow on the night of Saturday 1 April urging all workmen to strike four days hence. The people were exhorted 'to show the world that we are not that lawless, sanguinary rabble which our oppressors would persuade the higher circles we are, but a brave and generous people determined to be free.' Whether the placards were genuine is still in dispute. What isn't in doubt is what actually happened on the following Wednesday.

From the time the placards went up there was heightened tension. Reports of young men making pikes and marching in the streets reached the ears of Government. The failure of large sections of the workforce, 60,000 it was said, to 'clock in' on the following Monday simply added to their fears. Come the 5th there was a huge military presence in the centre of Glasgow. The 'Radicals', gathered on the outskirts of the city and reported to be 7000 strong, decided discretion was the better part of valour and chose not to enter the city.

And there matters would have rested had not a hardy core opted to march along the Forth & Clyde Canal and seize Carron Ironworks with its precious store of guns. They got no further than Bonnymuir before they were intercepted by a troop of hussars, veterans from the Napoleonic Wars. Four of their pitifully small number were wounded and 47 taken prisoner; three were subsequently hanged. The mass-protest fizzled out. But the 'Radical War' marked a turning-point in Scotland's history. It was the first flickering of a common resolve among the nation's workforce, a resolve that would persist, and ultimately find expression in the formation of the Labour Party later in the century.

The industrial heartland of the Central Belt was not the only area benighted by the economic crisis. The Highlands and Islands too were gripped by recession. Over half the Scots fighting in Wellington's armies, 40,000 men, had come from the *Gaidhealtachd*, the Gaelic-speaking areas of Scotland. Now they returned to exacerbate an already parlous situation. The price of black cattle, their main income generator, had slumped, the bottom had fallen out of the kelp industry, and thanks to over-fishing in the shallower coastal waters the shoals that had helped sustain their ancestors for thousands of years had moved further out into the deep Atlantic swell. To compound the whole dire situation the population had actually grown, almost doubled in most areas, while the men had been away at the wars, and this despite the

drift towards the Central Belt and the rising tide of emigration to the New World. The soldiers came back to a familiar landscape, but one now clearly incapable of sustaining the people living on it.

The writing was on the wall even before the horrendous events that unfolded on the Sutherland estates between 1807 and 1821. Attempts had been made by Government and landlords alike to address the problem, by encouraging – and in a few isolated cases forcing – those living in the inland glens to relocate to the coast where new enterprises held out the promise of a better life. Some ventures were doomed from the start because of their sheer remoteness from the markets; they included David Dale's cotton mill at Spinningdale. Others flourished, particularly those linked to fishing. Ullapool, on Loch Broom, owes its origins to this time, thanks to the initiative of the British Fisheries Society in the 1780s. And while the men were away at the fishing, all along the coastal fringes their women and children harvested another rich produce of the sea, seaweed, burning it into an alkaline ash for use in the glass and soap industries.

Kirkwall, Sept 24. The brig *Nelly* of Newcastle, after having all her sails blown away on the west coast of Orkney, was forced ashore on the

◀ *Seven-year-old Christina MacVarish brings the firewood home to her crofthouse at Bracora, near Mallaig, around 1905. Barely a century has passed since this little girl was photographed, and yet today's boys and girls would scarcely recognise her life-style. She would have lived in a small thatched house with her mother (her father was drowned at sea when she was only two), her grandparents, brothers and sisters. Sharing the house with them were the family's · cows and calves, hens and chickens.*

In May, Christina and her brothers and sisters, along with the rest of the younger members of the township, would pack their belongings and head into the hills with the beasts to spend the summer on the family shieling, living and sleeping in the cramped hut and keeping an eye on the cattle as they grazed on the upland pasture. Every day, one of them would return to the family house with fresh milk. As the summer waned, all, beasts included, would return to the township once more.

'Uisgue Beaha'

~ SCOTLAND'S NATIONAL DRINK ~

'A creature of science – created by art'

▲ *In 1900 the nation 'rejoiced' at the news that the British Army had relieved Mafeking from the Transvaal Boers. Most would have toasted their heroes in 'Scotch', then by far the most popular spirit drunk in Britain; no doubt a few drams of 'Begg's' (seen here in an advertisement dating from 1902) were among them.*

Whisky is just a chemical, a mere mingling of water and barley with a smidgin of yeast thrown in for good measure. And yet the pure malt spirit that emerges has become Scotland's national drink, a drink that it has bequeathed to the world – 'Scotch'.

Scots have invented many wonderfully useful things, but whisky isn't among them. The word 'alcohol' comes from the Arabic *al-koh'l*, and it was in Arabia, in early medieval times, that spirit was first distilled to produce exotic perfumes. But the Scots and the Irish weren't that keen on smelling nice; they saw in the spirit a more fundamental quality, as an emboldening tonic, a reviver of tired bodies and minds. They called it *aqua vitae* in Latin, 'water of life'. In Gaelic it was *uisge beaha* (pronounced oosh-ke bay-ah) – whence 'whisky'.

Whisky and ale were natural by-products for a country people growing only oats and barley. For centuries, oats had been the 'food crop' and barley the 'drink crop', replacing the heather ale popular with our Stone-Age ancestors. Ale, being easier to produce, was the staple of the labouring classes, in town as well as countryside. It came in various strengths (as it still does), from strong ale to mere mouth-gargle, and was invariably brewed by women, one of the few positions of authority they held in medieval society:

> Twenty pints o' strong ale,
> Twenty pints o' sma,
> Twenty pints o' hinky-pinky,
> Twenty pints o' plooman's drinkie,
> Twenty pints o' splitter-splatter,
> And twenty pints was waur nor water [worse than water]!

(from the *gudewife of Lochrin's Peck o' Malt*)

The upper classes scornfully disdained the 'home-brew' and drank wine, mostly claret from Bordeaux.

Once the science (or art) of distilling the fermented malted barley had been mastered, whisky quickly took its place alongside ale as the 'bevvy' of the labouring classes. It was a simple enough thing to make, requiring little room and no complicated apparatus. Soon the little pot stills with their characteristic coiled 'worms' were common sights not only in Highland crofthouses (it was said there were two things a Highlander liked naked, and one was his malt!) but in the cottages and town tenements of the Lowlands also. Edinburgh alone in 1774 could boast over 400 stills bubbling away behind its respectable street frontages. As wine-making was to the French, so whisky-distilling became to the Scots.

The hobby was not without its perils. Distilling was after all a chemical process involving fire, and the disaster that befell an Inveraray widow in 1680, when her 'pot' set alight to her furniture and burnt her house down, was no isolated incident. But the greater risk was running the gauntlet of the taxman. Duty was first imposed on whisky in 1644, and as the rate was progressively raised, so more and more people turned to illicit distilling and smuggling. Throughout the eighteenth century, it became a real headache for the Government, who resorted to tougher measures and more aggressive policing. Even Robert Burns, a man known to like a dram or two, was employed as an exciseman for a while; obviously a civil servant's pay was better than being the country's foremost poet!

We'll mak our malt,
and brew our drink,
We'll dance, and sing,
and rejoice, man;
And mony thanks to the
muckle black De'il
That danced awa' wi'
the Exciseman.'

(From Robert Burns's *The De'il's Awa' Wi' The Exciseman*, 1792.)

The crunch came in the 1820s with the passing of the Illicit Distillation and Excise Acts. Almost overnight, it would seem, whisky distilling moved from being a private activity to becoming a large-scale venture capital industry, taking its place in the industrial revolution alongside its 'big brothers', iron, steel and coal. In just two years the number of legal distilleries more than doubled, to 263, and the legal output of whisky rose from 3,000,000 to a staggering 8,000,000 gallons a year. By 1830, as the redcoats at Corgarff barracks packed their knapsacks ready to march back to Fort George, their work of rooting out illicit distillers and smugglers in remote Strathdon completed, every man, woman and child over the age of 15 was consuming on average one pint of whisky per week.

By now whisky was becoming fashionable in the houses of the 'high and mighty' as well as in the hovels of the humble, thanks to Sir Walter Scott taking the opportunity presented by George IV's visit to Scotland in 1822 not only to encourage the wearing of the tartan but also the drinking of the dram. Whisky began to replace brandy as the fashionable post-prandial tipple.

Demand would surely have outstripped supply had Aeneas Coffey, an Irishman, not invented his 'continuous still' in 1830, which, unlike the traditional 'pot still', required no cleaning out after every 'running'. Coffey's still also produced grain whisky, a lighter, less fiery drink than the malt whiskies created in the four established centres, the Lowlands, Highlands, Islay and Campbeltown. Campbeltown was known as the 'double-bass' of the orchestra because it had the strongest, peatiest flavour; the violin section was claimed by the more subtle Highland malts of Speyside.

As the taste for whisky grew, so the industry developed. It had to – the drinks business was as 'cut-throat' then as it is today. New ideas to keep the 'punters' buying were tried, including Andrew Usher's brainchild of 1853, 'blended whisky', a subtle mixture of 'single malts' (malt whiskies produced from one distillery) and grain whisky. His *Usher's Old Vatted Glenlivet* has the distinction of being the world's first 'blend'. Attractive

packaging and aggressive promotional campaigns were launched.

Whisky as a drink has changed out of all recognition since Mr Usher's time, thanks in part to the improving craft of the distiller but also to Government intervention; during the Great War legislation was introduced requiring that whisky be matured for at least three years. The industry, too, has endured wild fluctuations in its fortunes in the intervening years. Yet somehow it has survived the privations of the Great War, the threat from 'prohibition' overseas in the 1920s and grim recession at home in the 1930s. In recent times it has even seen something of a revival in its fortunes, earning two billion pounds a year in export sales and providing 60,000 jobs, many in rural areas where finding work can be hard.

But then that's what whisky helps you do, more than any other drink – it sees you through the hard times. As Robert Burns's drouthy Tam o' Shanter proclaimed:

Wi' tuppeny [ale] we fear nae evil;
Wi' usquabae, we'll face the Devil!

▲ *The Macallan workforce pose for the camera in 1917. The pretty Speyside complex at Craigellachie, in Morayshire, was one of 79 new distilleries licensed to produce whisky in the 12 months following the passing of the Excise Act in 1823. Most of the output went to slake the thirst of the fast-expanding population in the industrial Central Belt; but quite a lot went to those same industrial towns to meet a quite different 'thirst', as industrial alcohol, producing products from soap to surgical spirit.*

CROFTERS' COTTAGES, LOCH DUICH. 11,465. G.W.W.

▲ *These crofters' cottages beside Loch Duich, in Inverness-shire, would have been quite a recent 'housing development' when George Washington Wilson photographed them around 1890. Their forebears would have lived further into the hills, amid the heathery pasture, and not here on the margins of the land. But the land had become so congested by the early nineteenth century that it could barely sustain human life, and 'clearances' by the landlords, some of it voluntary, much of it ruthlessly enforced, saw a marked redrawing of the Highland map as the century wore on. Those reluctant to leave their homes for pastures new (chiefly to Canada from this particular 'airt'), were resettled beside inland lochs and sea shores. Into their ancestral lands moved the 'Cheviot and the stag'.*

people who for countless generations had toiled to make their homes among the heather simply weren't wanted any more.

The straggling crofting townships dotted about the coasts of the Highlands and Islands today give the impression of having been there from the beginning of time, their rubble walls seemingly an extension of the solid rock beneath. Yet most owe their origin to the troubled times of the early nineteenth century. Whole communities that had hitherto communally farmed the inland glens were uprooted and dumped on the coast to work individual crofts. While it might have solved the landlords' problems, it only worsened the plight of the tenantry, now shoehorned onto even smaller parcels of land that were even more incapable of sustaining human life. Thank goodness for the potato; the humble vegetable imported from the mountain slopes of South America thrived in the thin soils of the Highlands; crofters even grew it on the wall-tops of their blackhouses! As long as they had the potato to see them through the winter, all was not lost.

Then disaster struck. In 1846 the crofters were reduced to staring helplessly as the potato shaws withered and died before their eyes. A deadly blight had affected the fleshy tubers. The 1847 crop was even worse. Widespread death and disease would have been the order of the day, as was the case in Ireland where over a million souls died, had not Government, landlords and voluntary agencies combined to put in place a massive relief programme. It worked in the short term, but it also demonstrated that the crofting life could only be sustained if there were far fewer people.

So began the second wave of 'Clearances', greater and more ruthless than anything experienced previously. The families who had only recently been relocated to the coast were now forced to uproot once more and take to the sea, not as Patrick Sellar had envisaged as fishermen but as emigrants to the New World. What had hitherto been a steady trickle, mostly voluntary, now became a flood as

island of Enhallero [Eynhallow] and all the crew drowned. The vessel was loaded with kelp from the Highlands and bound for Whitby.
(*Edinburgh Evening Courant*, Wednesday Oct 6, 1779.)

The kelp industry, first introduced onto Stronsay in the Orkneys in 1722, had become big business by 1800 maintaining the landlords in their comfortable lifestyles, whether at their country seats or in their prestigious new residences in Edinburgh's New Town. It did little, though, to improve the lot of those who toiled to produce it.

Although some landlords were motivated by concern over the miserable lot of their tenants, others were spurred on by greed, convinced they could get a far better return for their investment by clearing the hills of unprofitable humans and replacing them with sheep. The words of Patrick Sellar, factor of the Duke of Sutherland's estates and without doubt the most despised of all those who did their landlord's bidding during the infamous 'Highland Clearances', speak volumes. Discussing uprooting thousands of families from their homes in Strathnaver to new crofting settlements strung along the rocky north coast of Sutherland, Sellar insisted on 'lots under the size of three acres, sufficient for the maintenance of an industrious family, but pinched enough to cause them to turn their attention to fishing.' It was all too clear; the

◀ At the heart of all crofts, as here in this Shetland crofthouse photographed in 1889, lay the fireplace, around which much of family life was carried on. The Gaelic for a living room/kitchen is aig an teine ('at the fire'). In an enchanting account for her school project, written as recently as 1964, a young Lewis girl told of how: 'During winter, many neighbours come in each night. We form a circle round the fire and discuss many subjects... Very often, after tea a cailleach [old woman] comes in for a ceilidh. You know just to gossip. I remember a few years ago, when my uncle was at home from Canada, people used to come every night. What times we had, singing . . . and many other sources of entertainment.' None of that entertainment included the 'telly', which only arrived in Lewis in 1971.

landlords found whatever pretext they could to clear the townships. In those famine-struck years, 20,000 Highlanders sailed for Canada alone – whole communities uprooted at one fell swoop. An eerie silence descended on the land, broken only by the sound of the new residents – sheep.

Just as many drifted south, to the factories and mines of the Central Belt and the rich farms of the south-east Lowlands. The policy worked. After 1850 the population of the Highlands began its inexorable downward spiral. The age-old bond between crofter and land, between tenant and landlord, was now being broken up in the steelworks and shipyards of the Clyde.

> *Ged thig anrach auneoil*
> *Gus a' chala, 's e sa cheo,*
> *Chan fhaic e soills on chagailt*
> *Air a' chladach so nas mo;*
> *Chuir gamhlas Ghall air fuadach*
> *Na tha fhuair 's a chunnaic mise:*
> *Thoir am fios so chun a' Bhaird.*

> Though a stranger, in his wanderings
> Comes to harbour in the mist,
> The hearth has no light shining
> Any more upon this coast;
> For Lowland spite has scattered
> Those who will not come again;
> Will you carry this clear message,
> As I see it, to the Bard.

(Uilleam MacDhunleibhe (William Livingstone) writing of his experience on Islay.)

WORKSHOP OF EMPIRE

In 1815 less than half the population, about 1,000,000 people, lived in the urbanised Central Belt. A century later, on the eve of the Great War, well over 80 per cent had gravitated there. Glasgow alone had grown sevenfold, to a staggering 750,000 souls. In just 100 years, Scotland had been transformed from a predominantly rural land to one of the most industrialised countries on earth – 'the workshop of the British Empire' – with Glasgow its undisputed 'Second City'. But how?

In 1801 in a field east of Glasgow, David Mushet, manager of the Calder Ironworks, stumbled across an unprepossessing-looking rock interspersed among the seams of coal – 'blackband' ironstone. Within 30 years James Beaumont Neilson

'The Silver Darlings'

~ THE SCOTTISH HERRING INDUSTRY ~

'Of aal the fish there iss in the sea, nothing bates the herrin';
the more you will be catchin' of them the more there is'

(The fictional musings of Para Handy, skipper of the Clyde Puffer, Vital Spark,
as told by Neil Munro in his Tales of Para Handy, 1906)

They appeared in the cool waters of the Minch in early May, by mid-June they were to be seen off the rocky coast of Shetland, and by September they were swimming south down the east coast towards Dogger Bank and away. They were 'the silver darlings', the shoals of herring, and they helped make Scotland's fishing industry.

Fishing had been in the blood from the very beginning of human life in Scotland; the delicate bones of cod and saithe found amid the middens at Stone-Age Skara Brae testify to that. In medieval times, the 'greit, innumerable riches' of the sea were seen as a lucrative source of income to those who would risk their lives in this hazardous duel with the deep. The towns strung like pearls around the coast of the Firth of Forth, from Eyemouth to Elie, made much from the Catholic Church's insistence on 'fish for Friday', and the desire to spice up the average Scot's dreary diet of porridge and kale.

But even as late as the eighteenth century, fishing was still by and large an extension of life on the land, not an industry in itself. As the crofter's family and cattle made their way to the summer pasture in the hills beyond the township, the crofter himself would

▲ *Female workers gut and cure fish on the quayside at Peterhead harbour, Aberdeenshire, around 1900. Many a sweetheart would follow her 'man' around the coast of Scotland and down into England during the summer months, waiting for him to land his catch and ensuring that it reached its destination as soon as possible. A 1902 Government report noted that whilst a typical Lewis family made around £3 a year from selling the produce from their croft, they could expect to make eight times that amount from the fishing.*

take to his boat and line-fish off the shallow coastal waters for cod, ling and haddock, and all would fill the long winter evenings mending nets and making hooks. It was ay thus.

It was the fisher-folk from the Continent who first exploited the rich potential offered by the vast herring-shoals that closed in on the waters of Scotland's east coast in late summer. While Scots stayed faithful to their shellfish-baited lines, the Dutch and Flemings and Germans would come across the North Sea in flotillas of boats and sweep 'the silver darlings' up

from the deep in nets. The trawling industry had arrived.

By 1800 the Scots too had begun to 'muscle in' on the act. The port of Wick, on Caithness's east coast, was developed in the 1790s to capitalise on the seemingly boundless natural supply of herring that had captivated the palates of many, particularly Eastern Europeans. Other harbours too joined in, and soon fleets of square-sailed boats of varying size and shape, not to mention name – Fifies, Scuffies, Baldies and Zulus – could be seen heading for the open sea in the evening twilight, and returning with their precious catches in the cold light of dawn.

Waiting patiently at the quayside were the wives and loved ones, not there simply to greet their return (though in a perilous industry that would be their first concern) but also to take the catch, gut and cure it and cram it into barrels filled with brine. Fishing, just as much as crofting and mining, was a family affair.

But it was also a precarious affair. In those early days at the beginning of the nineteenth century, herring fishing was restricted to a short, 10-week 'window of opportunity' provided by the herring themselves as they passed through the North Sea on their migration south. It was not enough to sustain a family for a whole year. And so the trawlermen took to shadowing the shoals, from the time in May when they appeared off the west coast to that day in late September when they disappeared beyond the port of Great Yarmouth. No longer would this be a night-time adventure but one demanding a summer-long attendance.

By 1850 Scotland's herring fleet was numbered in the thousands. Like swarms of midges they descended for weeks at a stretch on fishing ports barely able to accommodate them – Stornoway, Stromness, Stonehaven, St Monans and so on. In their wake followed the fish-gutters and barrel-fillers, a largely migrant workforce drawn from the crofting settlements and towns of the Highlands and Islands. It was not unknown for a fisherman to be followed

around the coast by his sweetheart supplementing the family income: 'It was all done for the love of oor menfolk', said one, Annie Selling. 'If we hadn't worked, they couldn't have sold their fish.' Life was as simple and as stark as that.

As demand grew, thanks in part to the invention of the 'deep-fat fryer' in the 1870s and the advent of the 'fish supper', so the industry grew with it. Fancy new steam trawlers appeared in Aberdeen in the 1880s, and by the turn of the century fish-processing had gone from being a 'here today; gone tomorrow' quayside activity to one largely concentrated in a few large factories back in the land where it all began, the north-east – Fraserburgh, Peterhead and Aberdeen. By 1914, 33,000 men manned the herring fleet, with almost twice

that number in onshore employment. They were heady days. And then it all started to unravel.

The eruption of the Great War started the rot. The German Grand Fleet blockaded the Continent and the industry's main market was lost. Until then 90 per cent of the fish had gone for export, most of it down the throats of Russians and Poles. Even with the First World War at an end, the Russian market continued to be denied to the Scots because of the Revolution. The industry began its steady decline. Today just 7000 people are employed in the industry, on and off shore. And over the almost-deserted quayside of Ullapool, where once Scotsmen landed their catches and Scotswomen packed 'the silver darlings' in barrels, today huge fish-processing ships from Eastern Europe, 'Klondykers', cast their long shadows.

▲ Wick harbour, Caithness, 'jam-packed' with fishing boats at the height of the herring season. This lasted no more than ten weeks before the shoals moved south; for the remainder of the year, a few boats rattled around the harbour 'like peas in a drum'.

▶ *The men sweating away in the boiler house at the Cowlairs engineering works, in Glasgow, helped make Glasgow the 'boiler house' of the Empire. By the end of the nineteenth century, the Clyde was exporting heavy engineering products, such as the railway locomotives rolling off the Cowlairs' production line, all over the world, and 'Clydebuilt' became a by-word for quality and price. But therein lay the seeds of its destruction in the twentieth, for that success was largely down to the pitifully low wages paid to the skilled workforce – 'a mere pittance' a United States Congress report of 1872 called it. It has been estimated that a Clydeside worker was paid around 13 per cent less than his opposite number in London.*

had perfected his 'hot-blast' smelting process at the Clyde Ironworks using that same rock. The invention proved as revolutionary as Abraham Darby's coke-smelting technology perfected at Coalbrookdale a century earlier. By preheating the blast of air before it was forced into the furnace, Neilson's process dramatically cut the cost of making iron pig, enabling entrepreneurs to exploit the 'new' blackband ores that shared the bowels of the Central Belt with the coal that had hitherto been confined to heating salt-pans, steam engines and domestic hearths. 'Blackband' and 'King Coal' made a powerful double-act, and the iron they spewed from the furnaces as a result was robust and easily cast into all manner of objects, great and small.

Almost at a stroke Neilson's invention propelled Scotland into the forefront of world industry, transforming its economy from one based on traditional industries like textiles to one driven by heavy engineering. Within ten years of Neilson taking out his patent in 1828, the number of furnaces in the Central Belt had mushroomed from 25 to over 100, most of them in Lanarkshire – Airdrie, Motherwell, Shotts and Wishaw – some in Ayrshire. So fiery was the sky over Coatbridge that one reporter urged sightseers to visit at night 'when

the flames produce a lurid glow similar to that which hangs over a city when a great conflagration is in progress.' A more cynical wag summed up the dubious delights of Coatbridge more bluntly: there was 'no worse place out of hell'.

> An' the flame-tappit furnaces staun' in a raw,
> A' bleezin', an' blawin', an' smeekin' awa,
> Their eerie licht brichtenin' the
>   laigh hingin' cluds
> Gleamin' far ower the loch an'
>   the mirk lanely wuds.

(From Janet Hamilton's *Gartsherrie*, 1850.)

The output of the new iron works, and later the steel works, spawned new engineering industries, as enterprising Scots realised the potential. You name it – modest machine tools, monstrous engines and mighty ships; they were soon rolling off the production lines and into the domestic and world markets. The phrase 'Clyde-built' became synonymous with quality as Scottish engineering skills earned respect across the globe. From that time Scotsmen have often figured as canny engineers in works of fiction, from Kipling's *M'Andrew* to *Star Trek*'s 'Scottie'.

One of the most significant products was the railway locomotive with all its associated rolling stock and rails. The first railway line in Scotland had been in use for exactly a century when George IV (1820-1830) visited Scotland in 1822, the first British sovereign to stand on Scottish soil in 171 years. But the coal wagons trundling along the stone blocks and wooden rails from the Earl of Winton's 'Great Seam' at Tranent to the harbour at Cockenzie were pulled by horses, not steam. The invention of the 'iron horse' in the 1820s, and the substitution of iron for wooden rails, changed all that. No sooner had William IV (1830-37) ascended the throne than the first locomotive-driven railway in Scotland was opened between Glasgow and Garnkirk to its east.

Soon steam locomotives capable of reaching frightening speeds of 30 mph were rocketing past the snail-paced boats on the canals, and threatening the stagecoach for supremacy as the number one means of transport. New routes were being rapidly developed: 1838 – Dundee to Arbroath; 1839 – Glasgow to Ayr via Paisley and Johnstone; 1840 – Glasgow to Kilmarnock by way of Ardrossan; 1841 – Glasgow to Greenock. On 21 February 1842 Scots got their first intercity service when Queen Victoria (1837-1901) snipped the ribbon at the opening ceremony of the Glasgow to Edinburgh line. By the time the Empress of India had reached 30 in 1849, trains were trundling over the Border – the North British Railway (the old 'NB' of blessed memory) from Edinburgh as far as Berwick, and its arch-rival, the Caledonian, linking both metropolises via Carstairs and Carlisle with the capital of the Empire itself, London. Another knot in the Union was tied.

The Scots took to the rails like ducks to water. Even before the 'NB' was formed in 1844, an incredible 3,000,000 journeys had been made. Hearts of towns were ripped out to accommodate bustling passenger stations and busy goods yards; among the biggest casualties were Edinburgh's Trinity College Church, replaced by Waverley Station in 1848, Glasgow University's medieval

campus in the High Street, sold off in 1863 for a goods yard, and once-mighty Fort William, flattened in the 1880s as the 'NB' stretched out its tentacles towards distant Mallaig. The landscape, too, was transformed as railway companies cut through hills and crossed valleys from Whithorn to Wick. Not even the disastrous collapse of Sir Thomas Bouch's Tay Bridge one foul December night in 1879, in which 79 passengers aboard the 17.27 from Burntisland lost their lives, could diminish the public's passion for the railway.

The railway locomotive shop at the Cowlairs engineering works in Glasgow (above); and (below) locomotives for export being loaded onto a ship at Plantation Quay, Glasgow. Steam 'locos' and the iron rails they ran on were shipped all over the world in the latter half of the nineteenth century.

'The Beautiful Game'

~ FOOTBALL ~

'fitba' crazy, fitba' daft'

(From the song by Jimmie McGregor, 1960)

In the 1870s the working man won something that has remained dear to him to this day – Saturday afternoon off. It is no coincidence that in that same decade the sport of football took off 'big time'. What better way to forget your work, your wife and wains, albeit for just a few precious hours, than to spend it with your mates 'at the fitba'; followed by a few pints of beer in the pub.

Scots had been playing football for centuries before Queen's Park Football Club, first winners of the Scottish Cup, was formed in 1867. But the 'uppies and downies' brand of football, played by entire communities from Jedburgh to Kirkwall, was more organised rioting than organised sport. If it was sport you wanted, and you had the time to indulge – which most working men hadn't – then try golf or curling. If you were working class then throwing quoits would fit in better with your busy schedule.

'One of the peculiar diversions of the gentlemen is the Goff. The diversion of Curling is likewise peculiar to the Scots. The natives are expert at all other diversions common in England, the cricket excepted.'
(William Guthrie, in his *New Geographical Grammar*, 1774.)

Quite how modern football emerged is shrouded in mystery, but by the 1850s young men were being encouraged to participate in organised 'diversions'. Boys in 'public' (that is, private) schools took to picking up the inflated pig's bladder and running with it as well as kicking it – what became known as 'rugby football'. 'Association football' was more a working-class thing.

▲ *Celtic Football and Athletic Club first XI in their inaugural season 1887-8. 'Celtic' went on to become the first side from the U.K. to win the European Cup, in 1967.*

Queen's Park FC sprang from a local Young Men's Christian Association (YMCA), ironic in a way, for in those early years of the game the Church generally frowned on the diversion as being just that, a 'diversion' from the young men's church-going habit: 'the Saturday evening sporting paper is the young man's Bible', fulminated the elders gathered for a meeting of the Dumbarton Presbytery in 1891.

Dumbarton's own Vale of Leven FC had been a founder member of the Scottish Football Association (SFA) on its inception in March 1873, along with other long-departed names such as Clydesdale, Dumbreck and the late-lamented Third Lanark Rifle Volunteer Reserve. But others from those early days have survived and blossomed – Heart of Midlothian (1873), Hibernian (1875), and of course Glasgow Rangers (1872). They had to hang around awhile, though, before the other half of the 'Old Firm', Celtic, joined in 1887.

The United Kingdom is unique in being the only 'country' with four international sides, but in those formative years it could so easily have gone differently. The Football Association (now the English Football Association) had been formed 10 years before the SFA, oddly enough by a Scot, William MacGregor, with every intention of it being a British Football Association. But these were stirring times in British politics, not least in the debate about Home Rule, in Scotland as well as in Ireland. The Scottish football fanatic, player and supporter, saw his sport as much a reflection of national pride as one of local rivalries.

The first 'international' between Scotland and England kicked off at 2 pm on St Andrew's Day, 1872, in Partick, Glasgow, in front of 4000 enthusiastic supporters; it ended goalless – and amicably! The entire Scottish team that day, kitted out in their now famous dark-blue jerseys and white shorts (except they wore more respectable 'knickerbockers' then), were all Queen's Park players. And when it came to selecting a permanent stadium for Scotland's home matches in 1903, it was understandable that it should be Hampden Park, Queen's Park's ground, that was picked, such had been the club's role in making the SFA a success. Since then there have been many memorable encounters between the 'auld enemy', not least the famous 5-1 thrashing of England by the so-called 'Wembley Wizards' in 1928.

Local matches were played, and supported, with equal intensity. The game itself had emerged at a time when public transport was becoming more accessible and affordable, making it easier for working men to travel to 'away' games (though none was as easy to get to as the Dundee 'derbies', separated as the two clubs were from each other by just the width of a street). But it has been the long, and often bitter, rivalry between the 'Old Firm' that has dominated the Scottish game.

Rangers had already been playing for 15 years when Brother Walfrid, headmaster of the Sacred Heart School in Glasgow's East End, formed The Celtic Football and Athletic Club. We could be forgiven for thinking that the two were always 'at each other's throats' from the word 'go', two clubs – one 'Establishment', the other 'Irish' – playing within a couple of miles of each other in the sectarian furnace that was west-central Scotland in the later nineteenth century. But we would also be mistaken. Although there was rivalry

from the outset, it was a friendly rivalry such as was typical between all clubs. It wasn't until the Belfast shipbuilding giant, Harland & Wolff, appeared on the Clyde in 1912, bringing with it its bigoted discrimination policy against Catholics, that the sectarian jealousy was begun that has become the hallmark of the 'Old Firm'; the fact that Celtic were winning everything in sight at the time didn't exactly help cement friendly relations!

Football has come a long way since then, and seen a lot of changes – professionalism, multi-million pound transfer fees, and proper crossbars where once there was just a tape. The greatest day in Scottish football (unless you were a 'Gers fan, perhaps) came in 1967 when Celtic's famous 'Lisbon Lions' lifted the European Cup; their illustrious manager, Jock Stein, was a Protestant. Sceptics will say the game isn't what it

used to be in the 'good old days' like 1938 when 92,000 fans crammed into Hampden to see East Fife play Kilmarnock in a Cup Final replay. But beneath all the glitzy new 'strips' and under all those snazzy hair-cuts, it remains basically the same old game: 22 players kicking a bladder around a field. It beats fighting. I for one would rather have 'Wembley 1967' than 'Flodden 1513' any day.

And where is the fitba' that
 I played and saw,
The fair shou'der charge and
 the pass aff the wa'?
There was nae 4-3-3, there
 was nae 4-2-4,
And your mates didna kiss
 whenever ye'd score.
Is the game, like big Woodburn,
 suspended sine die?
(A verse from Adam McNaughtan's *The Glasgow That I Used To Know*.)

▲ *England versus Scotland 1936. Walker places the ball beyond Sagar, the English goalkeeper, to earn a 1 - 1 draw.*

▲ *Producing mighty ocean-going vessels such as the S.S. Aquitania, seen here under construction at John Brown & Co's shipyard in Clydebank in 1911, became the basis of the Scottish economy as the nineteenth century drew to a close. A whole raft of support skills and industries depended heavily on the success of the riveters. By 1913, one third of the U.K.'s shipping tonnage was slipping out of the Clyde and onto the oceans of the world.*

I must now conclude my say
By telling the world fearlessly without
 the least dismay
That your central girders would not
 have given way
At least many sensible men do say
Had they been supported on each
 side with buttresses . . .

(Lines from William McGonagall's poem describing the Tay Bridge Disaster. McGonagall, a former Dundee handloom weaver, became the world's most famous bad poet!)

The locomotives rolling off the assembly line in Glasgow's Springburn works pulled their loads not only across Britain but all over the world. They were transported to the furthest reaches of the Empire and beyond in that other great engineering product of the Clyde, the steamship. From the day in 1812 when the passenger steamer *Comet* sailed out from its home yard in Port Glasgow to herald the world's first commercial steamship service, the Clyde's future as the world's greatest shipbuilding centre – ever – was assured. Thousands of them slid from the shipyards into the River Clyde's murky waters and onto the oceans.

Steamship building didn't take off quite as meteorically as the locomotive industry, reaching its peak only in the closing decades of that century. Until the opening of the Suez Canal in 1869 drastically reduced the distance to the eastern outposts of Empire, progress was hampered by the inadequacy of the steam engine to make the long haul around the Cape of Good Hope. But thereafter sailing clippers like the Dumbarton-built *Cutty Sark* were put in their place. Engineers like Robert Napier, 'the prince of marine engineers', perfected the engines, scientists such as Lord Kelvin invented instruments like compasses that could work in the metal-hulled ships, and the workers acquired new skills as platers and riveters. By the end of the century, the Clyde was turning out half of the United Kingdom's marine engines and a fifth of the world's ships – cargo vessels, liners, and of course battleships.

None of those railway locomotives or ships would have been built, though, had it not been for the ceaseless burrowings of the colliers. Without them the 'Industrial Revolution' would not have been possible. Stanley Jevons, an economist of the day, shrewdly observed: 'coal stands not beside, but entirely above all other commodities. It is the material source of the energy of the country – the universal aid – the factor in everything we do.' 'Black rock', as coal used to be called, had been howked from the bowels of the earth since the twelfth century. But the modest industry begun by the white-clad Cistercian monks of Newbattle Abbey, in Midlothian, fittingly within sight of the pit-head gear at Lady Victoria Colliery, Scotland's Mining Museum, was 'revolutionised' beyond all recognition during the course of the nineteenth century.

In 1799 Parliament declared an end to serfdom,

the degrading practice that had been the tarnished hallmark of the coal and salt industries for the best part of 300 years. Even so, as the new century dawned colliers' wives and families still crawled along the labyrinthine tunnels, hauling their coal hutches and breaking their backs lifting heavy loads up the rickety ladders to the fresh air above – a task likened to climbing Ben Lomond each day with a hundredweight (65 kg) of Kendal mint-cake in your backpack.

A century on and the coal industry was a different world altogether. Where once a few thousand had toiled to supply barely a ton of coal each year, now almost 150,000 miners, all men, emptied the earth of 42 million tons – 10 tons per day for every man, woman and child in the country. Gone now were the child-propelled hutches, and the ladders swarming with women; into their place had come pit-ponies, destined to live their entire lives underground, and iron cages hoisted by powerful steam engines, coal-fired naturally. Where before mine shafts had sunk to 160 ft (50 m), now they plumbed depths of 1600 ft (500 m) and more.

Not everyone mined coal, or tapped molten iron and steel from the fiery furnace, or dripped

with sweat in the locomotive works, or cheered as their handiwork glided into the Clyde; far from it. Countless others continued to work the land to produce the food for the new working class, or laboured in by-now well-established industries like textiles.

In 1815, nine out of every ten working Scots were employed in the textile industry. In Ayrshire they specialised in lace, in Paisley silk shawls, in Border towns like Galashiels and Hawick woollen knitwear and tweeds, in Dunfermline fine linen, and in Dundee of course jute – one of the three 'Js' (the others being 'Jam' and 'Journalism') for which Dundee is famous. So overwhelmingly important was the jute industry to the town on the Tay that it became known as 'Juteopolis'.

But here, as with the coal industry, times were changing. As the nineteenth century wore on, competition from overseas, and wars here, there and everywhere disrupting supplies and markets, forced the industry to cut its costs or perish. Unlike mining and heavy engineering, which required plenty of muscle, cotton-spinning, lace-making and thread-weaving were just as easily done by women, and children as well for that matter, and at much less cost. By 1880, two out of every three workers in an industry employing 100,000 people were women and children. In Dundee, almost the entire workforce was female, leading one observer in 1912 to note that 'the husbands stay at home dry-nursing; the woman

The granting of Saturday afternoons off to Scotland's workforce in the 1860s led to more time for leisure and recreation, and one way of enjoying yourself on Clydeside was to go 'doon the watter' on a paddle-steamer. Everyone benefited – the holiday-makers who sailed on them, such as those seen above embarking at the Broomielaw, in Glasgow, around 1890; the riveters like those pictured left working in John Brown's Clydebank shipyard and the Scottish economy that relied increasingly heavily on the shipbuilding industry as its saviour.

'The Man in the Cloth Cap'

~ JAMES KEIR HARDIE ~

'No noble task was ever easy'

(Motto on the first membership card of the Scottish Labour Party, 1888)

It was an inauspicious start to what turned out to be a most remarkable life – born illegitimate to a Lanarkshire farm-girl in 1856. But by the time he passed away at his modest Ayrshire home 57 years later, 'the man in the cloth cap' was fêted as the founding father of the Labour Party.

The reference to the cloth cap is one of the few myths that has crept into the life of James Keir Hardie; he much preferred a deer-stalker. He was just 10 when he was sent down the pit. There his skill as a communicator soon surfaced and at the age of 23 he was embroiled in his first 'action', the 'tattie strike' of 1880, so called because the members of the Lanarkshire Miners' Union were reduced to scrabbling around for potatoes in order to survive. The young Hardie's involvement forced him to move to Ayrshire, but here too he was soon involving himself in the struggle of the newly formed Ayrshire Miners' Union.

Even so, Hardie was still a confirmed Liberal, as were most of his class. It had been the Liberal Party that had achieved so much for the working man, such as the Reform Act of 1868 extending the right to vote to all male urban householders, the abolition of child labour and improved working conditions for women, compulsory education for all 5-to-14-year-olds and public health reforms. As James Keir Hardie took his seat as secretary of the Ayrshire Miners' Union, William Ewart Gladstone, Liberal Prime Minister and 'Grand Old Man' of British political life, whose parents were also Scots, was settling into his favourite armchair in Downing Street, London,

contemplating what further measures he could introduce to better the lot of the British working man.

But when, over the winter of 1886-7, Hardie felt the stone-hearted contempt of the coal-barons at his old Blantyre pit, and witnessed the brutality of the police and the military as they set about his brother miners, he knew in his heart

▲ *Keir Hardie displays his oratorical skills at a peace rally in Trafalgar Square, London, at the outset of the Great War.*

that Liberalism could no longer stand up for the working man. What was needed was working men like himself in Parliament fighting their own corner.

The perfect opportunity seemed to arise early in 1888 – a by-election in the safe Liberal seat of Mid-Lanark. Hardie put his name forward as a Liberal 'working-class' candidate on a radical ticket. It was too much for the local Association who 'parachuted in' a wealthy London-based Welsh barrister instead. Hardie, undaunted, broke with the party and put himself forward as an 'Independent Labour' candidate. The fact that he lost, and lost heavily (Lib: 3847; Con: 2917; Ind. Lab: 617),

somehow seems irrelevant now. What his standing did was attract nationwide interest. The word 'Labour' had entered the political arena.

Within weeks of his defeat, Hardie helped form the Scottish Labour Party (motto: 'no monopoly – no privilege'). The aim as Hardie saw it was to free the Scottish workers 'from the bondage of commercialism'. It is far from clear what Hardie knew of Karl Marx's political philosophy, or indeed whether he had even read *Das Kapital*. What is abundantly clear is that Hardie was no confrontationalist. Although the ultimate aim might have been 'the cooperative ownership by the workers of land and the means of production', and despite emotionally charged words like 'agitate' and 'organise' appearing on the first S.L.P. membership cards, Hardie's socialism was 'an alliance of all good men against the evil intent of capitalism', not all-out class war. Perhaps he knew deep down in his heart that the Scots weren't quite ready for out-and-out socialism. After all, his heavy defeat at Mid-Lanark was largely down to his brother miners staying loyal to the old and familiar Liberalism. An associate of Hardie's once remarked: 'whilst the large majority of the miners are socialists, that is unknown to themselves'. But that wasn't going to deter Hardie; as the S.L.P. membership card warned: 'no noble task was ever easy'.

In the event the Scottish Labour Party failed. A rag-bag of competing interests, from Highland land reformers to Scottish home-rulers, jumped on the bandwagon. Hardie, dispirited, moved to London. His reputation went before him, and in the

1892 general election he was returned as the Member for West Ham, the first MP to sit for the Independent Labour Party. His place in the pantheon of the British Labour Party was assured.

But like many an MP before and since, his was a 'here today – gone tomorrow' existence. In 1895 the electorate of West Ham sent him packing, and he returned to his native land. He found it little changed. If anything, the rising popularity of the Conservatives in England, following a major split in the Liberal Party over Irish home rule, caused many workers to stay faithful to Liberalism. Hardie soon returned south, this time for good. On 27 February 1900 he formed the Labour Representation Committee, and later that year the electors of Merthyr Tydfil took him to their Welsh hearts. At last he represented a mining constituency such as he had aspired to in 1888, and unlike West Ham this time he stayed put.

But if there was one year that James Keir Hardie would perhaps recall with most pride it would be 1906. In that year he helped found the modern Labour Party. In the general election of that year 29 Labour MPs were returned to the House of Commons, and those proud representatives of the working class had no hesitation in declaring Hardie the first chairman of the Parliamentary Labour Party. Not bad for an illegitimate ex-miner. The only cloud was the abject failure of his own Scottish workers to return more than two MPs, for Dundee and Glasgow Blackfriars. Only in the aftermath of the Great War would the Scottish working-class 'rise like lions' and wrest the political centre ground from Liberal and Tory alike.

What if Hardie had beaten Wynford Philipps to the Liberal candidature of the Mid-Lanark seat in 1888? Would the Labour Party have come into being? Or would the Liberals and their arch-rivals the Tories still be slugging it out for the right to represent 'the people'. We shall never know. What we do know, with our benefit of hindsight, is that the whole face of British politics was irrevocably changed when 'the man in the cloth cap', James Keir Hardie, fervent socialist, ardent pacifist, passionate feminist, but above all idealist, stood up in front of audiences across the land, held them in thrall and made them think about what it was to be 'socialist':

Come now, Men and Women, I plead with you, for your own sake and that of your children, for the sake of the downtrodden poor, the weary, sore-hearted mothers, the outcast, unemployed fathers – for their sakes, and for the sake of our beloved Socialism, the hope of peace and humanity throughout the world – Men and Women, I appeal to you, come and join us and fight with us in the fight wherein none shall fail.

---

goes out to earn wages: what an inversion of civilisation!' Little surprise then to learn that it was in Dundee that women first took formal strike action when the Dundee and District Mill and Factory Operatives Union 'downed tools' in 1885.

At the outset of the industrial revolution in the 1780s, Scotland was a land where power and privilege were the preserve of the few, servility and suffering the sad lot of the many. But even before the Dundee women vented their collective spleens in 1885, the working class had already wrung a few improvements in pay and working conditions from their grudging employers. Now they were arming themselves for another tilt at the twin windmills of political democracy and workers' rights.

STATE AND SOCIETY

On a chilly March morning in 1890, Edward Prince of Wales officially opened the Forth Rail Bridge, 'the eighth wonder of the world'. To this day it stands as a fitting memorial to the Victorian economy, and the three pillars on which it was founded – coal, iron and rail. The future king's simple act that morning marked the culmination of a half-century of Scottish industrial supremacy that saw the nation's products dispersed throughout the world. But at what cost; 57 men had fallen to their deaths in the River Forth's icy depths, and another 461 were seriously injured, in

▼ Scotland's industrial society was founded on coal, from coalmines such as Prestongrange Colliery, in East Lothian. The first shaft was sunk in 1829; the last shift was brought back up to the surface in 1960.

▲ The suburb of Garngad, in Glasgow, makes for a grim picture. Yet such were familiar sights in the industrial heartland of west-central Scotland throughout much of the later nineteenth and early twentieth centuries. Wars here, there and everywhere may have resulted in the tragic deaths of so many Scots, but far, far more died in the 'slumlands' of Glasgow, Greenock and elsewhere, from such killers as cholera, typhoid and the dreaded TB – tuberculosis.

the eight years it took to construct the bridge – 518 more casualties to add to the many thousands who had already suffered producing Scotland's industrial miracle.

Labour was plentiful; that was the 'mantra' murmured by employers and what bought Scotland her industrial miracle. There were exceptions to the rule. Robert Owen's philanthropy towards his workers in the cotton mills of New Lanark at the outset of the century is legendary; Walter Crum's enlightened attitude towards his workforce at his calico-printing works in Thornliebank, Paisley, as the century drew to its close scarcely rates a mention today. But whereas Crum's workers undoubtedly benefited from their employer's 'profits-sharing' scheme and their involvement in the planning of the 'model' village which Crum built for them, the jury is still out as to precisely what Owen's motives were – outright philanthropy? 'Incentivisation' of the workforce?

Or simple paternalism, an unwavering conviction that he knew what was best for the poor wretches in the lowest orders of society? One thing is clear. Notwithstanding all Owen did to improve the lot of the children in his factory village, they still had to crawl beneath the clanking, shaking looms picking up fluff.

Working conditions for those fortunate to be in employment were mostly appalling – six days a week, 14 hours a day, with two extra days off a year if they were lucky. 'Six days shalt thou labour and do all that you are able; On the Sabbath-day wash the horses' legs and tidy up the stable', was a jingle popular with Fife ploughmen in 1903. The excessively long hours applied equally to children and women as they did to men, and if the workers had not risen up and the state not intervened, the bosses would have had it so till the end of time. Take wee John Myles, a Dundee flax mill worker by the time he was seven, who was at his work by

05.30 and away no earlier than 19.30, with two half-hour breaks for breakfast and lunch. Or the case of two teenage girls sweating in temperatures as high as 150 degrees Fahrenheit in a Kelty brickworks in 1904, shifting 6000 bricks a day for the princely sum of 2s 3d, the price of a half-bottle of whisky.

If labour was plentiful, then life was cheap. There is no way of knowing the true list of casualties who suffered to create Scotland's economic miracle. There is no Scottish National Industrial Memorial standing alongside the Scottish National War Memorial in Edinburgh Castle. If there was, the former would surely contain the longer roll of honour. Take coal; in Victoria's Scotland, 800 men were killed or seriously injured on average every year, 207 men and boys in a single incident at the Blantyre pit in 1877, Scotland's biggest mining disaster. So commonplace had the death-toll become by 1900 that newspapers had long ceased running separate pieces and were simply listing the names of the dead. Not for nothing was it said that there was 'blood on every ton of coal'.

As if spending 14 hours a day in appalling working conditions wasn't bad enough, spare a further thought for those labouring there as they returned exhausted to their homes of an evening. Edinburgh's medieval 'high-rise' tenements had long had an unenviable reputation for crampedness and inadequate sanitation, but they were as nothing compared to the new tenement jungles rising up in the industrial heartland of west-central Scotland. Official statistics like the 1861 Census are the more shocking because of the stark reality they expose: 34 per cent of all homes in Scotland had just one room (the 'single end'), 37 per cent had just two rooms (the 'but-and-ben'), and 1 per cent of families lived in homes without any windows. Just imagine a husband and wife and their family, from teenagers down to babes in arms, living, eating and sleeping all in one room measuring 14 by 10 – feet not metres!

The problem was at its worst in Glasgow simply because of the monstrous growth of the place from provincial cathedral city to big-time metropolis. Illness, disease and death were frequent visitors to the wynds and closes. Over 4000 people were

killed at one fell swoop during the cholera epidemic that ravaged the country in 1853, a disaster that prompted the city fathers to build the Loch Katrine Water Works. In breeding grounds such as these, little wonder that one child in five never got the chance to celebrate his or her first birthday, or that half of the city's wains died before they were five.

And as the landless from the Highlands entered the city, and as the immigrants from famine-ravaged Ireland came too, all desperately seeking work and housing, so the overcrowding got worse, and with it the hardship and squalor it spawned. In the middle years of the century the average life

▲ *Glasgow 1868; amid such squalor was Scotland's economic miracle made – low expectations, low wages and low esteem.*

'Votes for Women'

~ SCOTLAND'S SUFFRAGETTES ~

'We do not want to usurp anything, but to do our proper part in helping on the world's reform'

(Jane Taylour, honorary secretary of the Galloway branch of the National Society for Women's Suffrage, in a speech to the Kirkwall branch, 1871)

On 6 May 1999, 48 women were returned as Members of the Scottish Parliament (MSPs) – 48 out of 129 all told, or 37 per cent. But had that election been held when it should have been, 75 years earlier, before the Great War scuppered the chances of the Scottish Home Rule Bill becoming law, there would have been precisely no women representatives, just a sea of bearded faces and top hats across the benches.

It took the appalling brutality of that war, and more particularly the contribution women made to the winning of it, that finally shook the male-dominated British Establishment into granting women the right to vote in general elections. Even then it was grudgingly given – to women aged 30 and over – at a time when most males over 21 had had that privilege for three decades and more. It would be another 10 years before women and men would have equal suffrage (suffrage, 'a power to vote', from the Latin *suffragium*, 'vote'). It had been a long hard road.

'She advances, it is true, when he advances; but it is no less true that she is always kept some steps behind him.'

Marion Reid's perceptive words were written just 11 years after some 65,000 Scotsmen had been added to the electoral roll as a result of the 1832 Reform Act. At a stroke of William III's pen, another two per cent of the population now found they had the right to vote for those who would be in authority over them. But the clamour for a wider suffrage continued unabated, and it wasn't all male-

dominated. In 1867, the year before another 150,000-odd Scotsmen (urban householders) were added to the register, an Edinburgh branch of the new National Society for Women's Suffrage was formed. By 1874 there were branches from Laurencekirk to Lerwick. It wasn't long before the contribution 'the fairer sex' might make to the nation's well-being was being recognised, when the

▲ *A suffragette is arrested during a demonstration in Dundee around 1910. The city on the Tay was a hotbed of feminism.*

passing of the 1872 Education (Scotland) Act permitted women not only to vote for members of the newly established School Boards, but actually to stand for election as well. Well, it wasn't too risky, was it, letting ladies get involved in children's affairs? As one Glasgow hack wrote in his newspaper at the time, it was an area 'in which ladies can be useful and do some service to the State, without in any way sacrificing the bloom of their womanhood.'

Bless him, to think so selflessly of the women-folk! He wouldn't appear, though, to have visited Dundee, and

seen the ladies there 'sacrificing the bloom of their womanhood', sweating away in the jute mills for most of the hours God sent them, and for a pittance, before returning home tired and exhausted to look after their unemployed husbands and sickly wains.

Despite such entrenched and unenlightened attitudes, the tide was now turning inexorably in the women's favour. With the growing and vociferous support of 'new' men like Keir Hardie, they won the right to vote in local elections (1882; although to qualify they had to be over 30 and either unmarried or widowed) and subsequently the right to stand as candidates in those elections (1895). They even won the right to go to university in 1889. But it was all very slow-going, and somewhere up the hill their patience snapped.

It snapped not long after the huge Liberal landslide in the 1906 general election, a victory that should have enabled Sir Henry Campbell-Bannerman, Glaswegian and Prime Minister of his country, to deliver his promise to enfranchise women. He didn't. All he secured was their right to vote and stand in burgh council elections, a right curiously denied them in 1895. But as far as national politics went – nothing.

It was the last straw. In 1908 the 'fur gloves' came off. The Scottish headquarters of the militant Women's Social and Political Union, founded by Emmeline Pankhurst, Britain's best-known 'suffragette', opened in Glasgow. Shortly afterwards, Dr Elsie Inglis, one of the first women to graduate from a

Scottish university, launched her Scottish Women's Suffrage Movement in Edinburgh. The temperature of the debate rose, and with it the women's anger. Suffragettes poured acid into pillar boxes, smashed windows, and set light to a variety of buildings, including Ayr racecourse and Leuchars railway station – and, most bizarrely of all, the pretty village kirk at Whitekirk in East Lothian. They were even accused of attempting to capture that bastion of male virility, the Wallace Monument in Stirling! The authorities closed the Palace of Holyroodhouse to the public for fear they would destroy that too.

It was all to little avail. Even as the dark clouds of war thundered in from the Continent in 1914, their efforts had wrung no concessions out of the Liberal government. Male chauvinism still ruled; when Dr Inglis offered her medical services to the War Office at the outbreak of hostilities, she was politely told by the faceless civil service bureaucrat who interviewed her: 'My good lady, go home and sit still'. She didn't, of course, and instead set up a chain of all-women hospitals and ambulance stations along the western front. Her stubbornness, and that of thousands like her, won in the end. In 1918, as Lloyd George began to build his 'homes fit for heroes' in the euphoria that followed the war, women finally won their right to vote and stand in general elections.

They didn't waste any time exercising that power. Eunice Murray has the distinction of being the first woman to stand in a general election, as an Independent for Glasgow Bridgeton in 1918; she came third. But it was the Conservatives (or Unionists as they were called then) in 1928 who gave Scotland its first woman MP, when Katherine Atholl, Duchess of Mar, became the parliamentary representative for the good people of Kinross and West Perthshire. What irony, for neither the party nor its first woman representative in Parliament had ever had much enthusiasm for women's rights. But then neither did Labour's first woman MP, Jennie Lee, who joined Katherine Atholl in the House of Commons the following year. However, it says much for both women, and for the entry of women generally onto the centre-stage of British politics, that they were committed first and foremost to the rights and concerns of all their constituents, and not just the newly enfranchised women.

Auld nature swears, the lovely dears
Her noblest work she classes O;
Her 'prentice han' she tried on man,
An' then she made the lasses O.'
(Robert Burns in *Green Grow The Rashes*, 1784.)

---

expectancy for Glaswegians actually dropped, from 42 to 37 for men, and for women down five to 40. One seasoned visitor was so appalled by what he saw he was moved to write:

I have seen human degradation in some of its worst places, but I can advisedly say that I did not believe until I visited the wynds of Glasgow that so large amount of filth, crime, misery and disease existed in one spot in any civilised country.

The arrival of the Highlanders simply exacerbated an existing problem; the arrival of the Irish added a new ingredient to the already volatile brew – sectarianism. For those crossing the Irish Sea were both Catholic and Protestant. There was no love lost between the two traditions, the 'Orange' (named after the Protestant King William of Orange) and the 'Green' (from Ireland's nickname, the 'Emerald Isle'), whilst they were in Ireland; neither side saw any reason to 'kiss and make up' once on Scottish soil.

Irish immigrants had begun to have an impact on Scottish society before 1800, mainly as seasonal workers making the short sea-crossing to eke out their paltry wages by labouring on Lowland farms and in the factories of the Central Belt. Orange 'lodges' soon began to spring up in towns around Glasgow, the first at Maybole by 1800. (The first Scottish 'twelfth of July' parade, to commemorate 'King Billy's' victory over the Catholic James VII at the Boyne in 1692, held in

▼ *Female jute-weavers work at their Dundee looms. In sharp contrast to the male-dominated heavy industries on the Clyde, Dundee's workforce was overwhelmingly female.*

▲ *Forget your Clackmannanshire collieries and Clydeside shipyards! It was the Carron Iron Company that became the icon of Scotland's industrial revolution. Founded as early as 1759, it not only launched the revolution; it led from the front for the rest of its long life. The company that gave James Watt his big break in 1766, and locked out Robert Burns in 1787, went on to become the largest ironworks in Europe, employing a workforce of over 2000 and casting anything from cannonballs to telephone kiosks. It was a sad day for Scotland when the famous Carron name slipped into the pages of history in 1982.*

*'We cam' na here to
    view your warks
In hopes to be mair wise,
But only, lest we gang
    to hell,
It may be nae surprise!'*

(From Robert Burns's Written on a window of the inn at Carron, *1787)*

Glasgow in 1821, was a flop by all accounts.) By 1830 'ghettos' of Catholic and Protestant immigrants, the former outnumbering the latter by three or four to one, were beginning to develop. Resentment grew, not just between the two immigrant communities but between the Catholic incomers and home-grown Scots.

It has to be said that religion was more the catalyst than the cause, as is often the case. The Scots were a proud Presbyterian lot who not only detested 'popery' but feared it too. But the root cause of the tension was the increasing economic and social hardship felt by working-class Scots as they saw their jobs taken by incomers prepared to work for drastically lower wages. Such was the inspiration behind a sinister poster that appeared in the quiet Fife port of Kinghorn in 1845:

NOTICE IS GIVEN that all the Irish men on the line of railway in Fife Share must be off the grownd and owt of the countey on Monday the 11th of this month or els we must by the strenth of our armes and a good pick shaft put them off. Your humbel servants, Schots men.

Such latent tensions began to surface in the following year as a massive tidal wave of immigrants swept up the Clyde in the wake of the great famine; more than 30,000 arrived in Glasgow in four months in 1847. By 1850 Glasgow was home to 10 per cent of all of Britain's Irish immigrants. All were starved and destitute; the overwhelming majority were Catholic. The strain on Glasgow, and on the industrial towns around, was too much and resentment frequently bubbled up into open conflict. A century and a half later and Scotland still bears the scars of that rivalry between the Orange and the Green.

Oh! It is the greatest mix-up the
    world has ever seen,
Ma faither he wis Orange, an' ma
    maither she wis Green.
(A traditional Glasgow song.)

The increasingly dire situation of the urban working class could not continue if Scotland was to sustain its economic miracle. Something had to be done, but by whom? The employers didn't see it as in their interest to improve the lot of their workers; there were plenty more where they came from. And the workers themselves, for all they had been forming 'trades unions' in individual factories for years, somehow lacked the collective will to unite for the common cause.

Ironically, in an age when *laissez-faire* 'leave well alone' was the order of the day, it was the State that took the initiative. Despite vociferous opposition from sections of society opposed to State intervention, including not just privileged individuals who would have to pay more in taxes, but corporate bodies like town councils and the Church of Scotland who resented growing interference from 'Big Brother', government commissions were set up to investigate and report on a whole raft of issues, from child-employment to public health. Legislation followed, slowly but surely.

As early as 1833 the first measure designed to control child labour appeared on the Statute Book; Althorp's Act set a minimum age of nine for children working in cotton mills, and limited the working day of those aged under 13 to eight hours. A modest move, but one in the right direction at least. In 1842 the Mining Act put an end to the degrading practice of sending women and children down the pit, and further Factory Acts attempted to protect more of the vulnerable and exploitable in society. But passing laws was one thing; policing them was another. Until the introduction in 1851 of a formal register of births, marriages and deaths, it was well-nigh impossible to confirm someone's age. Employers cavilled at this unwanted intervention in their affairs, but there was little they could do other than search for, and generally find, loopholes in the law.

The Church of Scotland too was concerned at this growing 'meddling' by the State. It was an unseemly row over patronage, the right to appoint ministers to parishes, that led directly to the 'Disruption' of 1843, when two-fifths of the clergy and a third of their congregations 'walked out' to form a Free Church of Scotland, independent of the State. As a result the squabbling rump of clerics left behind lost much of its credibility for most of what remained of the century, and was powerless to stop the State taking over responsibility for poor-relief and elementary education, the two main planks in the Kirk's mission since the Reformation.

For the best part of three centuries, Kirk sessions the length and breadth of the land had toiled hard to help the needy in society, and educate its young children, and they had every right to be enormously proud of their achievement. The Scots had a reputation for being one of the best educated nations in Europe – some would say the best – and as statistics are the yardstick that dictate education policy today, then a simple statistic from 1855 confirms that the Scots were certainly streets ahead of the English when it came to literacy. The marriage registers for that year show that 87 per cent of husbands and 77 per cent of wives in Scotland were able to sign their names, compared to just 70 per cent and 59 per cent respectively south of the Border! But the overwhelmingly pastoral nature of society in Knox's day had by now become intensively urbanised, and quite simply the Kirk could no longer cope. Poor law and education legislation largely relieved it of both, and by the Great War compulsory education for all five to 14-year-olds, free school meals, school inspectors and 'nit ladies' had become part-and-parcel of Scottish life.

This growing intervention by the State in the

'It's a man's world' – well, it certainly was in Scotland's Central Belt in the later nineteenth century, with its reliance on heavy industry. Men such as the one pictured here, toiling in the mighty Carron Ironworks, near Falkirk, were the workforce on which Scotland's claim to being the 'Workshop of the Empire' had been built. But these skilled and semi-skilled men were among the poorest paid in the country, and with the huge growth in the population of the Lowlands throughout the century, were constantly in fear of losing their jobs. Only in the more traditional, lighter industries, such as textiles, were women, and children of course, tolerated. But all that would be changed as a new century dawned and a world war helped create the conditions for a new society.

way Scots lived their lives was officially recognised in 1885 with the creation of the Scottish Office and the appointment of the Duke of Richmond as Secretary for Scotland. (Since the abolition of the post in 1746, responsibility for Scotland's affairs had been subsumed by the British Home Secretary.) But in one vital area, that of workers' rights, there had scarcely been any progress at all. The arrival on the stage of someone far removed from the priviliged world of Charles Henry, Duke of Richmond, and former ADC to the Duke of Wellington, would change all that. Cue James Keir Hardie.

In the aftermath of Waterloo, and with the spectres of the American and French Revolutions still fresh in their minds, successive British governments had inched forward in extending political democracy to a wider electorate. The great Reform Act of 1832 enfranchised Scotland's 'middle class' – over 60,000 people (all men naturally!). Now a thumping two per cent of the population was entitled to vote and stand for Parliament. Even this was too much for some.

There was little desire on the part of the privileged few in society to see the many rewarded for their pains; no good could possibly come of it.

▲ When the Glasgow publisher, Walter Blackie, met Charles Rennie Mackintosh in 1902 to discuss designs for a house in the Dunbartonshire town of Helensburgh, he told him that he 'rather fancied grey rough cast for the walls, and slate for the roof; and that any architectural effect should be secured by the massing of the parts rather than by adventitious ornamentation'. When, two years later, Mackintosh handed Blackie the keys to his new 'des. res', The Hill House, he replied: 'Here is the house. It is not an Italian villa, an English mansion house, a Swiss chalet, or a Scotch castle; it is a dwelling house'. Blackie was clearly delighted at his choice of architect, for he lived at The Hill House for the rest of his days. And courtesy of the National Trust for Scotland, we too can visit and enjoy this undoubted Mackintosh treasure.

That was what 'fuddy-duddies' like Lord Cockburn felt as they saw the industrial society grow, and with it the clamour for 'workers' rights'. In a diary entry for 1848, the year Europe was aflame with revolution and the Chartist spirit was sweeping Britain, Cockburn warned that 'a manufacturing population, of which about a half is always hungry, and the passions of this hunger always excited by political delusion, it is not easy to see how wealth and sense are to keep their feet.'

How dare the masses demand things like the right to the vote, and what is more be allowed to do so in secret! What was all this stuff and nonsense about MPs being paid, of the removal of the property qualification before you could stand for Parliament, of annual elections? Cockburn and his like could only see the end of civilisation as they knew it resulting from the dark shadows of the 'enlarging and darkening tree' of populism.

All Lord Cockburn could do was wring his hands. All the employers needed to do was sit on theirs. While there was plenty of cheap labour, there was little need for them to change. As for the workers themselves, it was always going to be an uphill struggle. We might be forgiven for thinking that Scotland has long been a socialist country,

some would say its very cradle, but until the emergence of Keir Hardie and other like-minded spirits as the nineteenth century drew to a close, Scotland by and large was a liberal (and Liberal with a capital 'L') society, very much for self-help and against hereditary privilege; all good Enlightenment stuff. 'Cooperation, not confrontation' was the order of the day.

And that approach had wrung a few concessions out of the employers and the State. Elements of the Factory Acts, which had largely addressed female and child employment, did at least rub off onto the male workforce, like the granting in the 1860s of a half-day holiday on Saturdays for many categories of workers; now they would be able to attend the new sporting entertainment that was all the rage – football! In 1868 the right to vote was extended to all urban male householders, adding another 100,000 names to the electoral roll. In 1885 the names of their rural counterparts were added also, thereby enfranchising that other long-abused element in society, the crofters. Now, only 40 per cent of the male population remained without the vote, and all the women of course.

But the bloody events of the '80s and '90s changed all that, as the workers' hopes for improved pay and working conditions were cruelly dashed beneath the stamping hooves of the hussars' horses – in the Blantyre miners' strike over the winter of 1886-7, for instance, and the Caledonian Company railway workers' strike of 1891. It was the first of these that finally drove Keir Hardie to abandon his Liberalism and become an outspoken propagandist for socialism. From the moment Hardie helped found the Scottish Labour Party in Glasgow on 19 May 1888, the Liberal Party, in the ascendancy over their arch-rivals the Tories for much of the century, was forced onto the back foot in Scotland. From the time he formed the British Labour Party in London on 27 February 1900, Liberalism was forced onto the defensive across the United Kingdom as a whole.

But no sooner had the new century dawned than a far greater menace threatened the stability, even the very existence, of the United Kingdom. The two political heavyweights, Liberal and Tory, and the newcomer in the parliamentary ring, Labour, had all to put aside their differences for the moment to take on the armed might of Germany.

'Glasgow by Design'
~ CHARLES RENNIE MACKINTOSH ~

'Move a Mackintosh chair in a Mackintosh interior and you alter the whole ensemble'
(Alan Crawford, in Charles Rennie Mackintosh, 1995)

Charles Rennie Mackintosh was much more than an architect of buildings, he was the 'complete' designer, turning his hand to everything – interior decor, furniture and furnishings, the lot. In his marital home in Glasgow, even the cat was 'colour-coordinated'!

The Glasgow Mackintosh was born into in 1868 was a metropolitan dynamo. If there had been a 'European City of Design and Engineering' then, as there is a 'European City of Culture' today, Glasgow would have won year after year. Whilst great engines rolled off the production lines, and whilst mighty ships slid into the Clyde to head for all corners of the globe, so new designers, technicians and craftsmen were needed in the drawing offices and workshops of the factories and shipyards.

And that was where the young Mackintosh, son of a Dennistoun 'bobby', was headed. By the time he was nine, he was a pupil at Allan Glen's Institution (now embedded in the University of Strathclyde), founded in 1850 by a wealthy benefactor 'to give a good practical education'. There the talented youngster honed his skills in technical drawing and engineering design. His artistic bent developed soon after, at night classes in Glasgow School of Art.

Within ten years of entering architectural practice in 1889, Mackintosh designed a new Art School for his former Governors. It has become his most famous building, many would say his finest. Although Mackintosh spoke emotionally of 'the monuments of our own fathers', there is precious little sign of it in the Art School.

Mackintosh wrote of clothing 'modern ideas with modern dress', and that is what he gave us in his Art School. It proved too 'modern' for his fellow Glaswegians, and they rejected him, by and large. Only his genius as an interior designer, and more specifically the commissions he got from Miss Catherine Cranston and her 'tea-rooms', sustained him through the early years of the new century. In the two years leading up to his departure from Scotland in 1914, his total output comprised just one commission, for a ladies' hairdressing salon in Union Street, Glasgow! What's that about a prophet being without honour in his own country? Disillusioned, Mackintosh turned his back on architecture and design, and increasingly indulged himself in his painting. And that was what he was doing when he died in 1928.

But in time Glaswegians became more comfortable with their native son's innovative creations. In 1950 the Corporation carefully removed into storage the fittings from his Ingram Street tea-rooms rather than see them flung into the skip along with everything else. In 1963 the University of Glasgow did much the same with the contents of the Mackintoshes' home in Florentine Terrace. And despite determined efforts to flatten other Mackintosh creations in the name of progress, his Martyrs' Public School in Parson Street, the Scotland Street School and Queen's Cross Church survive largely unscathed.

Around this time the outside world too began to take Mackintosh to their hearts. The 'experts', where once they had used language such as 'bizarre' and 'a wee bit odd', now wrote admiringly of 'functional simplicity' and a 'fusion of puritanism with sensuality'. He came to be recognised as 'prophetically modern', a pioneer of Art Nouveau, respected equally for his architectural skills as for his decorative work. We consumers were also persuaded to 'buy' him. In the early 1930s, a revolving bookcase of Mackintosh's was sold by mistake; the purchasers thought they were buying a wireless aerial! Forty years on and Mackintosh chairs were fetching small fortunes at Sotheby's. It wasn't long before reproduction Mackintosh furniture was rolling off the production line, closely followed by Mackintosh mugs, Mackintosh mirrors, even a Mackintosh typeface. Some wag termed it 'Mockintosh'.

Looking back now, through all that 'Mockintosh' to the real Mackintosh, it beggars belief that he was seen as something of a failure in his own lifetime, by himself and by others. But he, more than any other individual of his time, took Glasgow, design-wise, from the nineteenth into the twentieth century, out from the Victorian and into the Modern era. Perhaps he himself was too much the artist, too much the purist, for his own creations to receive ready acceptance. He was more a sculptor than a practical designer. But it was his style that contemporary designers took and transformed into attractive but practical products more likely to appeal to the city's upwardly-mobile middle-class clientèle.

Mackintosh's style is now recognised as Glasgow Style. Allan Glen would have been justly proud of his pupil.

SCOTLAND AT WAR

(1914 - 1945)

'This country is at war with Germany'

(Prime Minister Neville Chamberlain speaking to the nation on 3 September 1939)

In 1914 Britain was plunged into the first of the two World Wars that cast their deathly palls over the twentieth century. This chapter records Scotland's contributions in those dark days, and the deep depression that scarred the intervening years of peace.

WAR . . .

Over 500,000 Scots fought in the Great War, a tenth of the adult male population. One in four never made it back alive. No country other than Serbia and Turkey made a bigger sacrifice. As the first troops left for Flanders shortly after war was declared on 4 August 1914, it was said that they would be back by Christmas. Little did they know that it would be Christmas 1918.

The statistics of the slaughter are as stark as the row upon row of neat headstones in the war cemeteries themselves. Mons 1914 – the 1st battalion Royal Scots Fusiliers, 1000 men, reduced to 70; Neuve Chapelle, March 1915 – the 2nd Cameronians (Scottish Rifles) cut down from 900 to just 150; Loos, September 1915 – most of the 15th Scottish Division lost in the opening minutes of battle; Somme, July-November 1916 – an estimated 6300 casualties, including men from the 2nd Seaforth Highlanders, the 5th Cameron Highlanders, the 2nd Gordon Highlanders and the 10th Argyll and Sutherland Highlanders, on the first day. And so on, and so on. And not just in Flanders' fields, but on the beaches of Gallipoli, 1915 (1200 Royal Scots and the commanding officer and half of his 1st King's Own Scottish Borderers as they attempted their landing), in Macedonia and Mesopotamia, Palestine and Egypt, on the high seas (including Jutland, May 1916) and in an entirely new theatre of war, the air. When the Kaiser's zeppelins appeared in the skies above Edinburgh one dark night in 1916, the noise of war returned to Scotland for the first time since Culloden 1746.

> When you see millions of the mouthless dead
> Across your dreams in pale battalions go,
> Say not soft things, as other men have said,
> That you'll remember. For you need not so.
> Give them not praise. For, deaf,
> how should they know
> It is not curses heaped on each gashed head?
> Nor tears. Their blind eyes see not
> your tears flow.

◀ *The storm clouds of war had just cleared when Alfred G. Buckham photographed this stunning view of Edinburgh in 1919. The Great War (1914-18) was the first conflict in which Scots had to fear attack from the skies. Indeed, the only occasion the castle's famous One O'Clock Gun was ever called on to fire in anger came in April 1916 when one of the Kaiser's zeppelins (airships) appeared over the port of Leith and began dropping its payload on the city.*

Scots; or for the countless more who joined the so-called 'pals' battalions, whole groups of men and boys from the same town, the same slums, all flocking to the same colours. Very few needed to be compelled in those early days, not even the employees of the Earl of Wemyss in East Lothian, who on 29 August threatened that 'if they do not enlist, they will be compelled to leave my employment'.

The whiff of adventure, the chance to escape the slums of the city, the mines, steelworks and dole queue and head abroad with one's mates was clearly the main reason. And the pay wasn't bad either – 7s a week for a single man rising to 22s for a married man with four of a family. And of course they would be back by Christmas! Some, alas, didn't even make it out of Scotland; in May 1915 , 217 men of the 7th Royal Scots died in a horrific train crash near Gretna Green.

The Great War affected not only those who had to endure the carnage of the trenches; it touched those they left behind too. No one death was easy to accept, but the grieving can have been no more acute than in those communities who had waved farewell to the 'wee, hard men' of the 'pals' battalions, only to learn later that they had been gunned down almost as one. But no news can have been more devastating than that which reached the loved ones of the 500 men of Glasgow's Boys Brigade, who had helped form the 16th HLI in 1914 but who fell on the first morning of the Somme two years later; many were from the same street.

'La a bhlair's math na cairdean' ('Friends are good on the day of battle'), the simple Gaelic inscription on the monument to the fallen of the 51st (Highland) Division at the Battle of the Somme, 1916.

The Great War impacted not just on individual families and whole communities but on the entire Scottish people, both as it ran its bloody course and in its aftermath. The war itself was not without its good points; it brought a temporary halt to the

▲ *'Entrenched!' The year is 1917 and Scottish infantry crawl along yet another muddy Flanders trench, for yet another 'rendezvous with Death'. One in every four Scottish soldiers died in the trenches, 125,000 men – husbands, fathers, brothers, sons – out of a population of 4.7 million.*

'Another trench, another attack, another moment of wondering who would not come back.'

(Professor Christopher Harvie, in Scotland's Story, vol 46)

Nor honour. It is easy to be dead.
Say only this, 'They are dead.'
Then add thereto,
'Yet many a better one has died before.'
Then, scanning all the o'er-crowded mass, should you
Perceive one face that you loved heretofore,
It is a spook.
None wears the face you knew.
Great death has all his for evermore.
(Charles Hamilton Sorley's poem *When You See Millions of the Mouthless Dead*, written shortly before Sorley, an Aberdonian serving with the 7th Surrey Rifles, was killed at Ypres, July 1915.)

The readiness, eagerness even, shown by the young men of Scotland in accepting Lord Kitchener's call 'Your Country Needs You' in those first days and months overwhelms us who have the precious gift of hindsight and know all too well what horrors were in store for them; for the 20,000 men who hurried along to the recruiting office in Glasgow's Gallowgate before the month of August was out; for the thousand and more employees of Glasgow Corporation's Tramways Department who formed in a matter of hours an entire battalion of the Highland Light Infantry (the HLI), the city's local regiment; for the entire Watsonians XV who enlisted *en masse* in their city's regiment, the Royal

bitter political wrangling that had dominated the opening years of the century as everyone, the suffragettes included, rolled up their sleeves and rallied round. It brought, too, a welcome respite for the ailing heavy industries of the Central Belt. Suddenly there was an insatiable demand for guns and shells, ships and trains, plus newfangled tanks, submarines, airplanes, lorries and cars. The Clyde soon had the biggest concentration of war production in the U.K. It also gave women a real opportunity to show they were the equal of men, doing everything from making shells to 'clipping' bus tickets on the trams. Most welcomed them; only the skilled engineers feared for their employment prospects in the longer term.

The women soon showed their muscles in areas other than the factory. While the troops were marching off to war, thousands more men were descending on the Clyde 'from all the airts' to help the war effort – 20,000 within the first year.

Accommodation was soon at a premium, and the landlords quickly 'cashed in', hiking up rents by over 20 per cent. It was too much for the wives of the men 'at the front'. They began taking on 'the Landlord Huns', marching onto the streets waving placards reading, 'Our husbands are fighting Prussianism in France, and we are fighting the Prussians of Partick!', and barring their doors to the rent-collectors. Matters came to a head in November 1915 when the Govan shipyard workers downed tools and marched on the court where the rent-defaulters were appearing. Thousands more thronged the streets around. The trial collapsed and by Christmas the Government had given way and pegged rents for the rest of the war. The great Glasgow Rent Strike stands as a landmark in British social history, the first occasion a British Government listened to direct popular protest.

There were those who saw in the unrest the treacherous hand of pacifists determined to

▲ *They thought they would be home by Christmas 1914; and yet here they are still, the men of the 2nd battalion Royal Scots Fusiliers, in the Flanders trenches in 1915. Little did they know they were staring at another four years knee-deep in glore – and gore.*

'It was drizzling wet and vilely cold, the trenches in places thigh deep in clay and an awful mess of smashed barbed wire, mud and disintegrated German dead and debris of all sorts. In one trench our occupation for half-an-hour was hauling each other out of the tenacious and blood-stained mud.'

(Dr David Rorie, Royal Army Medical Corps, writing during the Battle of the Somme, 1916)

▲ 'At the going down of the sun we will remember them.' The rows of gravemarkers in Tyne Cot Cemetery, Belgium, overlook the desolate 'killing fields' of Flanders where the 11,871 soldiers buried here, the majority of them unknown by name, lost their young lives. The simple wooden crosses hastily erected in the aftermath of the horrendous Battle of Passchendaele, fought out in the closing months of 1917, simply overwhelm. Some good, though, came from the slaughter, for the utter futility of this battle, in which heavy casualties were sustained for just a few yards of bog, led to an increased clamour at home for an end to the bloodshed.

'slavery', raged David Kirkwood, then a little-known shop steward with Beardmore's, the iron and steel giant.

Up till then the Liberals had been the party of the working class. Not any more. The disillusioned workers in the munitions factories and shipyards were increasingly being drawn towards socialism by a new breed of trade unionist and political activist – men like Kirkwood, John Maclean and James Maxton – who saw no future in Liberalism. When they formed the Clyde Workers' Committee in early 1916, 'Red Clydeside' was born.

The Government was worried, so worried that in April 1916 it had nine shop stewards, among them Maclean, perhaps the most extreme of them all, rounded up and 'deported' to Edinburgh, where all was reasonably quiet. Within weeks Maclean, the Pollockshaws lad who had worked as a schoolteacher before being sacked in 1915 for his political beliefs, was prisoner no. 2652 in top-security Peterhead, serving the first of his four prison sentences for sedition and incitement to strike.

But Maclean and co. weren't to be deterred. Instead the course the war was taking persuaded more and more to support the cause they espoused – improved pay and working conditions, better housing, and of course peace through negotiation. They got some reward for their pains, including official recognition by a Royal Commission report into the vexed area of housing, published in 1917, that something had to be done urgently to address the problem of overcrowding. In the following year yet another Reform Act extended the right to vote to the remaining 40 per cent of the adult male population, those that were still living that is, and to certain women for the very first time. If there is any doubt where the patriotic loyalties of the 'Red Clydesiders' lay during the war with Germany, let them be dispelled by the declaration of David Kirkwood MP, Baron Bearsden himself: 'I was too proud of the battles of the past to stand aside and see Scotland conquered.'

undermine the war effort. They were mostly mistaken. There was an anti-militarist sentiment abroad, it is true, a distaste for war that festered and grew in intensity as the conflict dragged on and the full horror of the trenches revealed itself to the people back home. The feeling that the whole progress of the war was being grossly mismanaged, that the factory owners were making fat profits, fostered that unrest. But it was driven not by pacifism but by a determination by the workers to improve their lot. Even before the war they had begun venting their frustrations, nowhere more determinedly than at Singer's sewing machine factory in Clydebank in 1911 when the entire workforce of 12,000 men walked out in sheer desperation over pay and appalling living conditions, amongst the worst in Europe. The war simply brought the grievances more sharply into focus.

The delicate situation certainly wasn't helped by the Liberal Government rushing through legislation drastically curbing what few rights the workers already had. The Munitions of War Act 1915 was a particularly difficult pill to swallow, allowing unskilled men and women into the workplace to do the jobs of skilled men, and forbidding those same skilled men from leaving one employer for another   a condition akin to

'The Grand Scuttle'

~ SCAPA FLOW, 1919 ~

'I've got it! I believe they're scuttling their ships!'

(A lieutenant aboard one of the patrolling naval trawlers that June day in Scapa Flow.)

▲ *One of the 51 vessels of the German Hochseeflotte, sunk in 'the Grand Scuttle' of 1919, is raised from the murky depths of Scapa Flow, Orkney.*

The large anchorage of Scapa Flow, in Orkney, is fairly tranquil today, the peace broken only by the sound of seabirds and the storms that whip the waters into a frenzy without warning. It was not always so, and throughout the afternoon of 21 June 1919 an event took place there the like of which will never be seen again.

Following the capitulation of Germany in November 1918, and as the two sides were attempting to negotiate a peace settlement from within that railway carriage at Versailles, a problem had been identified – what to do with the German High Seas Fleet, the *Hochseeflotte*, in the meantime. They decided to 'intern' it in Scapa Flow, and by Christmas a grand total of 11 battleships, 5 battle-cruisers, 8 light cruisers and 50 torpedo boats lay at anchor in the Flow, watched over by Britain's Battle Cruiser Force. And there they remained, under Vice-Admiral von Reuter's command and with their guns and wireless equipment immobilised, most of their

fuel confiscated, and their skeleton crews unable either to go ashore or cross to a neighbouring vessel.

Meanwhile the peace negotiations dragged on, not helped by the Allies squabbling over who should get their hands on the German Fleet. Von Reuter decided for them. Four days before the Armistice period was set to end – at noon on 21 June – he somehow got word to his fellow captains that they should prepare to scuttle (sink) their ships.

As chance would have it, 400 schoolchildren from Stromness were on the Admiralty tender *Flying Kestrel* that day; they had been brought to see the amazing spectacle of the German Fleet riding at anchor on their doorstep. They were in for the treat of their lives. Shortly after noon, they watched in wonderment as the mighty *Friedrich der Grosse*, the German flagship at Jutland, rolled slowly over and sank beneath the waves, then another, and another. Some thought it was all a show put on especially for them! But no, this was serious business. By the time darkness descended, 51 ships had

gone to the bottom of the Flow. The folk around Scapa Flow that day had witnessed the greatest single loss of shipping in history.

Suddenly, without any warning and almost simultaneously, these huge vessels began to list over to port or to starboard; some heeled over and plunged headlong; their sterns lifted high out of the water and pointing skyward; others were rapidly settling down into the ocean with little more showing than their masts and funnels, while out of the vents rushed steam and oil and air with a dreadful roaring hiss, and vast clouds of vapour. The proud vessels slowly disappear with a long-drawn-out sigh.

(Eyewitness account by James Taylor, a 15-year-old pupil at Stromness Academy.)

▲ *The mighty German battleship,* Hindenberg, *sails into Scapa Flow under armed escort just ten days after the Armistice on 11 November 1918. In 1903, the British Admiralty had developed Rosyth as the main naval base for the Grand Fleet. But by the time war broke out, zeppelins were posing a new, aerial threat. The fear that a direct 'hit' on the Forth Bridge could potentially entrap the fleet forced the Admiralty to look elsewhere; hence Scapa Flow.*

▲ A break from the
fighting: soldiers of the
2nd battalion Argyll and
Sutherland Highlanders
relax for a brief moment
in their trench on the
Western Front. This
famous regiment sent
27 battalions to Flanders
in the Great War, and
won 78 battle honours.

That feeling of pride in the past, articulated by
Kirkwood and made manifest in the actions of
Scots, of whatever class or sex, endured through the
long and bitter struggle, and was finally rewarded
with victorious peace 'on the eleventh hour of the
eleventh day of the eleventh month' in the year
1918. H.G.Wells's 'war to end wars' was over.

. . . AND PEACE

But peace in Europe brought little peace to the
industrial heartland of Scotland. If anything it
made matters worse. While there had been war to
unite them, there had been remarkably little unrest
in the factories, mines and shipyards; but as soon as
the German menace had been seen off, the workers
who had tholed the wartime restrictions would not
go on putting up with being treated like the goods
and chattels of the capitalist bosses any more.

There were those who would dearly have loved
to follow in the footsteps of the Russian Bolsheviks
and seen Scotland become Communist, with
Glasgow its 'Petrograd'. William Gallacher, later the
Communist MP for West Fife, envisaged
Glaswegians 'tearing up Glasgow by the roots'.
Maclean was even appointed Soviet Consul on the
Clyde in the wake of the 'October Revolution'. But
their fellow Scots weren't so much interested in
political ideology as in 'bread and butter' issues
such as pay and conditions. Tom Johnston, a future
Secretary of State and friend of Maclean, wrote that
'the bulk of the workers regard the John Macleans
as "decent enough, but a bit off".'

Scarcely was the war over than there was
confrontation. In January 1919, the Clyde Workers'
Committee called a strike in support of a 40-hour
week; 80,000 men walked out, and it would seem
that most of them tried to squeeze into George
Square, Glasgow, on Friday 31 January to further

'Their Name Liveth'

~ SCOTLAND'S NATIONAL SHRINE ~

'The souls of the righteous are in the hand of God.
There shall no evil happen to them. They are in peace.'

(The words on the frieze around the walls of the Shrine, taken from Apocrypha 3, 1-3)

At the eleventh hour of the eleventh day of the eleventh month in the year 1918 an Armistice was declared with Germany. The Great War had at long last ground to its gory and inglorious end in the killing fields of Flanders. A year on, as the first anniversary of 'the war to end war' approached, the Government hastily commissioned Sir Edwin Lutyens to design a Cenotaph, to be the focus of a solemn observance in the British capital. The simple lath and plaster memorial was recreated in stone in time for the second Armistice Day parade in 1920. The Scots meanwhile had to wait a further seven years before their national memorial was ready.

But it was neither bureaucratic procrastination nor lack of will that was the cause of the delay – far from it. Scotland had been planning her monument to the fallen even before the Great War had run its course. It was worth the wait, for the Scottish National War Memorial in Edinburgh Castle is one of the most moving and humbling places on Earth.

The outpouring of emotion brought on by the appalling slaughter of the Great War led to Scots remembering their fallen heroes in all manner of ways. Across the land the 100,000 men and women who made the ultimate sacrifice were honoured on simple cenotaphs set up in public parks or prominent places in the parish, on decorative plaques and stained-glass windows, even in the building of memorial village halls.

Some were erected by 'the authorities', a great many more by church congregations, schools, commercial businesses, charities, and the regiments themselves of course; each one a poignant reminder of a loved one lost, a comrade who didn't make it through.

The nation's grieving and gratefulness was collectively enshrined in the Scottish National War Memorial on the summit of the Castle Rock in Edinburgh. This too was very much the people's memorial 'built by Scottish brains, Scottish hands and Scottish money'. The first subscription was one of £500 from a prominent businessman; the second, 2s 6d, was sent in by an ex-tinker who had served with the Black Watch in France. These and countless other donations received from all over the world helped to create a moving 'casket of memories'.

The starkness of the Memorial's exterior, with its symbolic images idealising the 'just war' – Justice blindfold with scales and a sword, Mercy as a warrior cradling a child, and above all a figure rising from a phoenix, betokening the survival of the human spirit – stands in sharp contrast to its striking interior – the Hall of Honour, emblazoned with the names, colours and Rolls of Honour of the 12 regiments, and of the other corps and services embroiled in the conflict; and, beyond, the Shrine itself wherein lies the steel casket containing the full Roll of Honour of the Scottish dead. The

walls are engraved with the names of battles that still resonate after all these years: Passchendale, Ypres and, most terrible of all, the Somme. Stone carvings, bronze sculptures and stained-glass windows capture every detail of that 'hideous conflict'; death in the trenches, at sea, in the air; soldier, sailor, airman, nurse, padre, munitions worker, land girl – even the animals who played their part, from huge elephants to tiny canaries and mice, 'the tunnellers' friends'. One could spend hours in wonderment, and still find more to amaze, to admire, to appal – but above all to remember.

Buried away among the myriad images of war is one tiny detail, so small you could be forgiven for not noticing it. And yet it is the most chilling detail in the entire Memorial. High up in a window in the Shrine is a rider on a white horse, with the armies of heaven following in his wake.

The rider's name is Faithful and True (from the *Book of Revelations*, 19, 15), who 'will defeat the nations, and rule over them with a rod of iron'. He wears a cloak, and on that cloak is a swastika. Hardly had the mortar set in the walls of the national shrine than the ancient symbol of good fortune began to appear in the skies over Europe, the insignia of a man who too sought to 'defeat the nations and rule over them with a rod of iron'. Those who had fallen in 'the war to end war' would soon be joined by comrades-in-arms from the next.

'Premier Scots'

~ SCOTLAND'S PRIME MINISTERS ~

'No one can give a more convincing representation of the weary Atlas than the Prime Minister'

(An anonymous writer's description of Ramsay MacDonald shortly before the Labour premier's formation of the National Government in 1931)

John Stuart, 3rd Earl of Bute, George Gordon, 4th Earl of Aberdeen and Archibald Primrose, 5th Earl of Rosebery were all scions of Scottish noble families. They had another thing in common too – they were all prime ministers of the United Kingdom. In fact Scotland can boast eight 'PMs':

John Stuart (b. Edinburgh 1713, d. 1792) – Whig, 1762-3.

George Gordon (b. Edinburgh 1784, d. 1860) – Conservative, 1852-5.

Archibald Primrose (b. London 1847, d. 1929) – Liberal ,1894-5.

Arthur James Balfour (b. Whittingehame, E. Lothian 1848, d. 1930) – Conservative, 1902-5.

Henry Campbell-Bannerman (b. Glasgow 1836, d. 1908) – Liberal, 1905-8.

Andrew Bonar Law (b. Canada 1858 raised Glasgow, d. 1923) – Conservative, 1922-3.

James Ramsay MacDonald (b. Lossiemouth 1866, d. 1937) – Labour, 1924; 1929-35.

Alec Douglas-Home (b. London 1903, d. 1999) – Conservative, 1963-4.

Throw in three more who had Scots blood coursing through their veins: William Ewart Gladstone (1868-74; 1880-5; 1886; 1892-4), born a Liverpudlian but whose father was a Leith merchant, Stanley 'the man you can trust' Baldwin (1923-4; 1924-9), whose mother was also Scottish, and Harold 'you've never had it so good' Macmillan (1957-63), whose grandfather was once a crofter. That is 11 out of 51 premiers in all – not bad for a small country.

The majority of these names probably mean little to many of us today. We might have heard of the Crimean War but not that it was George Gordon's ministry that mismanaged it. We will all be familiar with the Scottish

▲ *Arthur James Balfour, in his role as British Foreign Secretary, inspects troops during World War I. The East Lothian gentleman's three-year term as Prime Minister is largely forgotten now, but he will long be remembered for his 'Balfour Declaration' of 1917, in which he advocated a Jewish homeland in Palestine.*

Office but not necessarily with Archie Primrose's pivotal role in establishing it in 1885. The famous 'Balfour Declaration' of 1917 that proved crucial to the development of the Jewish state of Israel perpetuates the memory of the man simply known as 'A.J.' by his contemporaries, and the creation of the Republic of South Africa in 1910 is perhaps the greatest legacy of 'C-B'. Bonar Law, alas, has the unfortunate distinction of being Britain's 'unknown prime minister', who appropriately enough lies buried near to 'the unknown warrior' in Westminster Abbey. Douglas-Home will inevitably

also go down in history as a 'loser', to Harold Wilson in 1964.

But the name that stands out from all the others is that of James Ramsay MacDonald. The little lad from Lossiemouth should best be remembered for becoming the Labour Party's first prime minister in 1924. But 'a week is a long time in politics', as another prime minister famously declared, and it has been Ramsay MacDonald's fate that his name will forever be associated with his desertion in 1931 from the party he helped to found. His erstwhile Labour colleagues called it 'the Great Betrayal'.

Like the founder of the Labour Party itself, James Keir Hardie, James Ramsay MacDonald was born illegitimately to a farm-girl. And like Keir Hardie's mother, Ramsay MacDonald's mother sacrificed much to ensure that her boy had as good a start in life as any other boy. He grew into an alert and handsome young man whose ambitions soon outgrew his work as a farm-labourer and schoolteacher. By the time he was 20 he had forsaken his Morayshire home for London's bright lights where he took employment as secretary to a Liberal MP. But those were heady days in British politics, and MacDonald left the Liberals to throw in his lot with Keir Hardie's newly formed Independent Labour Party. When Keir Hardie established the Labour Representation Committee in 1900, MacDonald stepped out of the shadows to become its first secretary. He was set for a meteoric rise.

Within six years MacDonald was

Labour MP for Leicester and sitting alongside his leader, Keir Hardie, and his other 27 comrades on the opposition benches of the House of Commons. By 1911 his acclaimed skills as an orator had brought him to the leadership of his party. One day, if all went well, he might become leader of his country too. That day came far quicker than he expected.

It was not an easy ride. In 1914 his pacifist views compelled him to stand down as Labour leader, and in the general election of 1918 he lost his Leicester seat. But by 1922 he was back in the Commons as MP for Aberavon, and back as Labour leader also. And when a fellow Scot, the Conservative prime minister Bonar Law, died unexpectedly in 1923, and his successor Stanley Baldwin (another MacDonald on his mother's side!) called a 'snap' election early in the following year, Ramsay MacDonald found himself unexpectedly prime minister of his country, albeit at the head of a minority Government. In the few months that comprised his first ministry, MacDonald secured success abroad (diplomatic relations with Soviet Russia, and the inclusion of Germany into the League of Nations, the forerunner of the United Nations) and at home, most significantly with a new Housing (Financial Provisions) Act establishing the principle of State support for council housing. These were no mean achievements for a new prime minister of a new party.

It must have been with a similar expectation of success that MacDonald returned to Downing Street in 1929, this time with a majority. But no sooner had he unpacked his bags than the already ailing British economy was hit even harder by the 'Wall Street crash'. By 1931 MacDonald and his Cabinet were at loggerheads over the thorny issue of reducing unemployment benefit, and when MacDonald formed his 'National Government' with Conservative and Liberal support, a mere 15 of the 287 Labour MPs followed their leader. When MacDonald campaigned against his own party in the ensuing general election, he was immediately branded a traitor and expelled. He was effectively a 'spent force'.

MacDonald remained prime minister of his country for a further four years, but he became increasingly a pawn of Baldwin's Conservatives. In 1935 he 'threw in the towel' and died two years later. It was a sad end to a remarkable life that had begun so unpromisingly in Lossiemouth 69 years before. The man who had done so much to create the Labour Party, and by so doing diminish the power of the established forces in British politics, the Liberals and Conservatives, had succeeded only in alienating himself from them all.

their demand, so great was the press. Prime Minister Lloyd George, persuaded by his Secretary of State for Scotland that they were looking at a 'Bolshevist rising', had ordered a heavy police presence. They must have thought their worst fears were being realised when the Red Flag rose above the mass of cloth caps. The police baton-charged, the strikers retaliated, mostly with lemonade bottles, and mayhem ensued; they called it 'Bloody Friday'. On the following morning Glaswegians awoke to find their own tanks and machine guns turned not on the Germans but on them. Their presence cooled the temperature, but couldn't extinguish the flame. The fight continued, in the workplace and on the political soapbox. At the next general election in 1922, Labour won by a landslide in Scotland, taking 29 of the 74 constituencies, including 10 of the 15 seats on the Clyde; they had held just one before. 'New Labour – New Dawn.' As the eager MPs ran along the platform of St Enoch's Station to catch the London train, so the story goes, Jimmie Maxton shouted after them: 'Don't hurry for the train – it'll all belong to the people when we come back!'

'We'll soon change all this', whispered Kirkwood to his fellow Clydeside MP, John Wheatley, as they took their plush seats in the House of Commons along with the other 142 British Labour MPs. And the feeling that they could effect change must have seemed within their grasp when they unexpectedly took power following a

▼ 'A woman's place is in the home!' But not when there's a war on. These female workers produce shell cases in a Glasgow munitions factory during the First World War.

alike, as both try to pick up the pieces of their shattered worlds. But for Scots, particularly those who had toiled long and hard in the munitions factories and shipyards around the Clyde, the pain was particularly hard to bear.

Had the Great War not happened, the monolithic heavy industries of west-central Scotland would surely have gone bust earlier than they did. The cracks were showing even as the twentieth century dawned. The industrial society of the nineteenth century had bequeathed to the twentieth a consumer one. People from all walks of life and all classes had never been so well off, or had so much leisure time in which to spend their money. Since the 1880s Scottish workers had enjoyed the luxury of a week's holiday a year to go with their Saturday afternoons off. They wanted to buy things, consumer goods – not just Singer sewing machines but other 'luxuries' like telephones, radios, and the curse of the modern age, the motor car. And that was precisely what the industrial giants of the Clyde weren't making, by and large. The odd entrepreneur had diversified into 'consumer durables', like John Stirling with his 'Stirling' motor car in 1897, and the Argyle Motor Works in Alexandria which had opened to a great fanfare in 1906, only to be shut down seven years later and converted into a munitions factory. But these were exceptions. Most weren't disposed to innovate. They had become like huge dinosaurs, still casting their monstrous shadows over the land but increasingly unable to cope with the fast-changing world around them. 'Diversify – or die.' Most chose death.

The result was recession and rising unemployment. By the time of the 'General Strike' in 1926, 400,000 workers, one in seven, were idle. After the 'Wall Street Crash' of 1929 that figure had risen to one in five, and in certain 'black spots', like Airdrie, Dumbarton and Dundee, to as high as one in two. The only thing to prosper, it would seem, was the dole queue. The numbers leaving Scotland

▲ *In the autumn of 1915, the people of Govan, in Glasgow, swarmed onto the streets in protest at the hike in rents imposed by landlords seeking to benefit from the huge influx of workers into the city. The women and children pictured here may not have been the first 'militants' to protest, but the great Glasgow Rent Strike stands as a landmark in British social history as the first occasion Government listened to direct popular protest – their rents were 'frozen' for the duration of the Great War.*

'snap' election in 1924, a minority Government, maybe, but in government nevertheless. Their leader, Ramsay MacDonald, Lossiemouth born and bred, but like his revered predecessor, Keir Hardie, representing a Welsh mining constituency, wasted little time in implementing change. Before the year was out a Housing Act firmly establishing the principle of State subsidy for council housing was on the statute book, chased through Parliament by the indefatigable Wheatley. Alas, by the end of the year Labour too had been chased out of office by Stanley Baldwin's Conservatives. The one ray of sunshine Ramsay MacDonald glimpsed as he contemplated five clouded years in opposition was the fact that Labour was now firmly established as His Majesty's official opposition. The Liberals, who had dominated British political life for most of the nineteenth century, were now reduced to a paltry 40 seats and effectively a spent force; nothing is for ever, is it?

But no Government, whether Labour, Conservative or Liberal, could have envisaged the enormous hurt that would be visited on the nation so soon after the Great War, or done much to alleviate it, let alone prevent it. War inevitably brings pain in its wake, to victor and vanquished for a better life elsewhere grew, too; over 500,000 Scots emigrated to the 'New World' in the 1920s alone. During the 'Great Depression' of the early 1930s the population drift to London and the south-east of England started in earnest, a drain that has yet to be reversed.

There is no doubting times were hard and life tough in those dark days. By 1935 a quarter of all adult Scots were claiming Poor Relief from Ramsay MacDonald's increasingly beleaguered National Government. The male unemployed of Dundee were even reduced to having to clear their city's streets of snow before they could claim benefit. The downward spiral of the economy exacerbated the growing frustration of those most affected by it, frustration that occasionally erupted into open hostility – most memorably of course in the 1926 'General Strike' when the pitiful spectacle of Scot fighting Scot was seen on the streets of the country's political and industrial capitals.

In the working-class communities of the Central Belt, that frustration manifested itself most in attacks on 'foreigners', particularly those whose countries had been on the wrong side in the Great War – the Germans of course, but chiefly the Catholic Irish; except they were no longer Irish after the creation of the Irish Free State in 1922. The cancer of sectarianism wasn't helped by the Church of Scotland publishing a pamphlet entitled *The Menace of the Irish Race to Our Scottish Nationality*, extolling the virtues of a nation bound together by 'unity of race'. The rivalry between Protestant and Catholic, evident most amongst the supporters of 'the Old Firm', Rangers and Celtic, intensified as the cancer spread.

In political circles thoughts turned once more to freedom from the English yoke. Home Rule, whereby Scotland would control its domestic affairs within the framework of the United Kingdom, had long been a plank of Liberal and 'new' Labour policy, and the refounding of the Scottish Home Rule Association after the Great War encouraged several attempts by Labour MPs

to lay Home Rule bills before the House of Commons. David Kirkwood even set the hare running about returning the Stone of Destiny to Scotland as early as 1924. It was eventually returned 72 years later!

But in the 1920s the word 'nationalism' was increasingly being whispered abroad, and with it notions of full-blown independence. In 1921 Ruaraidh Stuart Erskine of Mar launched his Scots National League, the embryonic body that would in 1927 be recast as the National Party of Scotland, and on 20 April 1934 merge with another nationalist group, the right-wing Scottish Party, to become the Scottish National Party (SNP). The creation of the National Trust for Scotland in 1931 and the Saltire Society in 1936 were likewise manifestations of a desire to become more identifiably 'Scottish' as distinct from 'British'. The poet Hugh MacDiarmid, who helped found the National Party in 1927, only to be expelled a short time later for espousing Communist views, expressed the feeling of many like-minded souls when he wrote:

I want for my part
Only the little white rose of Scotland
That smells sharp and sweet –
And breaks the heart.

MacDiarmid would have no truck with 'Home

▲ *George Square, Glasgow, 31 January 1919, and the 'Red Flag' is raised aloft above the massed ranks of the cloth caps. The ending of the Great War had not so much brought peace to the industrial heartland of Scotland, more a resumption of the fighting between the 'bosses' and the 'workers'. The same flag flown here was no doubt waved just as proudly on St Enoch's Station in November 1922, following the general election, as the first Labour MPs from Scotland caught the Glasgow-London express.*

'Island on the Edge of the World'

~ THE EVACUATION OF ST KILDA 1930 ~

'We the undersigned hereby respectfully pray and petition HM Government
to assist us all to leave this island'

(From the letter signed by the entire adult population of St Kilda on 10 May 1930)

Far out into the Atlantic swell, 42 miles (66 km) north-west of Griminish Point on South Uist, lies the remote archipelago of St Kilda. It is uninhabited now, save for the wildlife and the soldiers manning the missile-tracking station there, one of whom spoke direct from the heart when he likened his island fastness to 'a dreary little dot of desolation'.

It was not always so. From time immemorial until the twentieth century, islanders had clung to St Kilda's rocky contours, eking out a meagre living from the thin soils and feasting on the fulmars, gannets and puffins nesting on the sheer faces of the storm-lashed cliffs. For centuries they had lived in almost total isolation, visited only by the odd Viking longship and occasional fishing smack.

Then in the nineteenth century came the tourists, attracted to this 'island on the edge of the world' by the musings of travel writers waxing lyrically about its 'mystical' inhabitants, whom they fêted as 'Britain's last indigenous people'. The inquisitive visitors came (weather permitting) and gawked at the strange 'noble savages' they had read about. It was as if they were visiting 'wild animals in the zoo', one of their number, the photographer Norman Heathcote, bemoaned:

they throw sweets to

them, openly mock them and I have seen them at their church door during service laughing and talking as if it was an entertainment.

Perhaps it was this uninvited arrival into their world that gradually opened up the islanders' eyes to the predicament they were in and the potential for a better life elsewhere. They had been beset for years by the remoteness of their situation and ravaged by illness and disease. In desperation, on 10 May 1930 they wrote to the Secretary of State asking to be resettled 'where there would be a better opportunity of securing our livelihood'. Their plea was granted, and on 29 August the 36

remaining islanders clambered aboard HMS *Harebell* with their few precious possessions. They carried with them also many memories but few regrets.

It has been a good move to bring us to the mainland, although the older folk like myself cannot refrain from thinking of the island where we were born and reared.

(74-year-old Finlay Gillies, inhabitant of St Kilda, reminiscing in December 1930.)

The evacuation of St Kilda was the last of the 'Highland Clearances'. But unlike all those that had gone before, this clearance had been achieved through the will of the people and not in open defiance of them.

▲ *St Kildans pose for the camera around 1890. By then, the islanders had become something of a tourist attraction – 'Britain's last indigenous people'. But within 40 years of this 'snapshot' being taken, the few remaining islanders 'on the edge of the world' had left it for a better life elsewhere.*

Rulers' – 'Ha'e nae hauf-way hoose, but aye be whaur extremes meet' he proclaimed in perhaps his most powerful poem, *A Drunk Man Looks at the Thistle*.

Notions like these compelled the London Government, be it Labour, Conservative or National, to take action in an attempt to alleviate the suffering and snuff out the unrest. Appalling housing and unemployment were recognised as the major causes of that unrest, and the inter-war period is littered with legislation designed to address them. No fewer than five Housing Acts followed Wheatley's, greatly increasing the programme of slum clearance in the cities and extending the number and range of houses available for rent. As the abandoned tenements in the centre were brought crashing to the ground, new estates sprouted up on the outskirts to replace them, like barnacles on a boat. Words like 'inner-city' and 'suburban' now became commonplace, and the bungalow (from Hindi *bangla*, 'house' – shades of Empire) the 'des. res.' of the 1930s. You could buy one for £400 +, but they did say the ceilings were so low all you could have for your tea was a kipper!

Alongside the new housing estates appeared purpose-built industrial estates, courtesy of the Special Areas Act of 1934 – places like Hillington, on the south-western edge of Glasgow, where Rolls-Royce set up a huge aero-engine factory that would shortly find a new market for its product. And it wasn't just in the towns that times were a-changing; throughout the Highlands and Islands two-storeyed houses were replacing the traditional thatched longhouses; the islanders dubbed the new lime-cemented residence *tigh geal*, 'white house', and it wasn't long before the antonym, *tigh dubh*, 'black house', came to be applied to its predecessor.

But one 'house' above all others best articulates both the fears and aspirations of Scots in those pain-filled years of peace. St Andrew's House, Edinburgh, completed in 1939, was the most

tangible expression of Scotland's long-held desire for a return to Home Rule. At no time since the Union in 1707 had the State been so powerful in Scotland, so instrumental in all affairs touching the lives of its people – housing, education, health, farming and fishing. Yet the Scottish Office and its Secretary of State were conspicuous by their absence, occupying an office in distant Whitehall. It made sense to relocate both to the country they were expected to serve. If it helped also to deflect demands for independence so much the better.

And that was how the Duke of Gloucester found himself laying the foundation stone for St Andrew's House in April 1937. No expense was spared, no opportunity lost, to declare Scotland's re-emergence on a truly national stage. The simple fact that Thomas Tait's 'unashamedly authoritarian' edifice bore a striking resemblance to the League of Nations' building in Geneva speaks volumes. But even as the Secretary of State, Colonel John Colville, was finalising moving himself and his 1300 + staff northward in the early autumn of 1939, the leader of another nation was ordering his troops eastward into Poland. On 3 September Britain found itself once more at war with Germany.

▲ *War once more; but thanks to the new-fangled aeroplane, there was now a real threat that war might visit its wrath on the homes of the people themselves. These Glasgow youngsters were among the 200,000 women and children evacuated from Scotland's inner cities as hostilities began.*

▲ *March 14, 1941, and the people of Clydebank leave their bombed-out homes; they were the lucky ones. The devastating two-night air-raid by the German Luftwaffe left over 1200 dead and another 1000 on the 'critical' list. Only eight homes escaped – eight from a population of 50,000!*

BACK TO THE FRONT

I am speaking to you from the Cabinet Room at No. 10 Downing Street. This morning the British Ambassador in Berlin handed the German Government an official note stating that, unless we heard from them by 11 o'clock that they were prepared at once to withdraw their troops from Poland, a state of war would exist between us. I have to tell you now that no such undertaking has been received and that consequently this country is at war with Germany.

The chilling words falling from Prime Minister Neville Chamberlain's lips that morning, 3 September 1939, crackled through the ether and entered the living room of almost every Scottish household. The 'wireless' (if you couldn't afford one outright, there was always the 'never, never' or hire purchase), first broadcast in Scotland in 1922 and so recently bringing joy and laughter into their lives, now brought the whole nation to stunned silence. The horrors of the last war still remained vivid in the minds of many; were they to go through all that again?

The war visited its wrath on Scotland within days of Chamberlain's announcement, as the first evacuees from war-torn Europe arrived wet and bedraggled on the quayside at Greenock, survivors

from the transatlantic liner *Athenia*, torpedoed far to the west of the Hebrides. In the following month sorrow and joy visited Scotland within days of each other. At one o'clock on the morning of 14 October, German U-boat *U-47* sneaked into the naval base at Scapa Flow, Orkney, and unleashed its murderous torpedoes on HMS *Royal Oak*, sending the veteran from the Battle of Jutland and most of its 833 sleeping crew to the bottom; it lies there still, an official war-grave. Two days later the citizens of Edinburgh watched in amazement as, overhead, the RAF fought out a 'dogfight' with German bombers hell-bent on destroying the Forth Rail Bridge and the Rosyth naval base in its shadow. The Spitfires of 602 (City of Glasgow) and 603 (City of Edinburgh) squadrons had the distinction of being the first to shoot down an enemy plane over Britain when a Junkers 88 crashed near Humbie, in East Lothian. Another, and unenviable, Scottish 'first' came in March 1940 when an Orcadian, James Isbister, who lived near Scapa Flow, became the first civilian casualty of the war in Britain, killed by a stray bomb. No matter who you were, what your age, or where you lived, it would seem, no one could escape from what became known as 'the people's war'.

World War II was truly a 'world war', and Scotsmen and women soon found themselves operating in every theatre – Europe, Africa, Asia and the Far East, over and under the oceans and in the skies. Many fought in battle, many more served as non-combatants – as merchant seamen in the perilous convoys, as medical staff behind the lines and the like. Their exploits, their sufferings and their joys would fill an entire library of books. Suffice it to say here that over 58,000 Scots laid down their lives in World War II for their country – and ours.

At home, Scotland was directly affected as never before. To the traditional need to provide men and munitions for the front were added new concerns – the threat of aerial bombardment, of sea-borne invasion from the east, and of the need to keep the

Atlantic and Arctic convoys going. Children, clutching their hastily gathered clothes and favourite toys, were evacuated from the vulnerable cities and towns to the relative safety of the countryside, there to encounter a world far removed from the one they had left behind. The story of the two little Glasgow brothers, left blubbing on the platform at Callendar Station because 'they were too appallingly dirty' nobody wanted to take them in, was repeated up and down the country as two quite different cultures were suddenly thrown together.

Those left behind in the cities and towns soon got into the routine of drawing their 'blackout curtains', of carrying their cardboard boxes containing their gas masks about with them, and of silently heading for the air-raid shelters whenever the sirens wailed. Mercifully, Scotland escaped the worst of the 'Blitz' thanks to its remoteness from German-held territory. Only when the Nazis took Norway in April 1940 were their bombers able to rain down their terror from the skies, on the naval bases at Scapa Flow, Invergordon and Rosyth, on east-coast cities like Aberdeen and Edinburgh, but most devastatingly of all on the industrial town of Clydebank over the nights of 13 and 14 March 1941; more than 1200 civilians lay dead, another 1100 were sorely wounded, and 35,000 left homeless, from a population of 50,000, as the Luftwaffe's 500 planes droned out of earshot.

In the face of such horrors, everyone wanted to 'do their bit'. They accepted rationing, including the dubious delights of Spam (spiced ham), as a necessity – even ladies' skirts became much shorter, to save cloth you understand! Many returned to the munitions factories, shipyards and mines that had never seen such activity since the Great War, including 22,000 'Bevin Boys' who responded to the call of Ernest Bevin, Labour's Minister of Labour in Winston Churchill's wartime Cabinet, and swarmed down the 384 pits then operating in Scotland; not one now remains. Those unable for whatever reason to enlist in the armed forces, the merchant navy or the 'reserved occupations', joined the Home Guard or LDV (Local Defence Volunteers) mobilised to defend the Home Front, or worked as ARP (Air Raid Precautions) wardens and firemen. Women too played their full part, in the WVS (Women's Voluntary Services), or as 'land girls' in

the WLA (Women's Land Army) and WTC (Women's Timber Corps). Others joined the ATS (Auxiliary Territorial Service), WAAF (Women's Auxiliary Air Force) or WRNS (Women's Royal Naval Service). Never in the field of human conflict had there been so many acronyms.

The gift of laughter was an important release in those dark days before the tide of war began to turn in the Allies' favour in 1944. Scotland became a fortress as all around her coastline concrete anti-landing craft 'dragons' teeth' and pillboxes, anti-aircraft ('ak-ak') batteries and submarine booms appeared almost overnight. She also became a giant aircraft carrier with airfields and seaplane bases

▲ *The first systematic aerial survey of Scotland was carried out in September 1939 – by the German Luftwaffe! This 'vertical' shows the Rosyth naval base, Forth Rail Bridge and RAF Donibristle. Shortly after this 'shot' was taken, fighter aircraft scrambled from RAF Turnhouse, near Edinburgh, shot down a Heinkel bomber during their first 'dog-fight' of the war over the roof-tops of the city.*

'Playtime'

~ LEISURE PURSUITS BETWEEN THE WARS ~

'a picture house for the masses, not the classes'

(A.B. King opening the Elder Picture House in Govan in 1916)

It was a bitterly cold night, 7 January 1929, but that did not dull the excitement, the sense of anticipation, as huge crowds queued to cram into the Coliseum in Glasgow's Eglinton Street. For this was the night the 'talkies' came to town: Al Jolson in *The Jazz Singer*.

As the music hall had dominated public entertainment pre-war, so the cinema came to dominate the '20s and '30s. When Scotland's first purpose-built picture house, the Argyle Electric Theatre in Sauchiehall Street, Glasgow, opened on 12 May 1910, it was advertised as 'the new wonder of the day'. And so it proved. It wasn't long before music halls were showing films instead, and new picture houses were sprouting up all over the country. Even a 'Wee Free' kirk in Cumberland Street, Glasgow, was transformed into the Paragon Cinema!

By the mid 1930s, Paisley had eight cinemas and Coatbridge four – even tiny Anstruther had two. But Glasgow was 'Cinema City', with 114! No city anywhere else in the world outside the United States could boast as many 'silver screens' per head of population as Glasgow. A survey by the Carnegie Trust in 1938 found that four out of five young unemployed Glaswegians went to 'the flicks' at least once a week. It was escapism, a break from the dole queue, a chance to believe you were a dashing Douglas Fairbanks or the adorable Mary Pickford. It was also the perfect place to do your courting. In an age when a third of the population still lived in homes with two rooms or less,

the warm, dark interior of the cinema presented a rare moment where couples could be alone, particularly on wet nights. Just how much of the 'movie' those occupying the famed 'double seats' at the back saw is questionable!

> Don't you remember
> how towards these smoky screens
> youth stared with wild eyes?
> The organist picked out in marble,
> the plush carpets,
> houses such as we never owned

(From *Early Films* by Iain Crichton Smith.)

But before you could make full use of those double seats, you had to have a partner, and one of the most popular ways of meeting one was to go dancing. Those same Carnegie pollsters discovered that 'the search for a mate and dancing go hand in hand'.

Dance halls began to be the 'in' places to be just before the Great War but took off once peace had returned, as

first 'Jazz' and then 'Swing' got the toes tapping. Once again Glasgow led the way, with 11 top-class dance halls by 1930. Dancing and cinema-going complemented each other perfectly, for many films included breathtaking dance routines, most memorably those starring Fred Astaire and Ginger Rogers – their first, *Flying Down to Rio*, took the country by storm in 1933.

Almost as appealing as a rumba on the dance-floor or a kiss and a cuddle in the cinema was a hike in the country or a trip to the seaside. Fresh air was in short supply in the tenement slums of the inner cities and the smog-bound industrial towns, and every opportunity was taken to escape. The coming of the railway, the paddle-steamer and the humble bicycle, invented by a Dumfriesshire man, Kirkpatrick MacMillan, had brought the countryside closer to the town (one Victorian minister moaned that the 'boneshaker' was taking people *past* his church door and not *to* it) but few outside the upper and middle classes had either the time or the money to avail themselves readily of the opportunity. The advent of Saturday afternoons off and week-long holidays as the new century dawned, together with a little more loose change in the trouser pocket and purse, enabled many more folk to 'have a break'. Whole families – 'ma, pa an' the weans' – would catch the train, coach or steamer and head 'doon the watter' to the seaside for a day, or a week if you were lucky, of sun,

▲ *A band entertains passengers aboard the King Edward as it leaves the Broomielaw, in Glasgow, to go 'doon the watter', to Dunoon, Rothesay or wherever.*

▲ 'Cinema City': Glaswegians had 141 picture houses to choose from between the two World Wars, including the old Paramount Theatre in Renfield Street, captured here in a blaze of lights. Scots went to the 'flicks' far more frequently than their U.K. counterparts, on average 38 times a year.

heart out! And afterwards, why not head back into the city centre, take in a show (Walt Disney's first feature-length movie *Snow White and the Seven Dwarfs* was showing at 'the flicks') and finish up with a curry in the newly opened Taj Mahal Indian Restaurant, Scotland's first.

There was another attraction at the Exhibition, a 'Peace Pavilion'. Casting his shadow over the proceedings in Bellahouston Park was 'the grim reaper', for war had once more become a real threat. Rearmament had newly ridden to the rescue of Scotland's ailing heavy industries, as it had in the years leading up to the Great War, but as welcome as the work was, no one wanted war. Prime Minister Neville Chamberlain, soon to fly to Munich and a date with destiny, expressed the desire of all when he wrote in his foreword to the Exhibition brochure:

We are pledged to work for peace and progress in the world, and it is my hope that this Exhibition will make its contribution to that end.

He was to be bitterly disappointed.

sea, sand and . . . well, fish suppers and ice-cream, actually. Single men and women meanwhile often preferred to take to the hills, walking and climbing, and sleeping in hostels provided by the Scottish Youth Hostel Association (SYHA). Founded in 1931 with the aim of helping 'all, especially young people of limited means', the SYHA by the outbreak of World War II could claim over 30,000 healthy members, and the strains of 'the hostellers' song' could be heard the length and breadth of the land:

Come tramping by lochan,
 by forest and glen,
Come shoulder your pack,
 bend your knee to the ben,
Come north to the mountains,
 by crag and by scree,
Or south to the Lowlands – come
 tramping wi' me.

A century and more of migration from the country to the town had been halted as the nation's youth returned to the glens whence their ancestors had come.

But no matter how great the draw of the mountains and the 'tangle o' the isles', in 1938 Bellahouston Park, Glasgow, was *the* place to be. For that

was the year of the great Empire Exhibition, a stunning extravaganza designed to showcase the 'best of Scottish' to the world, and take people's minds off the depression that had traumatised the country for more than a decade. Forget the Millennium Dome; the Empire Exhibition was enormous, covering 175 acres (71 ha) and attracting well-nigh 13 million visitors. Highlights included a gigantic 'Palace of Engineering', two 'Palaces of Industry' and a 'National Fitness Pavilion' (Glasgow's equivalent of the Dome's 'Body Zone'). But the two attractions that stole the show were a full-blown recreation of a Highland township, 'The Clachan', complete with real-life Gaels, and an amusement park organised by a then unknown entrepreneur called Billy Butlin. Over all loomed the mighty 'Tower of Empire', 300 feet (91 m) of shining steel, Clyde-built naturally – Disneyland, eat your

▲ Young people queue outside the Locarno dance hall, in Glasgow's Sauchiehall Street, in the expectation of a good evening's dancing – and maybe a 'click' as well, if they were lucky. The following weekend might then hold out the prospect of a visit to the Paramount, and those famous 'double seats' at the back for a wee bit kiss n' cuddle!

▶ On the very threshold
of war, Glasgow hosted
a huge Empire Exhibition
in Bellahouston Park
(pictured here on the
front cover of a special
Glasgow Herald
supplement). Over 100
pavilions, as well as two
great 'palaces', to
engineering and industry,
promoted the concept
of 'modern living' using
the latest technological
wizardry and gadgetry.

The 13 million people
who visited the Empire
Exhibition marvelled
at the sleek, shimmering
lines of the concrete and
glass exhibition spaces,
designed by such up-
coming Scots architects
as Basil Spence (of
Coventry Cathedral fame)
and Jack Coia (famed for
his post-war churches).
The top attraction,
though, was 'Tait's Tower',
a futuristic 300 foot
(92 m) tower named
after its designer,
Thomas Tait, the architect
of St Andrew's House,
Edinburgh, into which
the Scottish Office
had recently moved.

All who visited must
have been greatly
impressed by this
'modern' world, but they
had another World War
to fight before they could
embrace it.

sprouting up from the Mull of Galloway to Muckle Flugga. Prestwick became like modern Heathrow, the busiest airport in the world, as RAF Wellingtons and USAF Flying Fortresses constantly touched down and took off again on their way to bomb the industrial heartland of the Third Reich. Remote sea lochs that had barely seen a fishing trawler in years now played host to hundreds of vessels as they rendezvoused for the Atlantic and Russian convoys, – Loch Ewe in Wester Ross, for example, from where the ill-fated convoy PQ17 set sail in June 1942; of the 34 vessels beating their way to Murmansk in the Arctic Circle, 23 didn't make it.

Thousands of Allied servicemen poured into Scotland, British commandos to the training grounds in the mountains of Lochaber, Norwegians to Shetland, the Polish Free Army centred on Kincardine, Canadian and Australian pilots to East Lothian, and the 'Yanks' seemingly everywhere, charming the girls with their cigarettes and stockings. Many were the love-affairs and many the tears when they left. Others stationed here weren't quite so enamoured with their lot, like one miserable so-and-so who found himself 'stuck' on Orkney:

No bloody sport, no bloody games,
No bloody fun, the bloody dames
Won't even give their bloody names,
In bloody Orkney!

There were others on Orkney who were equally homesick, Italian prisoners of war working on the Churchill Barriers. They too left their mark on Scottish culture, in the singularly beautiful Italian Chapel on Lamb Holm beside Scapa Flow, lovingly created from two Nissen huts. There were POWs elsewhere too, among them members of the Waffen-SS in Caithness and high-ranking German officers in the ageing splendour of Duff House, Banff. Some POWs settled here after the war, including the affable German Helmut Heipt, who married an Aberdonian quine and settled down to married life in Strathdon, and created the renowned 'venison sausage', a delicacy combining German 'know-how' and Scottish produce.

Scotland's contribution to the war effort was met in so many other ways as well. Had it not been for the pioneering genius of Brechin-born Sir Robert Watson Watt, a descendant of the James

Watt, and his device for 'Radio Detection and Ranging', or RADAR, which he discovered in 1935, would we have won the Battle of Britain in 1940? Would any of the Atlantic convoys have got through, or the bombers have found their targets in the darkness over Germany? And who were the men responsible for putting those planes in the air? Step forward Maxwell Aitken, 1st Baron Beaverbrook, the Scots-Canadian who became Churchill's Minister of Aircraft Production in May 1940, and Air Chief Marshal Hugh Dowding, 'Stuffy' to his friends, the Moffat lad who masterminded the Battle of Britain itself.

But wars are fought and won mostly by soldiers, sailors and airmen risking their lives in the front line. And Scotsmen aged 18 to 51 went in their hundreds of thousands to fight shoulder to shoulder with comrades from other parts of the United Kingdom, from Europe and the Commonwealth. From that black day in June 1940 when General Fortune's 51st (Highland) Division were forced to surrender to Rommel at St Valéry-en-Caux, shortly after the débâcle at Dunkirk in which the 52nd (Lowland) Division had been caught up; through the bitter fighting across the North African desert and up through Sicily and Italy with Montgomery's 8th Army; through the appalling slaughter and unimaginable sufferings in the jungles and prison camps of Malaya and the Far East following the surrender of Hong Kong and the fall of Singapore to the Japanese; to the final onslaught on Germany that began with the D-day landings on 6 June 1944, and in which the 15th (Scottish) Division joined with the 51st and 52nd to form part of Montgomery's 21st Army Group.

Then fare weel, ye banks o' Sicily,
Fare ye weel, ye valley and shaw.
There's nae Jock will mourn the kyles o' ye,
Puir bliddy swaddies are wearie.

(From Hamish Henderson's moving song The 51st Highland Division's Farewell to Sicily.)

Such was the service and sacrifice Scotland's sons made to achieve that final victory, VE Day (Victory in Europe), 8 May 1945. The church bells of Scotland, silent for the duration, rang out in celebration.

Once again Scotland would have to set about the task of rebuilding.

THE GLASGOW HERALD

EMPIRE EXHIBITION
SCOTLAND 1938

SCOTLAND.COM

(1945 - 2003)

'This project is part-funded by the European Union'

RECONSTRUCTION

Six years after the Second World War, a little-known American company set up business in unlikely surroundings on the outskirts of Greenock. IBM is there yet, employing over 2000 people making personal computers and peripherals and turning over well-nigh £2 billion a year. It has since been joined by electronics giants from all over the world, Compaq, Ferranti, Motorola and the rest; not for nothing is the Central Belt nicknamed 'Silicon Glen'. Today the Glen employs upwards of 70,000 people from Ayr to Dundee. No one could have predicted that as they picked up the pieces in 1945.

Reconstructing post-war Scotland was never going to be easy. Once again, as in 1918, the chief problem was Scotland's over-dependence on its heavy industries, coal, iron and steel, and shipbuilding. This was fine so long as Europe was undergoing major reconstruction following the war, but by 1955 Europe had put itself back together again. The emergence of the Far Eastern countries onto an increasingly global economic stage simply made Scotland's predicament worse.

If only the politicians had listened to the words of their own advisers. In 1962, J.N. Toothill submitted his report, *Inquiry into the Scottish Economy*, to the Scottish Council Development and Industry (SCDI), which had been set up after the War to help reconstruct Scotland. In it he wrote: 'It is chiefly to the scientific-based industries that we must look over the next few years.' James Clerk Maxwell, Lord Kelvin *et al.*, would have drunk to that.

But Toothill was largely ignored. With the ink still drying on his signature, the decision was made to build Ravenscraig Steelworks in Motherwell and a steel strip mill in nearby Gartcosh; both closed 30 years later. In 1965, soon after the creation of the Highlands and Islands Development Board, an aluminium smelter went into production on the site of the Invergordon naval base (it closed in 1981) and a paper pulp mill at Corpach near Fort William (closed 1981 also). They would be joined on the scrap-heap by initiatives launched shortly before Toothill – BMC's lorry plant at Bathgate (opened 1959 – closed 1983) and Rootes' Linwood factory, near Paisley, where 'the people's car', the Hillman Imp, was made (opened 1960 – closed 1981). Harold MacMillan's proud boast that 'you've never had it so good' soon rebounded on the Tories when the people declared through the ballot box in 1964 that they'd never had it in the first place! By 1970, Harold Wilson's much vaunted 'white heat of technology' had all but cooled to freezing-point.

◀ *In the euphoria following the ending of World War II, the traditional heavy industries clustered around the Clyde still contrived to 'rule the roost'. But as the 'white heat of technology' began to cool in the 1970s, and their days were numbered, a new 'black' industry rode to the rescue – North Sea oil. Giant oil-rigs, such as the one pictured in the Cromarty Firth, not only helped engineer that difficult transition from 'Scotland.coal' to 'Scotland.com', but began to help halt the drift of Scots to the Central Belt after a period of 200 years. Scotland's centre of gravity had ever so slightly shifted.*

'To all the airts'

~ SCOTTISH EMIGRATION ~

'All the blood that flowed away
Across the ocean to the second chance'
(From The Proclaimers' Letter From America, 1987)

To emigrate would have seemed a natural thing to do in depressed, post-war Scotland. The prospect of a better life, in Canada, the United States, Australia, New Zealand, even the tiny, far-away Falklands, held its attraction for the industrial workers of the Central Belt, the fishermen from the north-east, and the Highland crofter. Many went because they had relatives to welcome them; others had made friends with their Commonwealth and Yankee comrades during the dark days of war who sang the praises of their homeland. All, though, left for the same reason – they wanted that 'second chance'.

Scots had been emigrating to the New World for over 200 years. Some left of their own accord, others were helped, many were pushed. Most of those who emigrated in the eighteenth century left because they wanted to. They headed mostly for North America, attracted by the prospect of sharing in the growing prosperity of the British colonies there. Some were Lowlanders, heading for the busy east coast ports. Typical were the Paul brothers from Kirkcudbrightshire. The elder, William, settled in Virginia around 1758 and set up as a tailor; his young brother, John, followed in 1774. We know the latter better as John Paul Jones, 'father of the American Navy'.

Many more were Highlanders, tempted out of their crowded crofts by the wide open spaces. Before the

▲ *Coastal steamers, like this one at Port Ellen, on Islay, around 1900, were used increasingly to take Hebrideans to Glasgow and Greenock, and to ships big enough to take them to a new life in the 'New World'.*

Declaration of American Independence in 1776, North Carolina was favourite, thanks to the colonising efforts of its Scots-born governor, Gabriel Johnston. Thereafter, Canada became the 'in' place, eastern Highlanders heading mostly to Nova Scotia, western Highlanders to Ontario, Lewismen to Quebec; by 1800 Orcadians were settling along the Red River in Manitoba. Paradoxically, the Highland landlords didn't really want their tenants to go, so useful were they to the lucrative kelp industry. Then all started to go horribly wrong as the Napoleonic Wars grew in intensity. The economy took a battering, and the bottom fell out of kelp. The heroes returning from Waterloo to the congested glens simply made matters worse. Suddenly, emptying those glens of people and replacing them with sheep had its attraction. Cue a second, and altogether different, wave of emigration.

I've looked at the ocean
Tried hard to imagine
The way you felt the
day you sailed.
(From The Proclaimers' Letter From America, 1987.)

In the nineteenth century, two million souls followed in their forebears' wake; most were Highlanders – and most were pushed. During the famines that bedevilled the 1840s and '50s, whole communities were plucked from the shore, like the seaweed they had once lifted, dropped into ships and despatched across the oceans. From Rum 350 souls, 'shipped' to Nova Scotia; from Raasay another 500; a story repeated across the *Gaidhealtachd*. Gordon of Cluny, who had purchased Barra from its bankrupt Macneil chief in an Inverness coffee-house in 1838, even offered to empty the island altogether and sell it to the Government as a penal colony! His offer was rejected, but that didn't stop him shipping most of his new tenants off to Quebec anyway. Their destitute condition on arrival so appalled the immigration authorities that the Government was forced to act. The 1851 Emigration Advances Act didn't go so far as to provide state-funded assisted passages – it simply enabled landlords to borrow public money at attractive rates – but at least it was a step in the right direction.

Now a penal colony at the opposite end of the world was catching the eye of prospective emigrants, and thanks to a bounty scheme designed to entice skilled workers thither, Scots began to sail for Australia. By 1850, 12,000 of them had settled in New South Wales. In 1853 the first Scots came ashore in New Zealand. The United States too, returned to the list of destinations, and that is where William Carnegie, a weaver from Dunfermline, and his wife made for in 1848, settling in Pittsburgh; their younger lad, Andrew, worked his way up from bobbin boy to steel magnate and one of the richest men in the world. Such was the calibre of people lost to the 'auld country'.

The haemorrhage continued unabated through the nineteenth century, and through most of the twentieth also. So great was the misery at home after the Great War that the Government now began offering assisted passages, despite the ailing economy. The result – another 500,000 Scots, men, women and children, heading off into the sunset. By 1930, the population of Scotland had actually declined. The exodus resumed after the Second World War. Hardly surprising, when you could emigrate to New Zealand for a tenner! With carrots like that, who could resist the promise of 'the good life' under the New World sun. Yes, you missed the football, and the Sunday papers didn't arrive till the Tuesday, but that was but a small price to pay.

Today the 'phone books of the New World are full of 'Macs' and other Scottish surnames. But what other lasting effect has 250 years of emigration had on the welcoming countries and on Scotland? In Australia, despite the fact that two of the first three prime ministers had Scots' blood coursing through their veins, there is no real evidence of 'Scottishness'. The same is

true in New Zealand, even though the name 'Dunedin' derives from the old name for Edinburgh. As for the United States, although researching one's 'roots' has become a fascinating pastime for many, isn't it really more a question of America's influence on Scotland, given their consumerism impact on the rest of the world in the last century?

Only in Canada can there be held to be a 'special relationship', a bond that has survived the passing of time. Canada was much closer, physically, to Scotland, of course. By 1961 over two million Scots had emigrated there – three out of every eight Britons settling in Canada were Scots. But it wasn't just the volume of Scots, it was the pattern of settlement. Whereas those heading to the Southern hemisphere went as individuals or as a family, in the case of Canada whole communities uprooted from their native soil and transplanted to a particular 'airt'. This was certainly true of Highlanders, but it also applied to Lowlanders; no prizes for guessing where those settling in Lanark County, Ontario, or Carstairs, Alberta, hailed from. Even now, the Gaelic language and culture live on, in a very real sense rather than in the fabricated world of Highland Gatherings and Caledonian Societies, in places such as Cape Breton Island, where fiddle-music, step-dancing and the traditional ceilidh go on much as one imagines they have done since Scots 'washed up' there all those years ago.

Scots still emigrate to Canada, and the rest of the world, but the flood has dried to a steady trickle. The economic upturn at home in recent years has made the thought of leaving one's home and loved ones less attractive than it once was. If anything the trend is slowly being reversed, as the descendants of those early emigrants begin to return to the 'auld country'. Isn't it amazing how many sportsmen have discovered they have a Scottish granny? They do say the road runs in both directions.

▲ *A crowd of Hebrideans at a Glasgow dockside wave goodbye to their countrymen who are emigrating to Canada on board the* Matagama *in April 1923.*

▲ *Industrial landscape: smoke and steam belch forth from the steelworks at Ravenscraig, in the Clyde Valley, in 1979. Motherwell's skyline looks very different now that this industrial 'giant' is no more.*

Irvine no more.
(From The Proclaimers' *Letter From America*, 1987)

And yet the post-war rebuilding had started out full of hope. Churchill might have won the war but he definitely lost the peace. In the General Election that followed hard on the heels of VE-Day, Clement Attlee's Labour Party was swept into power with a huge majority. They had soon rolled up their sleeves and got down to the business of implementing their main manifesto pledge of taking State control of the major public utilities. First to be 'nationalised' was the Bank of England in 1946, then it was the turn of the coal and electricity industries in 1947, in 1948 the railways, canals, dockyards, road haulage and gas, and finally in 1949 the iron and steel industry, biggest 'giant' of them all (the Tories privatised it two years later). After a century and more of industrial subservience, 'the people' now controlled most of the means of production.

THIS COLLIERY IS NOW MANAGED BY THE NATIONAL COAL BOARD ON BEHALF OF THE PEOPLE

(signboard erected at all colliery pitheads in January 1947).

It was 'all go' in other areas of national life too. In 1945 the Scottish Tourist Board was born, and in the following year the Scottish Council Development and Industry (later to evolve into the Scottish Development Agency and Scottish Enterprise); both would come to Scotland's rescue in the years ahead as the country searched for new industries to replace the old ones. 1948 saw the creation of what was undoubtedly Labour's most inspired and successful 'nationalisation', the National Health Service (NHS). To be fair to the now-marginalised Liberal Party, they had begun the process way back before the Great War with their Old Age Pensions Act of 1908 and the setting up of the Highlands and Islands Medical Service in 1913, an NHS 'prototype'. And it was the report from another Liberal, William Beveridge,

These were profound disappointments for a nation recovering from the ravages of war. Such initiatives were instigated by governments of both hues, red (Labour) and blue (Conservative), for the best of reasons. What else were they to do to stave off a recession gripping the entire country, but most acutely the heavily industrialised area around Glasgow, once 'the workshop of the Empire' but described by Sir Patrick Abercrombie, author of the *Clyde Valley Regional Plan* in 1946, as having an 'atmosphere of industrial antiqueness'?

Some people helped by emigrating. On average 10,000 each year sailed for Canada alone in the first decade after the war. The introduction in 1948 of national service for all men over 18 (initially for a period of a year but rising to two by 1950 on the outbreak of the Korean War) also helped massage the unemployment figures, but no sooner was it abolished in 1957, in the aftermath of the Suez Crisis, than the dole queues rose alarmingly again, with 116,000 out of work by the end of that year. Bathgate, Linwood and the rest were seen as the answer; 'big is best' still ruled! And when they closed, the pain was even harder to bear.

Bathgate no more,
Linwood no more,
Methil no more

published in the dark days of the Second World War, that served as Attlee's 'blueprint'. The building of new hospitals like Dunoon General brought relief not just from pain but from unemployment too.

Hospitals weren't the only buildings to rise up anew in post-war Scotland. The heightened programme of 'slum' clearance in the thirties, put 'on hold' for the duration, was now 'on' again but with a different emphasis. Now mighty tower-blocks began to cast their long shadows over the old tenements, no shadow longer than that cast by the notorious Red Road flats in Glasgow's Balornock district. Fanfared as the tallest in Europe when they were built in the mid-60s, the 31 storeys (over 40 were originally projected!) housed a population the size of Dingwall.

But simply expanding the cities wasn't enough. Abercrombie's 1946 Plan had identified a shortfall of 600,000 houses in greater Glasgow alone, and recommended a 'planned decentralisation of both population and industry'. The answer was to decant Glaswegians to other towns, as far flung as Ayr and Haddington, and build new ones. East Kilbride 'New Town' was the first, begun in 1947 on a green-field site a short distance to the south.

Glenrothes (1949), Cumbernauld (1956), Livingston (1962) and Irvine (1966) followed. It was a painful readjustment, both for the communities uprooted from their inner-city tenement homes, and for those left behind. As the demolition men tore down the tenements, they tore out the heart of the inner city also.

O they're knocking doon the tenement
  next tae oors,
An sending us tae Green Belt trees an' floors.
But we dinnae want tae go,
An' we've surely telt them so,
O they're knocking doon the tenement
  next tae oors.

(From a Glasgow ditty of 1970.)

The move to the new multi-storey council estates was made the more painful because of the dearth of shopping and social facilities in the new 'concrete jungles'. Could you get a drink and have a flutter on the horses? Hardly. The socialist councils proved just as 'anti-drink and gambling' as the social reformers, such as Robert Owen at New Lanark, who preceded them, and Glasgow Corporation wasn't alone in forbidding such licensed premises anywhere on its estates. That maybe explains why the only buildings left standing in the flattened inner-city slum lands were 'boozers' and betting shops!

It wasn't just the Central Belt that felt 'the wind of change'. In the Highlands the landscape was changing too. Huge walls of concrete

▲ *There was scarcely room to 'swing a cat' in Peterhead harbour during the good old days of the herring industry (see the photograph on page 164), and there was still a living to be had when this picture was taken in 1999. But this once-vital industry is facing an uncertain future.*

◀ *Lochs such as Loch Glascarnoch, in Ross and Cromarty, pictured here, may be artificial, but they are now accepted as integral features of the 'wild' Highland landscape, and Scots are particularly grateful for the renewable energy they provide. But it wasn't always so, for hearts and minds had to be won over in the early days of the North of Scotland Hydro-Electric Board, set up during World War II. Today, Scots are similarly in two minds about another 'renewable', wind-power.*

'New Towns for Old'
~ CUMBERNAULD NEW TOWN ~

'Dreams are being built on a hill near Glasgow'
(The American Institute of Architects, 1967)

It is all too easy to deride the housing of the post-war years – 'bloody concrete', Prince Philip called it at the official opening of Cumbernauld New Town. But then it is all too easy to forget what housing was like, for most people, up till then – inner-city tenements for the most part, not the rat-infested slums of the turn of the century, but homes still lacking 'basics' such as hot and cold water and an inside 'loo'; if you had a bath, you kept the coals in it – that's what they said.

The housing problem post-war was a simple 'numbers' game, a 600,000 shortfall in greater Glasgow alone in 1946. Before the war they had tried everything – edge-of-town estates, decanting people to other ones – but still the problem persisted, not helped by wartime destruction; just seven Clydebank tenements had escaped unscathed during the blitz of 1941. New solutions were needed, as well as more of the same. The answer – build entirely new towns on green-field sites. Inspired! Not since Campbeltown, Fort William and Stornoway in the seventeenth century had Scotland had new towns.

In 1946 the Labour Government rushed through the New Towns Act. Within the year East Kilbride was sprouting up on the south side of Glasgow. Glenrothes in Fife, established in 1948 to house 'a self-contained and balanced community for working and living', was running a close second. With target populations of about 35,000 each,

▲ *The 'dream on the hill' – Cumbernauld New Town.*

they should help ease the problem considerably. But the problem persisted, and the decision to build a third, Cumbernauld, with a target population of 70,000, was taken in 1956. The architect invited to design the town centre, the tartan-suited Geoffrey Copcutt, later put the dilemma facing him succinctly when he reminisced about 'building a cheap town in severe conditions for a lengthening queue of Clydesiders.' We might think politicians and planners live in an ideal world, but they seldom do.

Copcutt and his colleagues broke with the 'tradition' established at East Kilbride and Glenrothes – of low-rise, low-density, 'neighbourhood' districts – and opted instead for a tightly compressed urban fabric, centred on what Copcutt called 'a single citadel-like structure half a mile long' consisting of 'highways and walkways, layers and ledges promising shelter, warmth and family freedom.' The architectural world coined a term

especially for it – 'megastructural planning'.

In the event, not all of Copcutt's vision was cast in concrete, and as the population projection expanded so too did the New Town. What has been described as a 'carpet' of low-rise housing and landscaping, punctuated by the odd 'vista stop' (tower-block to you and me), now swarms around Copcutt's concrete hive, their estate names – Kildrum, Muirhead, Park, Ravenswood and the rest – conjuring in the mind's eye images of rural idyll, in much the same way that 'Brae View', 'Rowan Cottage' and 'Tighnamara' did for the 1930s bungalow resident. If you haven't been there, you'll have seen it in Bill Forsyth's wonderful 1980 film *Gregory's Girl*.

In 1967 the American Institute of Architects visited Cumbernauld and awarded it their coveted R.S. Reynolds Memorial Award for Achievement in Urban Design. Soon experts from across the globe were trekking to the New Town 13 miles north-east of Glasgow to see for themselves this 'international exemplar of megastructural planning', the world's first multi-level covered-in town centre. In 1997 it was included in the 'Sixty Key Monuments built 1945-70' published in *Rebuilding Scotland*, and praised as 'Scotland's most significant ensemble of post-war urban architecture and planning'. I wonder what the residents think. As for me, I have trouble finding my way out of the place.

appeared, in massive dams like that at Lairg, on Loch Shin in Sutherland, built by the North of Scotland Hydro-Electric Board (NSHEB), set up in 1942 by the energetic and innovative Tom Johnston when he was Secretary of State during the war. On becoming its Chairman in 1945 he argued persuasively for the economic need for hydro electricity in the teeth of strong, and understandable, opposition to schemes that were seen as having a major detrimental impact on the sensitive landscape. Today we accept them as if they had always been there, and are grateful for the 13.5 per cent of renewable energy they pump into the National Grid. The debate now rages over another sustainable energy resource, wind farms. We don't like change, do we?

The planting of conifers aroused the passions too. It was in the trenches of Flanders that Britain's inability to produce enough home-grown timber had been woefully exposed; hence the setting up of the Forestry Commission in 1919. But it was after the Second World War that the 'blanket' planting of the Highland glens and the Southern Uplands with fir trees began in earnest, encouraged particularly by successive Labour Governments who saw in forests not only the potential to give much-needed employment in struggling rural areas but also the opportunity to open up more of the countryside to 'the people'. Today the income and employment derived from the 2.5 million acres (1,000,000 hectares) of Scotland now under State forests is still crucial to the rural economy, but it is the Forestry Commission's role as environmental guardian that has perhaps assumed the greater importance. Slowly but surely the coniferous blankets are disappearing as the native deciduous trees stage their comeback.

Trekking along the forest trails and fishing on the reservoirs were two ways of enjoying oneself in post-war Scotland. Lest the accounts of recession and unemployment, of uprooting and relocating, give the impression that the Scotland of the 1950s and '60s was all 'doom and gloom', life wasn't that bad – it just felt like it sometimes. Scots now enjoyed a standard of living far better than anything experienced previously. Salaries and

wages were higher, and the general health of the nation was improving, thanks to vaccination programmes, antibiotics such as streptomycin, and mass X-ray campaigns that identified 'killers' like cancer early on. Tuberculosis and poliomyelitis became things of the past, and prevention became as important as cure under the NHS.

Consumer goods such as motor cars and washing machines now came within the affordable reach of more and more Scots, but it was the television set that changed lives most. Perfected by a Helensburgh man, John Logie Baird, in the years between the wars, the 'telly' really took off with the live transmission of Queen

▲ 'The High Life'. With a shortfall of 600,000 homes in greater Glasgow alone in 1945, there was nowhere for people to go but 'out' – to 'new towns' like Cumbernauld – or 'up', as here in Shettleston in Glasgow. In the old four-storey tenements, you could communicate with your neighbours from window to window, but you couldn't do that from a 'high-rise'.

DEVOLUTION

The reality of Scotland's national identity had not been expunged by Union with England; it was merely stifled for a time. Despite a determination by Whitehall to rewrite the constitution by inventing the concept of 'North Britain', Scotland would not go quietly into history.

Ironically, given what was to happen subsequently, it was an arch-Tory, Walter Scott (1771-1832), who 'reinvented' Scotland. Through his poetry and novels, his 'scribblings' as he called them, he created a romantic image of his native land that quickly fired the imagination of his fellow countrymen and women. He reawakened their passion for their country, its history and its culture. No matter that his version was deeply flawed and heavily laced with myth, he engaged with his readers like no other before him.

Through the nineteenth century the debate grew as to how this Scottish identity could be sustained within the Union framework. The remoteness from London, and the inevitable feeling of remoteness from power that came with it, led to growing frustration. The fall-out from the Disruption in the Church of Scotland in 1843 didn't help, leading as it did to yet more centralisation, more power seeping to Whitehall. Worried that 'England' was fast becoming synonymous with 'Britain', a National Association for the Vindication of Scottish Rights was formed in 1852. It was short-lived, but its demise didn't mean the problem had gone away.

It came back to haunt Whitehall in the 1880s. This time Scotland 'piggy-backed' on another country's fight for self-determination, and the cry of 'Home Rule for Ireland' soon became 'Home Rule for All'. The Liberal Prime Minister Herbert Asquith, no Scot but MP for East Fife for most of his parliamentary career, declared in a debate in the Commons that he saw 'Irish Home Rule as the first step, and only the first step, in a larger and

▲ *Scots do not like change any more than other folk, but they are more prepared than most to stand up and be counted. Here they protest their inner feelings during the Miners' Strike of 1984/5. Today Scotland has no coal-pits left after 1000 years of mining, and the major sources of employment are the financial sector, 'hi-tech' industries, the oil industry and the service and tourism sectors. Tomorrow – who knows?*

Elizabeth's coronation in 1953. The little screen in the corner of the living-room soon ousted the cinema in the affections of the people and transported them to places they scarce knew existed. Perhaps the high expectations created by watching *Bill and Ben, Lassie* and *The White Heather Club* on television led to post-war Scots failing to appreciate how much better life was for them than for their parents.

Disenchantment showed itself in various ways – in an emerging rebelliousness among the youth, starting with the 'Teddy Boys' in the 1950s, and in a growing concern about nuclear weapons and particularly the arrival in the Clyde of US nuclear submarines in the early 1960s:

K - K - Kennedy, Kennedy, Kennedy,

K - K - Kennedy, we don't want Polaris!

(A frequently heard chant against the US base on the Holy Loch, near Dunoon)

It also expressed itself once again in demands for separation from England, not just for Home Rule, or 'devolution', but increasingly for out-and-out independence. When Robert McIntyre unexpectedly won Motherwell for the SNP in a by-election in April 1945 (he lost it a month later at the general election), it was the first 'warning shot' by 'the Nats' over the bows of the British Establishment.

more comprehensive policy'. Others weren't persuaded, seeing in Home Rule a devolution of power more apparent than real. The national socialist R.B. Cunninghame Graham was withering in his criticism: Home Rule promised 'only the pleasure of knowing that taxes would be wasted in Edinburgh instead of London.'

Cunninghame Graham, who in previous incarnations had been both a Liberal MP and the first President of the Scottish Labour Party, went on to become the first President of the National Party for Scotland (1928) and the first President of the SNP (1934). Herein lay the central dilemma of the nationalist lobby, a dilemma that dogs it still. It was an eclectic gathering of political persuasions embracing the whole spectrum from ultra conservative to extreme radical. The SNP wasn't alone in manifesting a 'Jekyll and Hyde' personality; Hitler's National Socialists were also struggling to square the circle of left and right; but whereas the 'Nazis' in Germany made the breakthrough and took power in the 1930s, the 'Nats' in Scotland did not.

Paradoxically, it was Labour's nationalisation programme after the Second World War that led to a greater clamour for self-determination, and ultimately devolution. Walter Elliot, Conservative Secretary of State in the '30s, perceptively remarked that 'nationalisation means de-nationalisation', by which he meant that instead of devolving power to the people of Scotland nationalisation would actually draw power away from them to Whitehall. But whilst the SNP argued amongst themselves (despite McIntyre's victory they fared badly in subsequent general elections), both Labour and Conservative chose to ignore the increasing demand that Scotland's role in the Union as a partner and not as a servant be properly acknowledged. Class was more important than nationality. Between 1950 and 1964 both main parties hogged the Scottish political limelight equally with about 46 per cent of the vote each; in 1951 they actually tied with 35 seats each; Jo Grimond ploughed a lone furrow for the once-great Liberal party in Orkney and Shetland. Britain's possible entry into the European Economic Community (we were finally let in in

1972) was a more burning issue for Scots than their country's role in the Union.

The SNP had their moments though, none more exhilarating than when Winnie Ewing snatched Hamilton from Labour in 1967. It rattled the party that had officially abandoned Scottish Home Rule ten years earlier. Their answer was to set up a Royal Commission on the Constitution; that should put the matter on the back burner for a while. But when Kilbrandon reported, to Edward Heath's Conservatives in 1971, it was unequivocal in its recommendation – devolution. Labour and Conservative were still equally divided. But with unemployment breaking records (it broke the dreaded one million barrier across the UK as a whole in 1971), the Scottish electorate was looking for scapegoats. In 1973 Margo MacDonald won Govan for the SNP. But even more humiliating for the 'big two' was the SNP's showing in the second general election of 1974. At last they made the breakthrough, securing 11 seats and over 30 per cent of the popular vote. Scottish politics was back to three heavyweights slugging it out in the ring. Devolution was back on the 'front burner'.

Within the year, Wilson's Labour Government had published its Devolution White Paper, promising 'assemblies' for Scotland and Wales. The 'wishy-washy' promise of a devolved power shared uncomfortably between a directly elected body and an 'unelected' Scottish Office failed to set the heather alight. In the March 1979

▲ Shop steward Jimmy Reid addresses a massed meeting of shipyard workers at John Brown & Co., Clydebank, in September 1971. The months of protest proved fruitless for Brown's (by then part of the Upper Clyde Shipbuilders group) was put into liquidation in 1972. The once-proud shipyard, that had created such masterpieces as the SS Lusitania (1907), HMS Hood (1920), the Queen Mary (1934) and the QE2 (1969), closed its doors for good.

'Black Gold'

~ NORTH SEA OIL ~

'It's Scotland's Oil!'

(The Scottish National Party's campaign slogan for the 1974 general election)

▲ *Lonely oil-rigs operating in the harsh environment of the North Sea, midway between Shetland and Norway.*

Scots started howking 'black rock' (coal) out of the East Lothian ground well nigh a thousand years ago. Exploiting Scotland's 'black gold' (oil) reserves began only in 1851, in West Lothian. Ten years before the world's first 'oil gusher' was drilled in Pennsylvania, USA, a Glaswegian, James Young, built a plant at Boghead to produce oil by destructive distillation of the oil shales beneath. It was an instant success, and soon 50,000 gallons of paraffin oil a year were being sold, much of it to 'oil' the wheels of industry. By the time his old student friend, David Livingstone, laid the foundation stone for a new works, at nearby Addiewell, 15 years later, James 'Paraffin' Young had become the world's first oil tycoon.

'Paraffin' Young launched a century of oil production on land. Shortly before the last drop of paraffin dripped from the production line in 1962, the first oil and gas reserves deep beneath the hostile environment of the North Sea were discovered. But in an increasingly global market it was no longer Young's Paraffin Light & Mineral Oil Company Ltd but multinationals like Amoco and British Petroleum who exploited the oil, to help fuel the world's motor cars and central heating tanks. When the price of crude oil quadrupled in 1973 as a result of the Arab-Israeli War, North Sea oil became an immensely valuable commodity almost overnight. By the time of the 1974 General Election, the Sullom Voe oil terminal was beginning to rise up from the Shetland rocks, and within two years the first oil gushed ashore onto the British mainland at Cruden Bay in Aberdeenshire. The centre of gravity of Scotland's population shifted ever so slightly away from Glasgow towards the North-East, and Aberdeen became Britain's 'oil capital'. But barely had the smell of fish faded from the streets of the 'Granite City' than the politicians began to argue as to whose oil it really was, Scotland's or Britain's.

It was a very good question. At a time when anti-devolutionists were arguing that Scotland couldn't possibly afford to go independent, here was Scotland earning goodness knows how much for the British Exchequer. Precisely how much was anyone's guess apparently. Estimates varied between £100 million a year (the Treasury) and £800 million (the SNP). In fact, by the time Margaret Thatcher took office in 1979, Scotland's oil was pumping £5 billion into the nation's coffers. And by the time of the ill-fated Poll Tax, the tax-take was a staggering £12 billion.

Geologists predicted that the wells would run dry within 20 years, but here we are 30 years later and still it flows ashore. But one thing we know for sure – it can't last forever. While we continue to reap the benefits of that exploitation, we are becoming increasingly conscious of global warming, and of exhausting non-renewable resources. Sustainability has become a keyword in our vocabulary, and wind-farms a familiar sight in our landscape. When James Hutton, 'the father of modern geology', was alive in the later eighteenth century, his world was full of windmills and watermills. But it was also one increasingly dominated by the steam engine, a device that certainly saved humans a great deal of energy but one that was just as assuredly draining the earth of its. In prophetic tones, Hutton warned of the danger of over-exploitation:

Man has the disposal of nature so much at his will. He must, by studying nature, learn what will most conduce to the success of his design. No part is indifferent to man.

We ignore his advice at our peril.

referendum, the 'ayes' stole it by just 1.9 per cent (32.9 per cent – 31 per cent). It wasn't enough. Thanks to the '40 per cent rule', whereby 40 per cent of the entire electorate, not just those bothering to turn up at the polling booths, had to say 'yes' (not even the 1975 referendum on Britain's continuing membership of the EEC had insisted on that), the Scottish Assembly on offer was dead in the water. Where would devolution go from here?

Enter Margaret Thatcher stage right. It has been said that Thatcher did more for the cause of devolution than any other person. As soon as she came to power in 1979 – ironically she was levered there through a pact with the SNP that led to Callaghan's Labour administration falling by one vote – she was in there wielding her famous handbag, lecturing the Scots, among others, about the evils of the dependency culture, the 'nanny state' as she liked to call it. They had to learn to stand on their own two feet, or else. And so she switched off the life-support system. Nationalised industries were sold back to the private sector, what was left of them that is. In 1950 there were 780,000 Scottish miners; by the time she resigned in 1990 they could be counted in their 100s, and now there is no deep-mining at all in Scotland. The same happened with the shipbuilding and steel industries. And council-house building was down from 35,000 in 1955 to a mere 468 in 1995.

Perhaps it had to come, maybe it was long overdue. But what made it unpalatable for most Scots was the manner of its doing. Scotland, the cradle of the Enlightenment, had long shown that it was a more socially inclusive society than England, with a greater sense of community. But a decade and more of having to accept the will of 'Middle England' at general elections took its toll. The patience snapped in 1989 when Margaret Thatcher introduced the Poll Tax in Scotland a year before the rest of Britain. The cry went up that she was using Scotland as a 'guinea pig'. It was her biggest single mistake, leading to her own downfall in 1990 and the ultimate demise of her party in Scotland. In the 1997 general election Tony Blair's 'New Labour' romped home with not one Scottish Conservative MP anywhere to be found. The date

of the election, 1 May, proved auspicious: it was the 290th anniversary to the day that Scotland had joined the Union.

Blair moved quickly to honour his pledge of offering devolution to the Scottish people. In a referendum in September that year they accepted with relish, 72 per cent voting 'yes' to their own Parliament once again, and 60 per cent to it having tax-raising powers; only in Dumfries and Galloway and Orkney did the people vote against the latter. Tony Blair declared it 'a good day for Scotland, a good day for Britain, and a good day for the United Kingdom'.

The result would have made one Scot very happy had he lived to see the day. John Smith, Blair's predecessor as Labour leader, would surely have led his party to victory that May Day had he not died so tragically early in 1994. Smith was the leading advocate of devolution, what he liked to call 'unfinished business'. In 1984 he wrote somewhat prophetically:

I have had – and have – a happy life in
Scotland. I started as a Highlander and
I suppose I am now much more a Lowlander.
I suspect, however, that these distinctions are
now becoming much less meaningful. I am
Scots, proud of it, and very glad to be able to
live in and enjoy my own country – all of it.

▲ *Margaret Thatcher's entry into no.10 Downing Street in 1979 very soon resulted in major tensions between the Scottish electorate and what came to be known as 'Middle England'. In 1989 she introduced the unpopular Community Charge (immediately named the 'Poll (head) Tax' by Scots) into Scotland a year ahead of its introduction into England and Wales. There were widespread protests, as seen here at a rally in Glasgow.*

'Talking Shops'

~ SCOTLAND'S PARLIAMENTS ~

'There shall be a Scottish Parliament – I like that!'

(Donald Dewar, First Minister of the new Scottish Parliament, opening the inaugural debate in May 1999)

On 6 May 1999, Scotland went to the polls. But this was no run-of-the-mill general election to send Members of Parliament (MPs) to the British Parliament in Westminster; the people were being asked to return MSPs to a new Parliament of Scotland in Edinburgh – the first to sit in almost 300 years. It heralded a new era in Scotland's history.

The word 'parliament' comes from the French *parler*, 'to talk', and that is what parliaments did – they still do! The first parliaments were gatherings of the 'great and good', the senior clergy and nobility – a House of Lords in all but name. In 1326 Robert I invited the royal burghs to send representatives also, a sign of the growing importance of the 'new towns' to the nation's economic well-being. We hear a new phrase to describe Parliament – 'the thrie estaitis', the Church, the Nobility and the Burgesses, in that pecking order, meeting as one body in one place.

> And heir be oppin
> proclamation, I wairne in name
> of his magnificence, The thrie
> estaitis of the natioun, That
> they compear [appear] with
> detfull diligence: And till [to]
> his grace, make thair obedience. And
> first I wairne the Spiritualitie [the
> Church], And sie the burgesses spair
> not for expence: Bot speid theme heir
> with Temporalitie [the Nobility].

(From the opening speech by Diligence in *Ane Satyre of the Thrie Estaitis*, by Sir David Lindsay of the Mount, premiered in

the Great Hall of Linlithgow Palace before James V and Queen Mary on Twelfth Night, 1540)

And that was how Parliament was

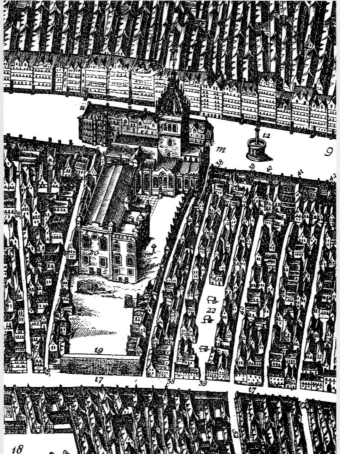

▲ *Scotland's first Parliament met in the Edinburgh City Fathers' Tolbooth (the building depicted on the far side of St Giles' in 1647) before moving to purpose-built premises (the far grander building this side of St Giles') in 1640; the cost – £127,000 Scots.*

composed in medieval times. It was another 200 years before lairds from the shires were permitted to elect 'one or tua of the maist qualifit and wyisest baronis to be commissionars'. Even then people from the smaller towns and most of the rural population were denied any representation until long after the first

Scottish Parliament was dissolved in 1707. And women weren't allowed to vote or stand until 1918.

The early parliaments met for only a few days at a time. Wherever the king was, that was where they gathered. But as Edinburgh became increasingly the capital from the reign of James III (1460-88), so parliament came to sit there more regularly, usually in the tolbooth, beside St Giles' in the 'Royal Mile', where the 'toon cooncil' also met. But the 'lack of convenient and fitt roumes' resulted in the building of a new, and doubtless very costly, Parliament House on an adjacent site. The new 'talking shop' was ready for business by 1640.

There was no age limit on those attending parliament, although occasionally individuals were disbarred if they were deemed to be 'past it'. Poor old Andrew Riddell of that ilk was voted out in 1628 when it became apparent to all that he had become 'very infirme in his persoun and his judgement not so rype and quicke as formerlie'. Another problem was the cost of sending representatives, for all expenses had to be met by the individual himself or the sponsoring burgh or shire. Sir Archibald Murray of Blackbarony, elected in 1658, simply refused to attend because he deemed the remuneration inadequate. Cost was more of an issue for those in the further-flung parts of the realm. The good people of Forres maintained they were unable to send anyone 'being but a little village, unless the inhabitants be stented [taxed] which dare not be medled with for the fear the most of them run away.' They astutely got round the problem by electing a Forres man already resident in Edinburgh.

Following the Union of the Crowns in 1603, Scotland was faced with an absentee monarch, and the ancient Honours of Scotland – the Crown, Sceptre and Sword of State – came to represent him in parliament. An elaborate procession, the 'Ryding of Parliament', was created to bear the Honours from their resting-place in Edinburgh Castle down to Parliament House, and an Act was deemed to have received the Royal Assent only when the King's Commissioner, the Lord Chancellor, touched the parchment with the Sceptre. The last time that happened was on 16 January 1707 when the 157 members, Burns's 'parcel of rogues' voted for Union with England, and most of themselves out of a job.

Fareweel to a' our Scottish fame.
Fareweel our ancient glory!
Fareweel even to the Scottish name,
Sae fam'd in martial story!
Now Sark rins o'er the Solway sands,
And Tweed rins to the ocean,
To mark where England's province stands;
Such a parcel of rogues in a nation!'
(Robert Burns's *Fareweel to a' our Scottish fame*, 1791)

After five centuries, Scotland's first 'talking shop' hung up the 'closed for business' sign. The 61 Scottish Members

▲ *The Royal procession in Edinburgh's High Street, on the occasion of the formal opening by Her Majesty Queen Elizabeth in 1999 of Scotland's second Parliament which meets in the Church of Scotland's Assembly Hall on Castle Hill, before moving to purpose-built premises at Holyrood in 2004; the cost – £375 million and rising.*

– 45 'Commoners' (up against 513 Englishmen!) and 16 Lords – included in the new United Kingdom Parliament packed their bags for London.

But the years of talking would not be so easily silenced. The clamour for 'Home Rule', whereby Scots would manage their domestic affairs while leaving 'foreign' matters to Westminster, grew in intensity as the nineteenth century ran its course, helped by the debate raging across the Irish Sea about Irish Home Rule. The creation of the Scottish Office in 1885, albeit in an office in Whitehall,

and the revival of the office of Secretary for Scotland after almost a century and a half failed to still the disquiet. The founding of the Scottish Home Rule Association in 1886 with both Liberal and 'new' Labour support led to the matter being raised time and again on the floor of the House of Commons, without success. The thorny issue of Scottish – and Irish – involvement with English matters (Tam Dalyell's famous 'West Lothian Question' of later years) came to dominate the debate. One solution was floated in 1911 by a future prime minister, Winston Churchill, who was then MP for Dundee; he drafted a bill setting up regional parliaments across the United Kingdom.

Strange to say, Scotland would probably have got Home Rule in 1914, before the Irish even, had not the Great War abruptly halted the passage of the bill through the Lords. Further false dawns, most notably in 1924 and 1979, followed until in 1997 Scotland at last secured control over its own domestic affairs once more. And so it was that shortly after that historic election in May 1999, 129 MSPs – 56 Labour, 35 SNP, 18 Tory, 17 Lib.Dems, one Scottish Socialist, one Independent Labour and one Green – took their seats in temporary premises on Edinburgh's Mound. The old Parliament House in the 'Royal Mile' had long ago been given over to Scotland's judiciary, and as I write its replacement is still struggling to rise from a hole in the ground at Holyrood. But the lack of a debating chamber doesn't stop them talking!

The future's bright. Torness Nuclear Power Station (above) glints in the East Lothian sun, whilst the titanium-clad Science Centre (opposite) shimmers in the heart of the city of Glasgow. All of us, whether we are employed at Torness or being entertained in Glasgow, have one thing in common – we are all products of our past. For the past is not 'a foreign country', it is where we came from.

MILLENNIUM SCOTLAND – AD 2000

A quick look back over the shoulder shows just how much Scotland has changed since the Second World War. No more do reeking furnaces light up the night sky, no more do black-faced miners emerge blinking into the daylight from the bowels of the earth. Few are the ships being launched into the water, and even fewer the crans of fish being lifted out of it. We weren't sure what would replace them, if anything, in those difficult post-war years. They were our traditional industries, that had always been with us – part of us, or so it seemed. That is why we tried so hard to cling on to them, with the Upper Clyde Shipbuilders' 'lock-in' of 1972, the miners' strike of 1984, and the rest.

But we didn't know then what we know now – that vast wells of oil were lurking beneath the bed of the North Sea, that you could generate energy sufficient to power whole cities from a tiny atom, that a plastic 'chip' no bigger than a postage stamp could bring the world together at the press of a button. Many a colliery's pit-head gear has gone for scrap, but who's to say that they haven't been recycled into those oilrigs bobbing about in the North Sea? Ravenscraig steelworks' giant cooling tower has been brought crashing to the ground, but four equally gigantic cooling towers have risen up at Chapel Cross nuclear power station, near Annan.

Not visible, but just as real, are those creations that shape our lives in other ways. Three hundred years ago Scotland was all on its own, a little country on the edge of Europe. Today it is not only part of the UK but in partnership, along with the rest of the UK, with so many other nations. In 1945 we joined with most of the nations of the world to create the United Nations. In 1949 we joined with the nations of the North Atlantic to form the North Atlantic Treaty Organisation (NATO).

And in 1972, arguably the most significant of all, we joined with most of the nations of western Europe when we were admitted to the European Economic Community (now the European Union). 'The 'auld alliance' is dead; long live the new one.' So much of Scotland's past seems to have been taken up with fighting. Now we prefer to talk. That must be better, that must be progress. Even the SNP has recognised that Scotland cannot stand alone in this shrinking world of ours; 'Independence in Europe' has become its cry.

Somehow, despite all this international fraternising, Scotland has managed to retain its national identity. It never became 'North Britain', and it won't become 'North-West Europe ' either. It remains emphatically Scottish, and recognisably so, with a national and cultural identity forged over thousands of years. But throw away those bagpipes, tear off the tartan, and toss away that caber, and you'll find that Scots are much the same as people everywhere – yesterday, today and tomorrow.

> Fir there's nane ava quite like us
> an why for shuid there be?
> Aw ither fowk are like theirsels
> and no quite like ye an me;
> an the ae thing that unites us
> aw the fowk, ilk quine, ilk man
> is oor different weys o singin
> the love for oor ain launs.

(From Stuart McHardy's *History – Wha's Story?*, 2001.)

'Singin the love for oor ain launs' is what I've tried to do in this book. It's been an incredible journey, taking millions of years and covering thousands of miles. And it continues yet, on into the future. What that future will bring is anyone's guess. I've just heard that Livingston has won its first game in the Scottish Premier League, not bad for a former works team called Ferranti Thistle. It just shows you – you never can tell what's round the corner.

CHRONOLOGY

BC

2,800,000,000	Scotland's oldest rocks are created near South Pole.
1,000,000,000	Scotland 'sails' north.
400,000,000	Scotland and England collide.
300,000,000	Scotland crosses the Equator.
65,000,000	Scotland splits from North America.
2,000,000	First Ice Age arrives – the 'Big Freeze'.
11,000	Last Ice Age ends.
9,000	First humans arrive.
6,000	Britain separates from Europe.
3,100	Skara Brae village built.
2,900	Maes Howe tomb built.
2,200	First metals appear – the 'Bronze Age'.
700	Iron appears – the 'Iron Age'.
200	First brochs built.

AD

79	Rome invades Scotland.
83	Roman legionaries defeat Caledonian tribes at Mons Graupius.
142	Rome builds Antonine Wall between Forth and Clyde.
297	First mention of the Picts in historical records.
367	Picts and Scots raid across Hadrian's Wall - part of the 'Barbarian Conspiracy'.
400	Traprain Law treasure buried.
450	Christian memorial – the 'Latinus Stone' – erected at Whithorn.
563	St Columba arrives in Argyll and establishes monastery on Iona.
597	St Columba dies on Iona.
600	Northern Britons defeated by Angles at Catterick.
603	Scots defeated by Angles at Degsastan.
638	Angles capture Din Eidyn and rename it Edinburgh.
650	St Cuthbert becomes a monk at Old Melrose.

685	Angles defeated by Picts at Nechtansmere.
794	First Viking raid on Northern Isles.
795	First Viking raid on Iona.
843	Union of Scotland and Pictland under Kenneth MacAlpin.
849	St Columba's relics removed from Iona to Dunkeld.
871	Vikings capture British stronghold of Dumbarton Rock.
904	Vikings defeated by Scots in Strathearn.
954	Scots capture Edinburgh.
1018	Scots defeat English at Carham.
1057	Macbeth killed at Lumphanan.
1072	William 'the Conqueror' invades Scotland.
1093	Malcolm III 'Canmore' killed whilst fighting in Northumberland.
1098	Scotland formally cedes Hebrides to Norway.
1113	First 'reformed' Benedictine monks in British Isles settle at Selkirk.
1136	David I takes control of Cumberland, Westmorland and Northumberland.
1157	Henry II reclaims northern counties. Border fixed at the Tweed-Solway.
1164	Somerled, 'King of the Isles', killed at Renfrew.
1263	Alexander III defeats Haakon IV of Norway at Largs.
1266	Treaty of Perth sees Hebrides returned to Scotland.
1286	Alexander III killed in fall from horse in Fife.
1290	Margaret, 'the Maid of Norway', dies suddenly in Kirkwall.
1292	John Balliol crowned king at Scone.
1295	pact signed between Scotland and France – the 'auld alliance'.
1296	Edward I of England invades and deposes King John.
1297	William Wallace and Andrew Moray lead Scots to victory at Stirling Bridge.
1298	William Wallace loses battle of Falkirk.

1305   William Wallace executed in London.

1306   Robert Bruce crowned king at Scone but then forced to flee.

1307   Robert Bruce returns.
        Edward I of England dies near Carlisle.

1314   Robert Bruce defeats English at Bannockburn.

1320   Letters sent from Scotland to Pope John XXII – the 'Declaration of Arbroath'.

1328   Treaty of Edinburgh brings first War of Independence to a close.

1329   Robert Bruce dies peacefully at Cardross.

1332   Scots defeated at Dupplin Moor.
        Edward Balliol crowned king at Scone.

1334   David II (Bruce) taken to France for his safety.

1341   David II returns and immediately raids northern England.

1346   David II captured near Durham and taken to Tower of London.

1349   Plague visits its wrath on Scotland – the 'Black Death'.

1356   David II released from captivity, bringing Wars of Independence to a close.

1371   Robert the Stewart becomes king – first of the 'royal Stewarts'.

1373   Parity between Scots and English money ends – start of 'inflation'.

1385   Richard II invades eastern Borders and puts it to the fire and sword.

1406   Prince James (future James I) captured by English and sent to Tower of London.

1411   Crown checks onslaught of MacDonald Lord of the Isles at Harlaw.

1412   St Andrews University founded, Scotland's first.

1424   James I returns to Scotland.

1437   James I assassinated by his own nobles in Perth.

1451   Glasgow University founded.

1457   Football and golf banned by James II.

1460   James II killed by one of his own guns at siege of Roxburgh.

1468-9 Orkney and Shetland transferred from Norwegian to Scottish sovereignty.

1470   Edinburgh made 'de facto' capital of Scotland by James III.

1472   Scotland's first archbishopric established at St Andrews.

1482   Berwick-Upon-Tweed ceded to England for good.

1493   Lord of the Isles forfeited and Lordship finally suppressed.

1495   Aberdeen University founded.

1500   Population estimated to be around 500,000

1503   James IV weds Margaret Tudor of England – 'marriage of the thistle and the rose'.

1508   First Scottish books printed in Edinburgh.

1513   James IV and 5000 Scots killed at Flodden.

1528   Patrick Hamilton burnt at St Andrews for heresy – start of 'the Reformation'.

1532   College of Justice (Court of Session) established.

1540   Crown of Scotland made by John Mosman for James V.

1542   James V dies after battle of Solway Moss. His 6-day-old daughter Mary succeeds.

1544   Start of the 'War of the Rough Wooing'.

1547   10,000 Scots killed at Pinkie.

1548   Young Mary Queen of Scots sent to France for her safety.

1559   John Knox returns to Scotland and preaches against Catholicism.

1560   Parliament passes Act of Reformation. First General Assembly meets.

1561   Mary Queen of Scots returns from exile to begin her personal reign.

1567   Mary forced to abdicate in favour of her infant son, James VI. First Gaelic book – Knox's Liturgy – published.

1581   First kirk presbyteries established.

1582   Edinburgh University founded.

1590   North Berwick witches burned at stake in Edinburgh.

1600   1 January adopted as start of calendar year (previously 25 March).

1603   James VI becomes James I of England also – the 'Union of the Crowns'.

1608   Scottish 'plantation' of Ulster begins.

1616   Parish school system established.

1621   Establishment of Nova Scotia.

1622-3 Country devastated by famine.

1633   Charles I crowned king in Edinburgh.

1638   National Covenant signed.

1643   Solemn League and Covenant agreed with English Parliament.

1644-5 Marquis of Montrose's campaigns on behalf of Charles I.

1649   Charles I is beheaded by Oliver Cromwell.

1650   Cromwell invades Scotland.

1651   Charles II crowned king but forced into exile shortly after.

1653	Scotland and England formally joined – the 'United Commonwealth'
1658	Cromwell dies.
1660	Charles II returns to throne but never returns to Scotland.
1663	Non-conforming ministers expelled. Start of conventicles and 'Killing Time'.
1666	Coventanters defeated at Battle of Rullion Green.
1679	Covenanters defeated at Bothwell Bridge by a royalist force.
1682	Advocates' Library (now National Library) founded.
1689	James VII deposed and replaced by William II and Mary II. First Jacobite Rising.
1692	Massacre of Glencoe.
1695	Bank of Scotland established.
1698	First expedition to Darien.
1700	Population reaches 1 million. Fire sweeps through centre of Edinburgh.
1707	Treaty of Union between Scotland and England – the 'Union of the Parliaments'.
1708	Second Jacobite Rising (aborted) follows Treaty of Union.
1715	Third Jacobite Rising follows coronation of George Elector of Hanover.
1719	Fourth Jacobite Rising ends at Battle of Glenshiel.
1725	General Wade arrives in Scotland and begins to build military roads.
1727	Royal Bank of Scotland founded. Last Scottish witch burned at Dornoch.
1734	John Cockburn experiments with new agricultural regime at Ormiston.
1739	First issue of the *Scots Magazine* published.
1744	Honourable Company of Edinburgh Golfers plays first 'medal' on Leith Links.
1745-6	Fifth – and last – Jacobite Rising ends at Battle of Culloden.
1756	Charlestown, Fife, becomes Scotland's first planned industrial community.
1759	Carron Ironworks founded.
1764	James Watt perfects his steam engine in Glasgow.
1767	Foundation stone laid for Edinburgh's New Town.
1776	Adam Smith publishes *Wealth of Nations*. David Hume, philosopher, dies.
1778	First Scottish cotton mills built at Penicuik and Rothesay.
1779	John Paul Jones's American fleet almost captures Leith.
1788	Bonnie Prince Charlie dies in Rome.
1790	Forth & Clyde Canal opens.
1792	Revolt in Strathoykel against sheep-farms. Robert Adam, architect, dies.
1796	Robert Burns dies in Dumfries.
1799	Serfdom banned in coalmines and saltworks.
1801	Population exceeds 1.5 million.
1807	First of the 'Highland Clearances' begins on Sutherland Estates.
1810	World's first savings bank opens at Ruthwell, Dumfriesshire.
1815	Royal Scots Greys lead Britain to victory at Battle of Waterloo.
1817	First issue of *The Scotsman* published.
1820	'Radical War' ends at 'Battle of Bonnymuir'.
1821	Population reaches 2 million.
1822	George IV first monarch to visit Scotland in 171 years. Caledonian Canal opened.
1828	J B Neilson invents 'hot blast' iron-smelting process at the Clyde Ironworks.
1831	Scotland's first steam railway service runs between Glasgow and Garnkirk.
1832	60,000 Scotsmen given vote. Cholera kills 40,000. Sir Walter Scott dies.
1838	Royal Caledonian Curling Club founded. Clydesdale Bank founded.
1842	Glasgow-Edinburgh 'intercity' train service launched.
1843	Disruption in Church of Scotland leads to formation of Free Church.
1847	Widespread famine results in 'Highland Clearances'.
1851	Formal registration of births, marriages and deaths introduced.
1853	First Scots settle in New Zealand.
1854	93rd Highlanders form 'thin red line' at Battle of Balaclava, in Crimean War.
1867	Scottish Society of Women's Suffrage established in Edinburgh.
1868	Charles Rennie Macintosh born in Glasgow.
1871	First Scotland v England rugby international played in Edinburgh – Scotland win.
1872	First Scotland v England football international played in Glasgow – result 0-0.
1877	207 people killed at Blantyre Colliery – Scotland's worst mining disaster.

1879	James Clerk Maxwell, physicist, dies. Tay Bridge collapses.
1883	Boys' Brigade formed in Glasgow by William Smith.
1885	Scottish Office created.
1886	Glasgow Underground opens.
1888	Scottish Labour Party formed. 'Highers' introduced into schools.
1890	Forth Rail Bridge opened.
1892	Scottish Trades Union Congress formed.
1906	Keir Hardie forms British Labour Party.
1909	Rosyth Naval Dockyard built.
1910	Scotland's first cinema opens in Glasgow.
1911	Population exceeds 4.5 million (over 1 million in Glasgow alone).
1913	Suffragettes burn Whitekirk.
1914	World War I begins.
1915	217 Royal Scots killed in train crash near Gretna. Glasgow Rent Strike.
1916	6000 Scots killed on first day of Battle of the Somme.
1918	World War I ends. Women given the vote.
1919	German Fleet scuttled in Scapa Flow. Forestry Commission set up.
1923	First radio broadcasting stations set up in Glasgow and Aberdeen.
1924	Ramsay MacDonald becomes first Labour Prime Minister. Housing Act passed.
1926	General Strike.
1927	Scottish National War Memorial in Edinburgh Castle opened by Prince of Wales.
1928	Sir Alexander Fleming discovers penicillin. First female Scots MP elected.
1930	36 islanders evacuated from St Kilda.
1931	National Trust for Scotland and Scottish Youth Hostel Association founded.
1934	Scottish National Party formed.
1936	Saltire Society founded.
1939	World War II begins. HMS *Royal Oak* sunk in Scapa Flow – 833 drown.
1941	Clydebank bombed – 1200 killed. Rudolf Hess, Hitler's deputy, lands near Lesmahagow.
1943	Aberdeen bombed – 43 killed.
1945	World War II ends.
1945	First SNP MP elected. Scottish Tourist Board created.
1946	New Towns Act passed.
1947	Prestwick Airport opens.

1947	Coal and electricity industries nationalised. First Edinburgh International Festival held.
1948	National Health Service created. Railways nationalised.
1949	Iron and steel nationalised.
1950	First performance of Military Tattoo on Edinburgh Castle Esplanade. Stone of Destiny removed from Westminster Abbey and taken to Arbroath.
1951	Population exceeds 5 million. IBM opens 'hi-tec' factory at Greenock.
1952	First television transmission from Shotts.
1957	Ravenscraig Steelworks built.
1959	BMC's Bathgate factory opens.
1960	Rootes' Linwood factory opens.
1961	US nuclear submarine base opens in Holy Loch.
1962	Last person hanged in Scotland at Craiginches Gaol, Aberdeen.
1964	Forth Road Bridge opens; so too Hunterston 'A' nuclear power station.
1965	Highlands & Islands Development Board established. Invergordon aluminium plant opens.
1967	Winnie Ewing wins Hamilton by-election for SNP.
1968	Church of Scotland admits women ministers.
1969	The Waverley Line between Carlisle and Edinburgh closes.
1972	Upper Clyde Shipbuilders' 'lock-in'.
1974	Sullom Voe oil terminal opens.
1979	Devolution referendum fails.
1983	Bathgate factory closes.
1984	Miners' Strike.
1988	Piper Alpha oil platform explosion kills 226. Pan-Am plane blown up over Lockerbie – 270 killed.
1989	Introduction of Poll Tax leads to angry protests.
1992	Ravenscraig closes. US pulls out of Holy Loch.
1995	Skye Bridge opens.
1996	Stone of Destiny returns to Scotland – officially this time!
1997	'Dolly the sheep', world's first clone, born at Roslin.
1999	Scottish Parliament sits for first time in 288 years.
2000	Donald Dewar, Scotland's first First Minister, dies.
2002	Scotland's women curlers (skip: Rhona Martin) win Gold Medal at Winter Olympics in February. Scottish Parliament passes the Community Care and Health (Scotland) Bill introducing free health care for the elderly.
2003	Second elections to the Scottish Parliament.

INDEX
Numbers in bold indicate illustrations

222

DEDICATION: IN MEMORY OF S.H.C.

Published in North America in 2004 by
Oyster Press, Anacortes,
Washington, U.S.A.

Distributed by Graphic Arts Center Publishing Company
P.O. Box 10306, Portland, Oregon 97296-0306, U.S.A.
Orders 800-452-3032

Produced by Colin Baxter Photography Ltd

Copyright © Colin Baxter Photography Ltd 2004

ISBN 1-932573-01-1

Printed in China

04 05 06 07 08   5 4 3 2 1

Text copyright © Chris Tabraham 2004

All photography copyright © Colin Baxter 2004, except for the following:

The Annan Collection, page: 171 (top)

Blair Castle Charitable Trust, page: 107

Board of Trinity College Dublin, page: 35

Bob Charnley Collection, page: 195

Bridgeman Art Library, pages: 53, 123

By permission of the British Library, pages: 70, 71, 80, 112

City Art Centre, City of Edinburgh Museums & Galleries, page: 118

Corbis, page: 210

Crown Copyright: reproduced by courtesy of Historic Scotland, pages: 60, 94

Crown copyright: Palace of Westminster Collection, page: 129

D.C. Thomson, page: 177

Dumbarton Football Club, page: 37

Falkirk Museum, pages: 178, 179

Gallacher Memorial Library, Glasgow Caledonian University, Research Collection, page: 191

Courtesy of Glasgow City Archives (Mitchell Library), pages: 66, 167 (top & bottom), 174, 175

Glasgow Museums: Art Gallery & Museum, Kelvingrove, page: 104

Glasgow Museums: The People's Palace, pages: 151, 194

Hulton Archive/Getty Images: pages: front cover (bottom right), 147 bottom, 168, 169, 171 (bottom), 172, 187 (bottom), 190, 196, 205

Imperial War Museum, pages: 184 (Q5100), 185 (Q49104), 186 (Q109523), 188 (Q48966)

Jim Proudfoot, pages: 77, back cover (top)

Master & Fellows, Corpus Christi College, Cambridge, page: 64

Mirrorpix, page: 213

National Archives of Scotland, pages: 79 (SP13/7), 97 (SP6/31)

National Galleries of Scotland, pages: 106, 119, 142, 182

National Museums of Scotland, pages: 23, 29, 44, 146

National Maritime Museum, London, page: 170

Pierpont-Morgan/Art Resource NY, page: 45

Popperfoto.com, page: 176, 187 (top)

Wendy Price maps copyright © Wendy Price Cartographic Services 2004, pages: 6, 30

Wendy Price map copyright © Wendy Price Cartographic Services 2004. Based on Mapping by Hallwag Kimmerly+Frey AG Switzerland, page: 6

Public Record Office Image Library, page: 160

RCAHMS, pages: 197, 214

The Royal Collection © Her Majesty Queen Elizabeth II, pages: front cover (middle right), 33

School of Scottish Studies, University of Edinburgh page: 163

Scotsman, pages: 211, 215

Scottish Fisheries Museum, page: 165

Scottish Life Archive, National Museum of Scotland, pages: 159, 161, 164, 204

Scottish Media Group, pages: 192, 193, 198, 199 (top & bottom), 201

Scottish Mining Museum, page: 173

Scottish National Portrait Gallery, pages: 10, 84, 100, 131, 138, 140, 144, 147 (top)

The Trustees of the National Library of Scotland, pages: 51, 55, 128, 141 (top & bottom)

University of Aberdeen, pages: 158, 162

FURTHER READING AND BIBLIOGRAPHY

GENERAL
J. Barbour 'The Bruce', Scottish Text Society, 1894
Brown, G. Mackay *Brodgar Poems*, Oxford, 1991
N. Buchan (ed) *101 Scottish Songs*, Glasgow, 1962
N. Buchan & P. Hall (eds) *The Scottish Folksinger*, Glasgow, 1978
A. Crawford *Charles Rennie Mackintosh*, London, 1995
I King & B Sinclair (eds) *Scotland's Story* (Glasgow, 1999-2000)
M. Lynch *Scotland: A New History* (London, 1991)
M. Lynch (ed) *The Oxford Companion to Scottish History* (Oxford, 2001)
E. Laird (ed) *The Sunday Mail Story of Scotland* (Glasgow, 1988)
A. Weir *Britain's Royal Families* (London,1989)
The Works of Robert Burns. Wordsworth Poetry Library, 1964

SPECIFIC – *Geology and prehistory*
I. Armit *Celtic Scotland* (London, 1997)
W. Baird *The Scenery of Scotland: The Structure Beneath* (Edinburgh, 1991)
G. Craig (ed) *Geology of Scotland* (London, 1991)
B. Finlayson *Wild Harvesters: The First People in Scotland* (Edinburgh, 1998)
R. Hingley *Settlement and Sacrifice: The Later Prehistoric People of Scotland* (Edinburgh, 1998)
C. Wickham-Jones *Scotland's First Settlers* (London, 1994)

AD 1 - 1000
D. Breeze *Roman Scotland: Frontier Country* (London 1996)
E. Campbell *Saints and Sea-Kings: The First Kingdom of the Scots* (Edinburgh, 1999)
A. Duncan *Scotland: The Making of the Kingdom* (Edinburgh, 1975)
S. Foster *Picts, Gaels and Scots* (London, 1996)
C. Lowe *Angels, Fools and Tyrants: Britons and Anglo-Saxons in Southern Scotland* (Edinburgh, 1999)
O. Owen *The Sea Road: A Viking Voyage Through Scotland* (Edinburgh, 1999)
A. Smith *Warlords and Holy Men: Scotland AD80-1000* (Edinburgh, 1984)

AD 1000 – 1560
G. Barrow *Kingship and Unity: Scotland 1000-1306* (Edinburgh, 1989)
G. Barrow *Robert Bruce and the Community of the Realm of Scotland* (Edinburgh, 1976)
D. Caldwell *Scotland's Wars and Warriors* (Edinburgh, 1998)
P. Dixon *Puir Labourers and Busy Husbandmen* (Edinburgh, 2002)

R. Dodgshon *The Age of the Clans* (Edinburgh,2002)
G. Fraser *The Steel Bonnets: The Story of the Anglo-Scottish Reivers* (London, 1974)
A. Grant *Independence and Nationhood: Scotland 1306-1469* (Edinburgh, 1984)
D. Hall *Burgess, Merchant and Priest* (Edinburgh, 2002)
R. Nicholson *Scotland: The Later Middle Ages* (Edinburgh, 1978)

AD 1560 – 1800
G. Donaldson *Scotland: James V-James VII* (Edinburgh, 1978)
R. Mitchison *Lordship to Patronage: Scotland 1603-1745* (London, 1983)
T. Smout *A History of the Scottish People 1560-1830* (London, 1969)

AD 1800 – present
O. & S Checkland *Industry and Ethos: Scotland 1832-1914* (London, 1989)
W. Ferguson *Scotland: 1689 to the Present* (Edinburgh, 1978)
B. Lenman *Integration and Enlightenment: Scotland 1746-1832* (Edinburgh, 1992)
T. Smout *A Century of the Scottish People 1830-1950* (London,1986)
C. Harvie *No Gods and Precious Few Heroes: Scotland 1914-1980* (Edinburgh, 1999)

ACKNOWLEDGEMENTS

The author wishes to thank the following for their help: my colleagues David Breeze and Doreen Grove for their very helpful comments, and Martin and Katie Bates and Liz Whitfeld for allowing me peace to write under the Mediterranean sun.

While we have made every effort to trace all copyright holders, we shall be glad to learn of any instances where acknowledgement is due. Extract from *1066 And All That* by W C Sellar and R J Yeatman reproduced by kind permission of Methuen Publishing Limited, London. Extract from A Guide to the Island Blackhouse, HMSO, 1978, reproduced by kind permission. 'Letter From America' Words and Music by Charles Reid and Craig Reid © 1987 Zoo Music Ltd. Warner/Chappell Music Ltd, London W6 8BS. Reproduced by permission of International Music Publications Ltd. All rights reserved. Extract from 'History – Wha's Story' by Stuart McHardy, from *Scots Poems to be Read Aloud*, ed. Stuart McHardy, reproduced with permission from Luath Press Ltd. Extract from *Early Films* by Iain Crichton Smith, Copyright © the Estate of Iain Crichton Smith; and extracts from 'The Little White Rose' and 'A Drunk Man Looks at the Thistle' from *Complete Poems* by Hugh MacDiarmid © the Estate of Hugh MacDiarmid; both by permission of Carcanet Press Ltd.

FRONT COVER: *Main photo:* The National Wallace Monument. *Top insert:* Calanais Standing Stones. *Middle Insert:* Battle of Culloden, by D. Morier. *Bottom Insert:* Workers and *Uganda* 1952, Clydeside. BACK COVER: *Top:* Battle of Bannockburn by J. Proudfoot. *Left:* Caerlaverock Castle. *Right:* Finnieston Quay crane, Glasgow